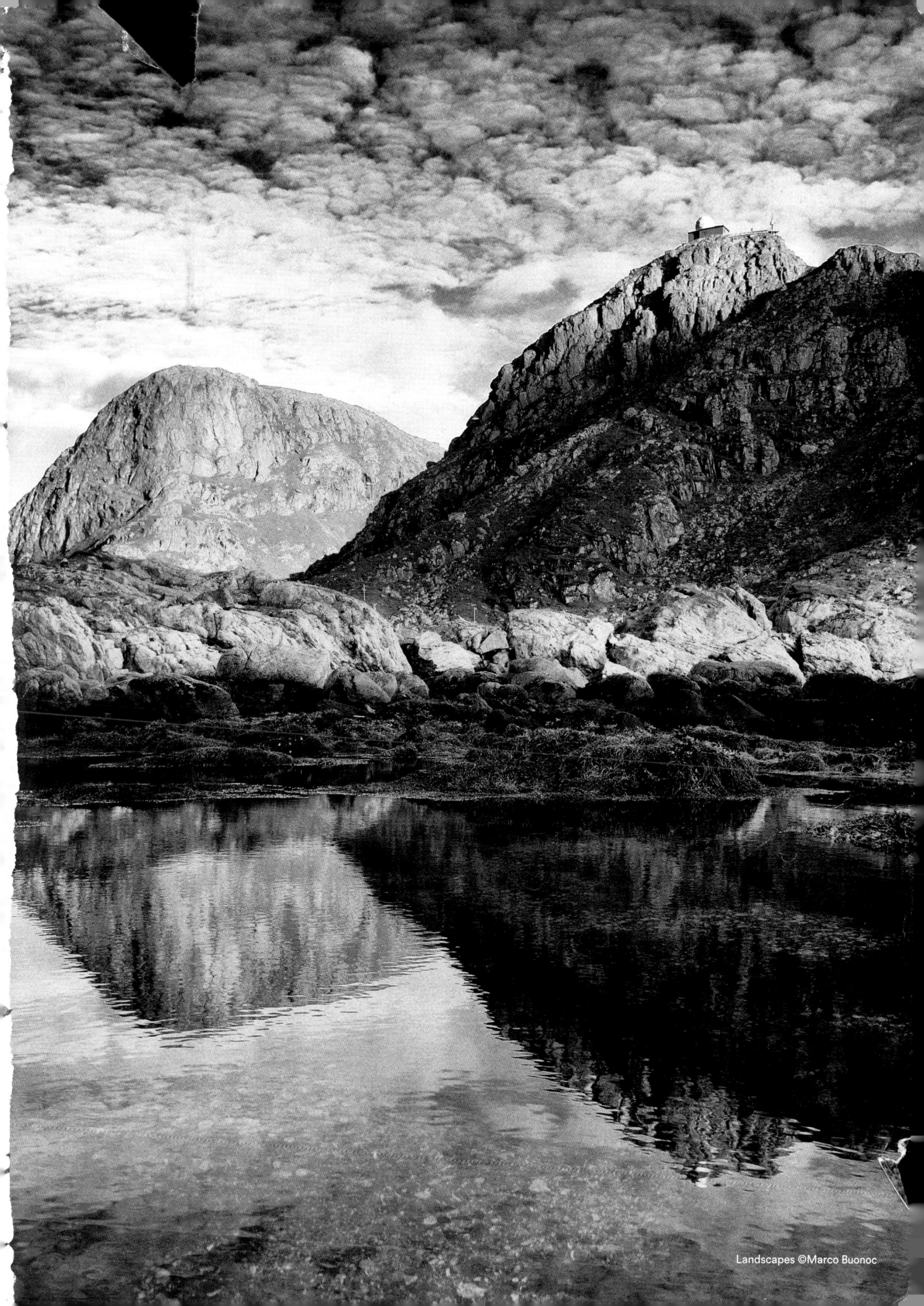

Landscapes ©Marco Buonoc

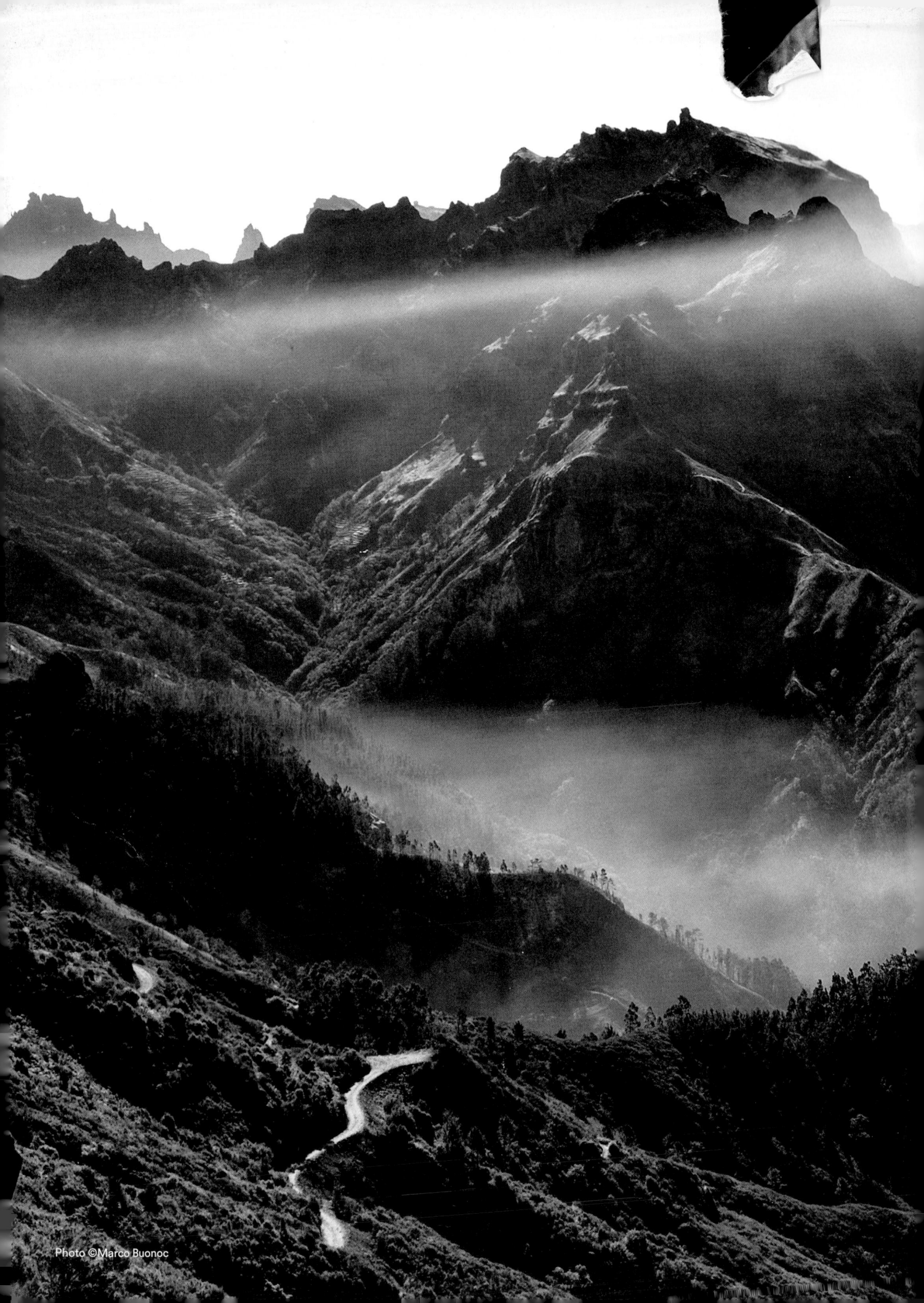

Photo ©Marco Buonoc

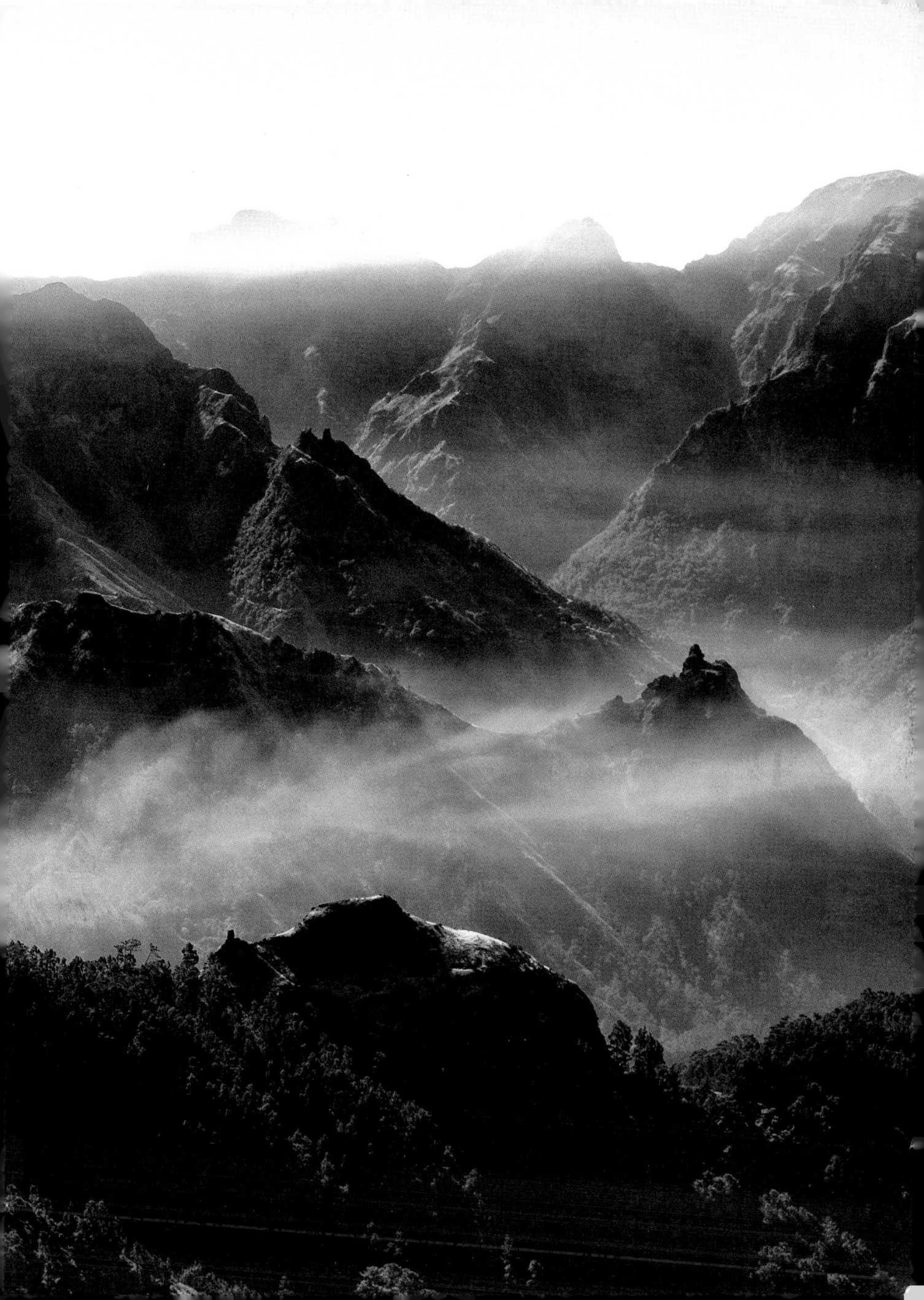

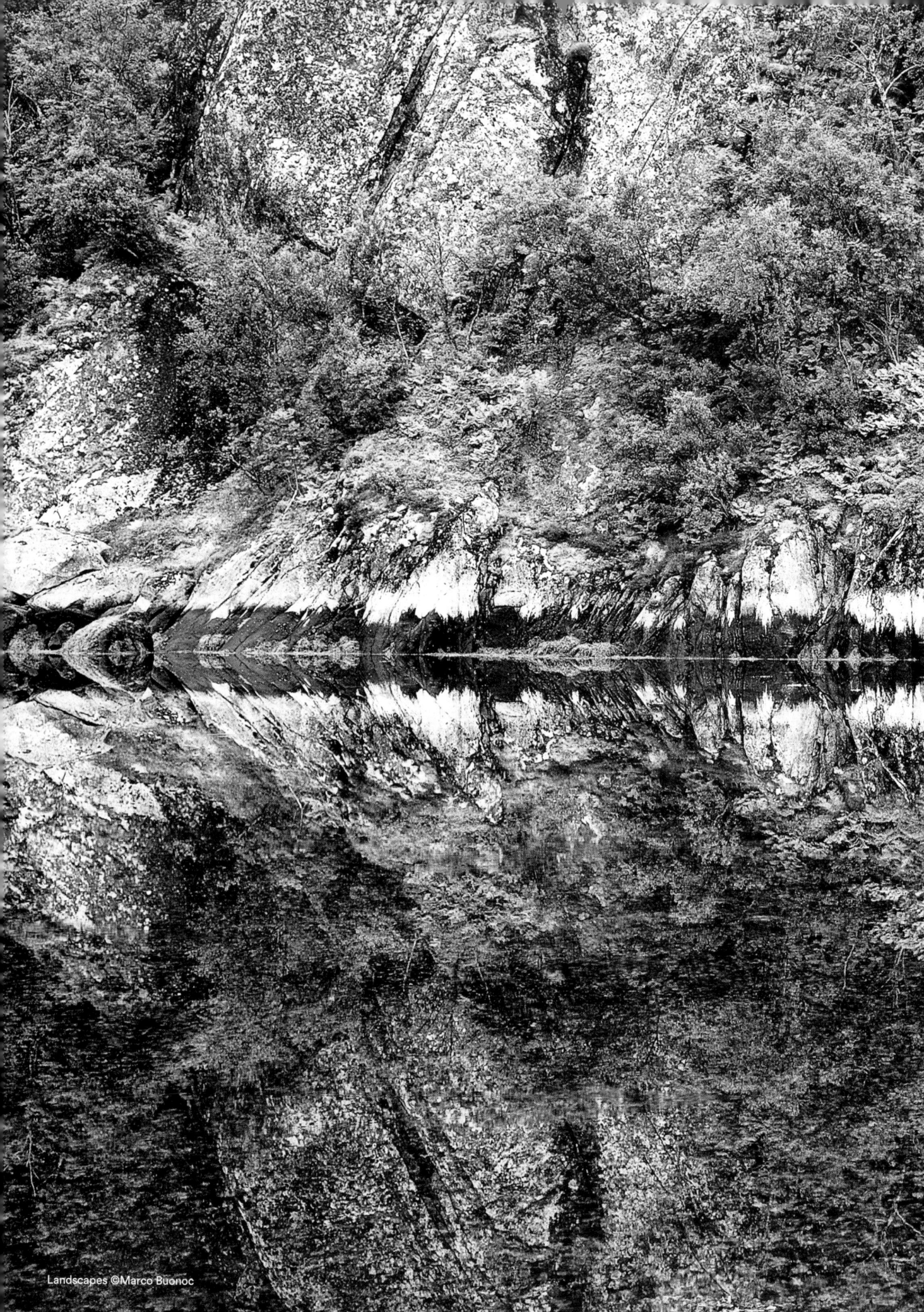

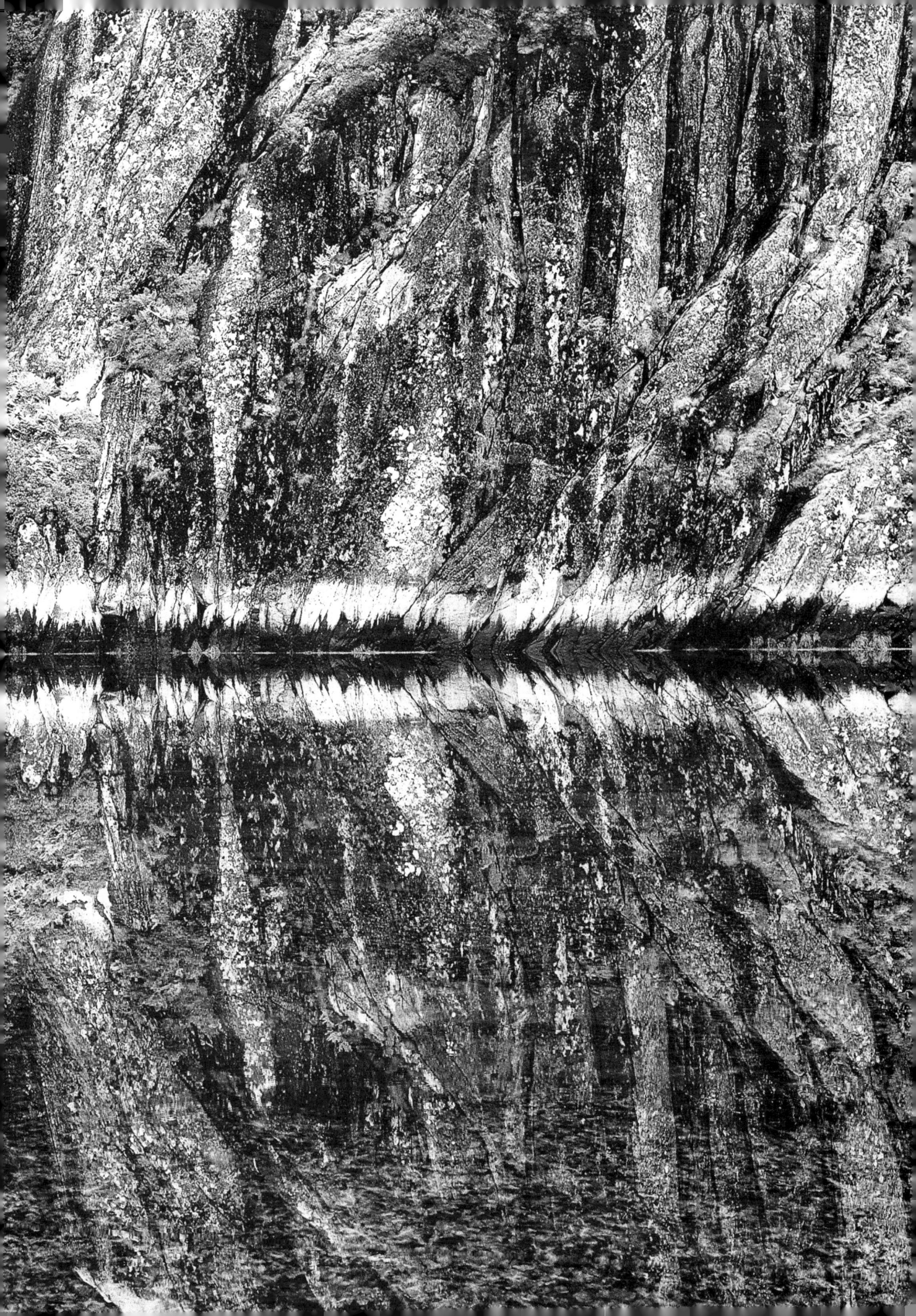

Monochrome Graphics

Maximum Creativity within a Minimum Budget
Maxi-créativité, mini-budget
Máxima creatividad, mínimo presupuesto
Máxima criatividade, orçamento mínimo

English preface revised by: Tom Corkett
Translators of the preface: Marie-Pierre Teuler French translation /
Jesús de Cos Pinto Spanish translation / Élcio Carillo Portuguese (Brazilian) translation
Cover design / revision of layout design: spread: David Lorente
with the collaboration of Victoria Arias

PROMOPRESS is a brand of:
Promotora de Prensa Internacional S.A.
C/ Ausiàs March, 124
08013 Barcelona, Spain
Phone: +34 932451464
Fax: +34 932654883
info@promopress.es
www.promopress.es
www.promopresseditions.com
Facebook: Promopress Editions
Twitter: Promopress Editions @PromopressEd

ISBN: 978-84-15967-30-9

Publisher: Lin Gengli
Publishing Director: Lin Shijian
Editorial Director: Sundae Li
Executive Editors: Casey Kwan, Ellyse Ho
Creative Director: He Wanling
Executive Designers: Amito Lau, Peng Lingbo
Proofreading: Sundae Li, Faith Dexter

Printed in China

Mono chrome Graphics

Maximum creativity within a minimum budget

Maxi-créativité, mini-budget

Máxima creatividad, mínimo presupuesto

Máxima criatividade, orçamento mínimo

EDITED BY
LING SHIJIAN

promopress

Contents

Black, White & Gray

BACK TO BASICS

Asphalt black, jet black, shadow black, Oxford black, ivory black, ebony, outer space, armadillo black, onyx, atrament, Baltic black, basalt, bister black, blackberry, coffee black, crow black, peppercorn black, tamarind, café noir, black bean, black olive, black leather jacket, burnt umber, native natural umber, deep native umber, midnight blue, ivory Prussian blue, Charleston black, eerie black, licorice, and black truffle; Champagne white, white light, cream, marble white, travertine, silver white, alabaster white, shale white, ghost white, baby powder, snow white, floral white, seashell white, corn-silk white, old–lace white, beige, linen, antique white, eggshell white, Dutch white, bone, vanilla white, flax white, Navajo white, Isabelline, magnolia, white smoke, ecru, glacial white, malachite white, lapis lazuli white, white with burnt umber, and China-clay white; Champagne silver, aluminum glaze, Rosa Caso's gray, natural gray, anthracite, ferric gray, light gray, charcoal, cool gray, warm gray, pearl gray, deep gray, medium gray, dim gray, Gainsboro, silver, Spanish gray, platinum, ash gray, battleship gray, cadet gray, blue-gray, glaucous, slate gray, puce, cinereous, rocket gray, taupe, and Davy's gray. To mention just a few.

▬▬ Within the fields of work in which we excel, we tend to develop an acute sensitivity for the things going on inside our contained microcosm. Only very few people request access to these miniature galaxies that are so important to experts. This is what makes our world one of such vast diversity. Whenever we seek out a specialist we get results, and through this we get a peek into this other world with all of its tiny details. The individual gifted enough to actually carve out a brand new scent who creates a new perfume—the so-called "nose"—is an example of this phenomenon. Countless nuances that remain hidden to an ordinary sense of smell can be perceived and tracked by the adept.

▬▬ It takes such an unusual ability and sensitivity to devise and market something that exceeds the demands and expectations of the common lot of people. Quality lies concealed within the details. Ultimately those details can be distinguished by a nonspecialist who can appreciate the difference between an average product and an outstanding one.

▬▬*For all these reasons, "black-and-white thinking" is not quite as simple as it might appear. Not for us designers.*

▬▬ In fact, we see it as launching pad. If we want to create a brand that is supposed to leave an impression, we first have to make our way to the base—to the foundation. We usually work with black on white, and yet black is not simply black, and white is not only white. There are endless possibilities that lie between the two, within the infinite palette of grays. One black corresponds to another like a laser-drawn line corresponds to a pencil stroke. We experiment with new ideas, play them out, and adjust and refine them. Sometimes even we are surprised at the outcome. Nothing can be judged quite so clearly and cleanly as a design in black and white. It has contrast and it has simplicity. In initially abstaining from a seminal color or entirely setting it aside, we as designers have a way of determining whether the work really functions or not—whether a logo actually fulfills its assigned purpose and attains its objective, or whether the language of forms is the right one and the balance is correct.

▬▬ We are aware of the importance of colors and the indispensable role they play in every sector of our lives, ranging from art and fashion to psychology and nature itself. What we are trying to establish is the fact that black and white and gray can be displayed in the selfsame variety, the selfsame richness of facets, and the selfsame complexity as all colors within the light spectrum. From the very first sketch to the final product, we exhaust everything this achromatic color scheme has to offer.

▬▬*Design in black and white, in other words, is not for the faint of heart. It is for those who aren't afraid to commit themselves, to reveal what they're capable of. Black and white are not neutral; they take risks. This is even truer of gray.*

▬▬ If black delivers the strength, white supplies the tenderness. Nonetheless, white can aggressively throw itself at the viewer, to such an extent that our eyes are forced to contract. Contrary to general opinion, white is the opposite of empty space; it is space filled with certainty. And where light transmutes to shadow is where gray makes its entrance. As Derek Jarman wrote, "Shadow . . . is the Queen of Colour. Colour sings in the grey." Black displayed on a radiant surface becomes a mirror or an opaque wall that absorbs all light. Black is mystical; it embodies elegance as no other color can. Its preeminence in the arts of photography and fashion is indisputable. In 1926 Coco Chanel invented the concept of the LBD or "little black dress," and ever since then the terms "elegant," "black," and "fashion" have been inseparable. Who knows, maybe it is simply the case that "black is the new black," and always will be.

▬▬ Ever since we have had an unlimited range of colors at our fingertips we have also been able to print them inexpensively and display them on film and photos—designs in black, white, and gray are no longer a compromise. To us, they are pure luxury: a truly winning color ensemble readily available for every brand that strives to appear classic, elegant, sophisticated, full of contrast, fresh, discreet, or perhaps purposefully simple—a corporate identity in which color doesn't draw one away from the essence, but instead underscores its intrinsic colorfulness. The shades we choose are further enhanced through the characteristics of the paper and other surfaces we use to display designs.

▬▬ Regardless of what shape they take, you will find in this book a collection of work that makes it clear just how much black, white, and gray are capable of. We are incredibly impressed with the printed compositions and works presented, and feel proud to be a part of this project.

Isabella Meischberger, Mike Rabensteiner / Bureau Rabensteiner

Noir, blanc et gris
RETOUR À L'ESSENTIEL

Goudron, jais, noir de fumée, noir de carbone, noir d'ivoire, ébène, espace interstellaire, noir animal, onyx, brou de noix, Dorian, basalte, ombre, cassis, café, aile de corbeau, noir d'aniline, cachou, café noir, haricot noir, olive noire, blouson de cuir noir, lignite, noiraud, charbon, bleu nuit, bleu de Prusse, noir d'encre, aubergine, réglisse et truffe noire. Albâtre, argile, azur brume, beige clair, blanc cassé, céruse, crème, blanc d'argent, blanc de lait, lin, blanc de platine, blanc de plomb, blanc de saturne, blanc de Troyes, blanc de zinc, blanc d'Espagne, ivoire, écru, blanc lunaire, neige, opalin, blanc-bleu, coquille d'œuf, cuisse de nymphe, blanc de Meudon, blanc de Chine, vanille, cire, magnolia, blanc banquise et blanc nacré. Ardoise, gris argent, argile, bis, bistre, bitume, châtaigne, étain oxydé, étain pur, fumée, grège, gris acier, anthracite, gris de Payne, gris fer, gris perle, gris souris, gris tourterelle, mastic, pinchard, plomb, taupe, tourdille, chinchilla, gris flanelle, gris Trianon, gris moyen, gris cendre, gris militaire et gris clair. Quelques nuances parmi tant d'autres.

■ Dans notre vie professionnelle, nous sommes sensibles aux détails et subtilités de notre spécialité. Très peu de gens cherchent à pénétrer les microcosmes réservés aux experts qui témoignent de l'incroyable diversité de notre monde. Lorsque nous rencontrons un spécialiste, nous prenons conscience des mille particularités de son univers. Une personne capable de mettre au point une nouvelle senteur et d'en produire un parfum inédit, est un exemple de ce phénomène. Seul un « nez » sera en mesure de percevoir les subtiles nuances d'une odeur qui seront imperceptibles pour le commun des mortels.

■ Il faut avoir un grand savoir-faire et une sensibilité hors du commun pour concevoir et commercialiser un produit qui dépasse les attentes du public. La qualité se cache parmi les mille et un détails qui parleront uniquement aux non-spécialistes capables de distinguer un produit banal d'un article d'exception.

■ *C'est pourquoi un mode de pensée « noir-blanc » n'est pas aussi simple qu'il y paraît. En tout cas pas pour nous autres concepteurs.*

■ Cette difficulté nous permet en fait de retourner à l'essentiel. Si nous voulons créer une marque qui produise un certain effet, nous devons retourner à la source, au point de départ. Le plus souvent, nous travaillons avec du noir et du blanc. Et pourtant, le noir n'est pas juste du noir et le blanc n'est pas simplement du blanc. Il existe un nombre infini de possibilités entre les deux, une immense palette de gris. Il y a autant de ressemblance entre deux tons de noir qu'entre un tracé au laser et un trait dessiné au crayon. Concrètement, nous commençons par tester quelques nouvelles idées, nous les développons un peu, puis nous les remanions et les affinons. Nous sommes parfois nous-mêmes surpris du résultat. Pour évaluer un concept de façon claire et nette, rien ne vaut une ébauche en noir et blanc. Elle allie contraste et simplicité. L'absence de couleur nous permet de voir si la proposition fonctionne ou pas. Par exemple, si le logo est conforme à l'objectif visé et produit bien l'effet désiré, ou si le langage des formes choisi est le bon et si le tout est équilibré.

■ Nous sommes conscients de l'importance de la couleur et du rôle indispensable qu'elle joue dans tous les aspects de notre vie, qui vont de l'art à la mode en passant par la psychologie et la nature elle-même. Nous essayons simplement d'établir que le noir, le blanc et le gris peuvent tout à fait représenter la même diversité, la même richesse et la même complexité que toutes les couleurs du spectre. Depuis l'esquisse initiale jusqu'au produit final, nous exploitons toutes les possibilités offertes par cette palette achromatique.

■ *Il est clair que le travail en noir et blanc demande une certaine force de ca-ractère. Ceux qui ont peur de s'affirmer ou de montrer ce dont ils sont capables feront bien de s'abstenir. Le noir et le blanc ne sont pas neutres : ils prennent des risques. C'est encore plus vrai pour le gris.*

■ Le noir transmet de la force et le blanc confère de la tendresse. Toutefois, le blanc est aussi capable d'agresser l'observateur au point de l'obliger à plisser les yeux. Contrairement à l'opinion générale, le blanc est le contraire du vide : c'est un espace rempli de certitude. Et lorsque la lumière se change en ombre, c'est là où le gris entre en scène. Comme l'a dit Derek Jarman, l'ombre est la reine des couleurs, et la couleur s'exprime dans le gris. Du noir affiché sur une surface brillante peut devenir un miroir ou un panneau opaque qui absorbe toute la lumière. Le noir a un côté mystique ; il incarne l'élégance, plus que n'importe quelle couleur. Sa suprématie dans les arts de la photographie et de la mode est indiscutable. En 1926, Coco Chanel a inventé la « petite robe noire » et depuis cette époque les mots « élégance », « noir » et « mode » sont devenus inséparables. Peut-être que le noir est simplement « le nouveau noir », et qu'il le restera à tout jamais.

■ Depuis que nous disposons d'une gamme illimité de couleurs, nous avons appris à les imprimer à moindre coût et à les tirer sur pellicule et sur papier photo : on ne choisit plus la combinaison noir, blanc et gris faute de mieux. Pour nous, c'est un véritable luxe ! C'est le trio gagnant disponible pour toutes les marques qui veulent projeter une image classique, élégante, sophistiquée, nuancée, fraîche, discrète ou une simplicité calculée. C'est la recherche d'une identité visuelle où la couleur ne détourne pas l'attention de l'essentiel et où, au contraire, elle renforce la personnalité intrinsèque de la marque. Les nuances que nous choisissons sont rehaussées par les caractéristiques du papier et des autres supports utilisés pour nos esquisses.

■ Le présent ouvrage renferme de multiples exemples de compositions qui montrent de quoi sont capables le noir, le blanc et le gris, indépendamment des formes utilisées. Les créations illustrées ici sont vraiment superbes et nous sommes fiers de faire partie de ce projet.

Isabella Meischberger, Mike Rabensteiner / Bureau Rabensteiner

Negro, blanco y gris

EL RETORNO A LO BÁSICO

Negro asfalto, azabache, sombra, negro de Paynes, negro marfil, ébano, negro profundo, negro pizarra, ónice, negro tinta, betún de Judea, basalto, bistre, zarzamora, café, ala de cuervo, regaliz, tamarindo, alquitrán, judía negra, oliva negra, cuero negro, sombra quemada, sombra natural, sombra natural oscura, azur, azul de Prusia, charol, negro luto, regaliz y trufa; blanco lino, luz blanca, nata, mármol, travertino, plata, alabastro, esquisto blanco, blanco sudario, talco, nieve, blanco camelia, blanco concha, barba de maíz, encaje antiguo, beis, algodón, blanco antiguo, cáscara de huevo, blanco de España, hueso, vainilla, lino, blanco Navajo, perla, magnolia, blanco humo, crudo, blanco hielo, blanco malaquita, nácar, blanco con sombra quemada y blanco porcelana; gris luna, aluminio, gris Caso, gris natural, antracita, hierro, gris claro, hulla, gris frío, gris cálido, gris perla, gris oscuro, gris neutro, Gainsboro, plata, gris arena, platino, ceniza, plata vieja, gris cadete, gris azulado, glauco, gris pizarra, gris morado, cinéreo, gris mezclilla, gris topo y gris de Davy. Por citar solamente unos cuantos.

■ Los humanos tenemos tendencia a desarrollar una aguda sensibilidad para las cosas que componen el microcosmos de nuestro campo de actividad. Muy pocas personas acceden a esas galaxias en miniatura que son tan importantes para los expertos, y eso es lo que hace que nuestro mundo tenga una diversidad tan vasta. Siempre que consultamos a un especialista obtenemos resultados y recibimos un atisbo de su mundo y de sus muchos y minúsculos detalles. Un ejemplo de este fenómeno es la *nariz*, como se llama al individuo que posee el talento de formular un aroma nuevo y crear un perfume, un iniciado capaz de percibir y rastrear incontables matices que permanecen ocultos al sentido del olfato de la mayoría de las personas.

■ Para concebir y comercializar algo que supere las expectativas y las demandas del común de los mortales se necesitan una sensibilidad y una habilidad semejantes a ésa. La calidad se esconde en los detalles. Y, al final, esos detalles son los que aprecia cualquiera que, sin ser un especialista, sepa distinguir la diferencia entre un producto corriente y otro excepcional.

■ *Por todas estas razones, el "pensamiento en blanco y negro" no es tan simple como pudiera parecer. Para nosotros, los diseñadores, no es así.*

■ De hecho, nosotros lo vemos como una plataforma de lanzamiento. Si queremos crear una marca que tenga que dejar una impresión, primero tenemos que dirigirnos a la base, a los fundamentos. Solemos trabajar en blanco y negro, pero ni el blanco es simplemente blanco ni el negro es solamente negro. Entre ambos hay infinitas posibilidades, dentro de la inagotable paleta de los grises. Un negro se corresponde con otro como una línea dibujada por láser se corresponde con un trazo de lápiz. Experimentamos con nuevas ideas, jugamos con ellas, las ajustamos y refinamos. En ocasiones, hasta nos sorprenden los resultados. Nada puede ser juzgado con tanta claridad y limpieza como un diseño en blanco y negro: posee contraste y simplicidad. Prescindir inicialmente de un color importante –o descartarlo definitivamente– es un sistema que usamos los diseñadores para determinar si nuestro trabajo funciona en realidad, para saber si un logo cumple el propósito asignado y alcanza su objetivo, y también para comprobar si el lenguaje de las formas es adecuado y el equilibrio es el correcto.

■ Somos conscientes de la importancia de los colores y del lugar indispensable que ocupan en todos los aspectos de nuestra vida, desde el arte y la moda a la psicología y a la naturaleza. Lo que intentamos demostrar es el hecho de que el blanco, el negro y el gris pueden desplegarse con la misma variedad, la misma riqueza de facetas y la misma complejidad que proporcionan todos los colores del espectro luminoso. Desde el primer boceto hasta el producto final, agotamos todas las posibilidades que ofrece este esquema de color acromático.

■ *En otras palabras, el diseño en blanco y negro no es para los que se desaniman fácilmente. Es para quienes no temen al compromiso y se atreven a demostrar de lo que son capaces. El blanco y el negro no son neutrales: asumen riesgos. Y lo mismo es incluso más cierto en cuanto al gris.*

■ Si el negro proporciona la fuerza, el blanco suministra la delicadeza. Y, sin embargo, el blanco puede arrojarse agresivamente sobre el espectador hasta el punto de obligarle a entornar los ojos. En contra de la opinión común, el blanco es lo opuesto al espacio vacío: es el espacio lleno de certeza. Y allí donde la luz se transfigura en sombra es donde el gris hace su aparición. Como escribió Derek Jarman: "La sombra ... es la Reina del Color. El color canta en el gris". Sobre una superficie radiante, el negro se convierte en un espejo o en un muro opaco que absorbe la luz. El negro es místico: encarna la elegancia como ningún otro color. Su preminencia en las artes de la fotografía y la moda es indisputable. Desde que, en 1926, Coco Chanel inventó el concepto del "vestidito negro", los términos *elegante*, *negro* y *moda* han sido inseparables. ¿Quién sabe? Tal vez por su simplicidad, "el negro es el nuevo negro". Y siempre será así.

■ Desde que disponemos de una gama ilimitada de colores y podemos imprimirlos de forma económica y mostrarlos en filme y en fotos, el diseño en blanco, negro y gris ha dejado de ser una solución de compromiso. Para nosotros es un puro lujo: una combinación ganadora de colores, siempre disponible para cualquier marca que anhele parecer clásica, elegante, sofisticada, llena de contrastes, fresca, discreta, o tal vez intencionadamente simple; una identidad corporativa en la que el color no nos distrae de la esencia, sino que subraya su colorido intrínseco. Las sombras que elegimos se refuerzan después gracias a las características del papel y de otras superficies que empleamos para mostrar los diseños.

■ En este libro encontramos una colección de trabajos que, con independencia de la forma que adopten, muestra de lo que son capaces el negro, el blanco y el gris. Las composiciones impresas y las obras aquí presentadas nos emocionan profundamente, y nos sentimos orgullosos de participar en este proyecto.

13

Isabella Melschberger, Mike Rabensteiner / Bureau Rabensteiner

Preto, branco e cinza
O RETORNO AO BÁSICO

Preto asfalto, azeviche, sombra, Paynes Grey, preto marfim, ébano, preto profundo, preto ardósia, ônix, preto tinta, betume da Judéia, basalto, bistre, amora, café, asa de corvo, alcaçuz, tamarindo, alcatrão, feijão preto, azeitona preta, couro preto, sombra queimada, sombra natural, sombra natural escura, azul, azul da Prússia, verniz, preto luto, alcaçuz e trufa; branco linho, luz branca, nata, mármore, travertino, prata, alabastro, xisto branco, branco sudário, talco, neve, branco camélia, branco concha, barba de milho, renda antiga, bege, algodão, branco antigo, casca de ovo, branco da Espanha, osso, baunilha, linho, branco Navajo, pérola, magnólia, branco fumaça, cru, branco gelo, branco malaquita, nácar, branco com sombra queimada e branco porcelana; cinza lua, alumínio, cinza Caso, cinza natural, antracito, ferro, cinza claro, carvão, cinza frio, cinza cálido, cinza pérola, cinza escuro, cinza neutro, Gainsboro, prata, cinza areia, platina, cinzas, prata velha, cinza cadete, cinza azulado, glauco, cinza ardósia, cinza arroxeado, cinéreo, cinza jeans, toupeira e cinza de Davy. Para citar somente alguns.

▬ Os seres humanos temos tendência a desenvolver uma aguda sensibilidade para coisas que compõem o microcosmos do nosso campo de atividade. Bem poucas pessoas têm acesso a essas galáxias em miniatura, que são tão importantes para os especialistas, e isso é o que faz com que o nosso mundo tenha uma diversidade tão ampla. Todas as vezes que consultamos um especialista obtemos resultados e recebemos um relance do seu mundo e dos seus inúmeros e minúsculos detalhes. Um exemplo deste fenômeno é o *nariz*, tal como é chamado o indivíduo que possui o talento de formular um aroma novo e de criar um perfume, um *expert* capaz de perceber e rastrear inúmeros matizes que ficam ocultos ao sentido do olfato da maioria das pessoas.

▬ Para criar e comercializar algo que supere as expectativas e as demandas do simples mortais necessita-se de uma sensibilidade e de uma habilidade semelhantes a essa. A qualidade esconde-se nos detalhes. E, afinal, são esses detalhes que agradam a todos e que ajudam a qualquer pessoa, mesmo que não seja um especialista, a diferenciar entre um produto comum e outro excepcional.

▬ *Por todas estas razões, o "pensamento em branco e preto" não é tão simples como poderia parecer. Para nós, os designers, não é assim.*

▬ De fato, nós o enxergamos como uma plataforma de lançamento. Se quisermos criar uma marca que cause um impacto, primeiramente temos que ir às bases, aos fundamentos. Costumamos trabalhar em branco e preto, mas nem o branco é simplesmente branco nem o preto é somente preto. Entre ambos há infinitas possibilidades, dentro da inesgotável paleta dos cinzas. Um preto corresponde a outro assim como uma linha desenhada por laser corresponde a um traço a lápis. Experimentamos novas ideias, jogamos com elas, as ajustamos e refinamos. Às vezes, até ficamos surpresos com os resultados. Nada pode ser julgado com tanta clareza e limpidez como um desenho em branco e preto: ele possui contraste e simplicidade. Prescindir inicialmente de uma cor importante – ou descartá-la definitivamente– é um sistema que nós, designers, utilizamos para determinar se o nosso trabalho funciona na realidade, para saber se um logo cumpre o propósito estabelecido e atinge o seu objetivo, e também para comprovar se a linguagem das formas é adequada e o equilíbrio está correto.

▬ Somos conscientes da importância das cores e do lugar indispensável que elas ocupam em todos os aspectos da nossa vida, desde a arte e a moda até a psicologia e a natureza. O que tentamos demonstrar é o fato de que o branco, o preto e o cinza podem ser desdobrados com a mesma variedade, a mesma riqueza de facetas e a mesma complexidade que proporcionam todas as cores do espectro luminoso. Desde o primeiro esboço até o produto final, esgotamos todas as possibilidades oferecidas pelo esquema de cor acromático.

▬ *Em outras palavras, o desenho em branco e preto não é para os que desanimam facilmente. É para os que não têm medo de compromisso e se atrevem a demonstrar do que são capazes. O branco e o preto não são neutros: eles assumem riscos. E o mesmo se pode aplicar, até com mais certeza, ao cinza.*

▬ Se o preto proporciona a força, o branco confere a delicadeza. E, no entanto, o branco pode ser lançado agressivamente sobre o espectador a ponto de obrigá-lo desviar o olhar. Contrariamente à opinião comum, o branco é o oposto ao espaço vazio: é o espaço cheio de certeza. E ali, onde a luz se transfigura em sombra, é o lugar onde o cinza faz sua aparição. Como escreveu Derek Jarman: "A sombra ... é a Rainha da Cor. A cor canta no cinza". Sobre uma superfície radiante, o preto converte-se num espelho ou num muro opaco que absorve a luz. O preto é místico: encarna a elegância como nenhuma outra cor. Sua prominência nas artes da fotografia e da moda é indiscutível. Desde que, em 1926, Coco Chanel inventou o conceito do "vestidinho preto", os termos *elegante*, *preto* e *moda* tornaram-se inseparáveis. Quem o sabe? Talvez por sua simplicidade, "o preto é o novo preto". E sempre será assim.

▬ Desde que passamos a dispor de uma gama ilimitada de cores e podemos imprimi-las de forma econômica e mostrá-las em filme e em fotos, o desenho em branco, preto e cinza deixou de ser um compromisso obrigatório. Para nós, é puro luxo: uma combinação ganhadora de cores, sempre disponível para qualquer marca que almeje parecer clássica, elegante, sofisticada, cheia de contrastes, fresca, discreta ou, talvez, intencionadamente simples; uma identidade corporativa onde a cor não nos distraia da essência, mas sublinhe o seu colorido intrínseco. As sombras que escolhemos se reforçam depois graças às características do papel e de outras superfícies que empregamos para apresentar os desenhos.

▬ Neste livro, encontramos uma coleção de trabalhos que, independente da forma que adotem, mostra do que são capazes o preto, o branco e o cinza. As composições impressas e as obras aqui apresentadas emocionam-nos profundamente, e nos sentimos orgulhosos de participar neste projeto.

Prólogo   Isabella Meischberger, Mike Rabensteiner / Bureau Rabensteiner

Black and White is a timeless combination of colors. Because of its monochromatic way of presentation, black and white process a certain charm beyond fathoming. It's been a popular choice for graphic designers for years. Simple, vintage, and sometimes elegant, black and white are the colors that capture viewer's attention by simply reducing colors to the basics to lead the focus back to the visual message a graphic design tries to express.

Water, ©Marco Buonoc

Gray is a neutral and balanced color between black and white. It is believed to be a cool, conservative color that seldom evokes strong emotion although it can be seen as a cloudy or moody color. Web designers and graphic designers often use gray as an innocuous background yet very few notice it can be a very powerful color to use with the right design concept in the right settings.

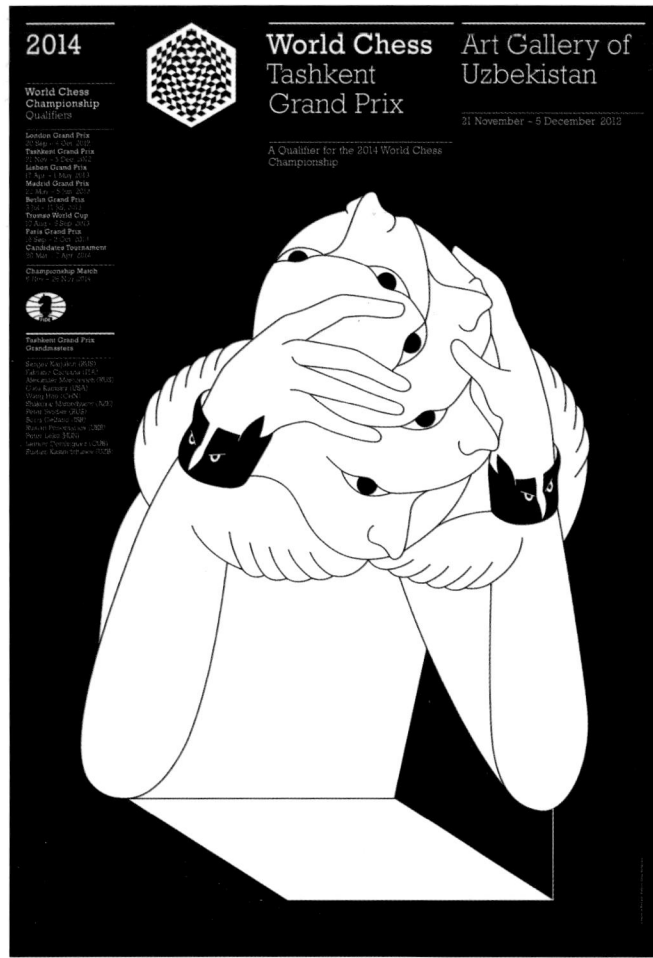

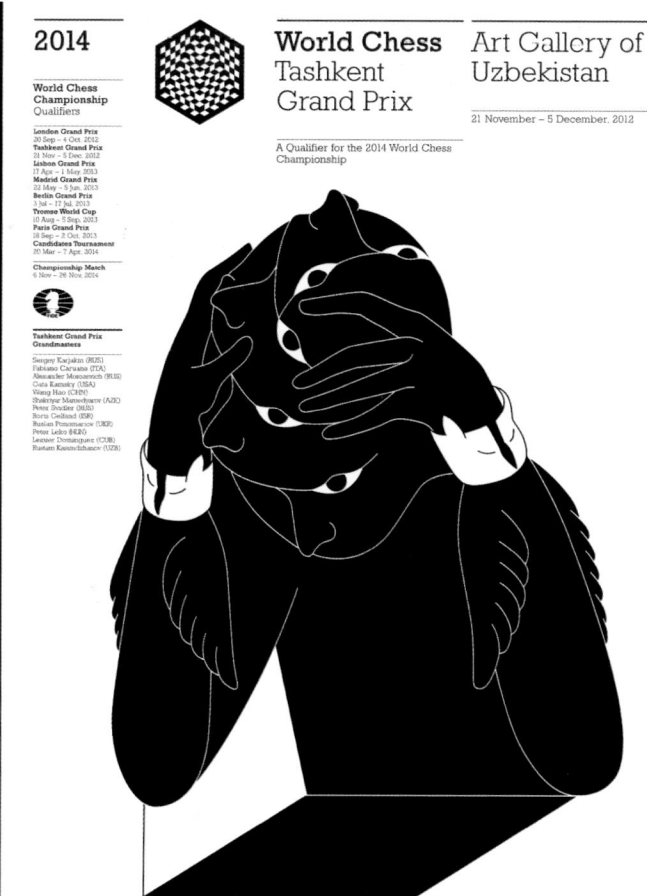

Andrew Paulson on Behalf of World Chess

United Kingdom

Pentagram Design
Design Agency

John Rushworth
Designer

World Chess
Client

To restore Chess's worldwide prominence, Pentagram partners John Rushworth, Daniel Weil and Naresh Ramchandani vitalized the World Chess brand by creating a system of names, an identity, a campaign and a gaming environment built upon the qualities of intelligence and intensity.

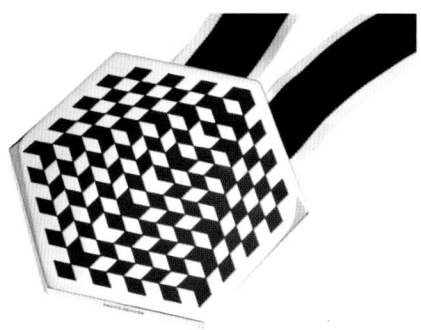

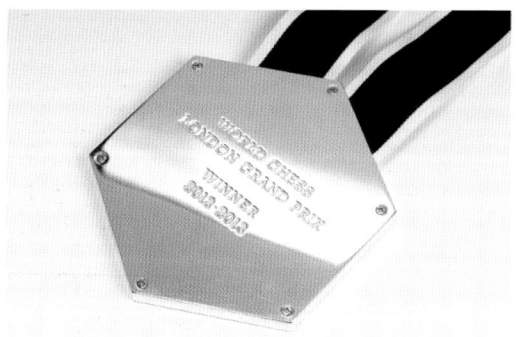

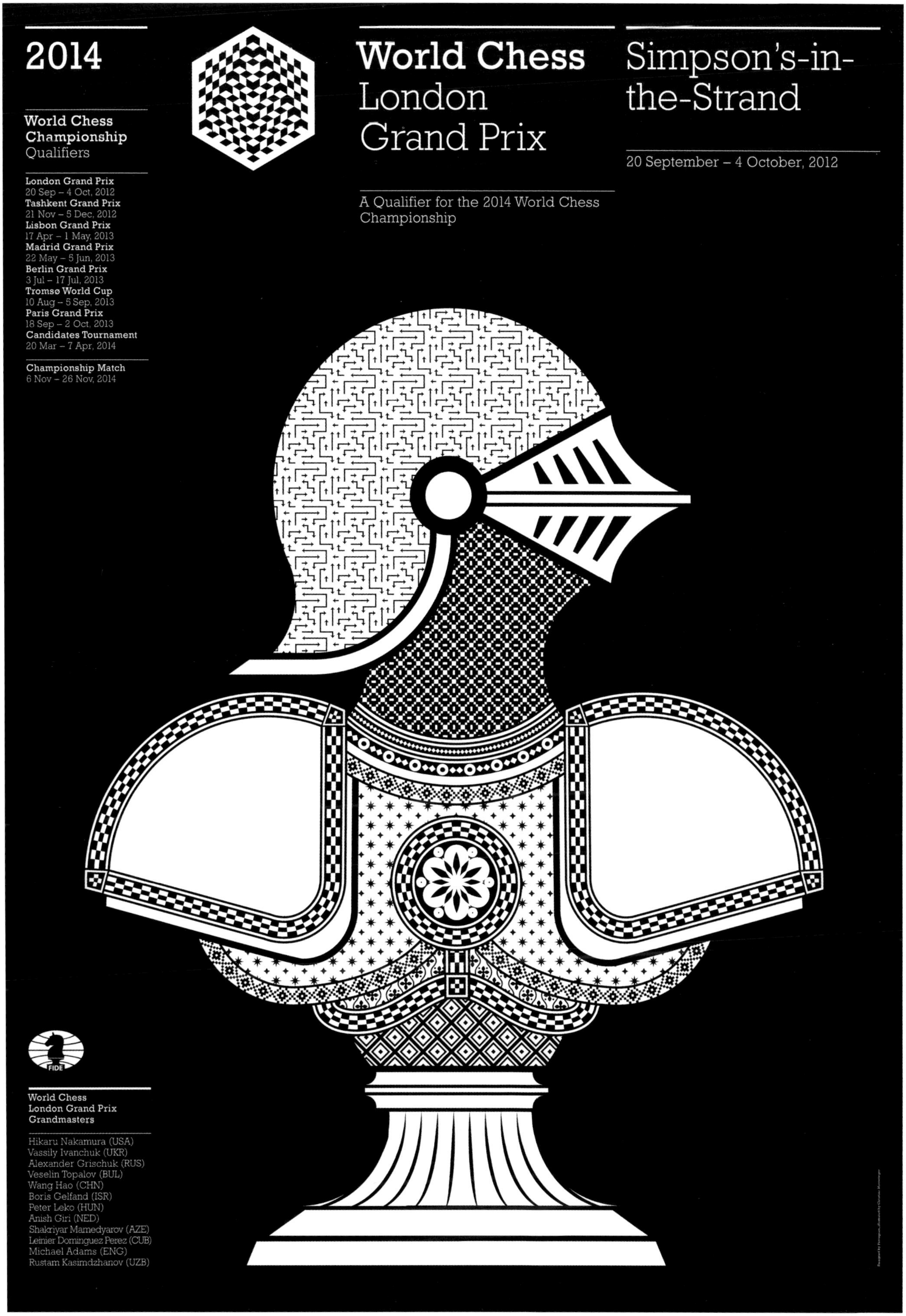

2014

World Chess Championship Qualifiers

London Grand Prix
20 Sep – 4 Oct, 2012
Tashkent Grand Prix
21 Nov – 5 Dec, 2012
Lisbon Grand Prix
17 Apr – 1 May, 2013
Madrid Grand Prix
22 May – 5 Jun, 2013
Berlin Grand Prix
3 Jul – 17 Jul, 2013
Tromsø World Cup
10 Aug – 5 Sep, 2013
Paris Grand Prix
18 Sep – 2 Oct, 2013
Candidates Tournament
20 Mar – 7 Apr, 2014

Championship Match
6 Nov – 26 Nov, 2014

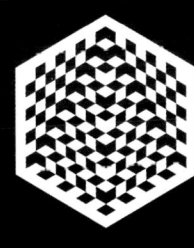

World Chess
London
Grand Prix

A Qualifier for the 2014 World Chess Championship

Simpson's-in-the-Strand

20 September – 4 October, 2012

World Chess London Grand Prix Grandmasters

Hikaru Nakamura (USA)
Vassily Ivanchuk (UKR)
Alexander Grischuk (RUS)
Veselin Topalov (BUL)
Wang Hao (CHN)
Boris Gelfand (ISR)
Peter Leko (HUN)
Anish Giri (NED)
Shakriyar Mamedyarov (AZE)
Leinier Dominguez Perez (CUB)
Michael Adams (ENG)
Rustam Kasimdzhanov (UZB)

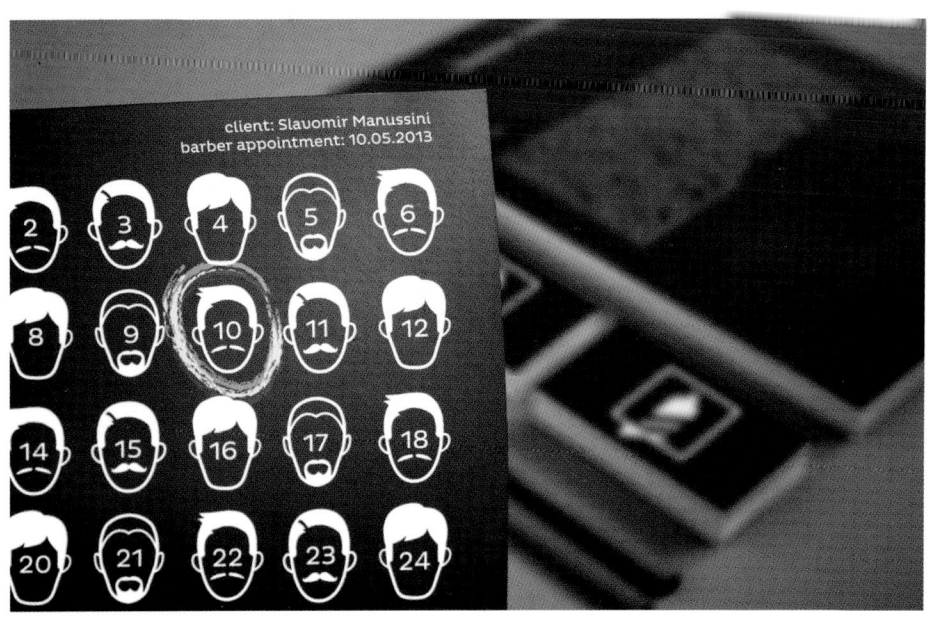

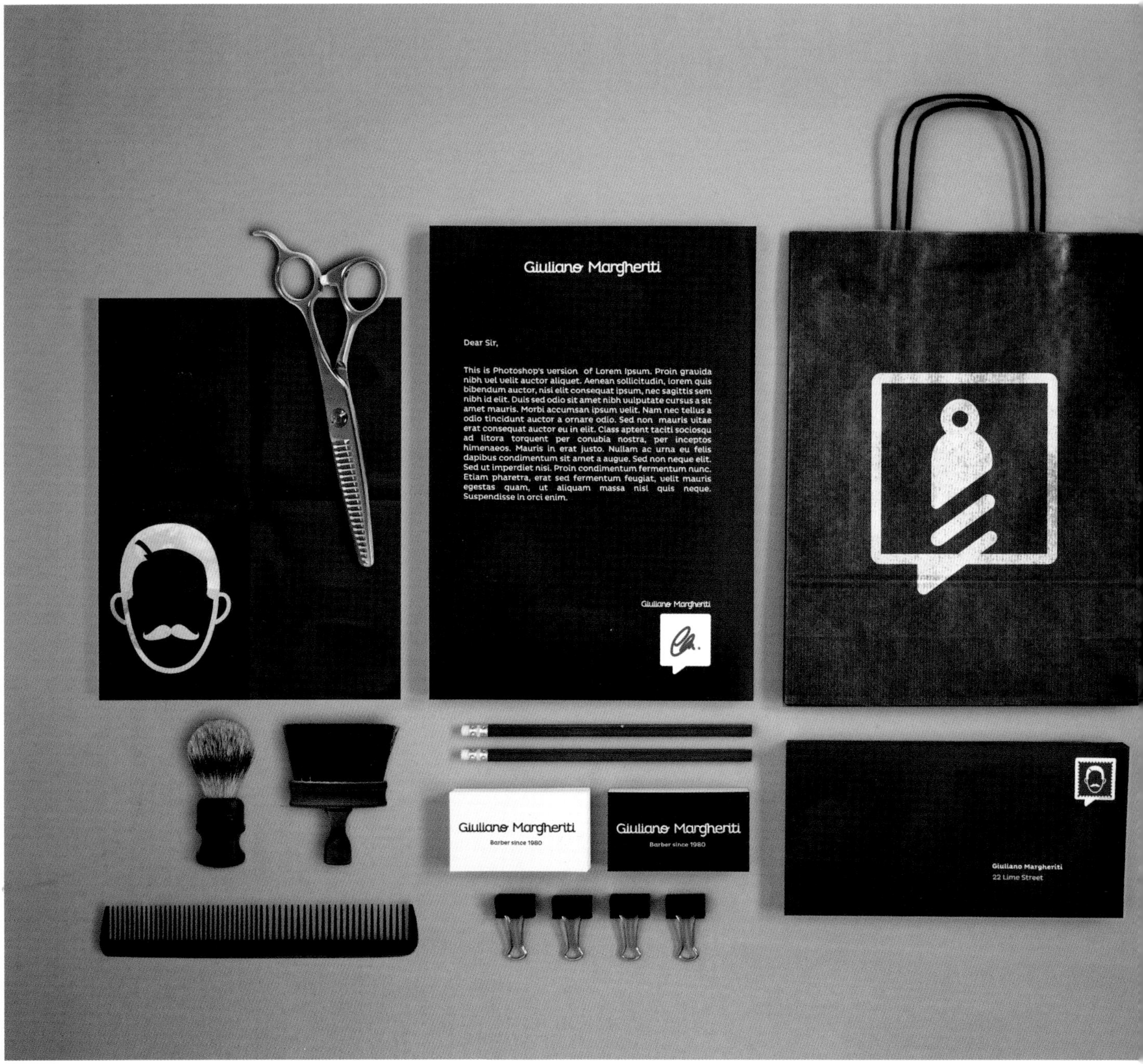

Giuliano Margheriti

Poland

Cosa Nostra Agency
Design Agency

Gracjan Wrzachol
Creative Director

Giuliano Margheriti
Client

This is the branding for an Italian barber – Giuliano Margheriti. The goal was to visually distinguish the client from other local barbers. The minimalist identity shines with elegance. In the promotion and advertising of the brand, the use of black and white colors depicts a classy brand image.

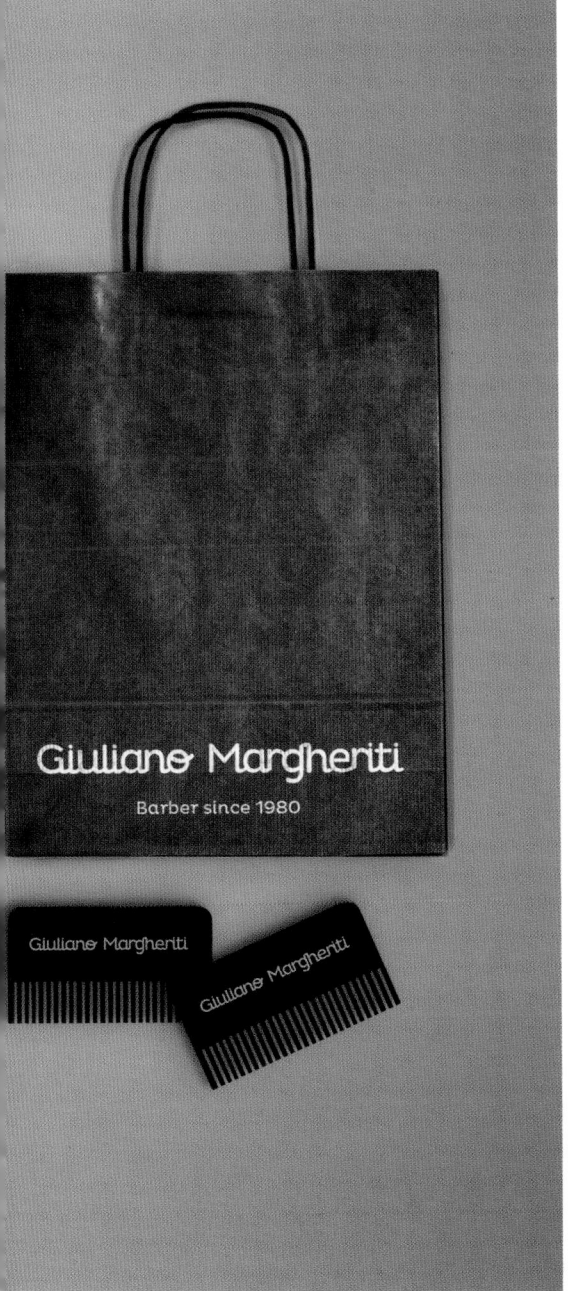

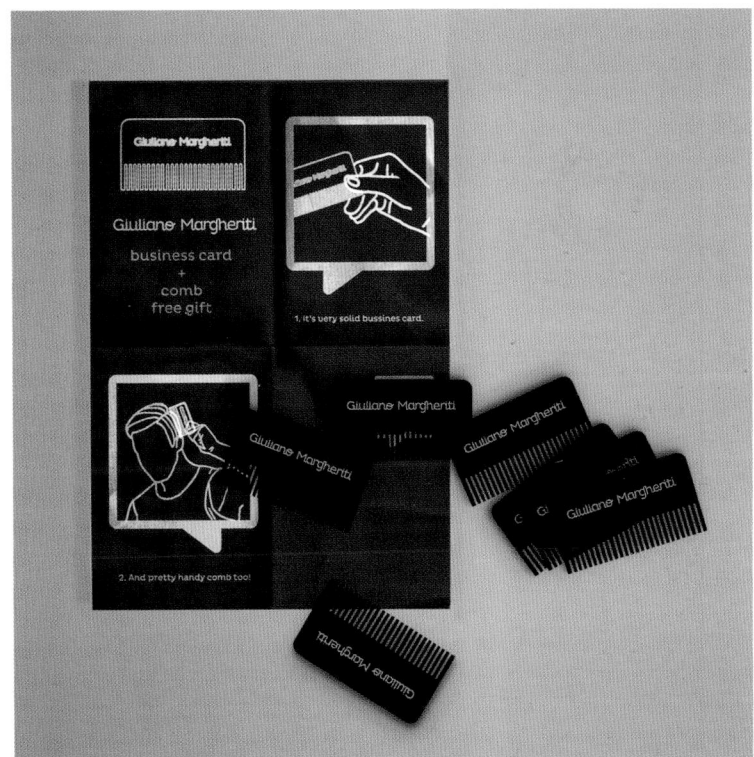

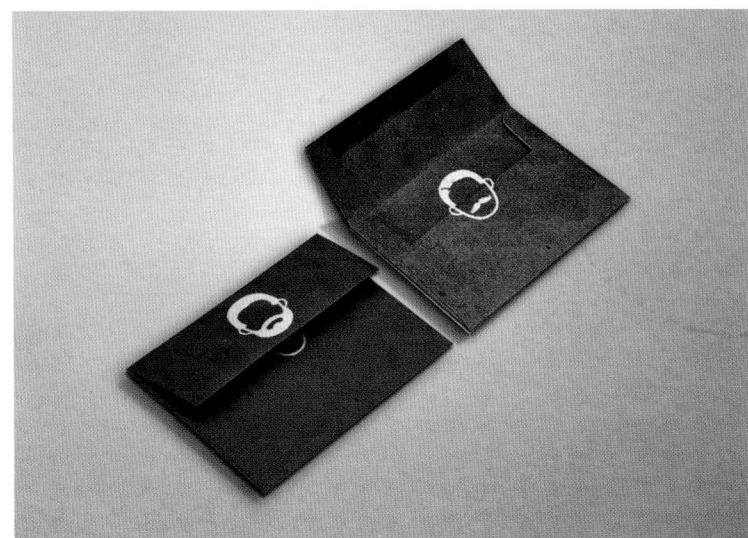

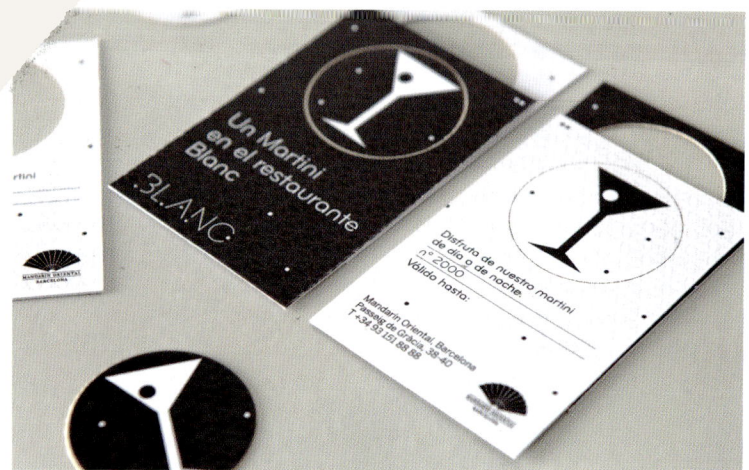

Restaurant Blanc
Spain

Alex Dalmau
Designer

Susana Gellida
Photographer

Hotel Mandarin Oriental Barcelona
Client

Restaurant Blanc is an establishment located inside the Barcelona Mandarin Oriental Hotel. At Blanc, bottles are made of aluminum and silkscreened with the restaurant's image, which is why the black and white palette used in the branding goes so well with the style of the restaurant.

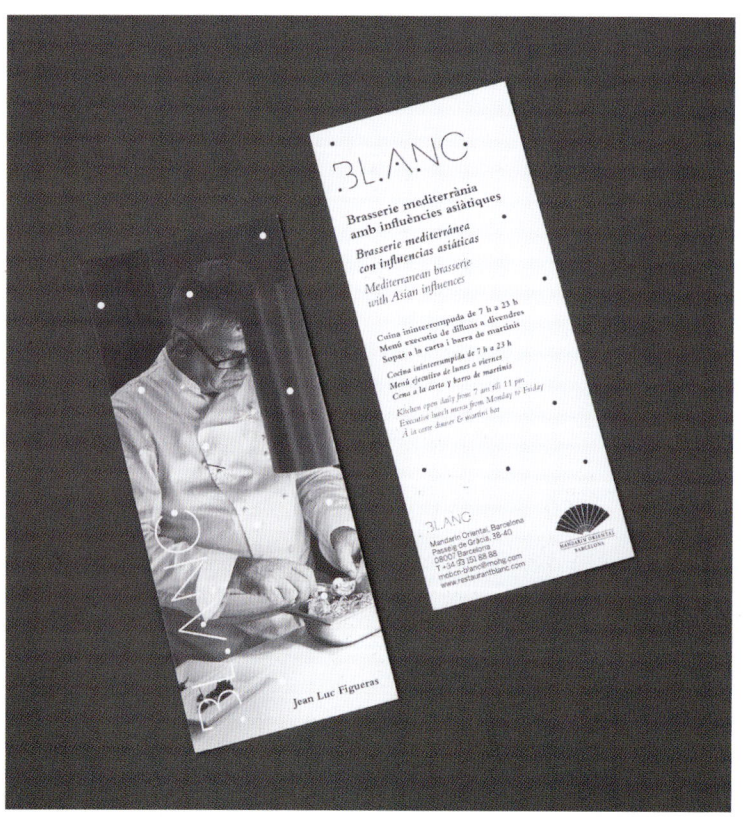

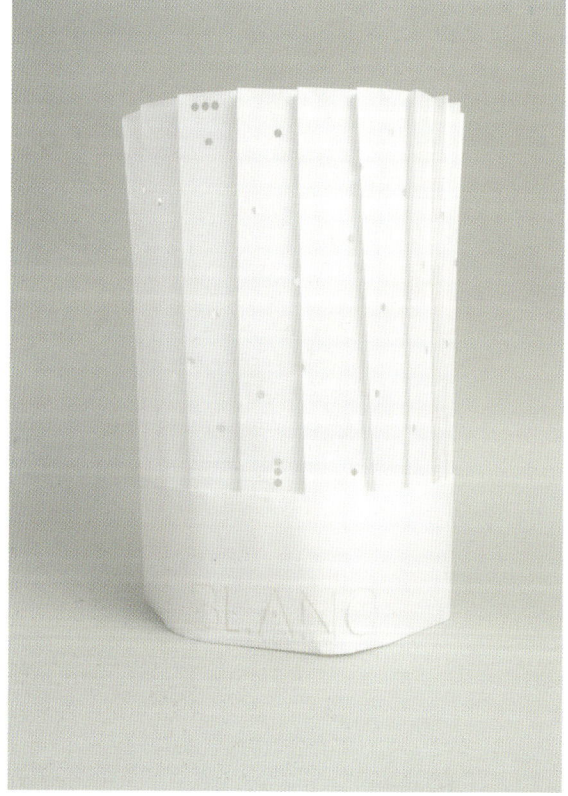

.BL.ANC

brasserie & gastrobar

VINOS BLANCOS POR COPAS
WHITE WINES FOR GLASS

D.O. Penedès
Crisalys de Torelló Xarel.lo 2010   6,00 €
Can Credo 2008   6,00 €

D.O. Costers del Segre
Els Eixaders Chardonnay 2008   7,00 €

D.O. Rías Baixas
Zíos de Lusco 2010   6,00 €

V.D.T. Castilla y León
Quinta Apolonia 2009   6,00 €

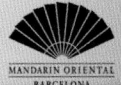

MANDARIN ORIENTAL
BARCELONA

.BL.ANC

brasserie & gastrobar

ESPUMOSOS POR COPAS
ESPUMOSOS FOR GLASS

D.O. Cava
Mont-Marçal Extremarium   5,00 €

A.O.C. Champagne
Bollinger Spécial Cuvée   15,00 €
Bollinger Rosé   28,00 €

VINOS ROSADOS POR COPAS
ROSE WINES FOR GLASS

D.P. Terra Alta
Mas Amor 2010 Rosado   7,00 €

A.O.C. Côtes de Provence
Domaine d'Ott Château
de Selle Coeur de Grain 2010   11,00 €

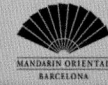

MANDARIN ORIENTAL
BARCELONA

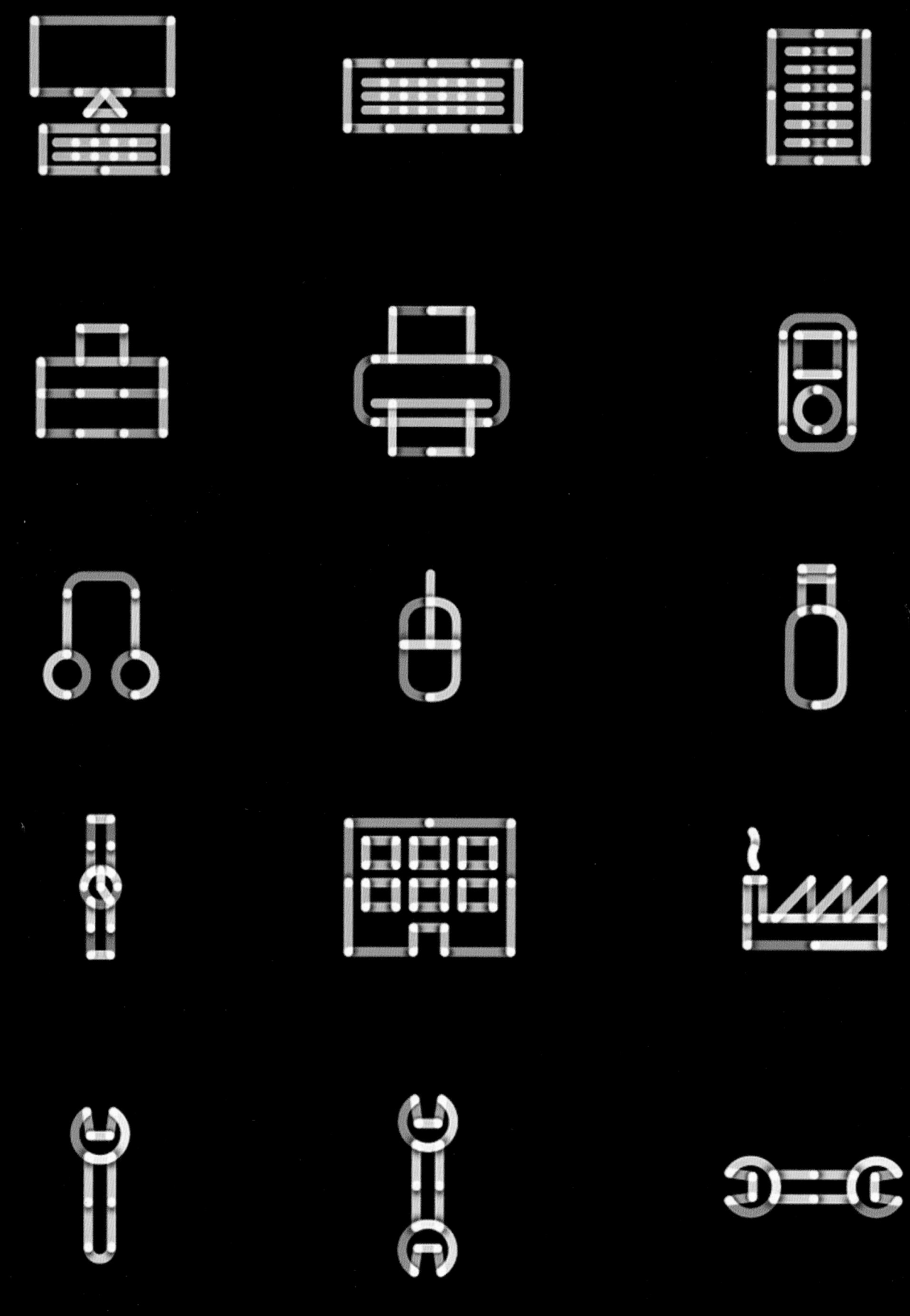

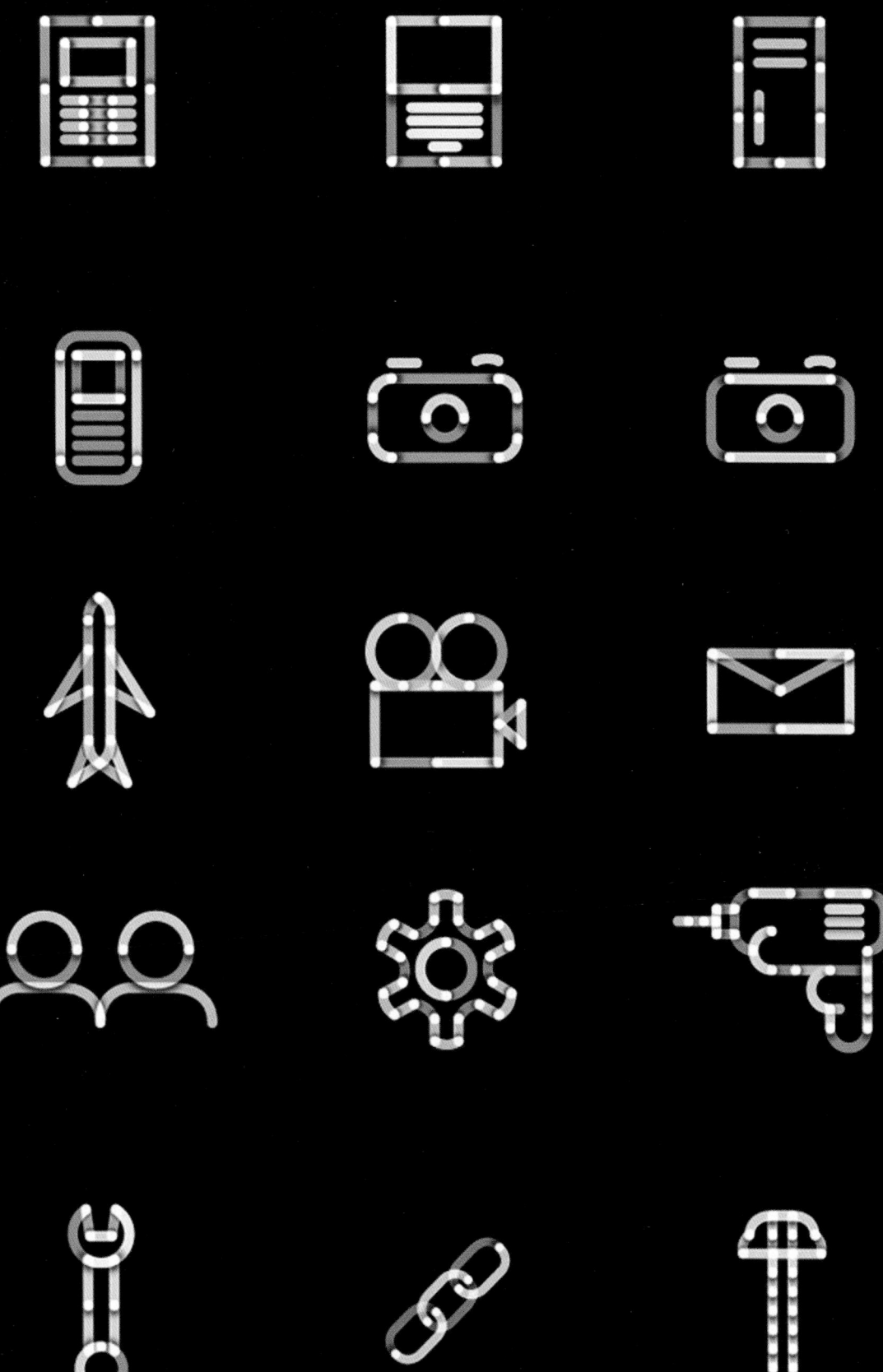

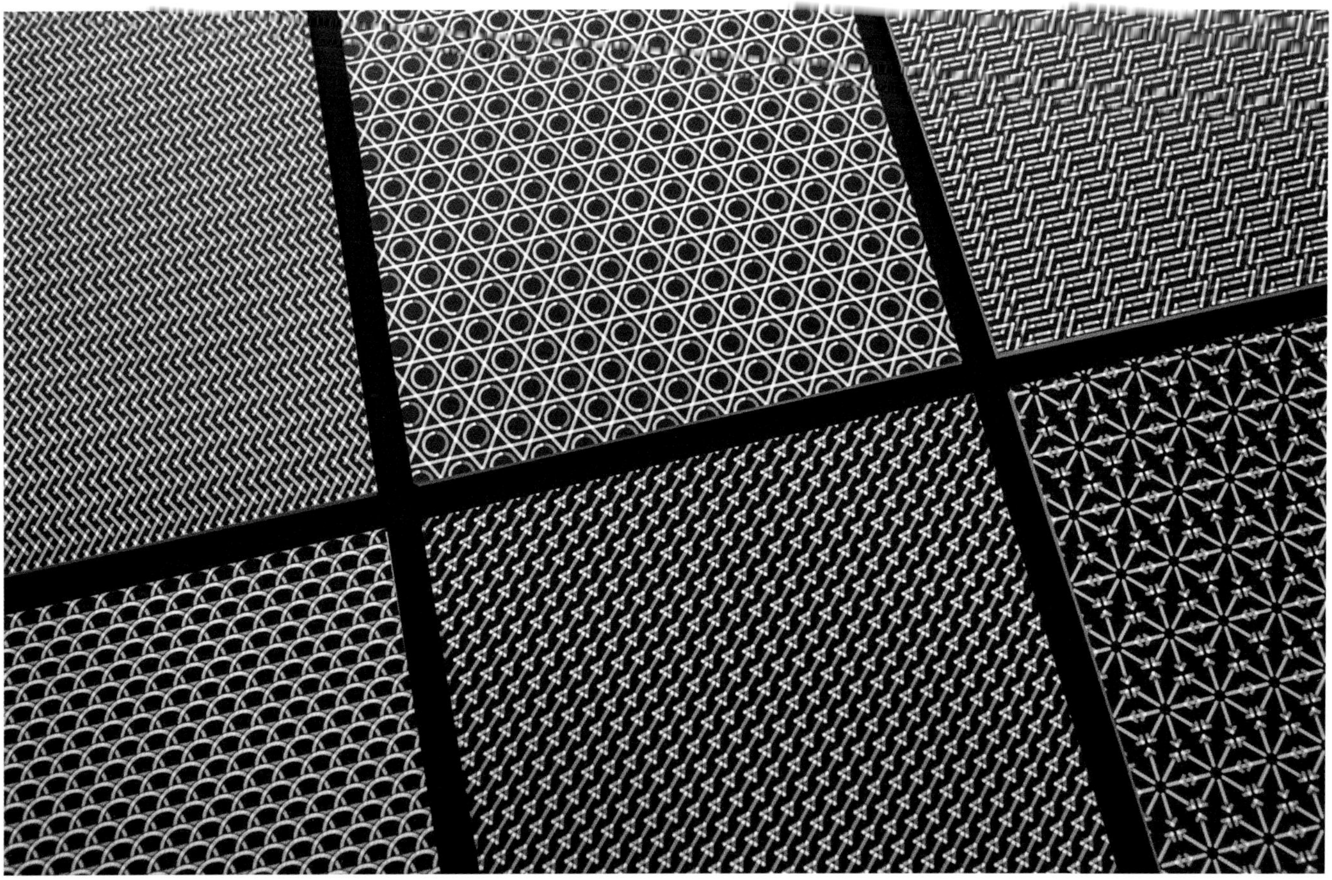

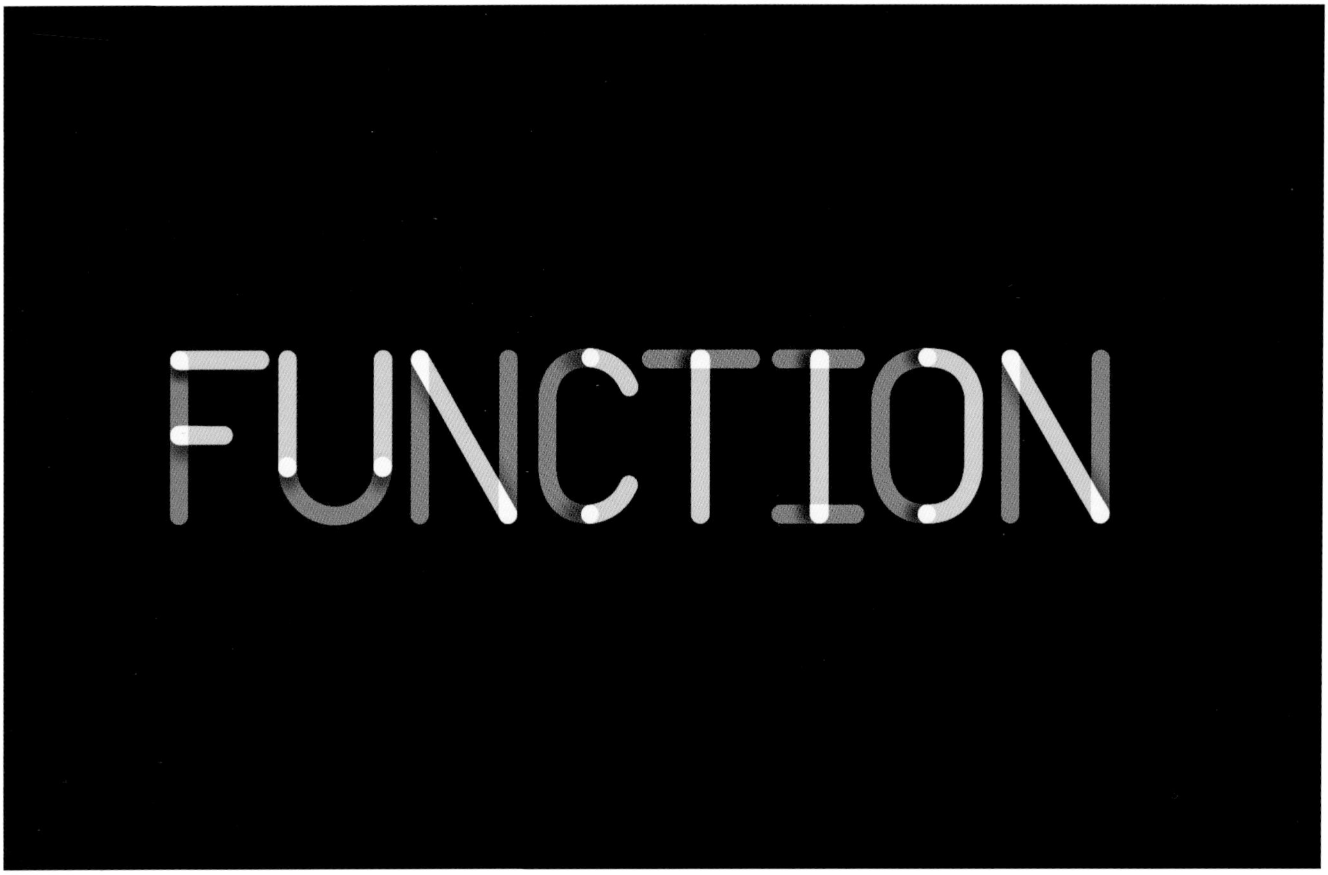

FUNCTION

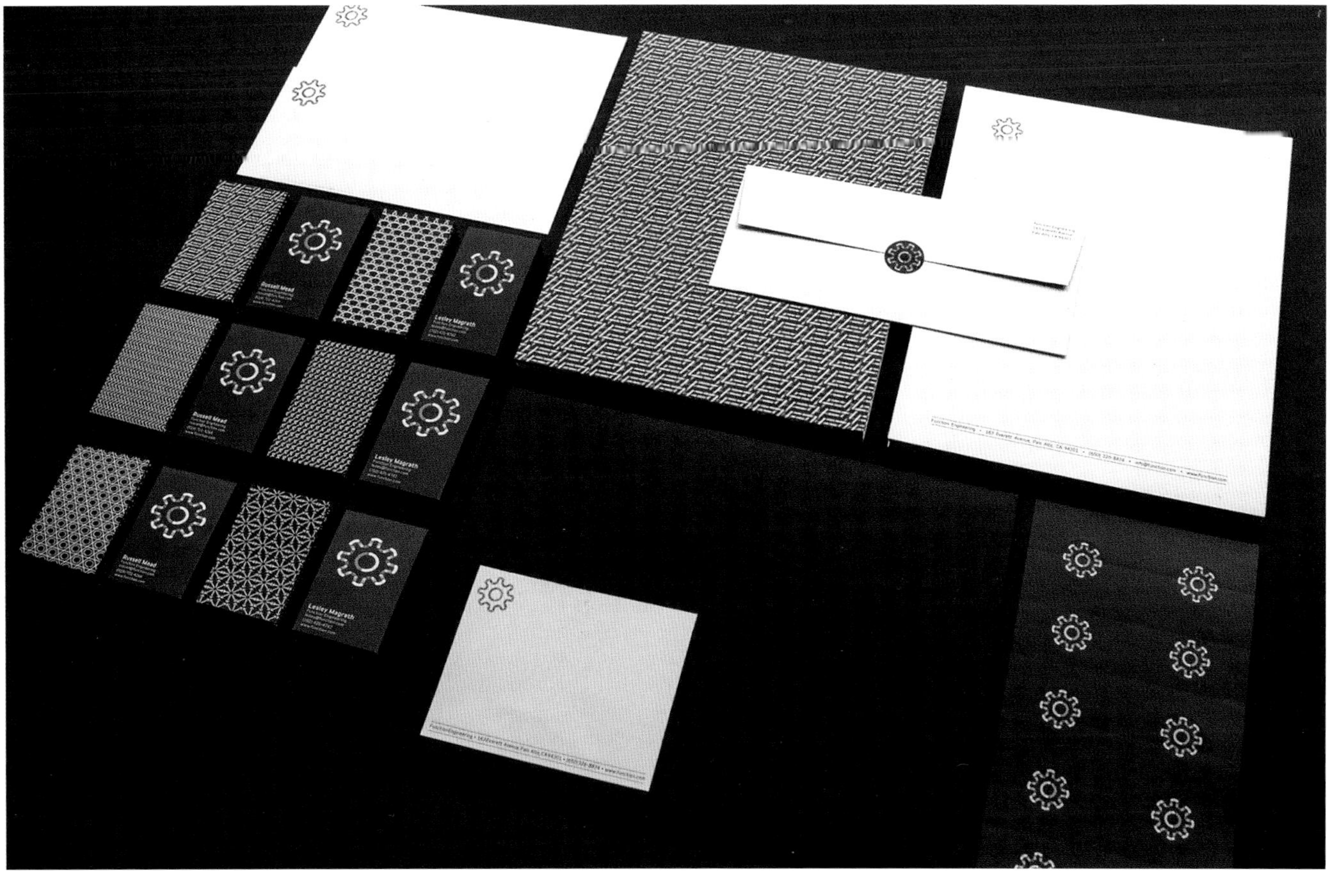

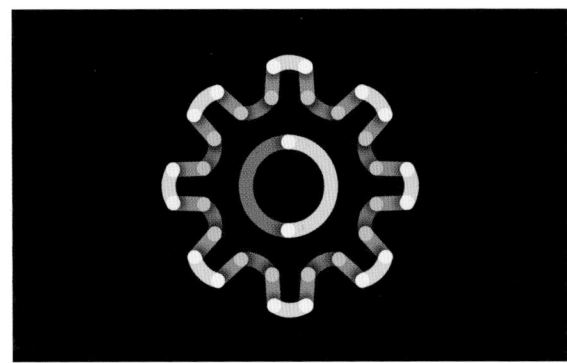

Function Engineering
United States

Wade Jeffree
Designer

Function Egineering
Client

Function Engineering specializes in mechanical design and engineering for product development. Narrowing in on Function's expertise in designing hinge and linkage mechanisms, the designer created a typographic system based on a hinge/pivot system, which was later expanded by creating a series of icons, illustrations, and patterns that can be used flexibly across various collateral in print and online.

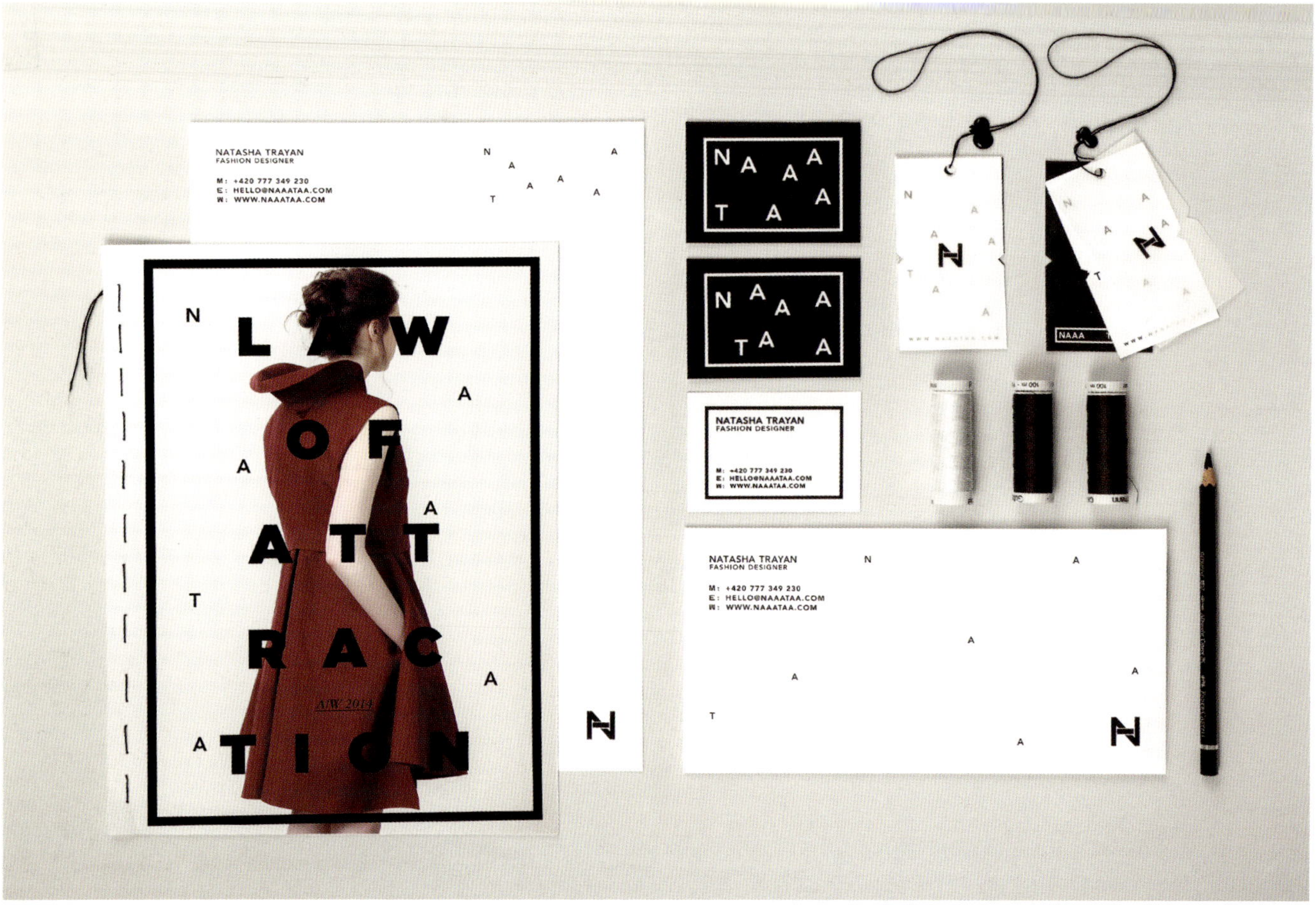

NAAA TAA
Czech Republic

Evan Dorlot
Designer

Natasha Trayan
Client

NAAA TAA is a unisex clothing brand in Prague. The designer interpreted all sides of each piece of her design by a unified identity: unique, minimalist, edgy and structural, using a system of modular typography in black and white that graphically accentuates the visual world created by the fashion designer.

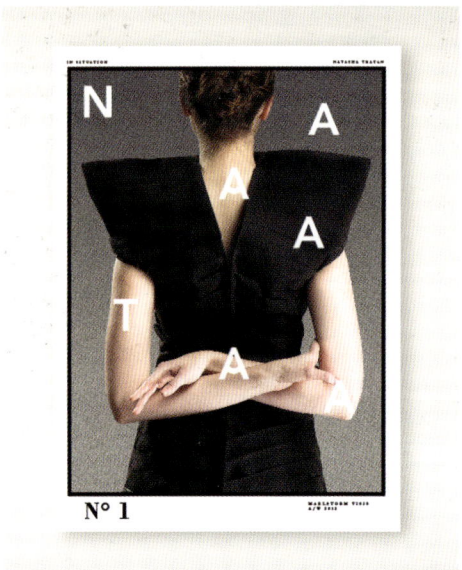

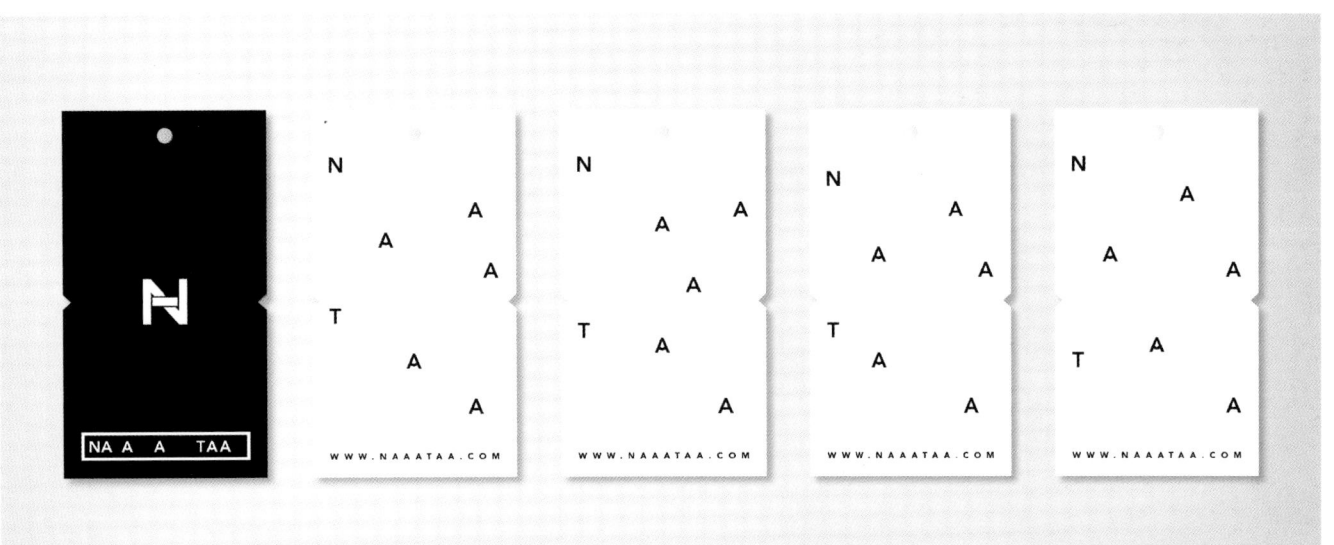

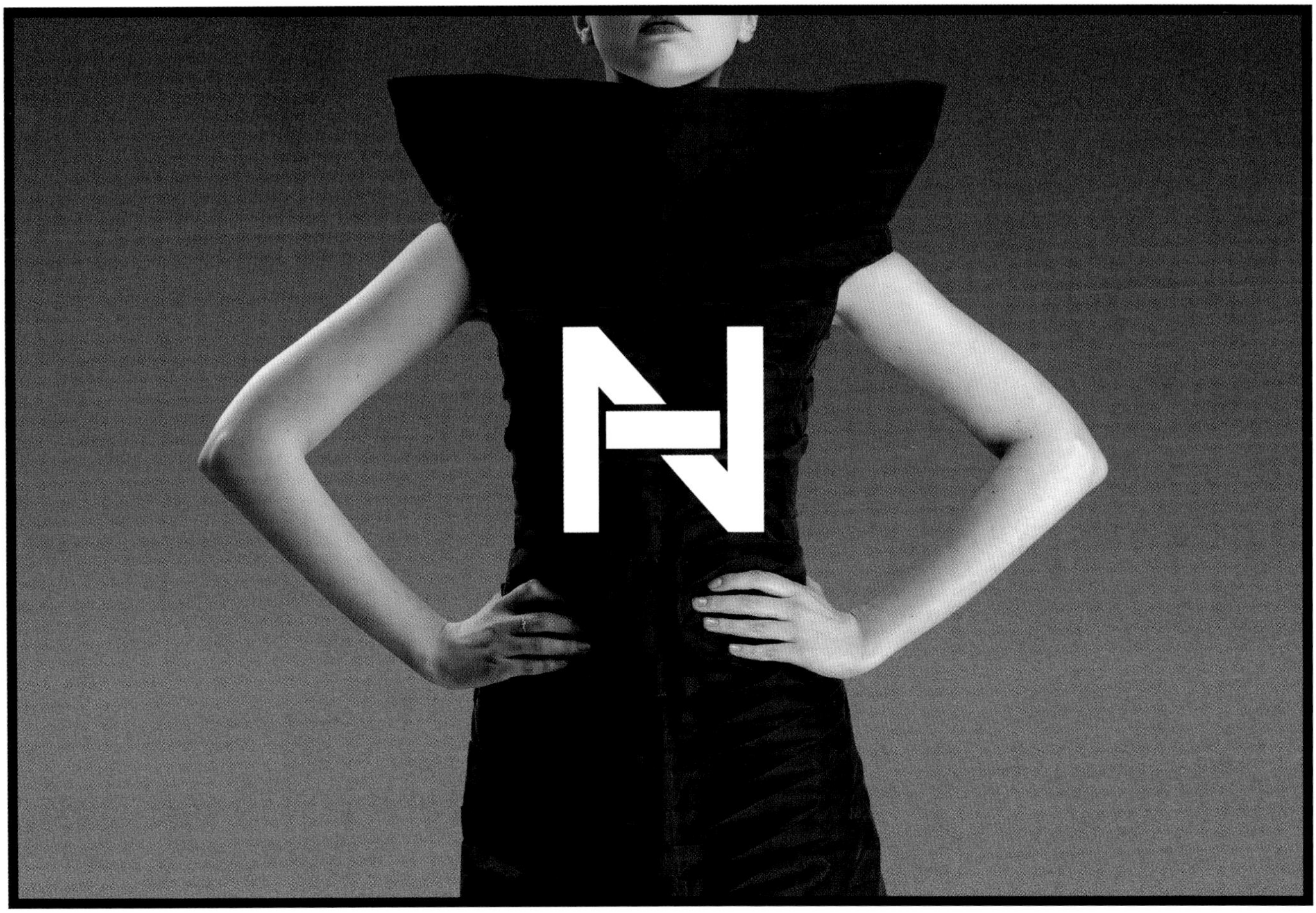

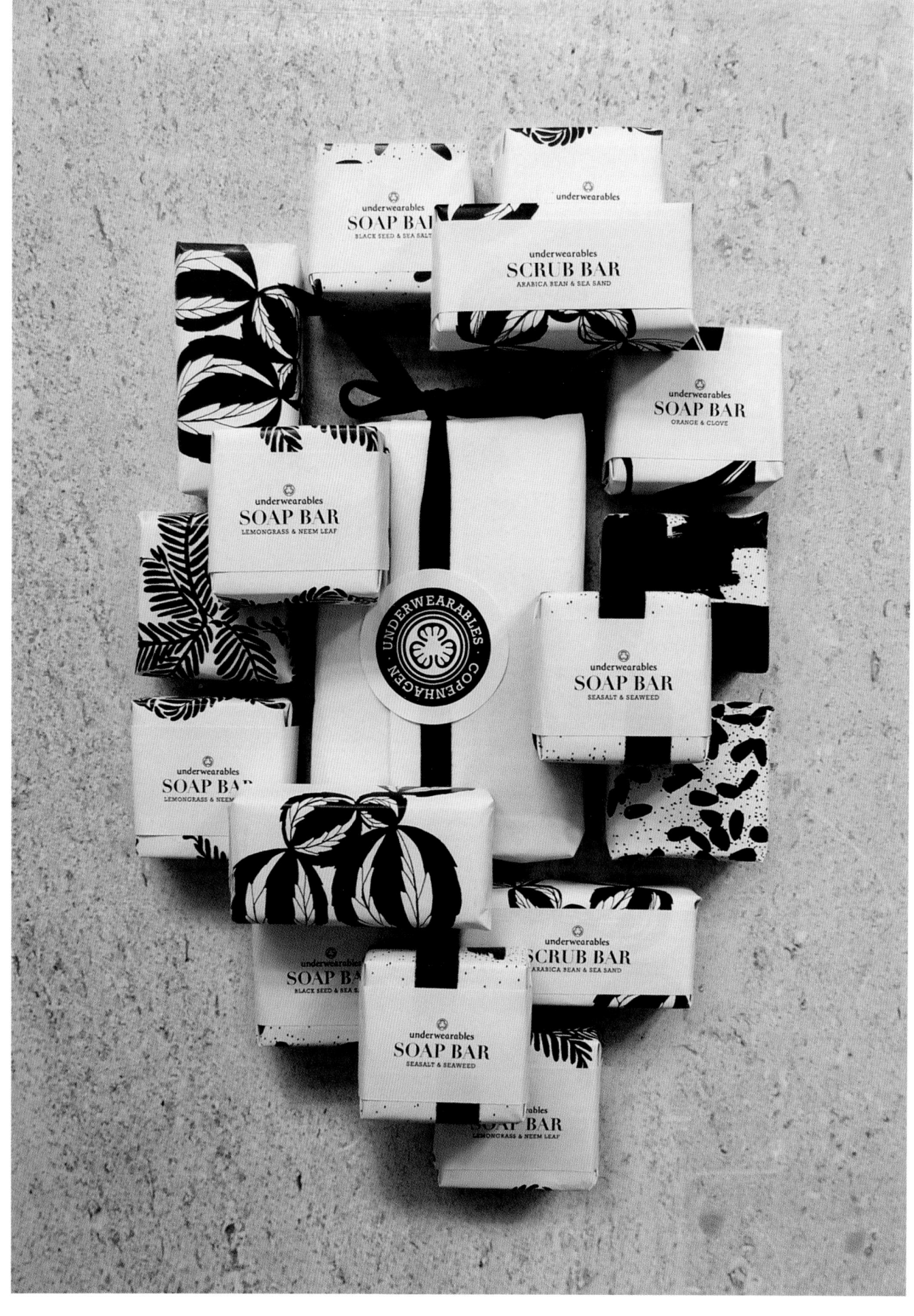

"Black and white is a fascinating and everlasting tale of light and darkness; what lies hidden in the light of day, becomes visible when the darkness falls."
—Spread Studio

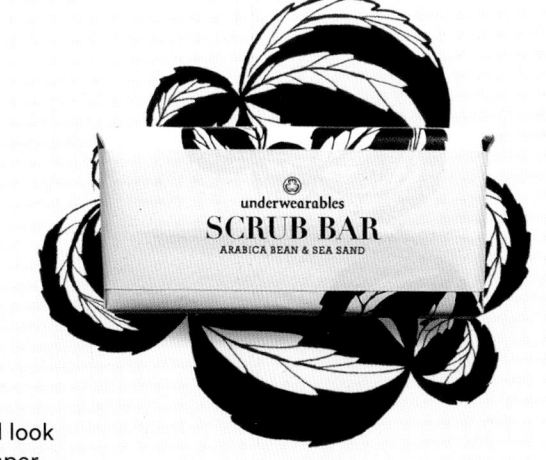

Underwearables Soap
Denmark

Spread Studio
Design Agency

Sidsel Solmer Eriksen
Designer

Underwearables
Client

The design focuses on a simple and crafted look by using Japanese black ink on recycled paper to display the ingredients in an engagingly poetic style. Like the handmade soap inside, the design features also a handmade style that can best be described as 'exotic minimalism' – a mix of origin and modernism that appeals to their consumers who enjoy contemporary minimalist life style.

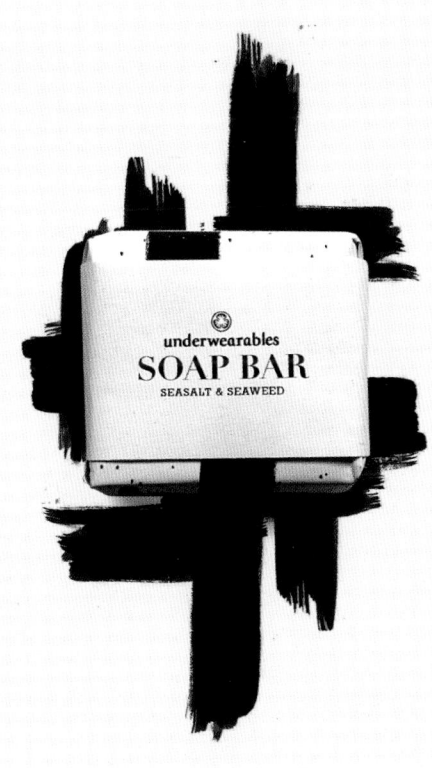

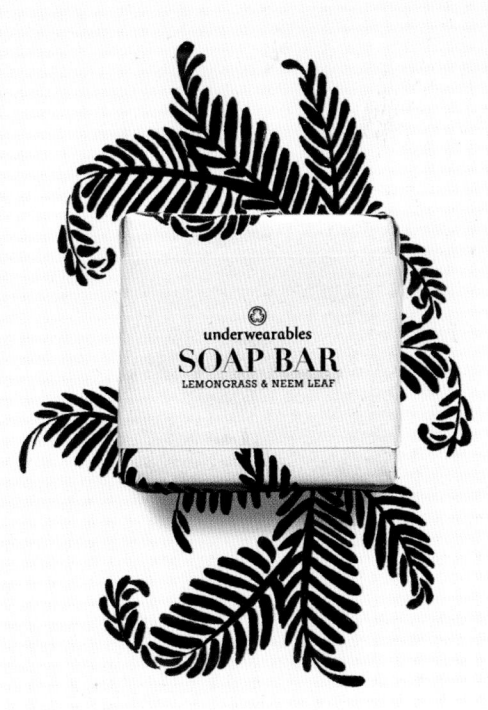

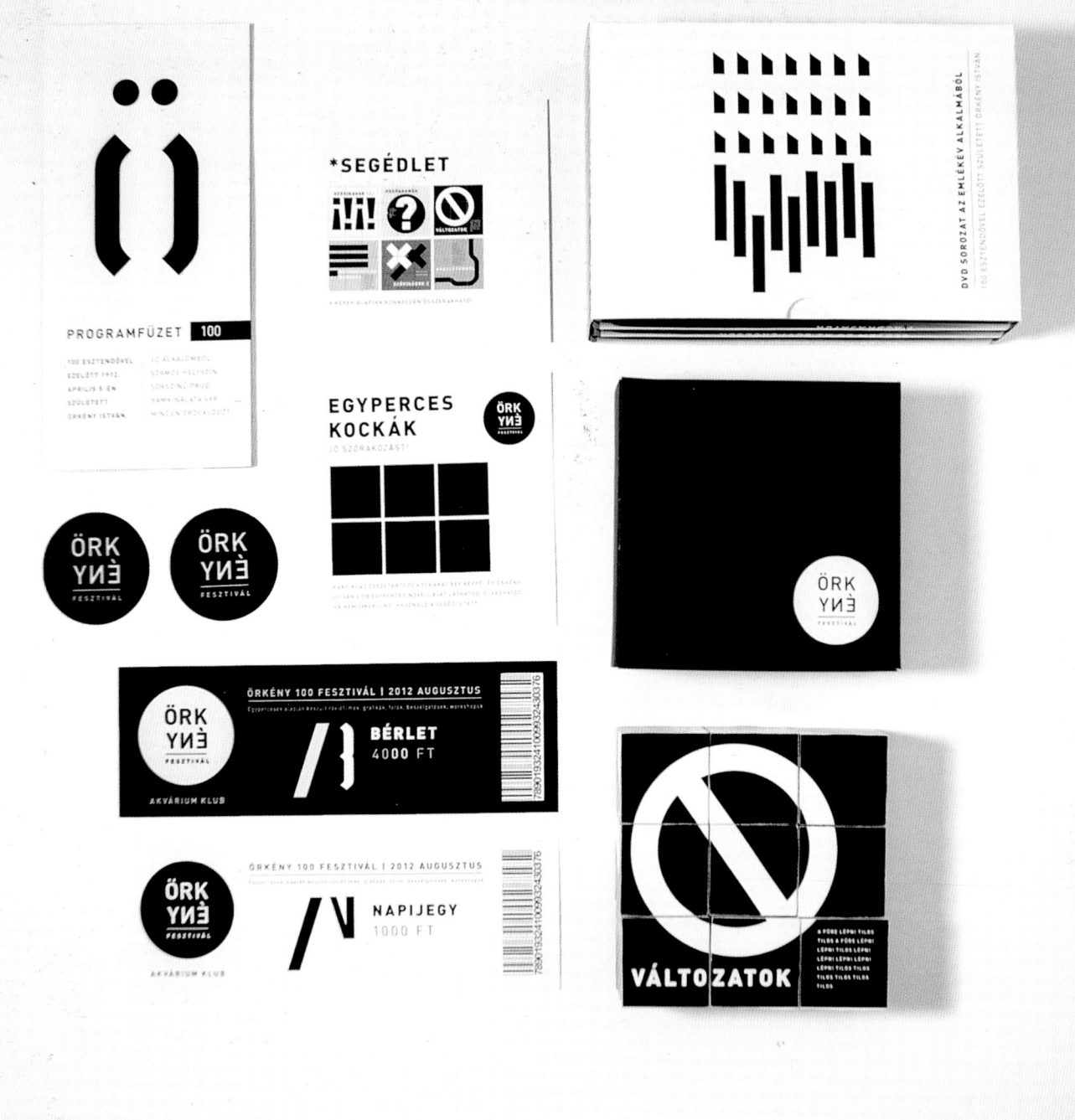

Örkény Festival Identity
Hungary

Enikő Déri
Designer

László Kőhegyi
Photographer

The occasion of the festival is a memorial year of the popular Hungarian writer Örkény István who lived in the 20th century. The concept was to create a complex project that would express the style of the writer. The designer used punctuation marks in every detail of the identity and highlighted the contrast between black and white.

ÖRK
YNÈ
FESZTIVÁL

100 ESZTENDŐVEL
EZELŐTT 1912. ÁPRILIS
5-ÉN SZÜLETETT ÖRKÉNY
ISTVÁN. AZ EMLÉKÉV
ALKALMÁBÓL ÖRKÉNY
100 KULTURÁLIS FESZ-
TIVÁLT RENDEZNEK
AZ AKVÁRIUM KLUBBAN.

AZ EGYPERCES
NOVELLÁK ALAPJÁN
KÉSZÜLT RÖVID-
FILMEK, GRAFIKÁK ÉS
FOTÓK BEMUTATÁSA,
KIÁLLÍTÁSA, TOVÁBBÁ
BESZÉLGETÉSEK
ÉS WORKSHOPOK.

AKVÁRIUM KLUB
2012 AUGUSZTUS

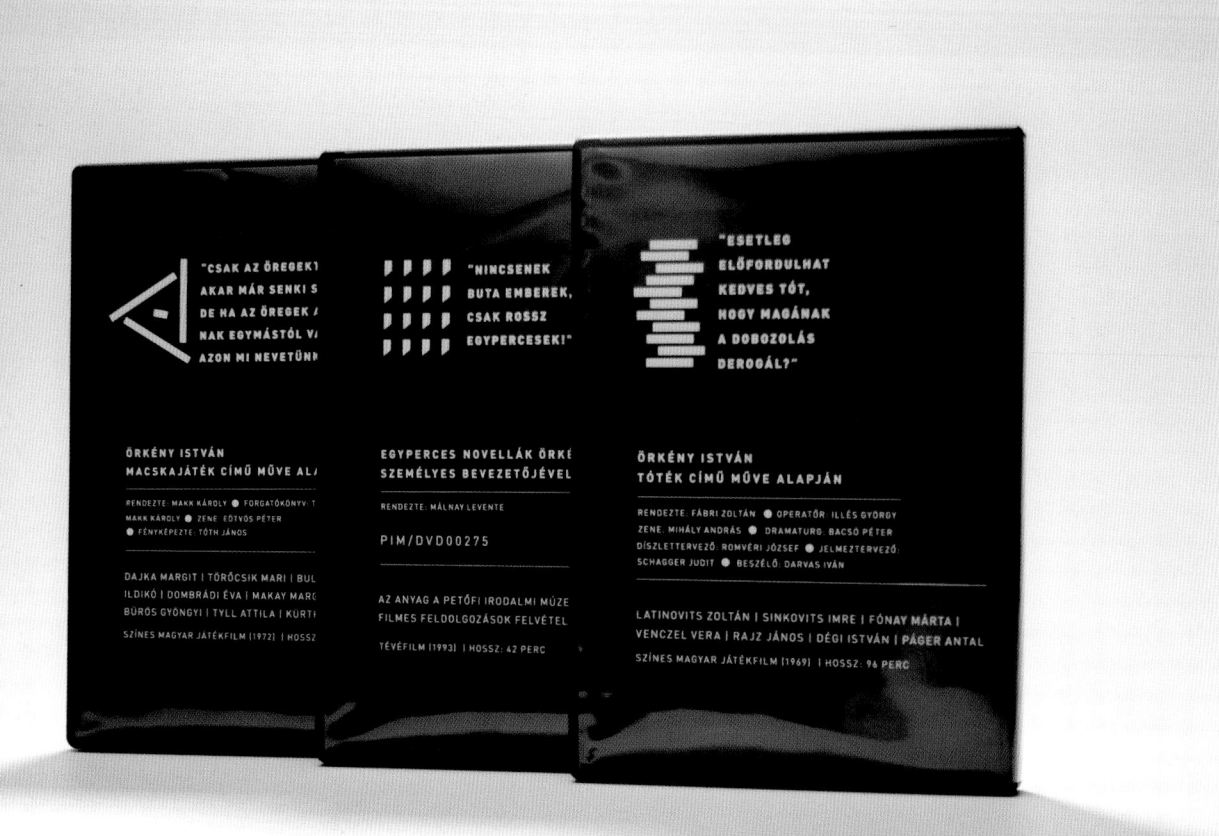

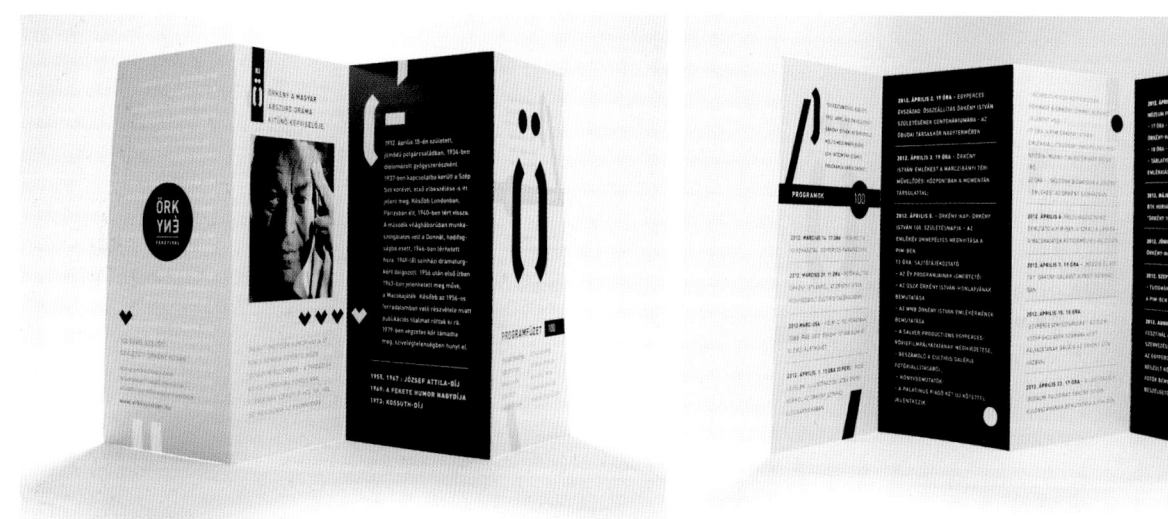

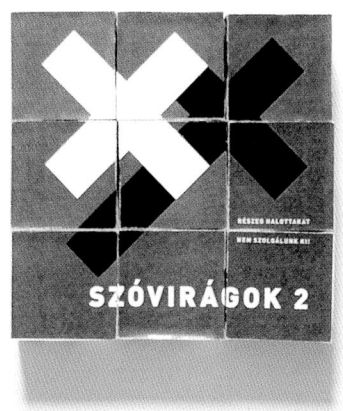

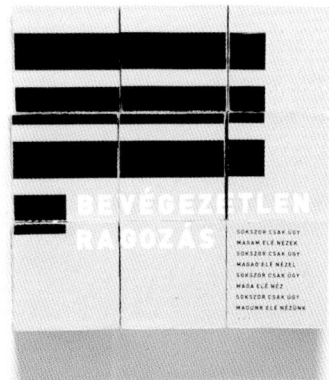

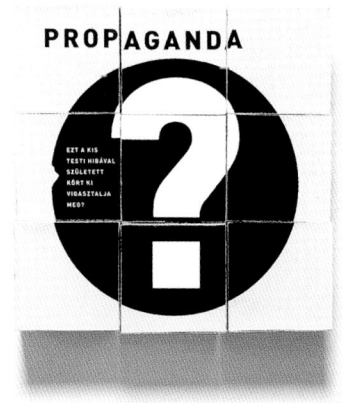

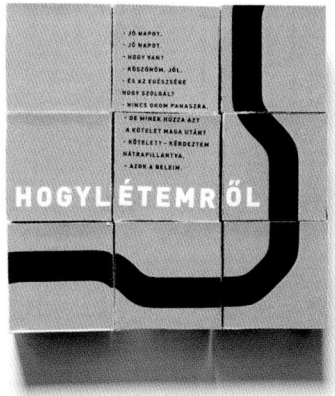

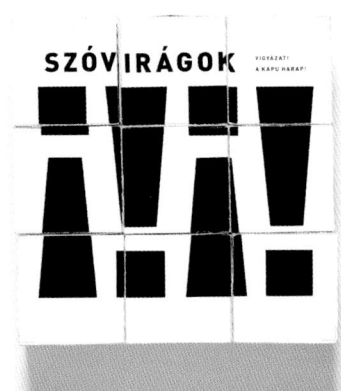

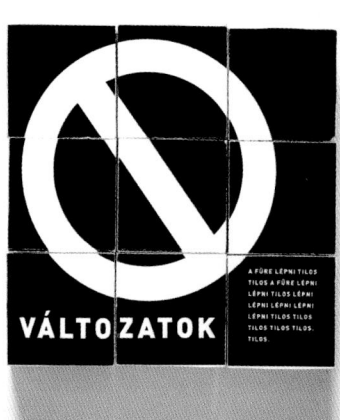

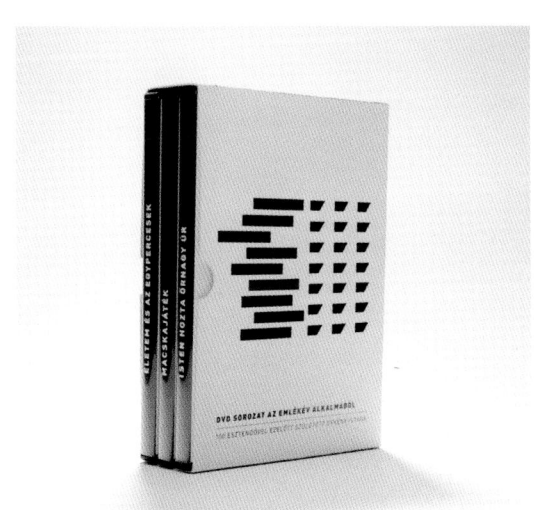

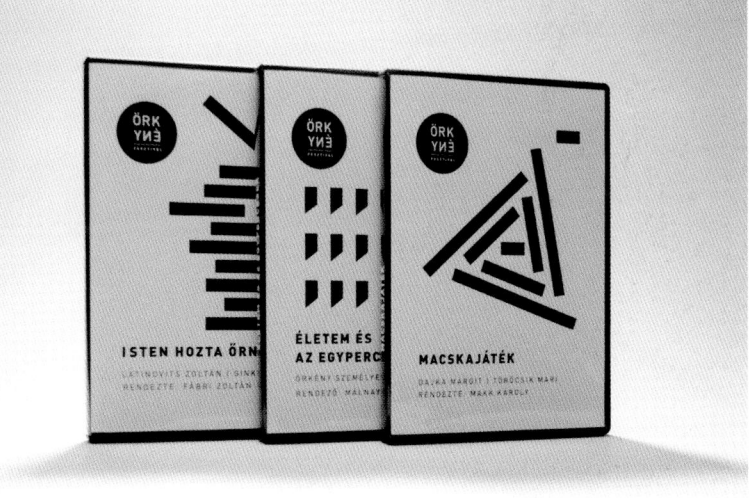

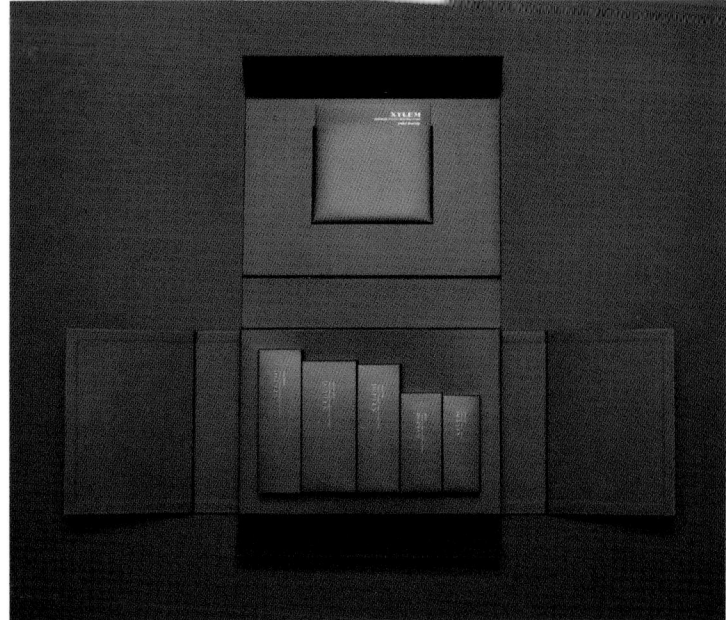

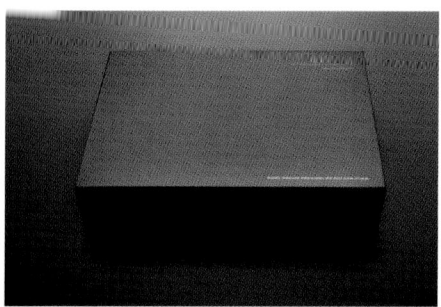

Xylem Packaging
United States

DEA/Studio
Design Agency

Dustin Edward Arnold
Designer

Xylem Advanced Organic Skin Solutions
Client

Xylem is a unisex organic skin care line with an upstream price point and a niche consumer base. The design takes on a minimalist and technology driven approach to the brand. The packaging prepares Xylem to become a cutting-edge brand while remaining true to its core values and philosophy.

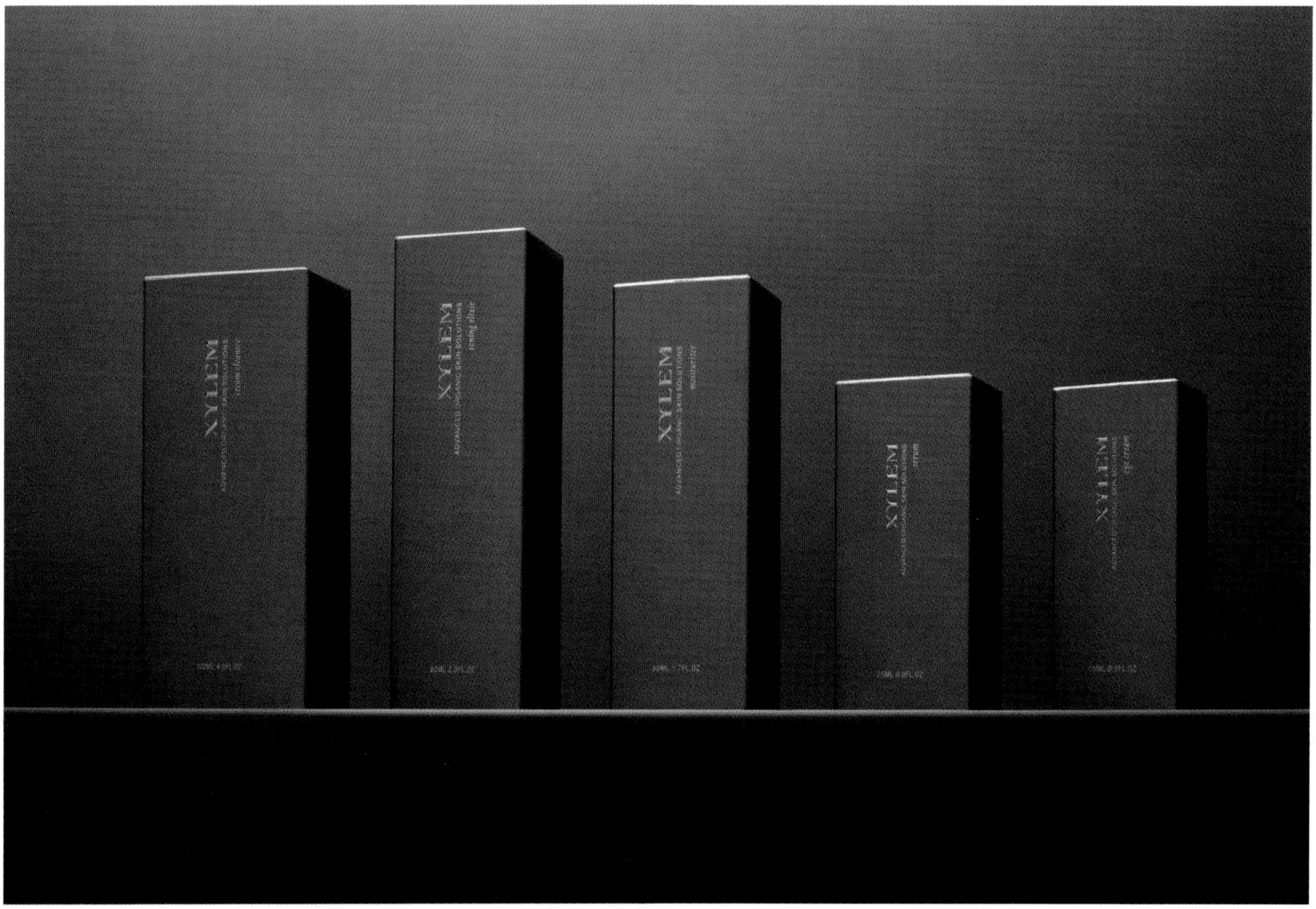

www.dustin-edward-arnold.com

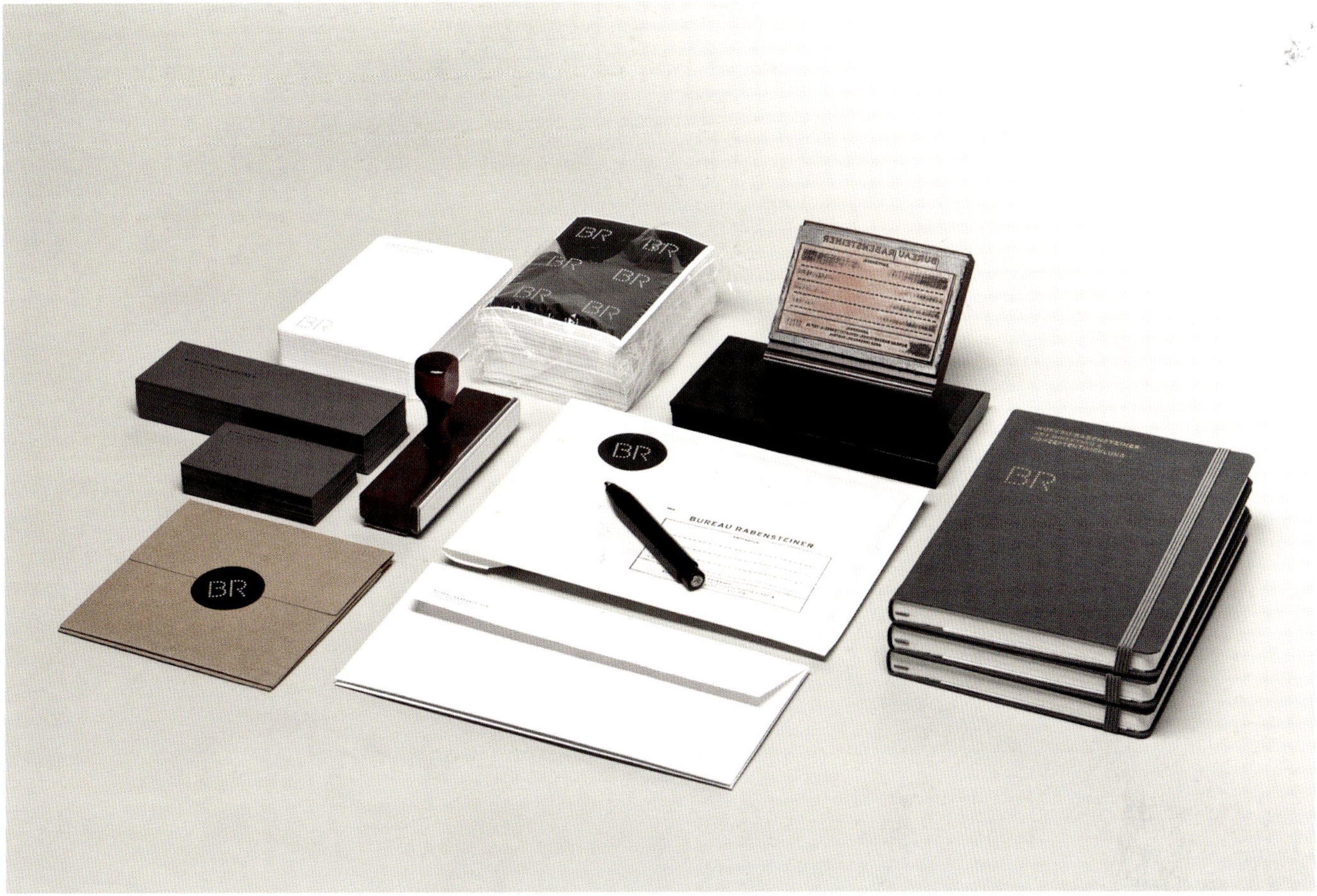

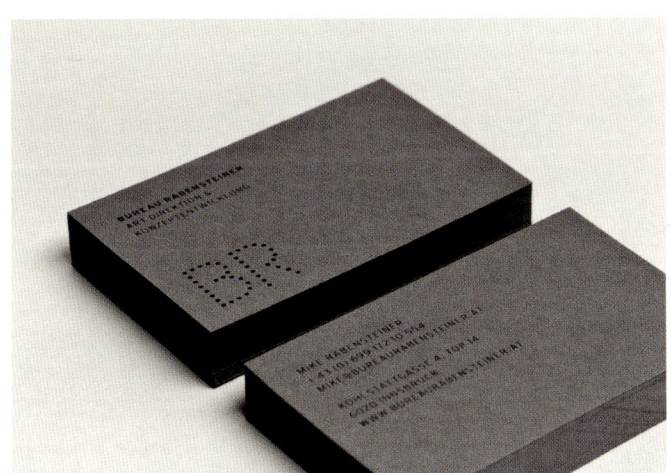

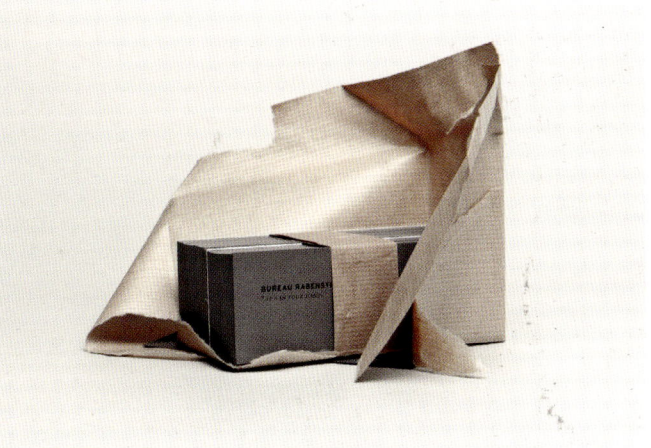

Bureau Rabensteiner
Austria

Bureau Rabensteiner
Design Agency

Mike Rabensteiner
Designer
& Photographer

Bureau Rabensteiner is known for its minimalistic and pure design, which is how they want their stationery to be like as well. They communicate their style in a simple and discrete way, timeless, a little old-fashion but peppered with a lot of details like wood handle rubber stamps, bookmarks and individual notebooks.

"Mainly, we use black to show strong expression, and use white to show something clear. Gray, the neutral color, is used to soften the overall impression."
—Atsushi Ishiguro (OUWN)

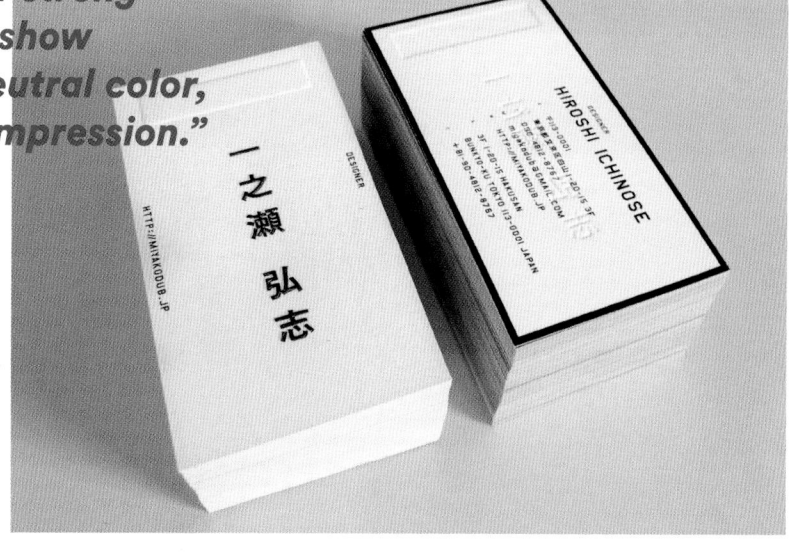

MIYAKODUB
Japan

OUWN
Design Agency

Atsushi Ishiguro
Designer

MIYAKODUB
Client

The brand identity was designed for the opening of the design office of MIYAKODUB, a Japanese designer. The design includes business cards, postcards and posters. The thick and black line is used to express the depth of the designer's thoughts and influence.

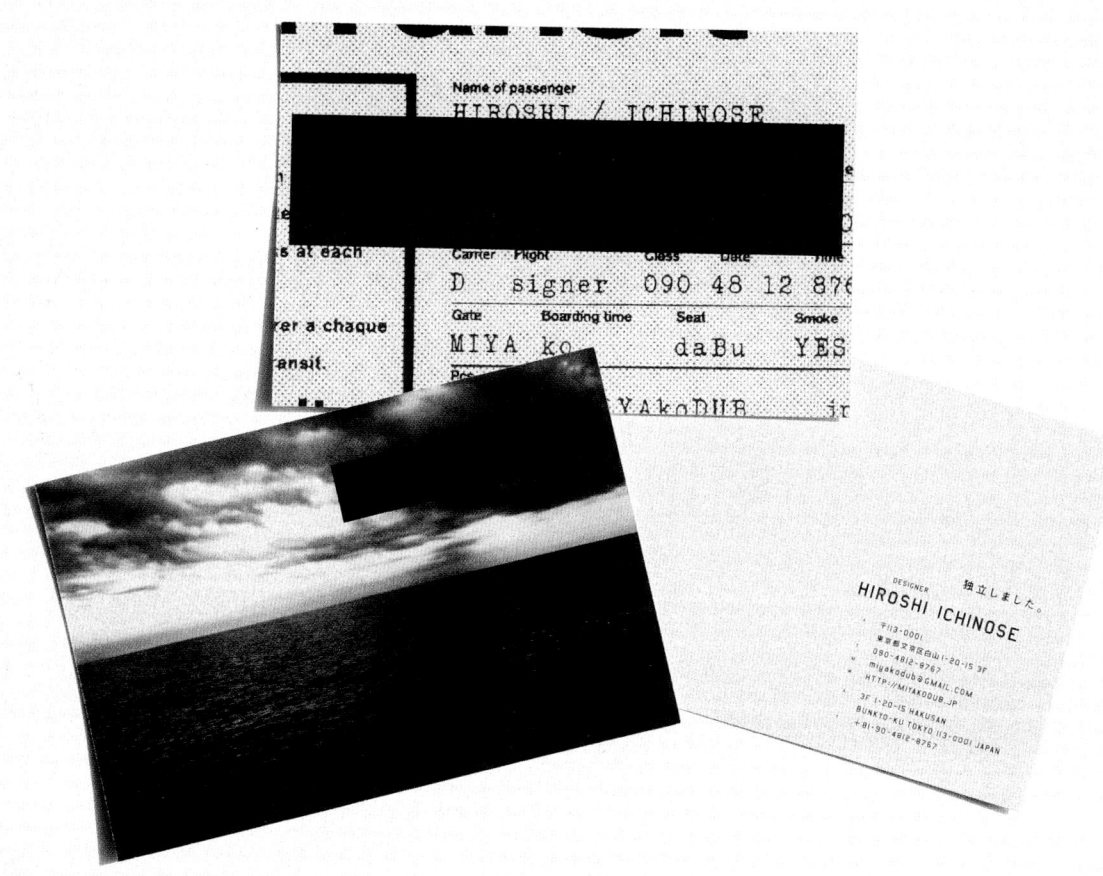

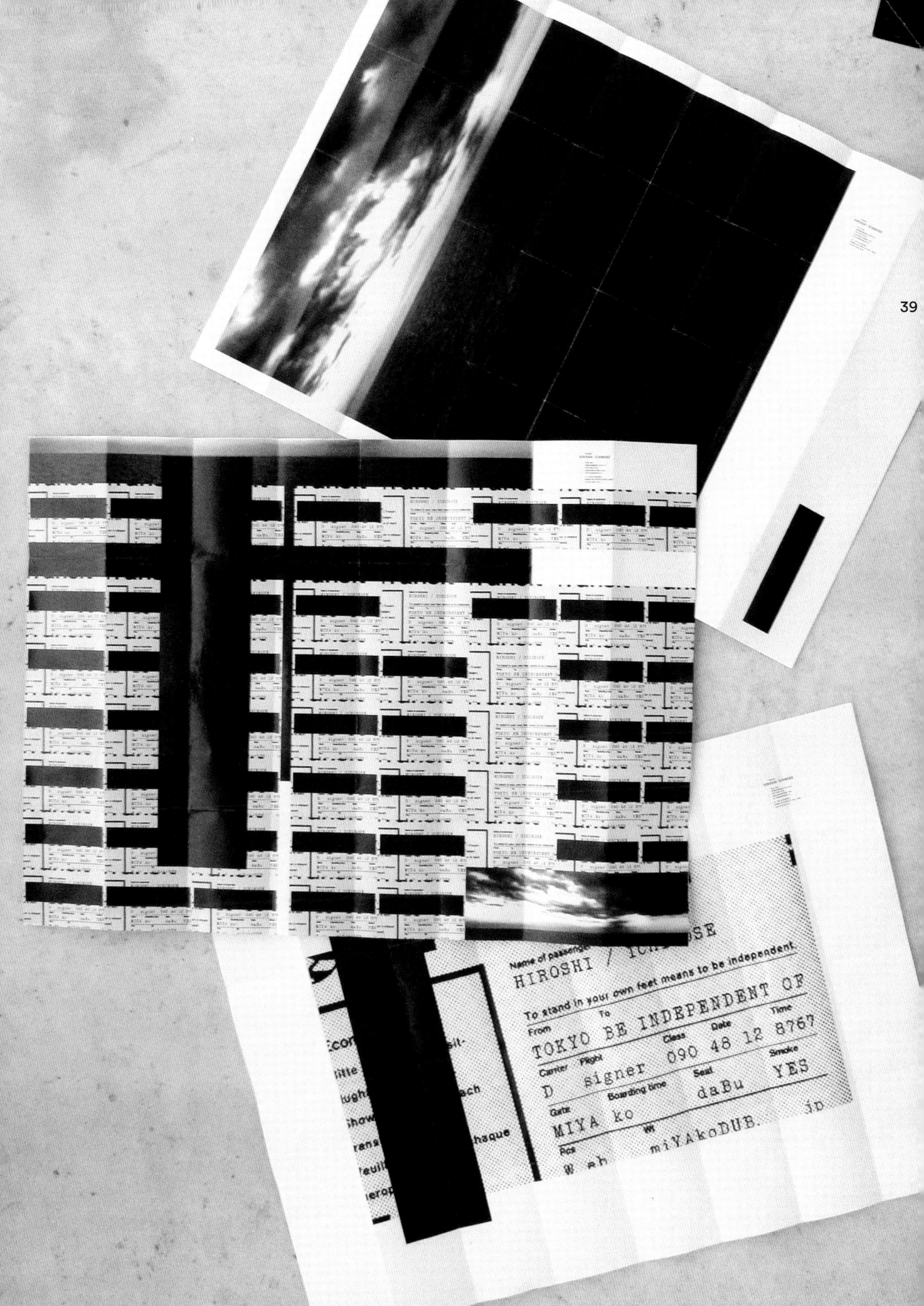

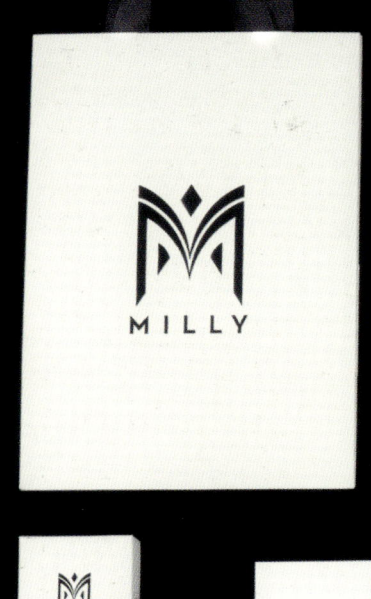

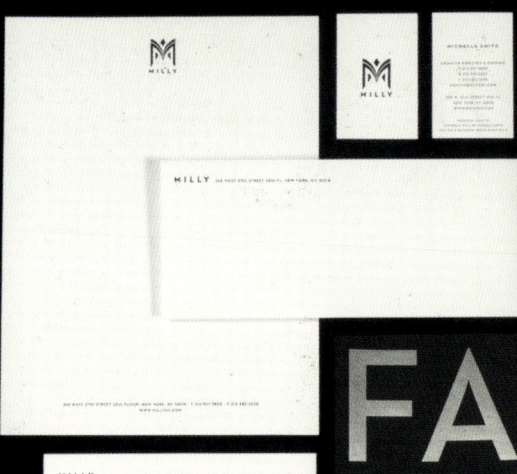

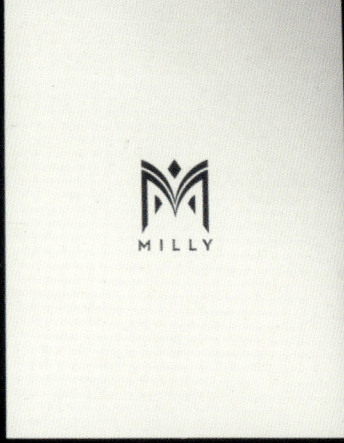

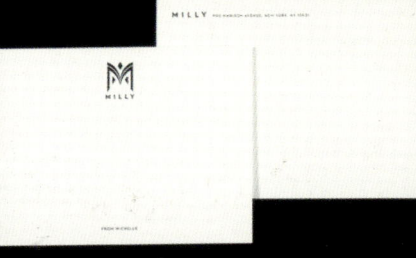

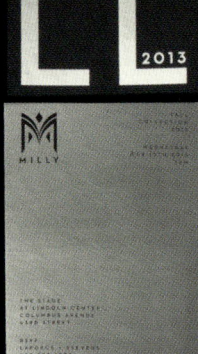

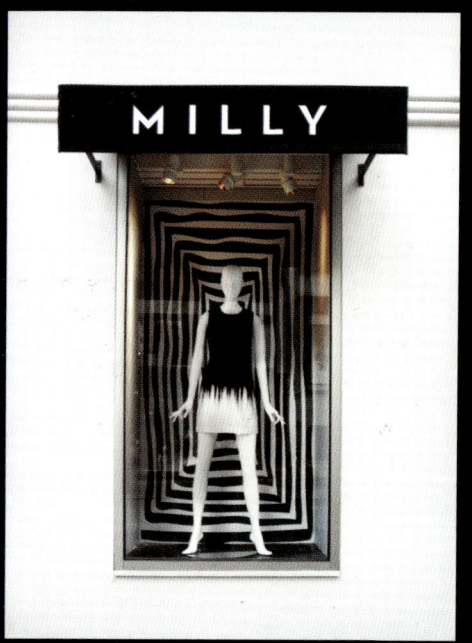

Milly
United States

Pentagram Design
Design Agency

Natasha Jen
Partner

Milly
Client

In the twelve years since New York label Milly was established, it has grown to epitomize bold contemporary women's fashion, and Pentagrams Natasha Jen was tasked with evolving the identity to match its stature. Replacing the existing pink script typeface, Jen and her team designed a mark that retained the femininity but instilled attitude and strength using a geometric sans serif font Neutraface set in black and white.

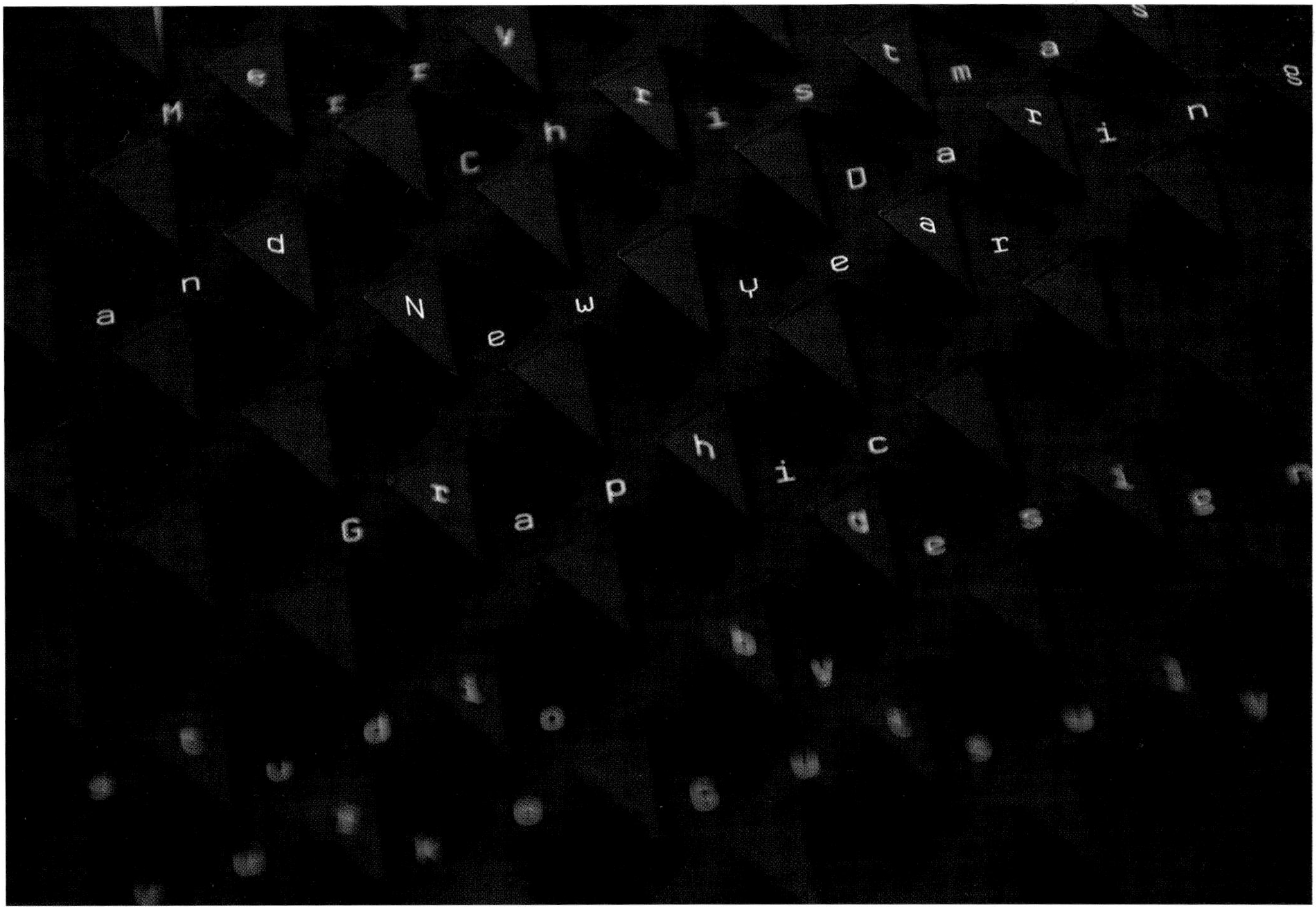

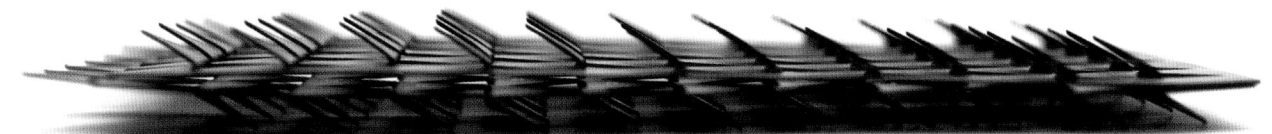

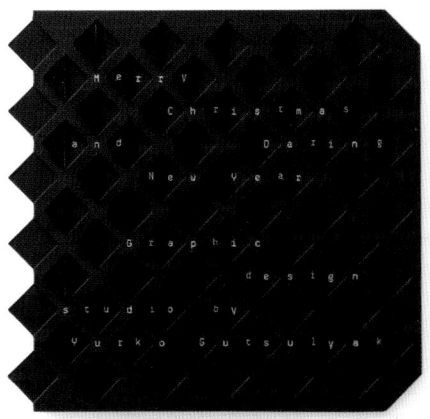

Dragon Card
Ukraine

**Graphic design studio
by Yurko Gutsulyak**
Design Agency

Yurko Gutsulyak
Designer

This New Year greeting is intended to be read and touched. With reference to oriental traditions, popular among Ukrainians, the designer's aspirations for a new year are embedded in a scrap of black dragon skin. The scaled texture was created by the interlocking layers of a gatefold.

www.gstudio.com.ua

PORTAL
Poland

Prograffic
Design Agency

Michał Stróż
Designer

PORTAL – Pracownia Architektoniczna
Client

Portal is a Polish architecture studio, the name of which originates from an architectural, decorative framing of a building entrance. The starting point was to create a clean and modern image, focusing on the structure of the form and the meaning of the word "construction". The whole system of identification was reduced to a single color to avoid distracting the perception of the idea, where the form itself is crucial. However, the color adds elasticity and lightness to the design while building up a solid brand image.

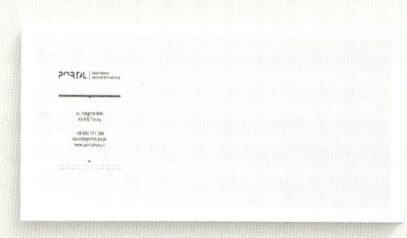

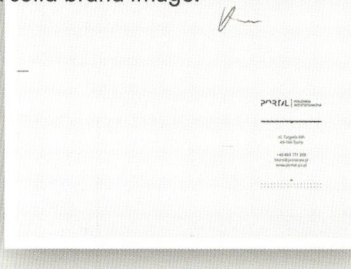

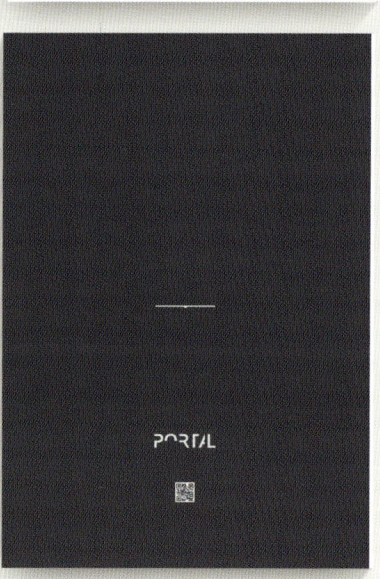

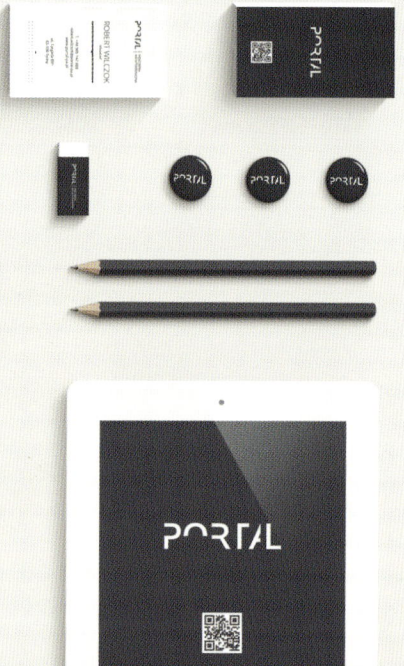

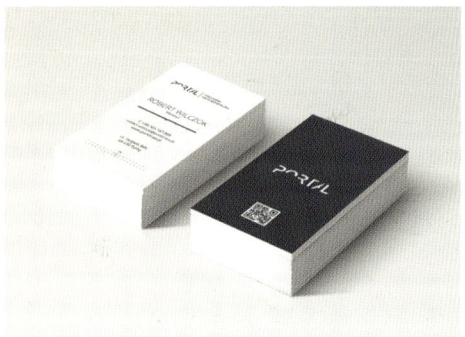

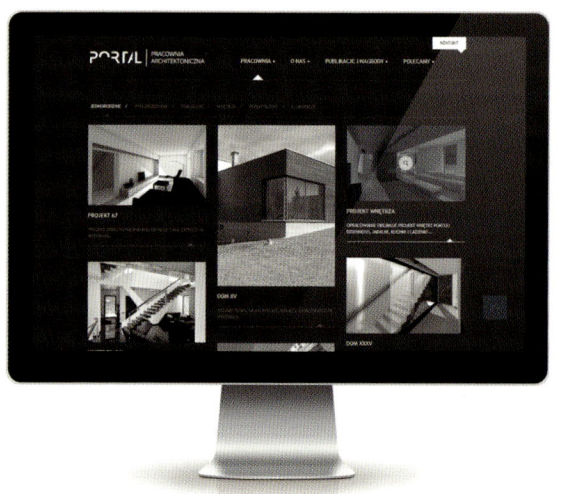

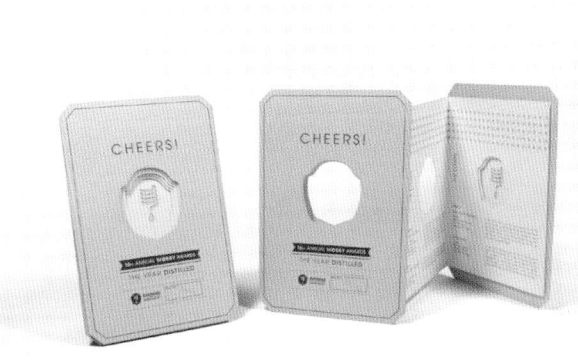
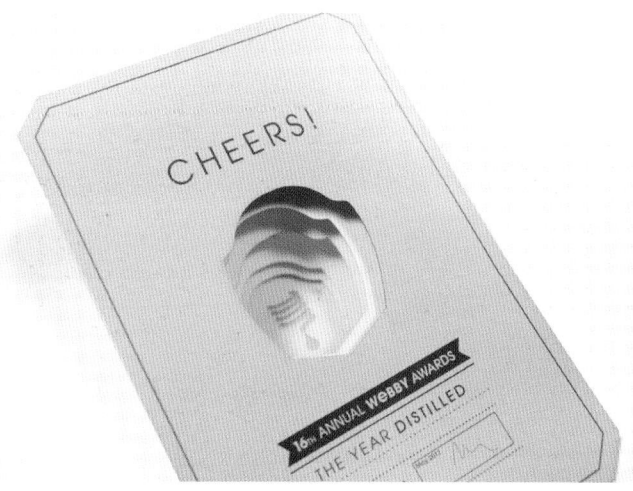

The Webby Awards Invite
United Kingdom

Shotopop
Design Agency

**Carin Standford &
Casper Franken**
Designer

The Webby Awards
Client

The invite package includes a Webby logo pop-up, a fully detailed event information booklet, a card explaining the five-word speech process and a swanky envelope. The basic color scheme was decided upon to bring out an elegant and straightforward look.

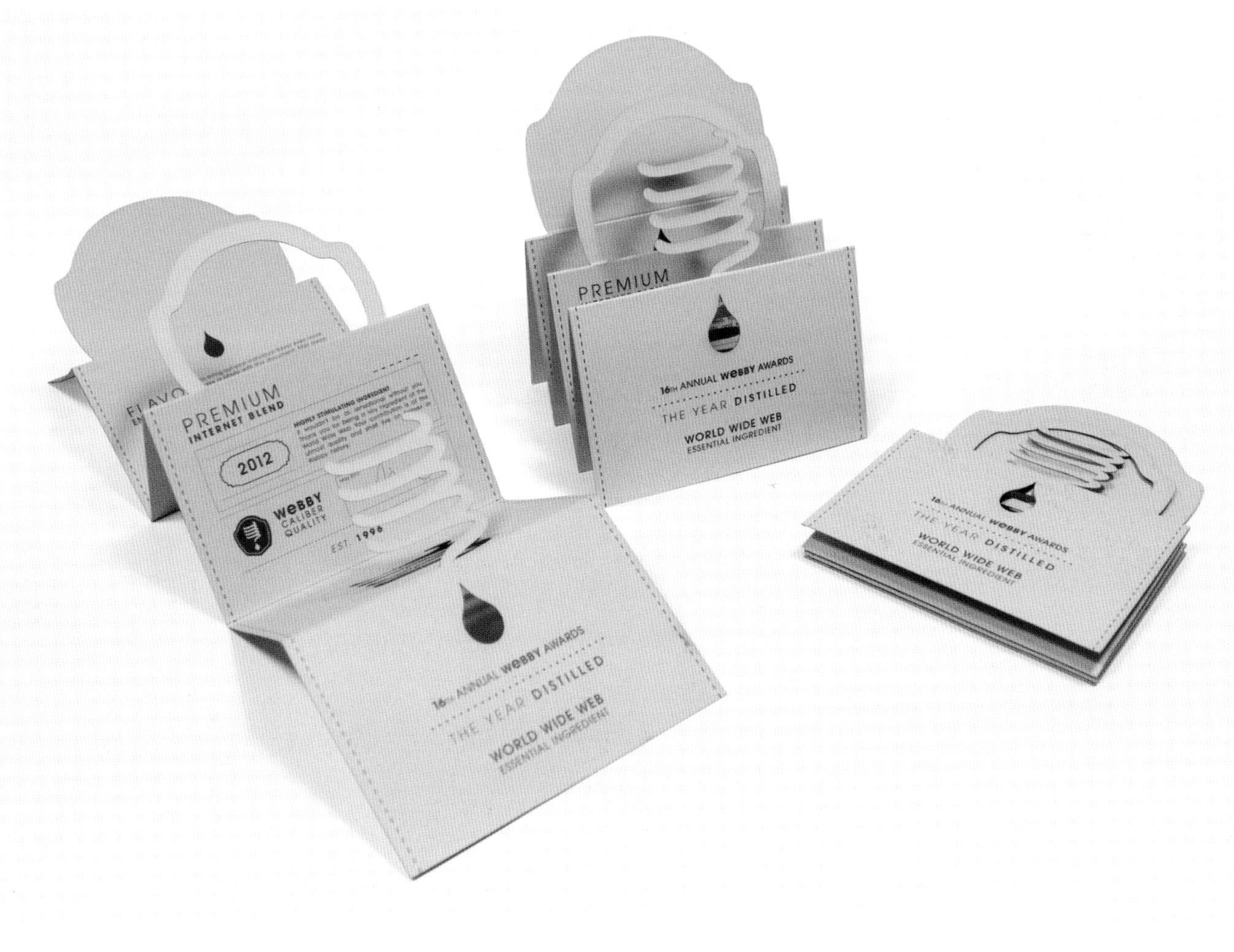

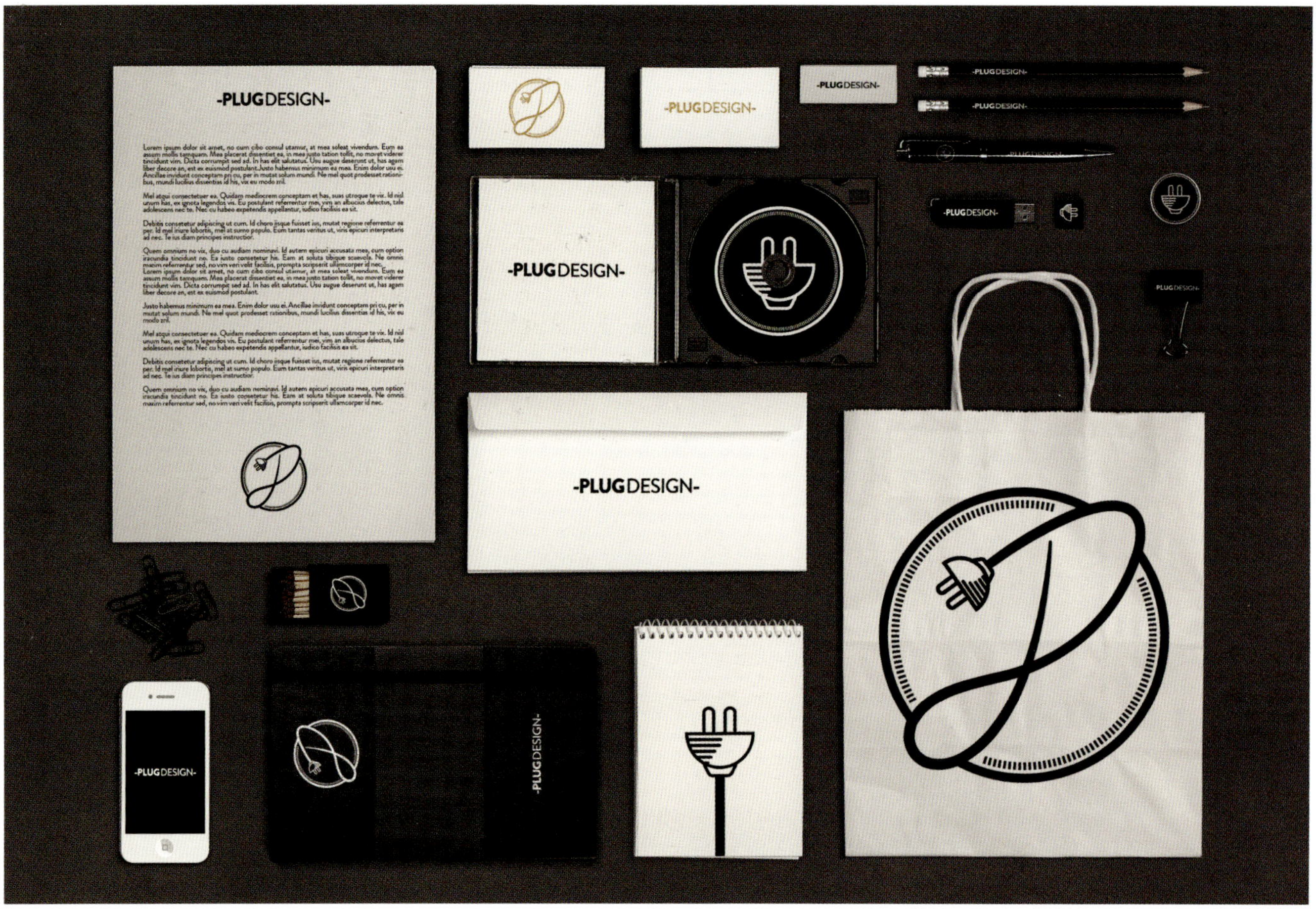

Plug Design
Mexico

Para Todo Hay Fans
Design Agency

Federico V. Astorga
Creative Director

Guillermo Castellanos Flores
Design Director

Moisés E. Guillén Romero
Art Director

Liliana Lucano
Client

This is the identity for Plug Design, an industrial design studio in Mexico focused on electronic design, technology and gadgets. The designer mixed the D and the P in one symbol to better convey the meaning of the brand and its name.

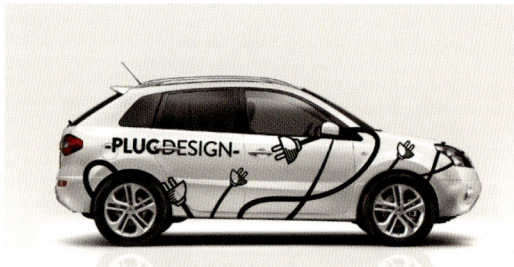

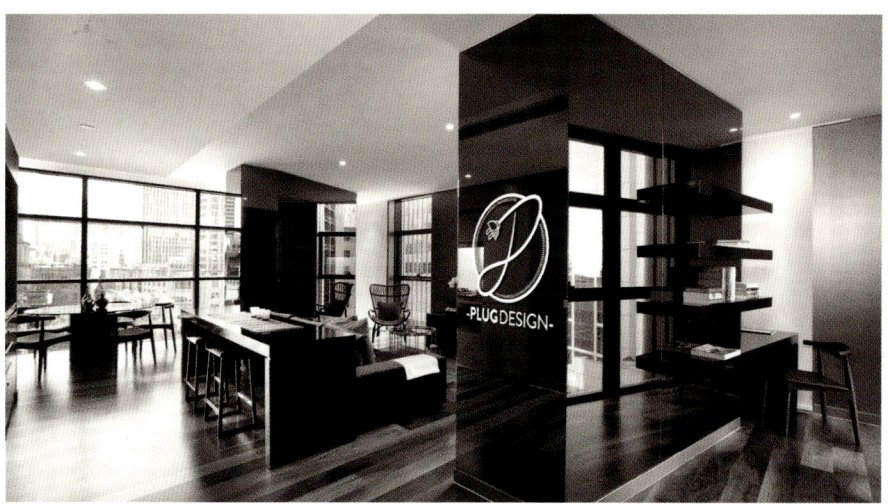

Gong

Korea

Sonu Jung
Designer

Café, gong
Client

Wildflowers are used as the main graphic shorthand in this beverage package to express the brand's focus on wellbeing and organic products. Gong means empty in Korea, which embodies the brand's philosophy – to give people an experience where they could take a five minutes break to empty everything in their mind. By using calligraphy, typography of Zen, and eco-friendly packaging materials, the designer captured oriental minimalism in the design.

45

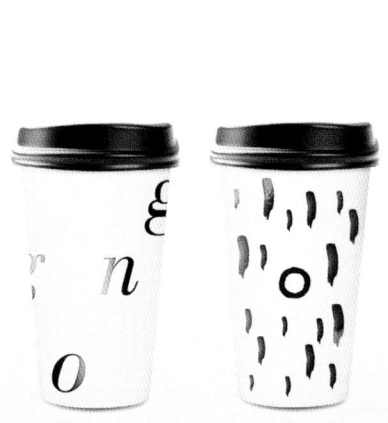
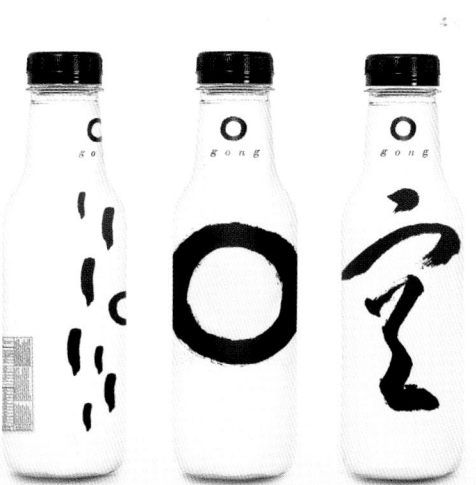

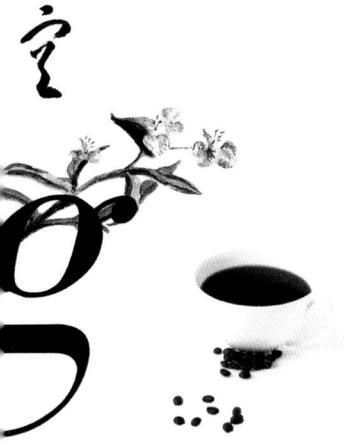
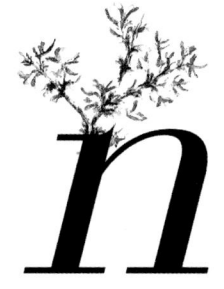

bran new beverage brand

공은 바쁜 삶에 지친 도시인들을 위한 야생초 음료이다. 야생초에서 추출된 각종 구성성분은 체내의 노폐물을 제거하고 신체기능을 활성화 시킨다. 공(空)은 비우다라는 뜻을 가지고 음료 의 기능적 특징을 설명함과 동시에 바쁜 일과의 무거운 부담, 스트레스 또한 함께 벗어내어 버릴 수 있는 삶의 여유와 휴식을 이야기 한다.

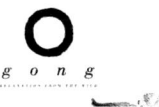
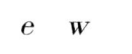

bran new beverage brand

"We see color as a powerful tool that helps provide personality to each project. We firmly believe in the power of black and white, and carry its flag along most of our projects."
—Manifiesto Futura

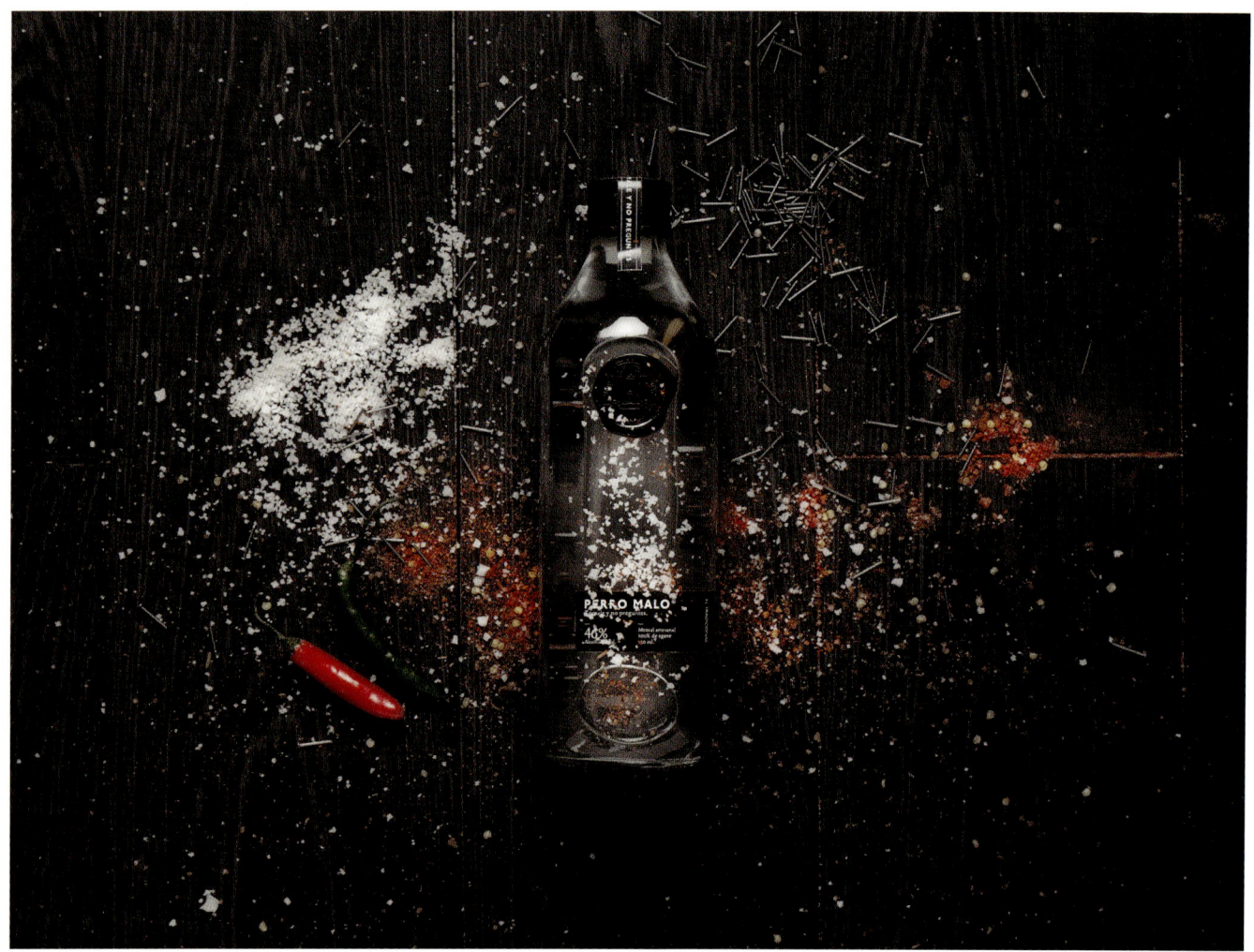

Perro Malo
Mexico

Manifiesto Futura
Design Agency

Mezcal Perro Malo
Client

This project was inspired by Cerberus the Roman and Greek mythology myth, which is the multi-headed "hell hound" that guards the gates of the underworld. This packaging represents the dark side or underworld. The designer took the concept and gave the packaging a mythical feel with the use of a dark black wooden box and a black matte bottle. The black on black wax seal echoes to every detail of the rest of the design.

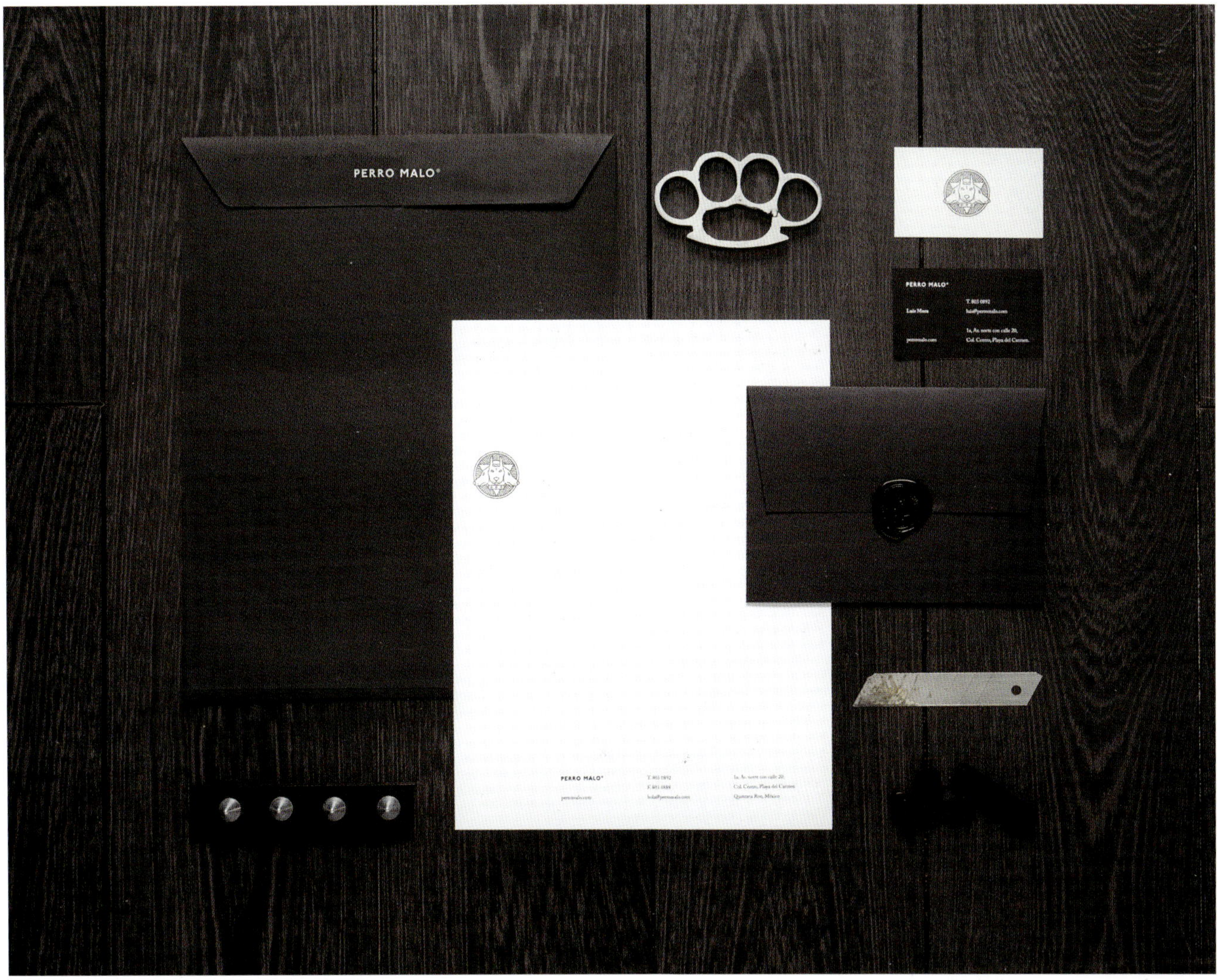

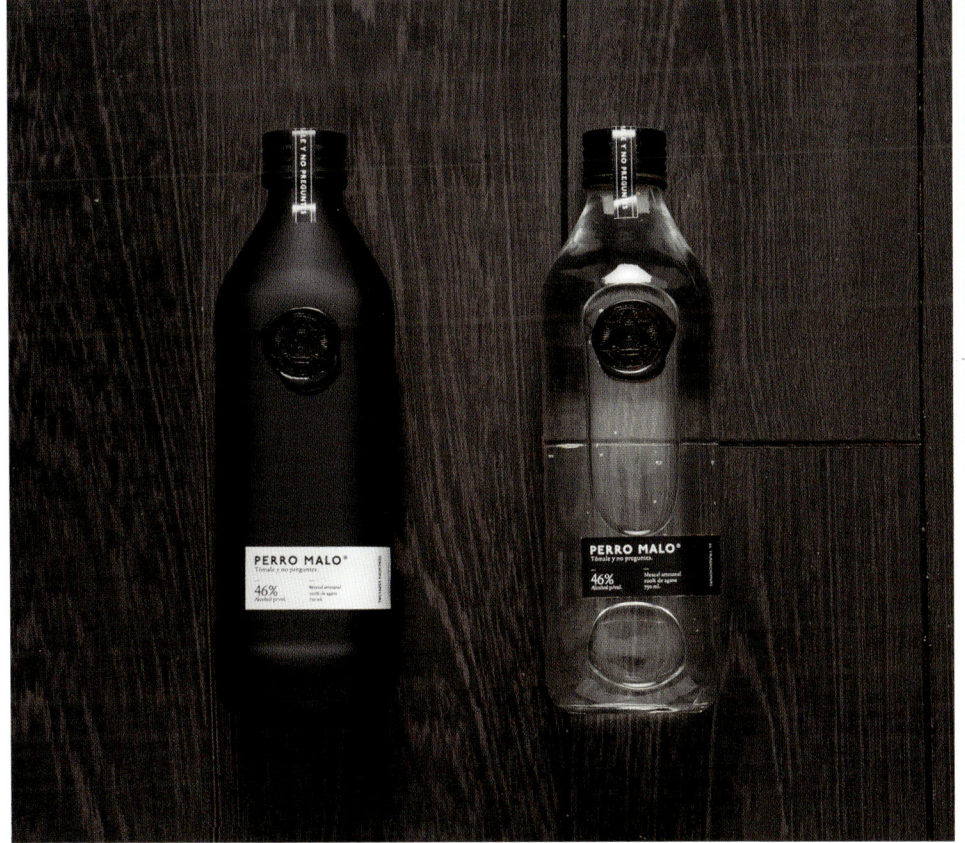

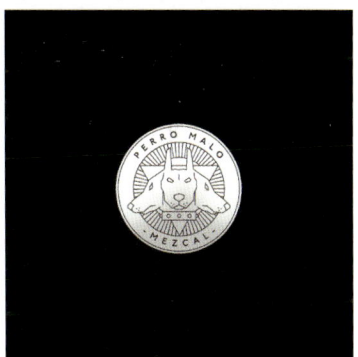

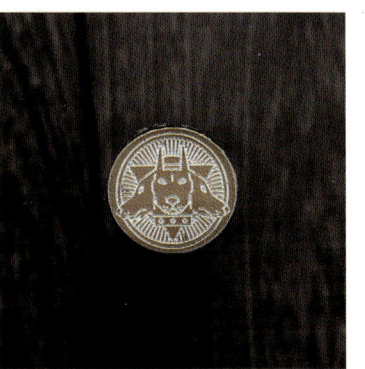

Den Sorte Skole – Lektion III
United Kingdom

Re-public
Design Agency

Søren Severin
Designer

**Dennis Westerberg,
Kristoffer Juel
Poulsen**
Photographers

Den Sorte Skole
Client

Lektion III is the third album released by the Copenhagen based DJ-collective Den Sorte Skole the Black School. To translate the vast complexity of Lektion III into any kind of figurative motif or illustration would only result in an inferior representation of the music. So the album cover is simply black, black like the vinyl records the music is created from; black like the gloomy mood of the melodies; and black like Den Sorte Skole itself.

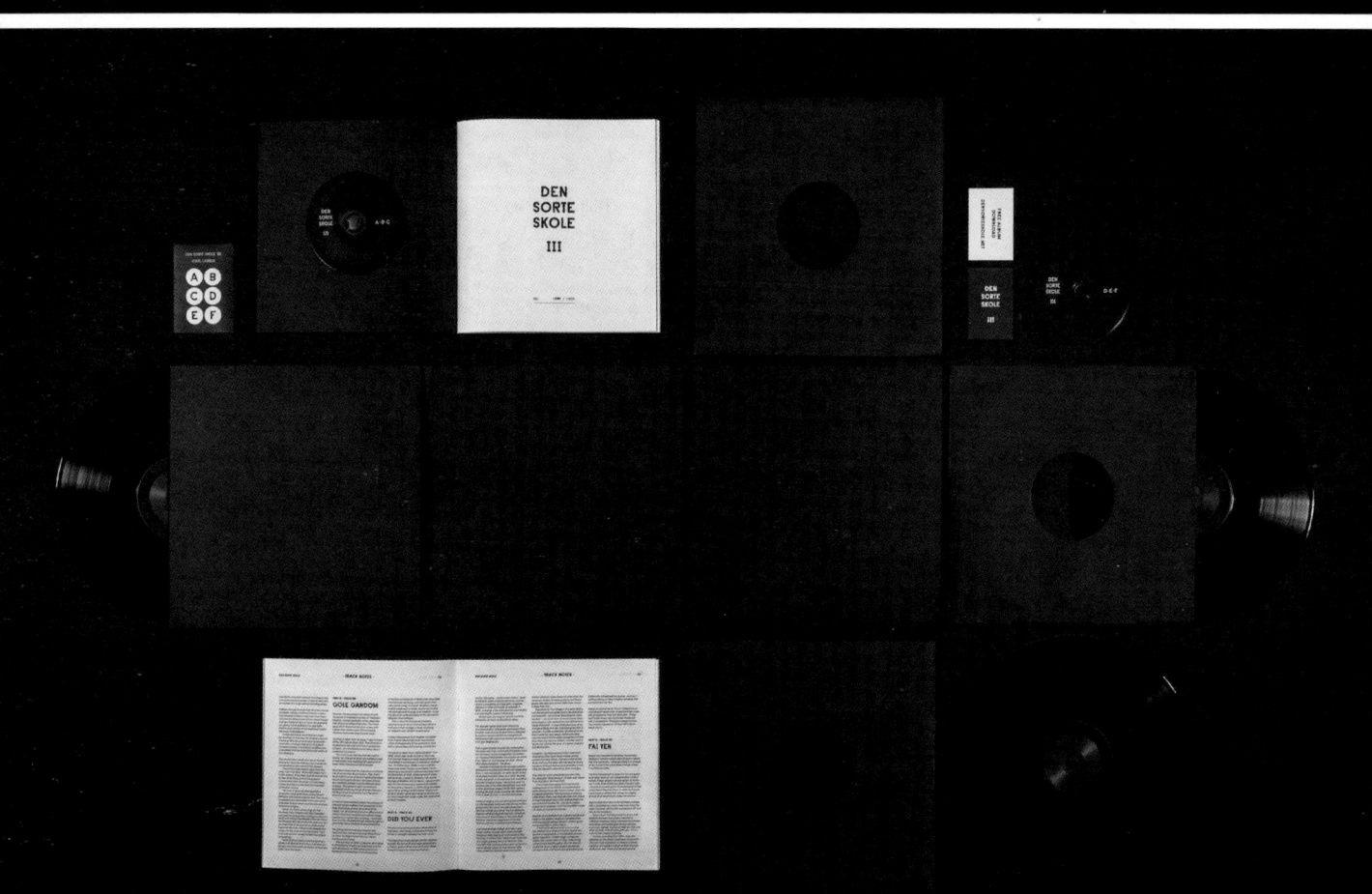

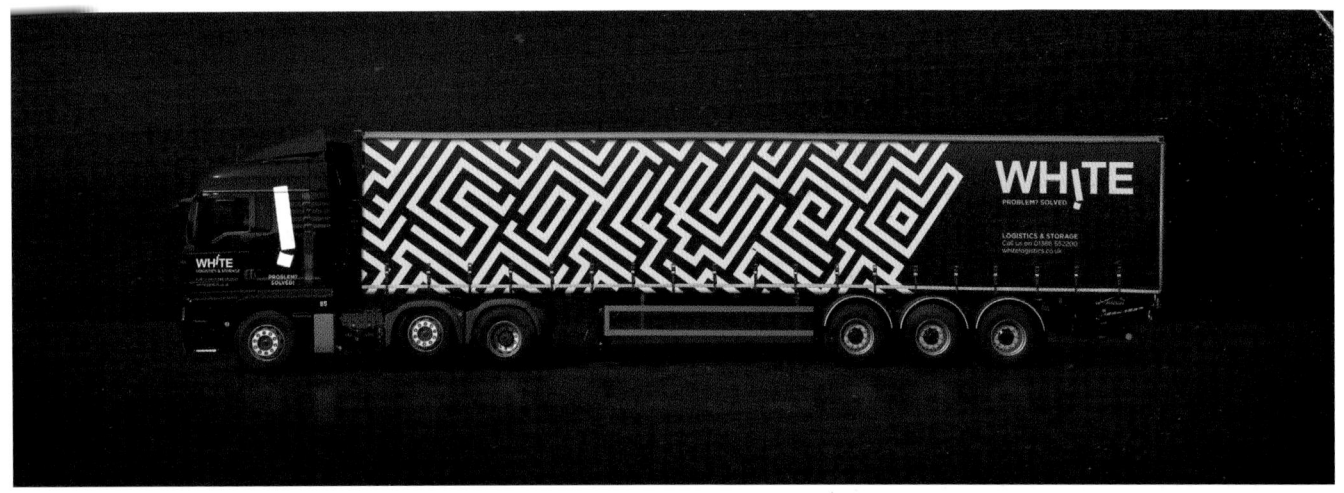

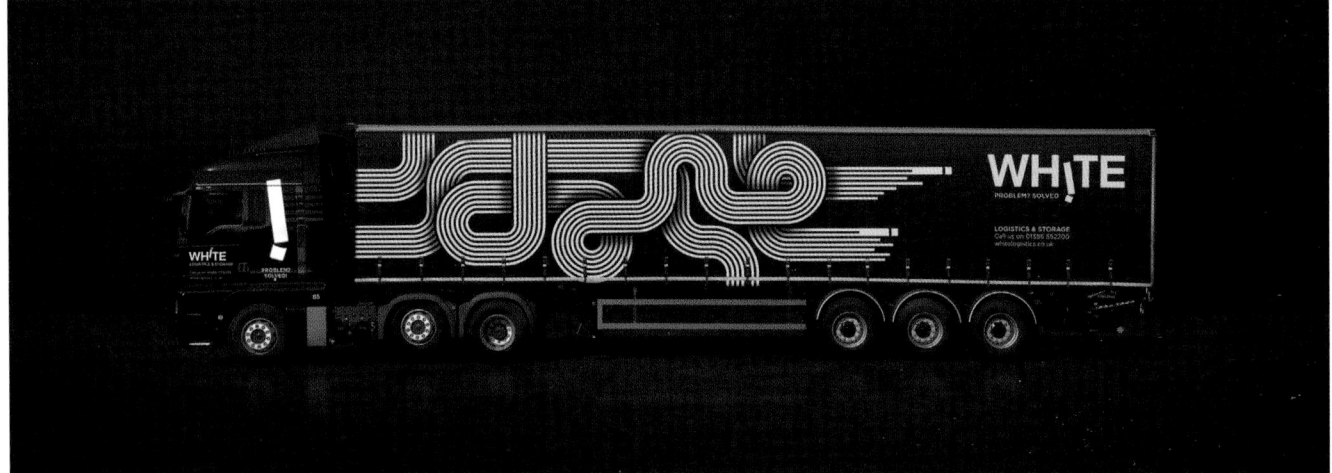

White Logistics and Storage
United Kingdom

The Allotment Brand Design
Design Agency

Paul Middlebrook
Brand Strategist

James Backhurst
Creative Director

Jonathan Oakes
Photographer

White Logistics is a family owned medium sized haulage business. The brief was to develop a brand proposition and identity that would communicate their drive and passion and put them on the map in the minds of potential customers. The straight-forward "black & white" problem solving approach to the identity brings to life a brand that is constantly on the move.

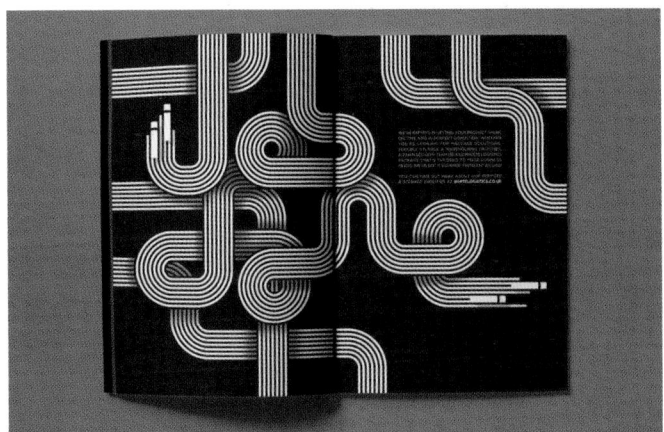

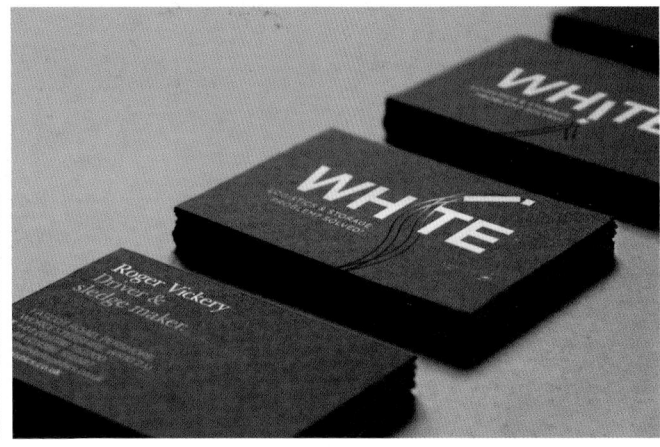

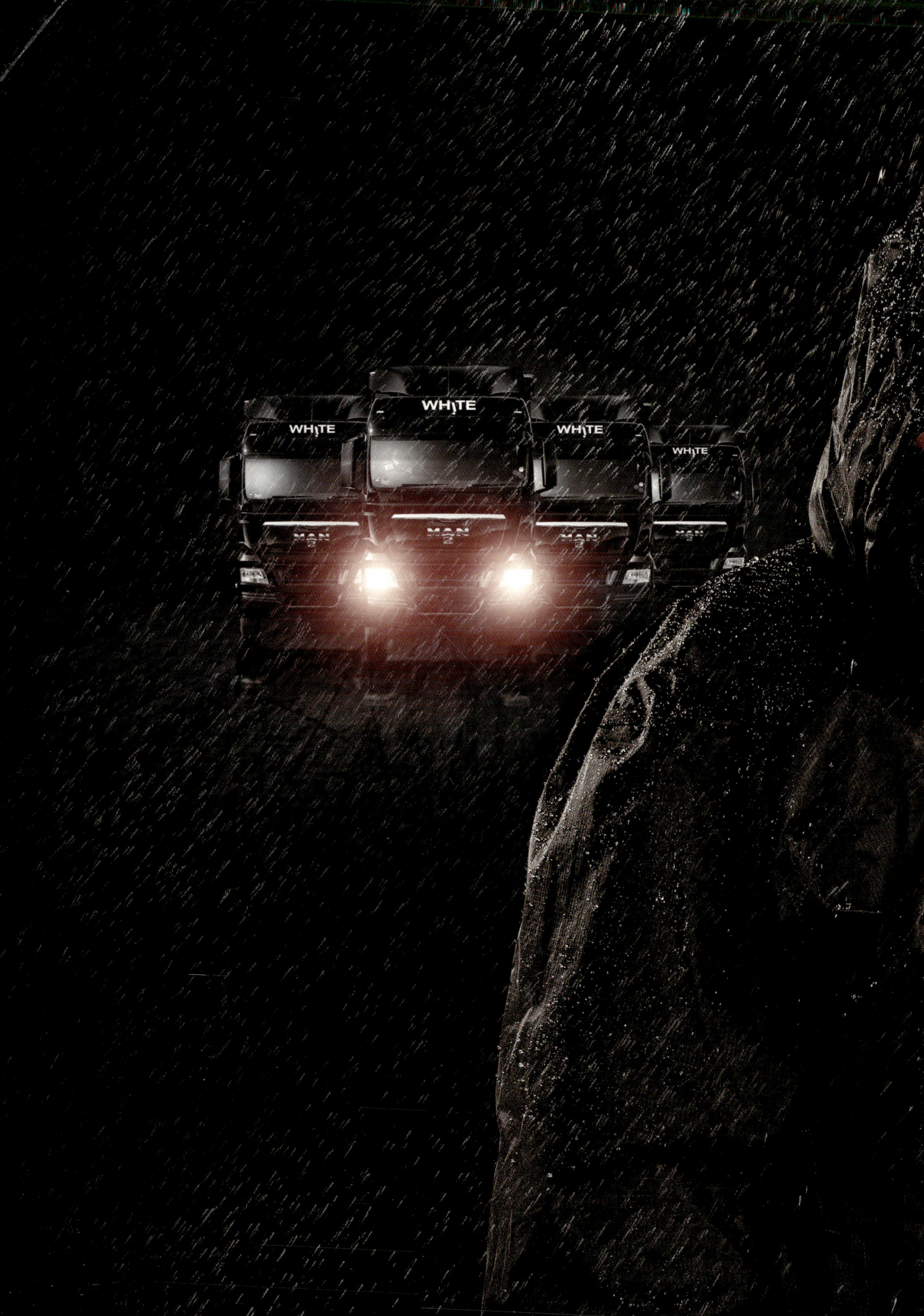

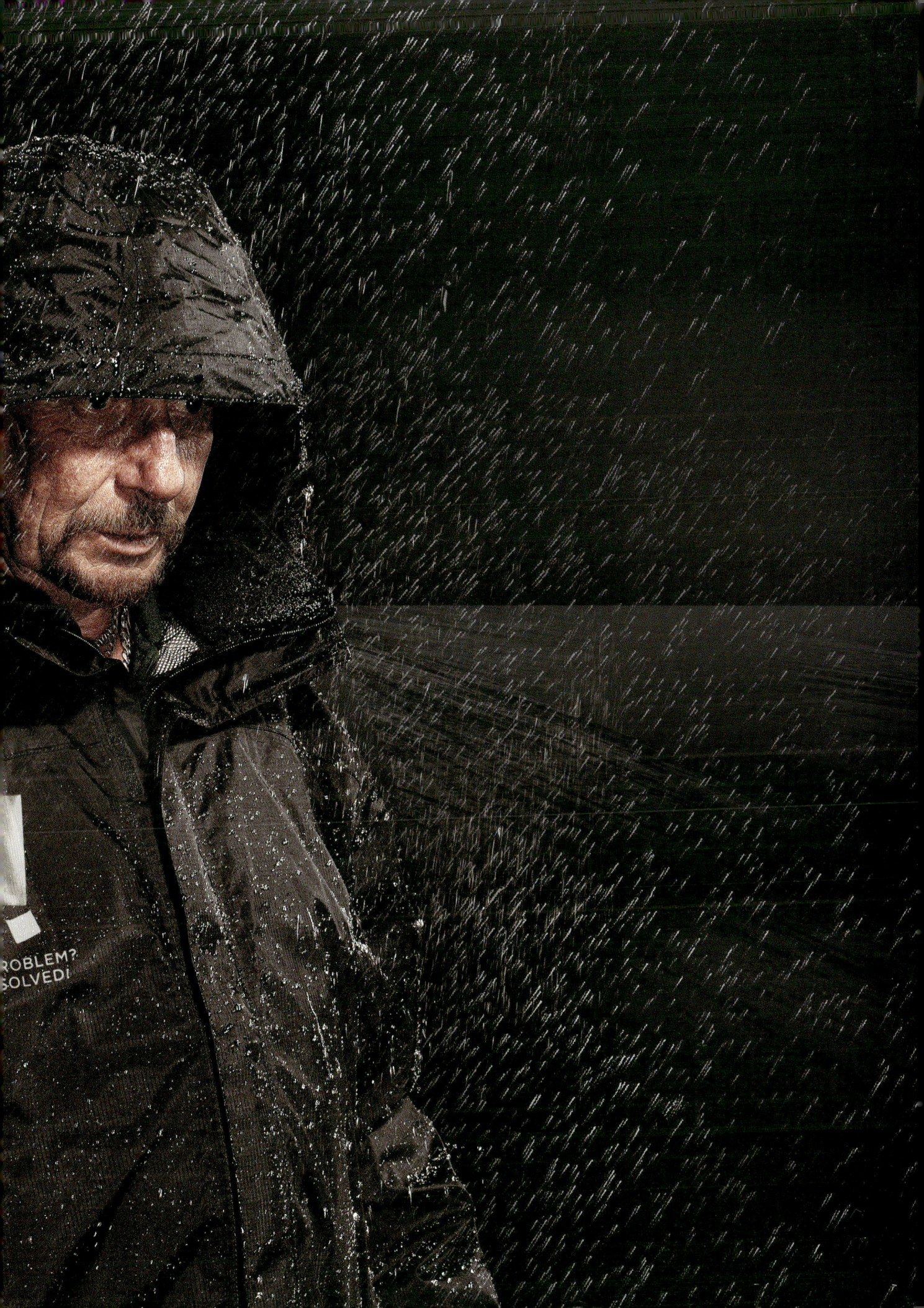

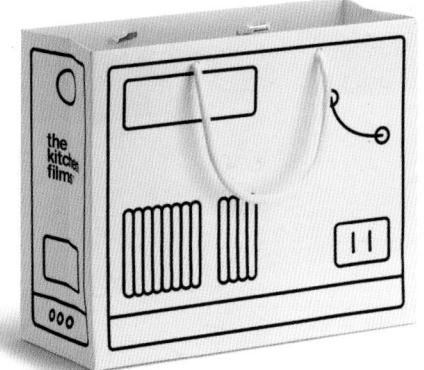
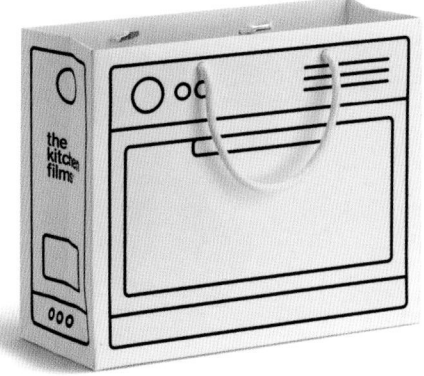

The Kitchen Films
Spain

ruiz+company
Design Agency

David Ruiz
Creative Director

Ainhoa Nagore
Art Director

Jorge Alavedra
Designer

The Kitchen Films
Client

This is the corporate identity for a production company, the Kitchen Films. The idea was to create a game based on the interaction among all of the lively pictograms pieces. The overall identity resembles the elements dancing in a kitchen to echo the brand name.

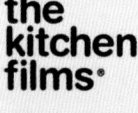

the kitchen films®

Álvaro Olalquiaga

Argensola, 18
28004 Madrid, Spain
T +34 917 020 143
M +34 677 450 728
thekitchenfilms.com
alvaro@thekitchenfilms.com

the kitchen films®

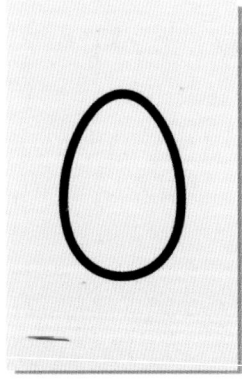
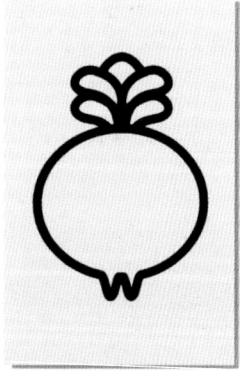
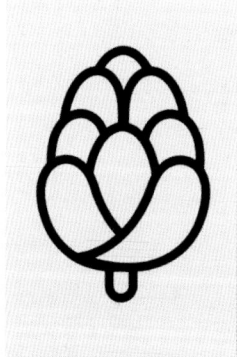
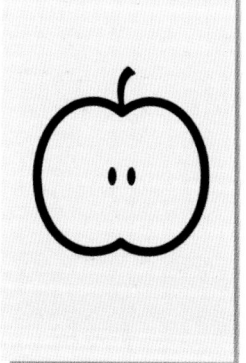

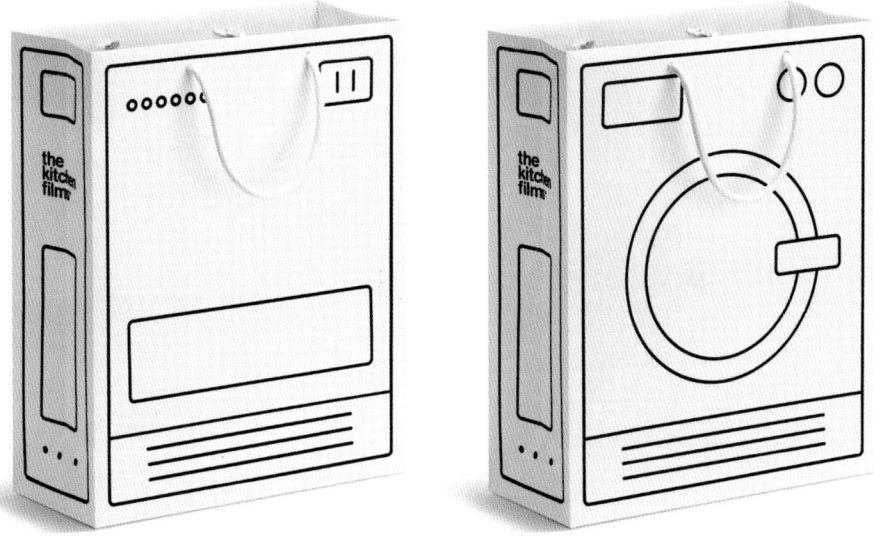

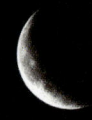

THE HARVEST OF THE MOON

Finest wine collection from California

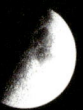

THE HARVEST OF THE MOON

Finest wine collection from California

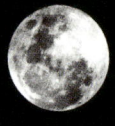

THE HARVEST OF THE MOON

Finest wine collection from California

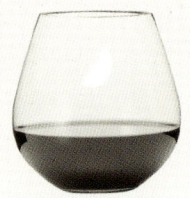

THE HARVEST OF THE MOON

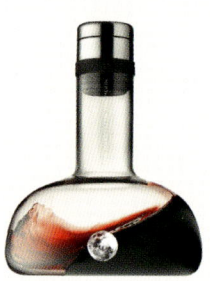

THE HARVEST OF THE MOON

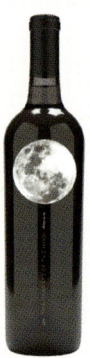

THE HARVEST OF THE MOON

"Space, texture and colors, in this order we make our choices; first we look at the space or form, then the texture, and at last the color. If a color is too dominant, it will rule the texture or form. Therefore, black and white is what we use most. As these are not dominant colors and will never ask more attention than the form itself."

—Jean-Maxime Brais (8 Bis)

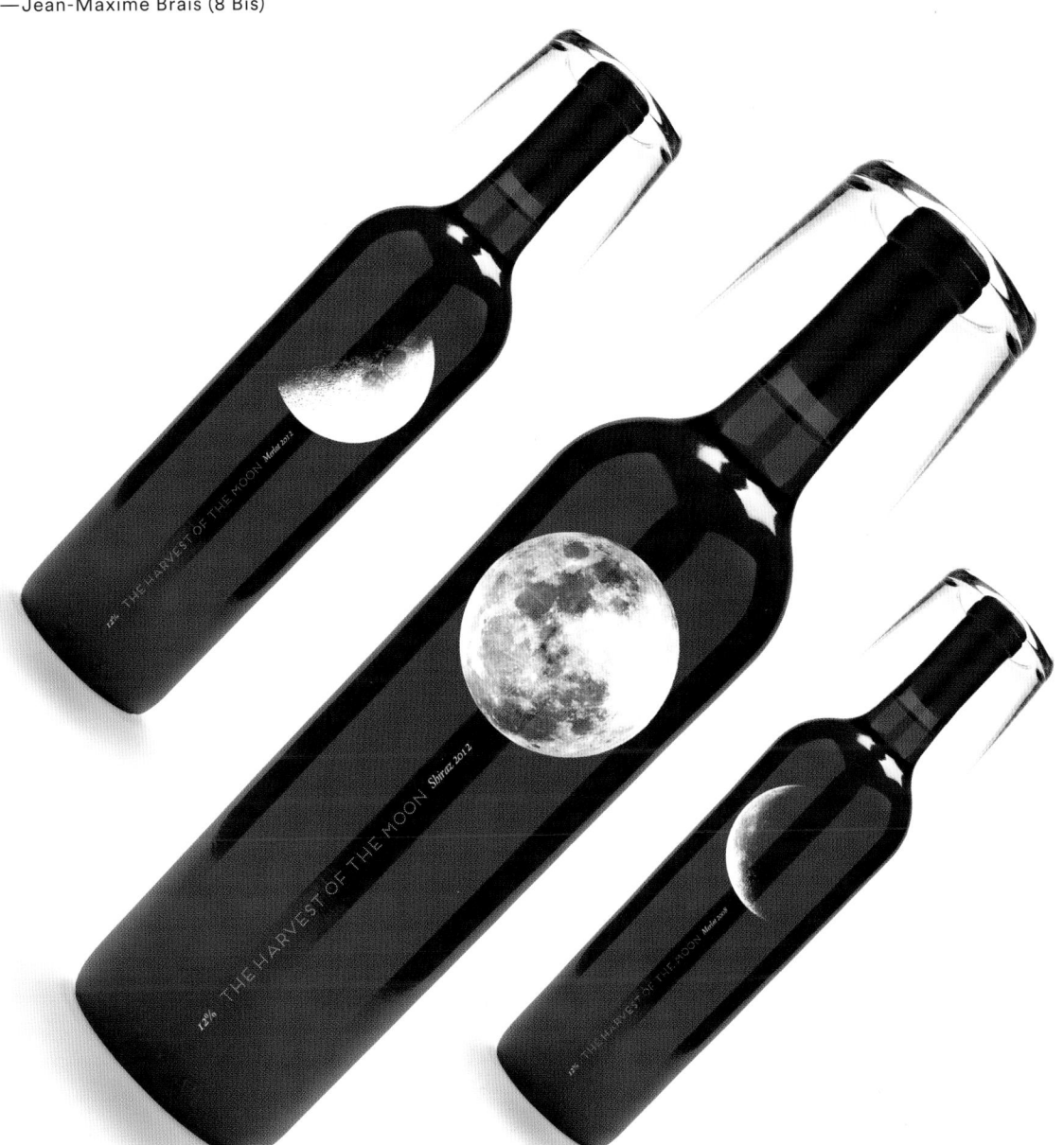

The Harvest of the Moon
Canada

8 Bis
Design Agency

Jean-Maxime Brais
Designer

The new branding and packaging was created for a new collection of Californian wine called "The Harvest of the Moon". The main inspiration came from the visual characteristics of moon travelling. The result is an iconic brand with an already strong potential recognition.

Vinosapiens
Mexico

Anagrama
Design Agency

Señor Sapiens
Client

Vinosapiens is an online wine shop that offers a great variety of organic and traditional wines and spirits. The naming is a combination of the words 'vino', the Spanish word for wine, and sapiens, the Latin word meaning wise. The happy wine bottle icon, along with the new name conveys an image of trust and friendliness. The circled marks on the stationery reinforce the idea of making wise choice as a form of wisdom. The uncoated black paper stamped with a touch of silver foil reflects the brand's good taste and excellent quality.

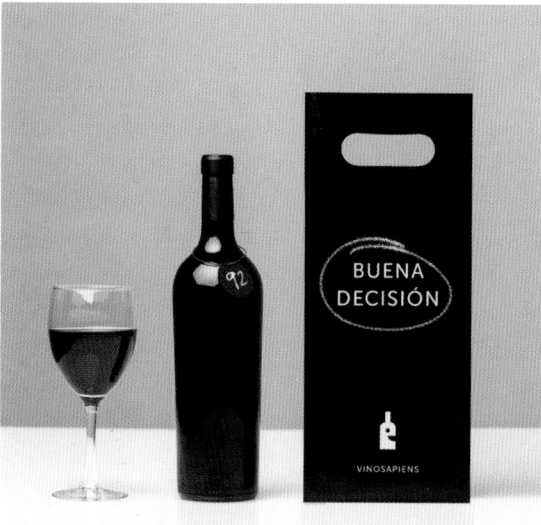

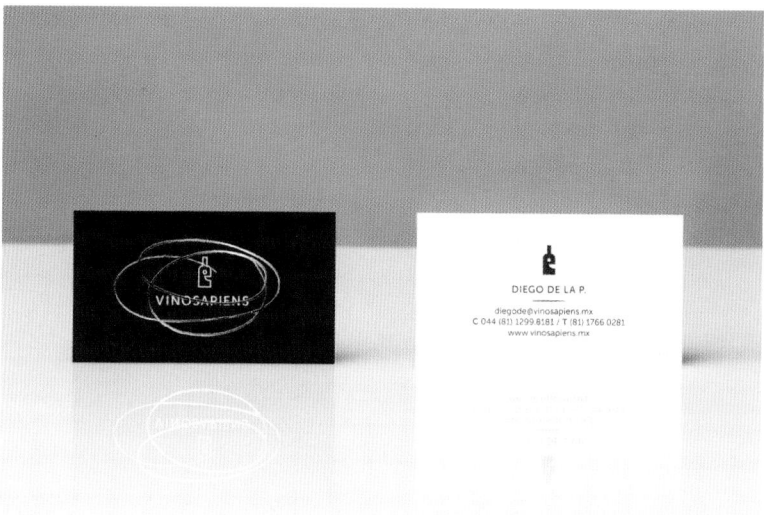

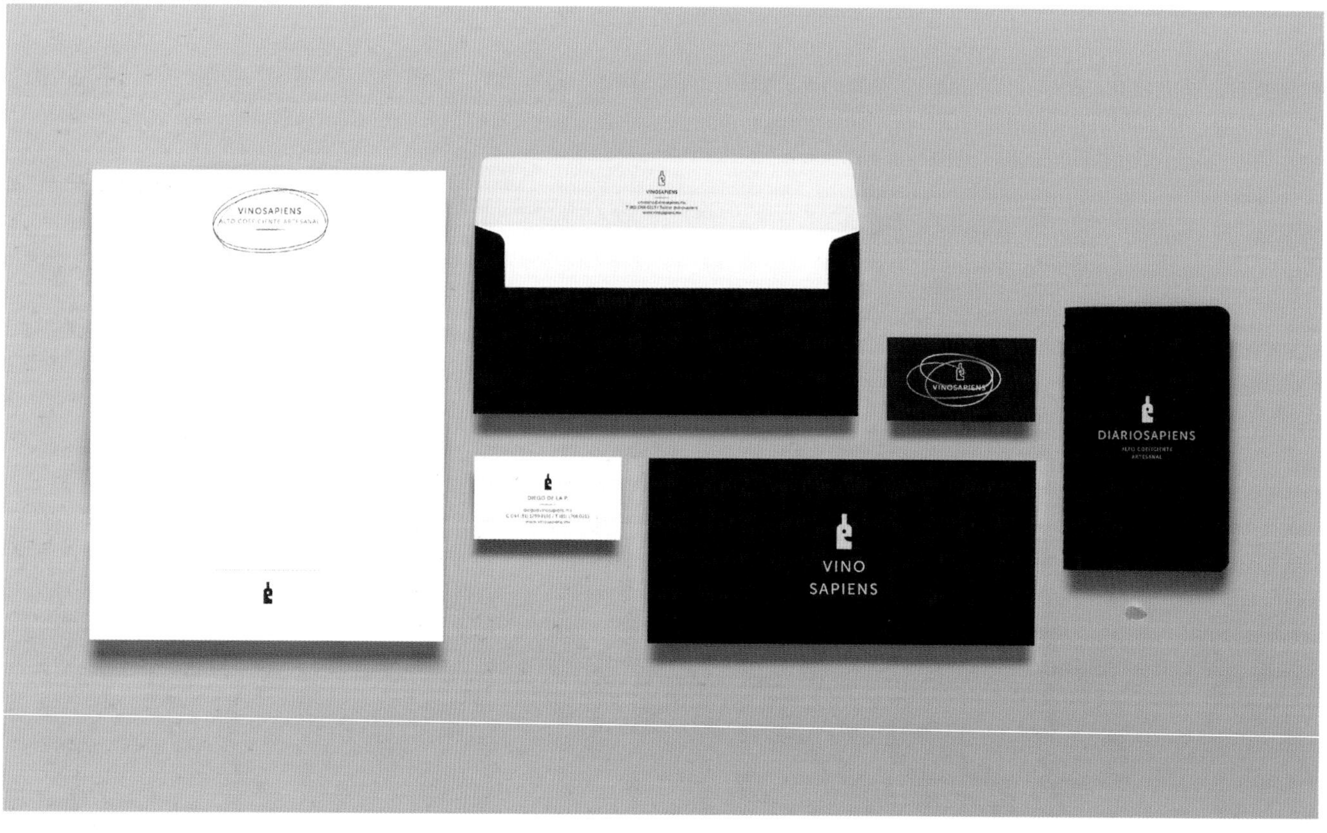

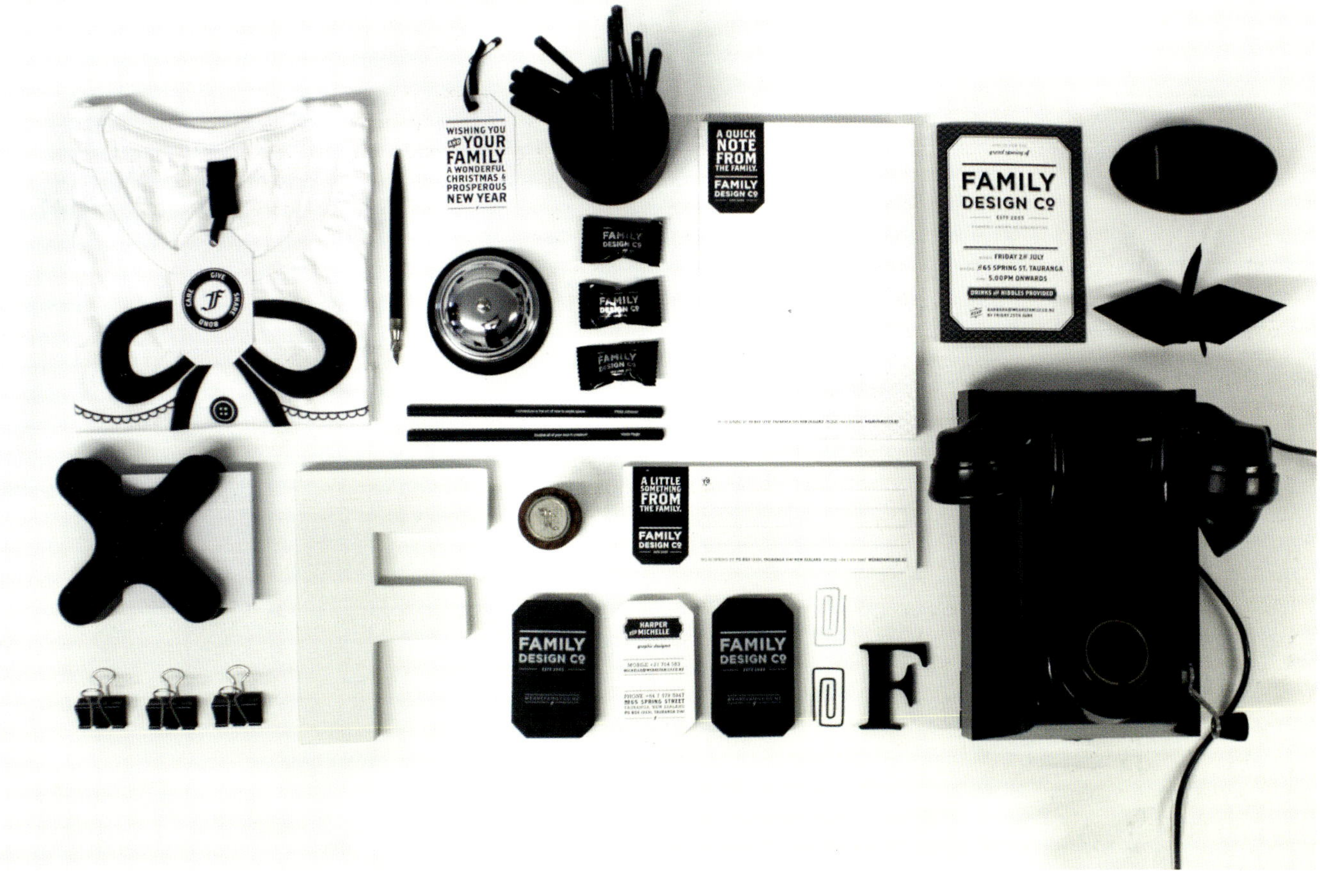

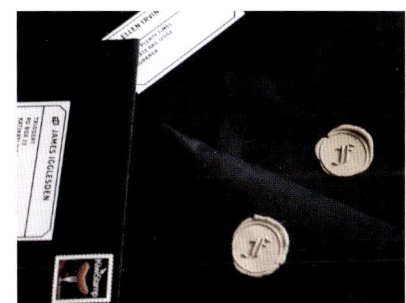

Family Design Co. Brand Identity

New Zealand

Family Design Co.
Design Agency

**Trent Sunderland,
Adam Herlihy,
Michelle Harper**
Designers

The business cards are specially crafted using hefty black card overprinted with white to achieve an old-world result that feels tactile and communicates uniqueness. The identity also includes notepads, address labels and envelopes made from quality offset stock.

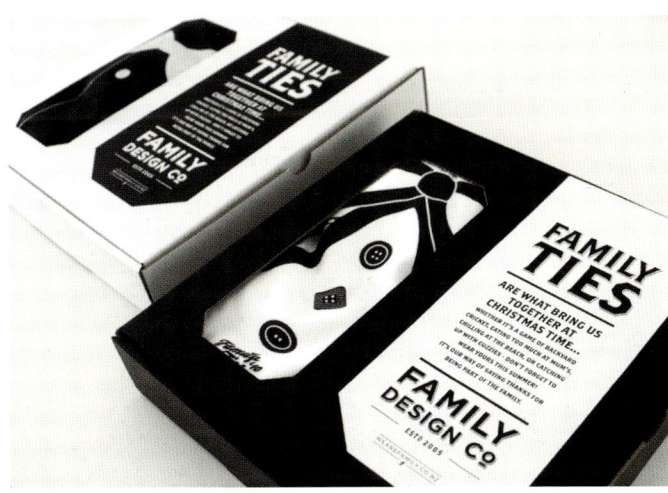

Stack Architects

United Kingdom

The Consult
Design Agency

Alex Atkinson
Creative Director

John-Paul Warner
Designer

Stack Architects
Client

The Consult developed a fresh brand identity and name for a dynamic practice headed up by Leeds-based architect Robert Bumby. The named "Stack" highlights most people's earliest experience of architecture – building block. A crafted typographical treatment was established alongside a stacked logotype and solid icon, forming a unique graphical look to the identity.

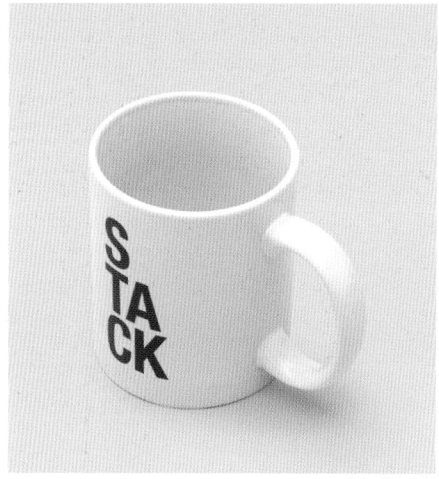

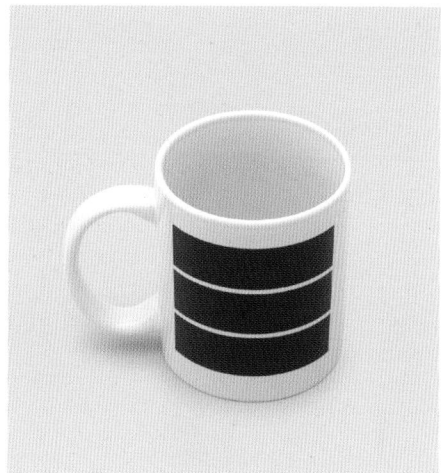

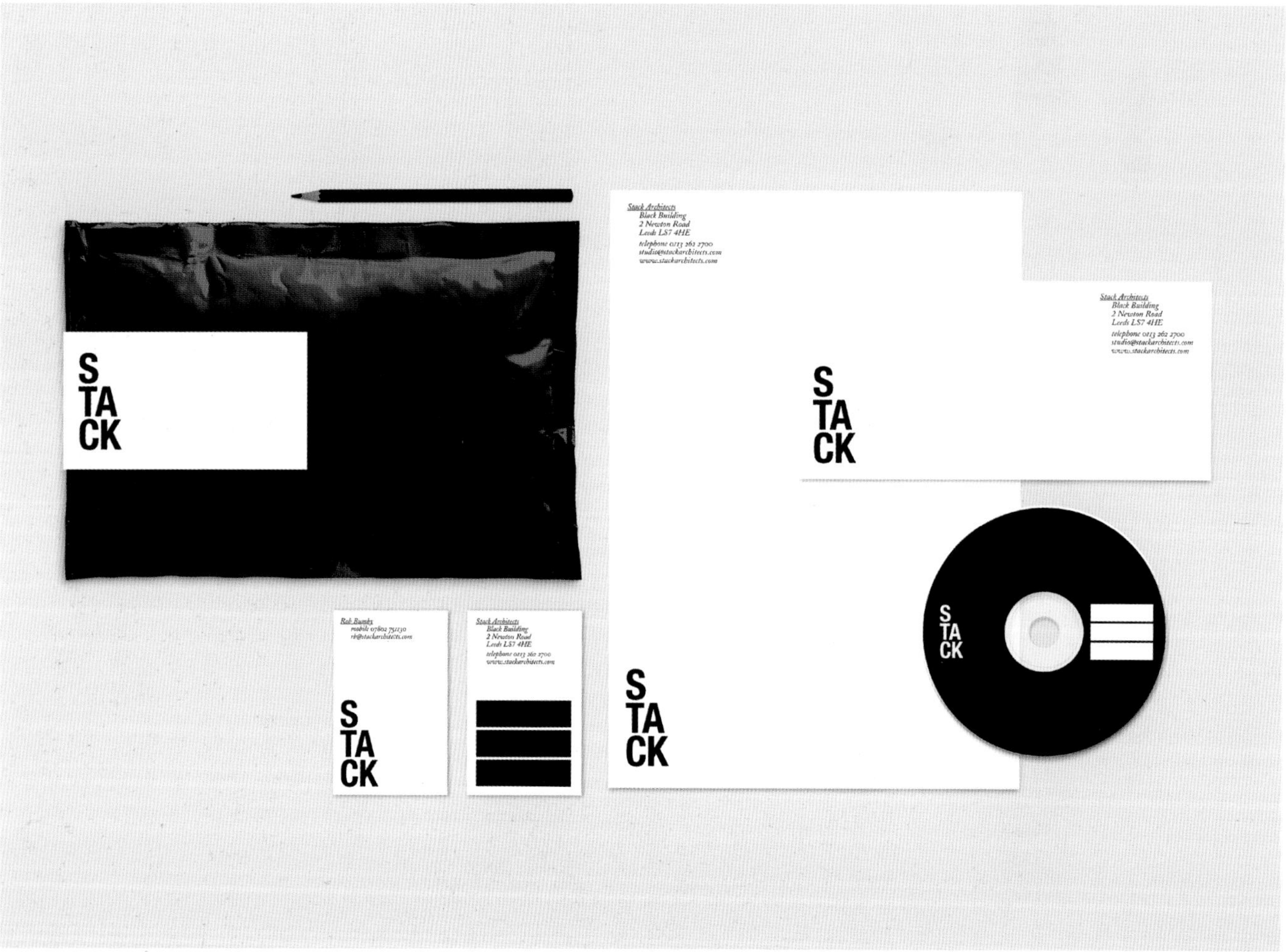

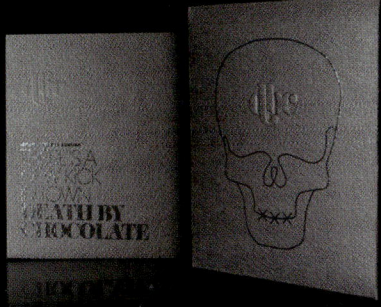
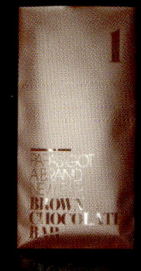
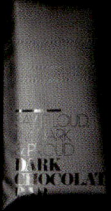
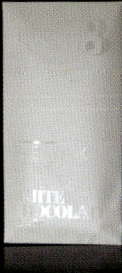

Death by Chocolate
Germany

Denise Franke
Designer
& photographer

Death by Chocolate is a corporate design and packaging concept for a chocolate brand. The aim was to create a unique packaging concept focusing on the myth of chocolate transferring it into a modern, rock and roll kind of context. The product ranges were finished with UV-Varnish and blind embossing. The skull refers on the one hand to the product name but also relates to the initial culture of chocolate. The mold which was used to make the skull is from Mexico, where once in a year the Day of the Dead is celebrated.

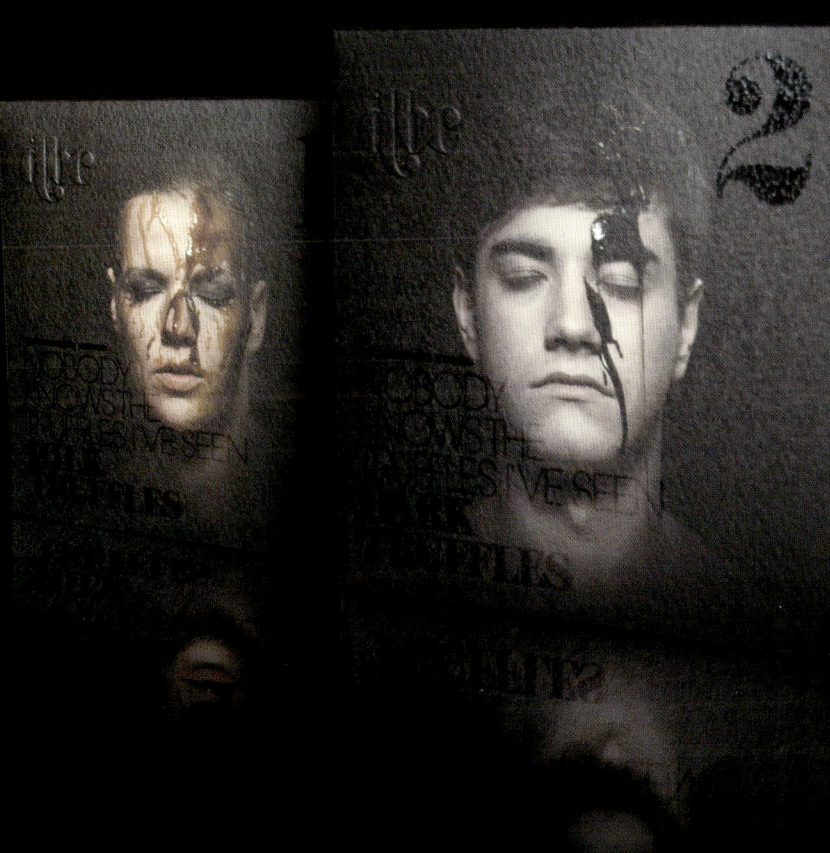
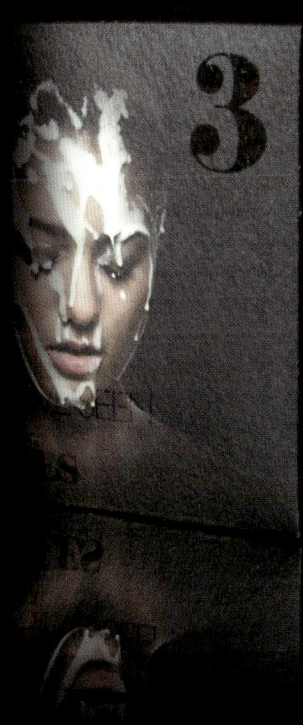

www.dfact.de

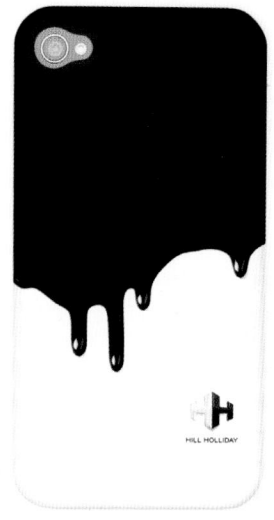
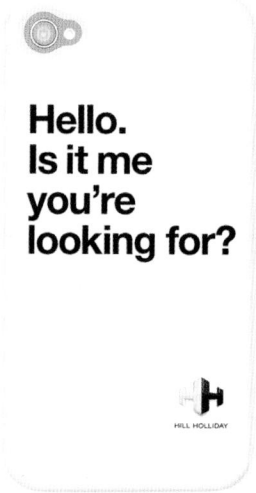
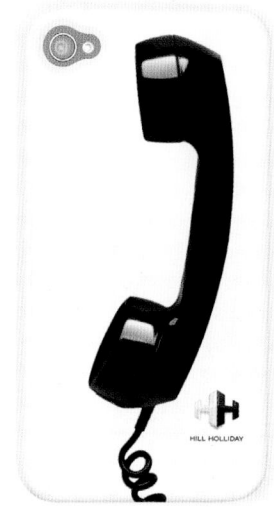

Hill Holiday

United States

Hill Holliday
Design Agency

Lance Jensen
Creative Director

**James Adamé,
Wesley Dorsainvil**
Designers

Hill Holliday
Client

This is the rebranding for Hill Holliday, an advertising agency based in Boston. The agency redesigned for themselves every touch point of their brand from business cards to interior design. The black and white colors constitute the dominant hue employed in the brand design, which match perfectly with all the applications of the brand to activate Hill Holliday's philosophy and commitment to excellence.

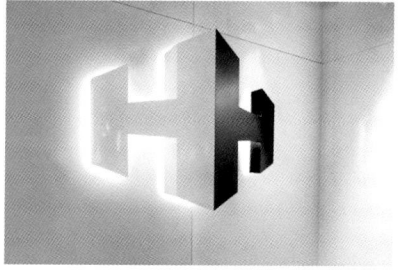

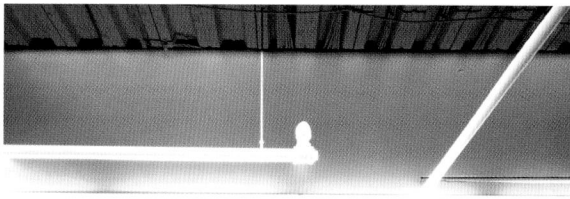

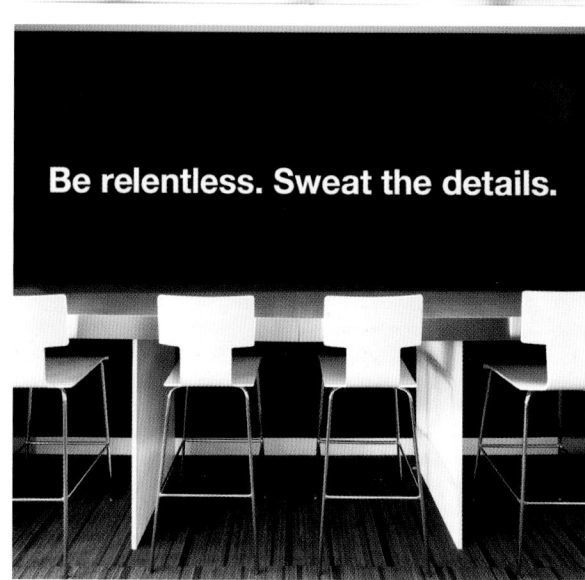

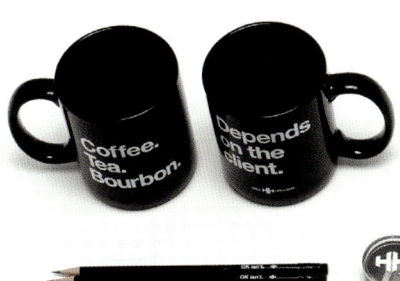

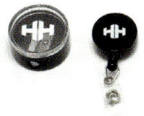
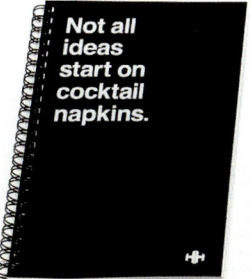
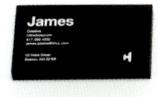
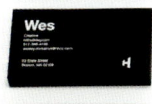
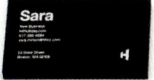
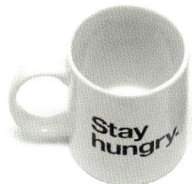
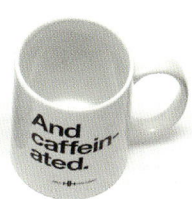
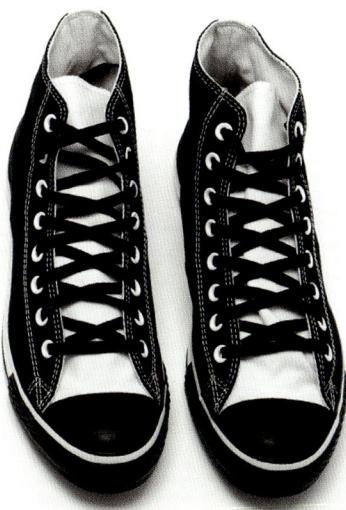

Coffee. Tea. Bourbon.

Depends on the client.

Stay hungry.

And caffeinated.

Kickin' it old school. On paper.

Wes,

Not all ideas start on cocktail napkins.

James

Wes

Sara

Sweat the small stuff.

OK isn't.

Sweat the small stuff and big stuff happens.

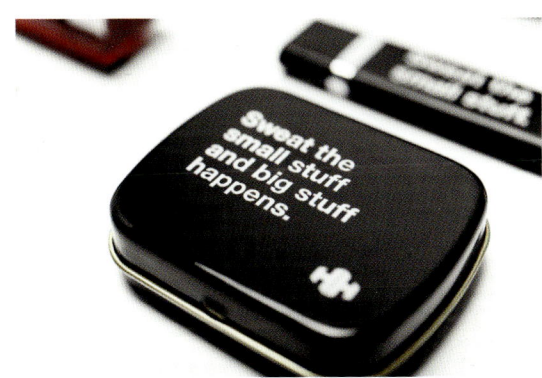

Sweat the small stuff and big stuff happens.

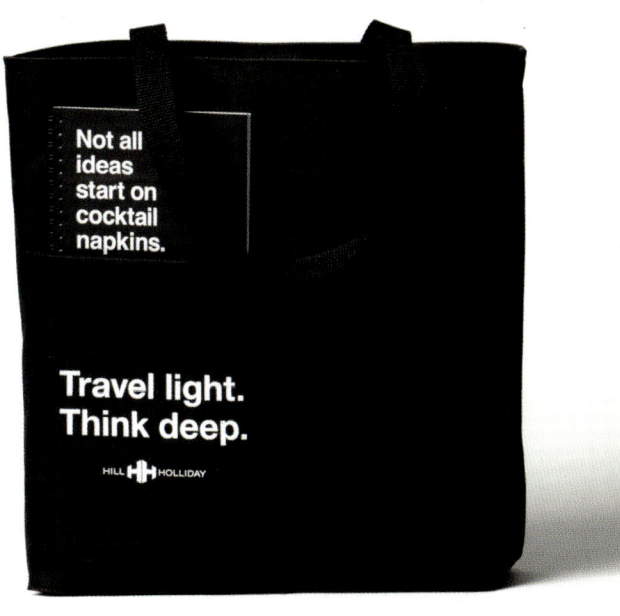

Not all ideas start on cocktail napkins.

Travel light. Think deep.

HILL HOLLIDAY

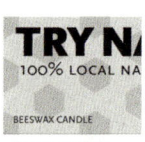
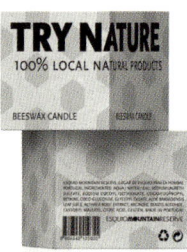
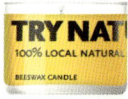
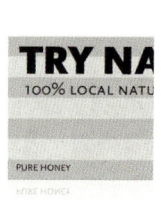
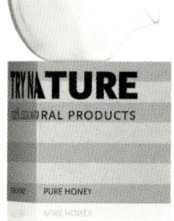
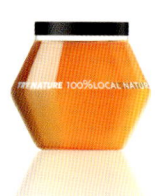

62

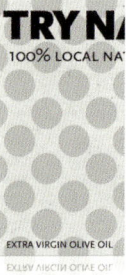

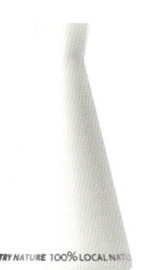

Try Nature
Portugal

**FEB Design
& FIBA Design**
Design Agency
& Photographer

**Marta Fragata,
Miguel Batista**
Designer

**Esquio Mountain
Reserve**
Client

This project avoids the unnecessary graphic features and applies low-impact, non-toxic, and sustainably produced or recycled materials to establish a fair relation between these local natural products, humans and nature. The one color printing and the use of halftone screen, reflects the low environmental impact that the Try Nature brand maintains and at the same time enhances the natural color of its products.

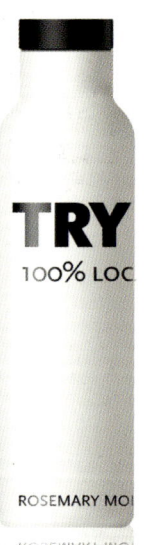
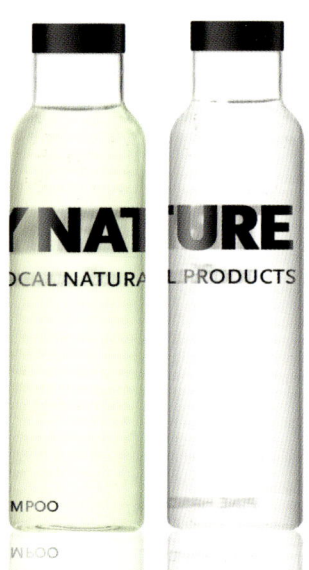
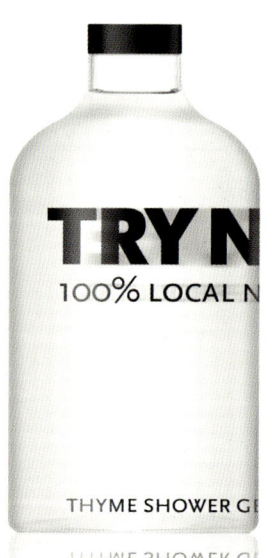
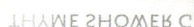
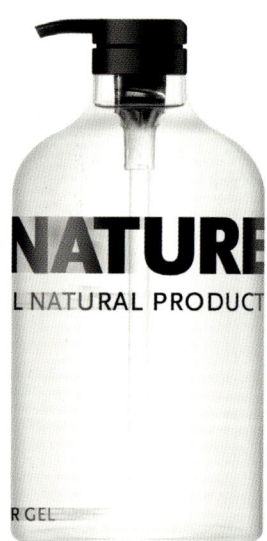

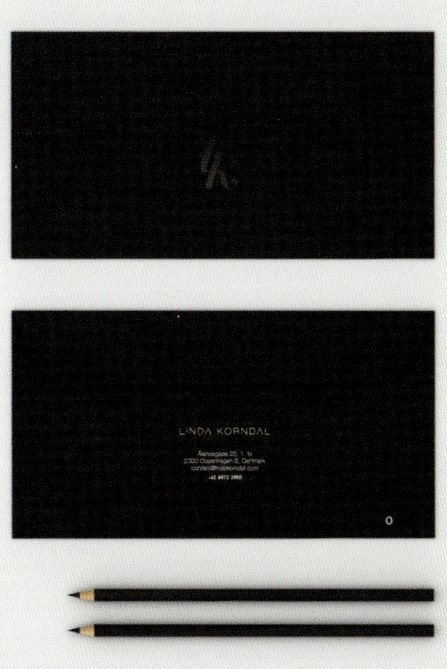
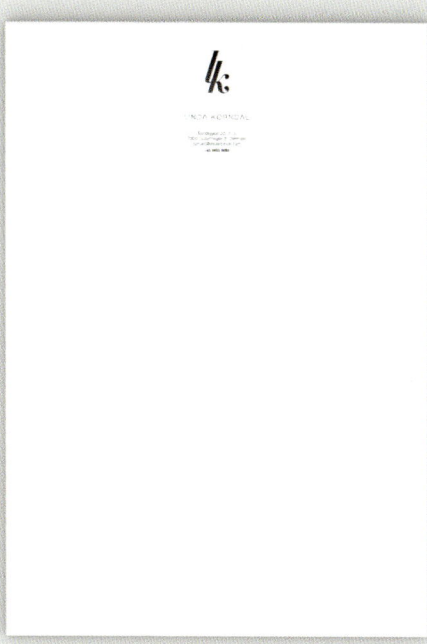
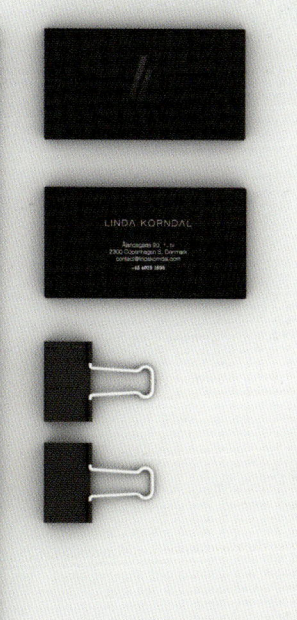

Linda Korndal

Italy

Emanuele Cecini
Designer

Linda Korndal
Client

This is an identity for Linda Korndal, an architect and designer from Copenhagen known for her clean and minimalist aesthetic.
The brand design, using a black and white palette and a classic serif typeface, reflects the client's characteristic approach to design and her meticulous attention to detail.

LINDA KORNDAL

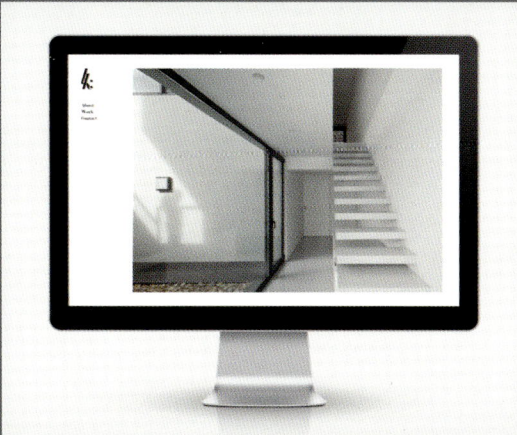
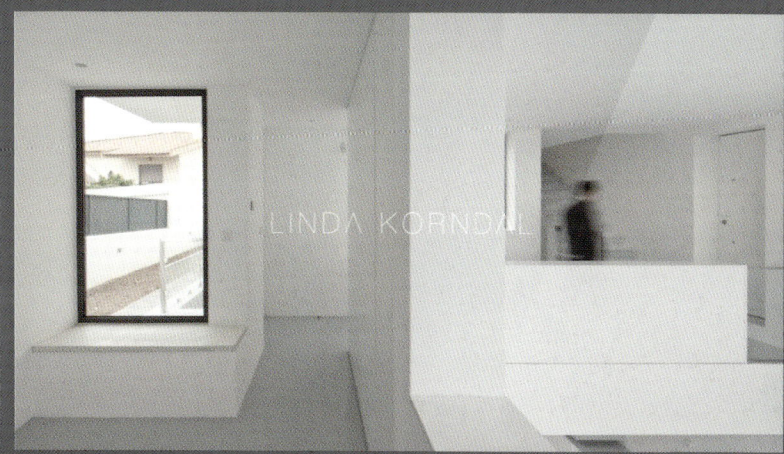

Paper Fastener
United Kingdom

Alex Kwan
Designer

The idea was to use simple shapes and minimal lines to achieve a clean look that would not look out of place in a modern office. Each design has a front and back appropriate to the object it holds. The design also describes how the objects are used to secure paper.

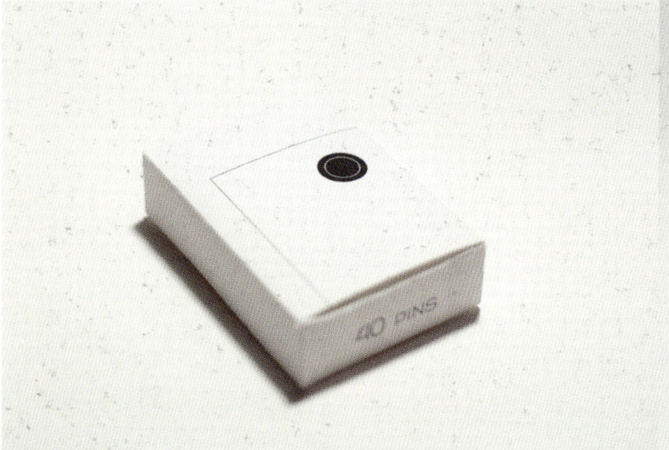

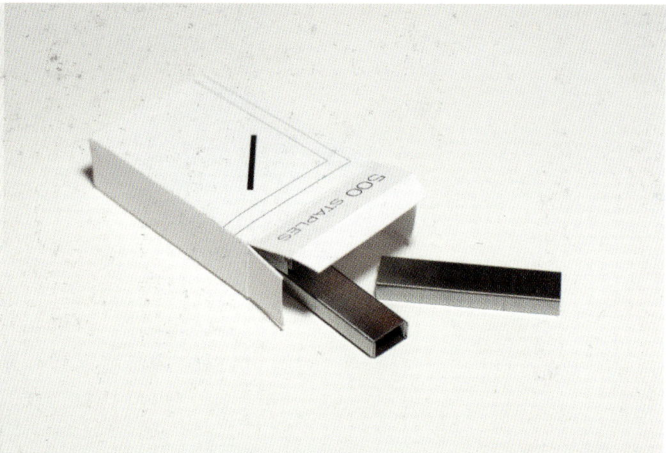

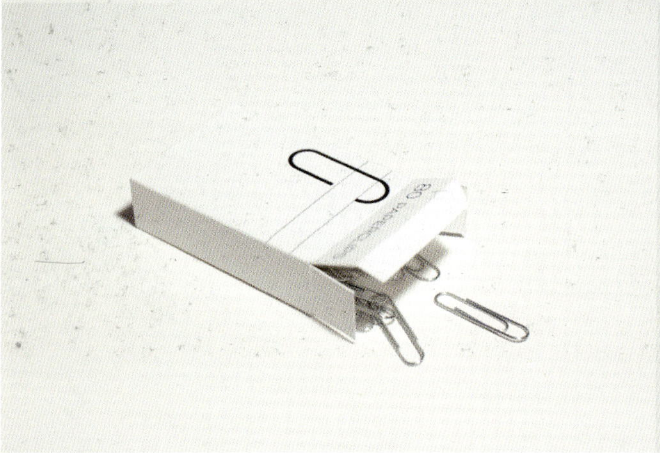

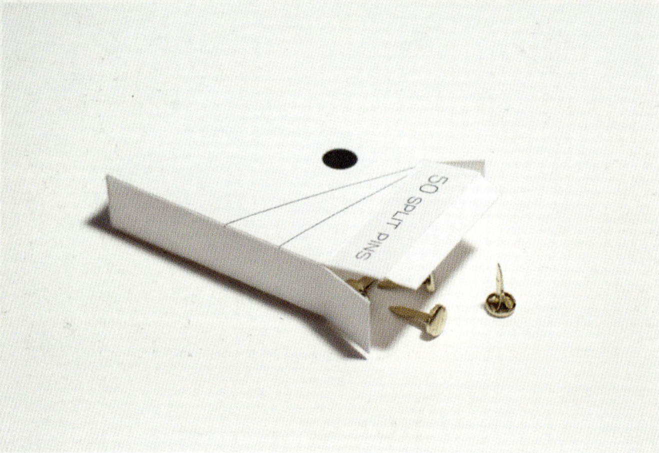

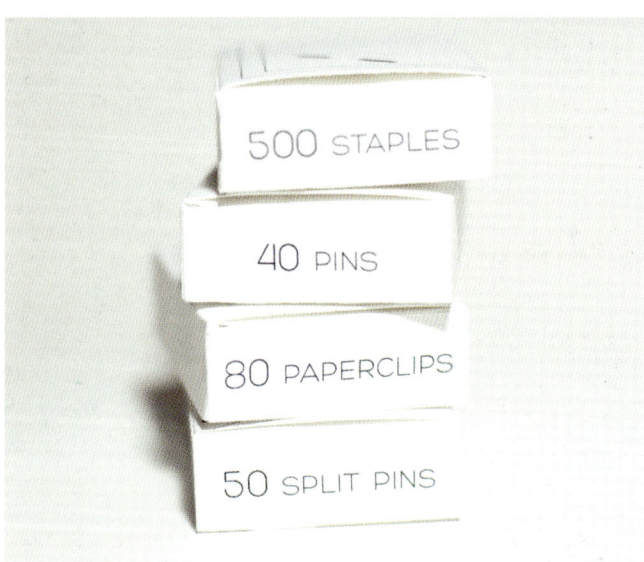

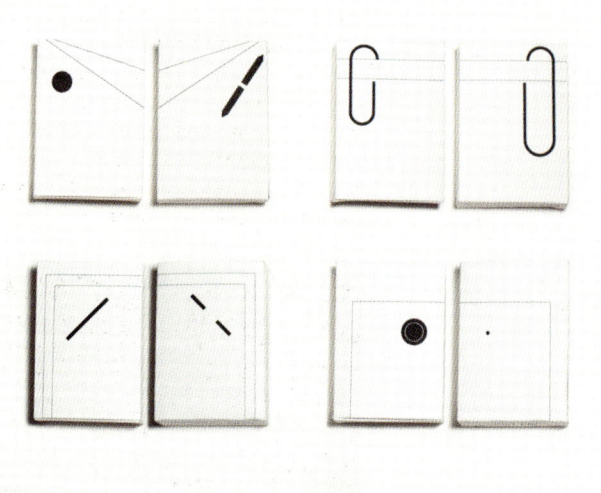

> *"Black, white and gray are the bases of my works, they have the sophistication and elegance that colors rarely bring to visual communication, and allow any color brought into the project to stand out."*
>
> —Baptiste Ringot (BLEED)

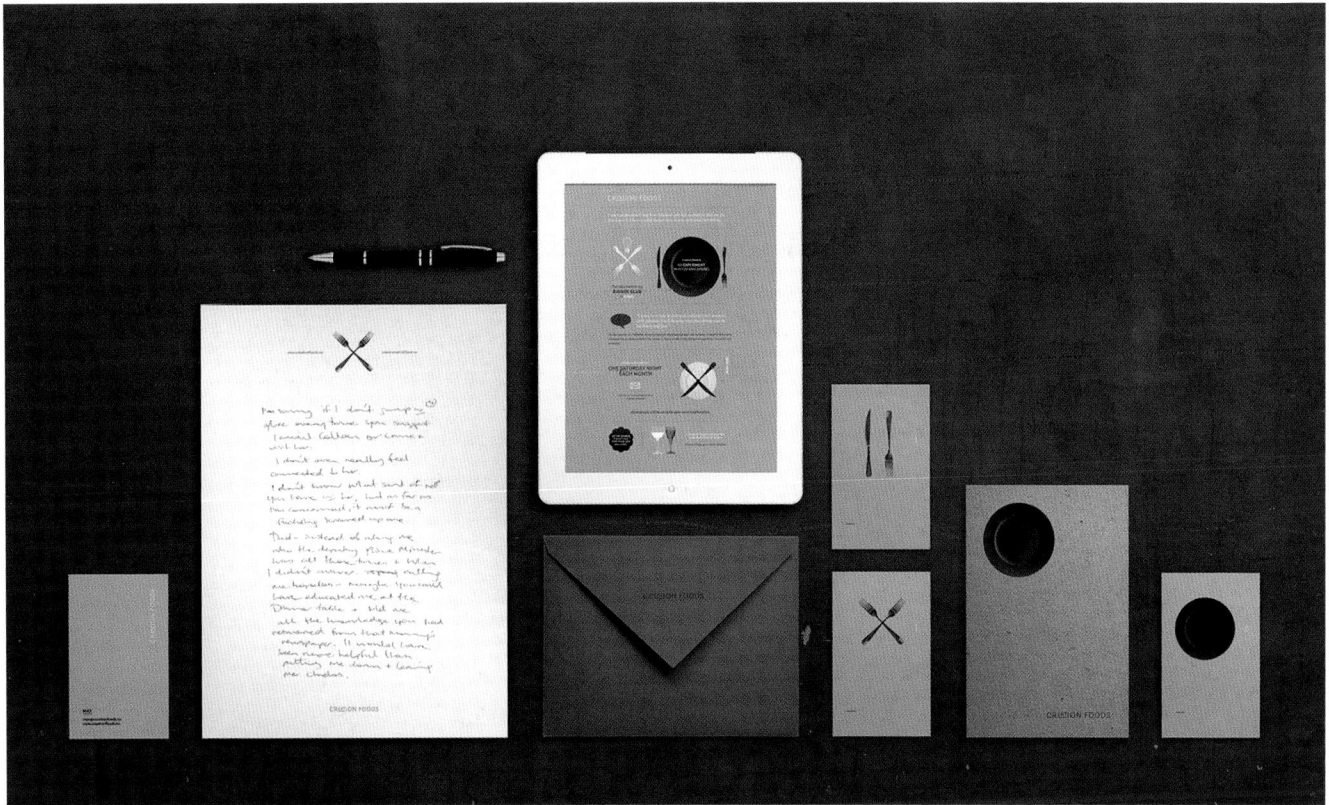

Creation Foods
Norway

BLEED
Design Agency

Svein Haakon Lia
Creative Director

Baptiste Ringot
Designer

Creation Foods
Client

The identity for Creation Foods, an underground and exclusive restaurant offering a surprising five-course set menu that promises an experience of quality and creativity, shows both high-end food and the rogue element in the concept, with the creation of a negative white plate and crossed knives and forks. The black, white and gray colors give the project a dramatic feel while keeping its excitingly charming secrecy and mystery.

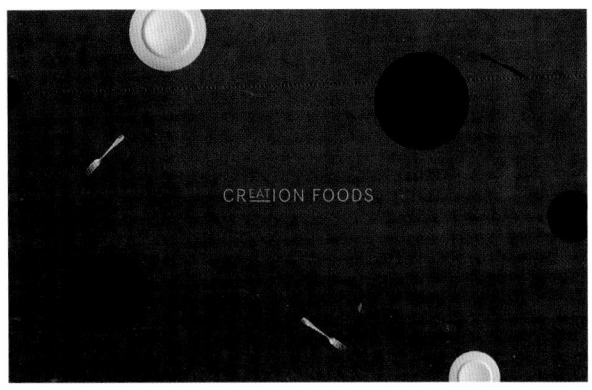

www.bleed.no

Monochrome Graphics

66

Drew Watts
Designer

The Pointe
Client

The Pointe is essentially a large studio space that changes uses ranging from dance lessons to corporate events to small concerts. The designer was tasked with creating a new brand that would highlight the industrial nature of the space as well as generate interest in the local arts and music culture. The concept was to create a brand that, like the space itself, is continuously changing and evolving. The circle transforms into the letter P which regularly changes positions, much like the furnishings in the studio. The icons shift on a gridded system throughout the branded elements revealing information and purpose.

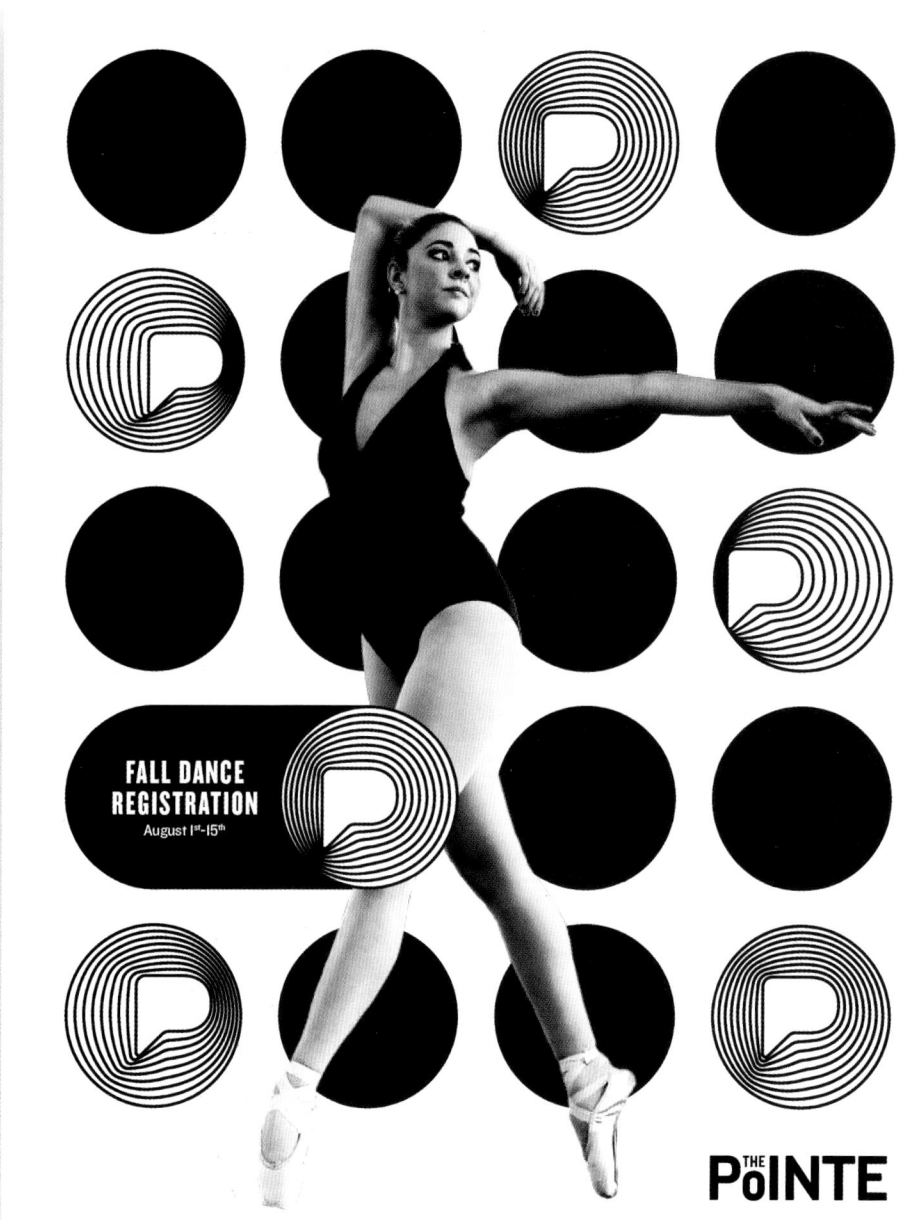

FALL DANCE REGISTRATION
August 1st-15th

THE PoINTE

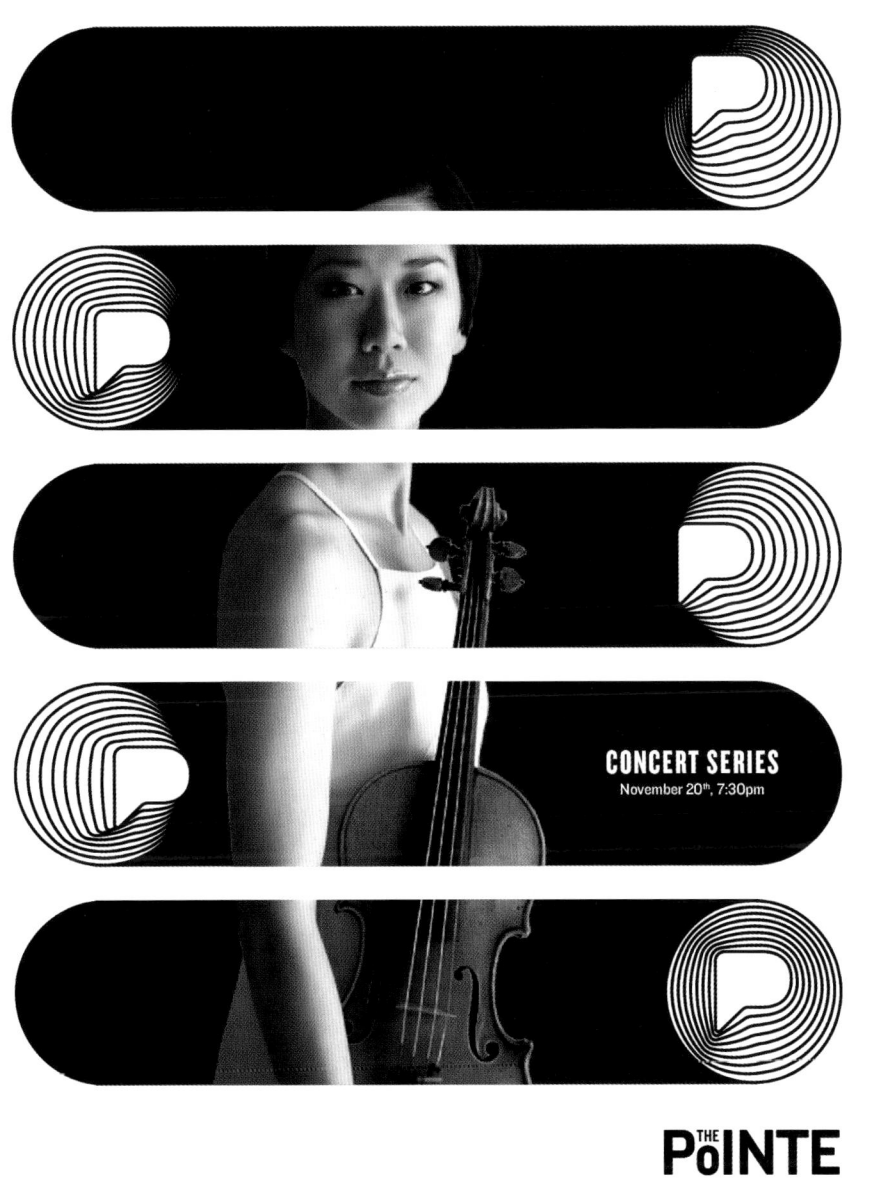

CONCERT SERIES
November 20th, 7:30pm

THE
PoINTE

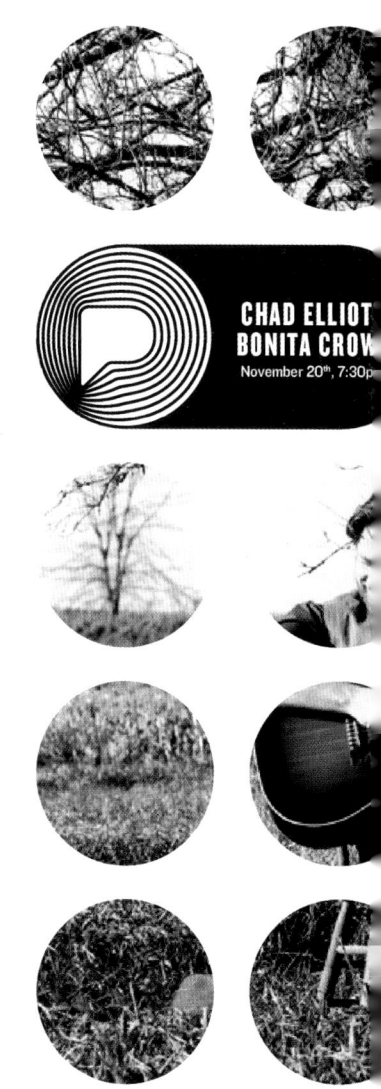

CHAD ELLIOT
BONITA CROW
November 20th, 7:30p

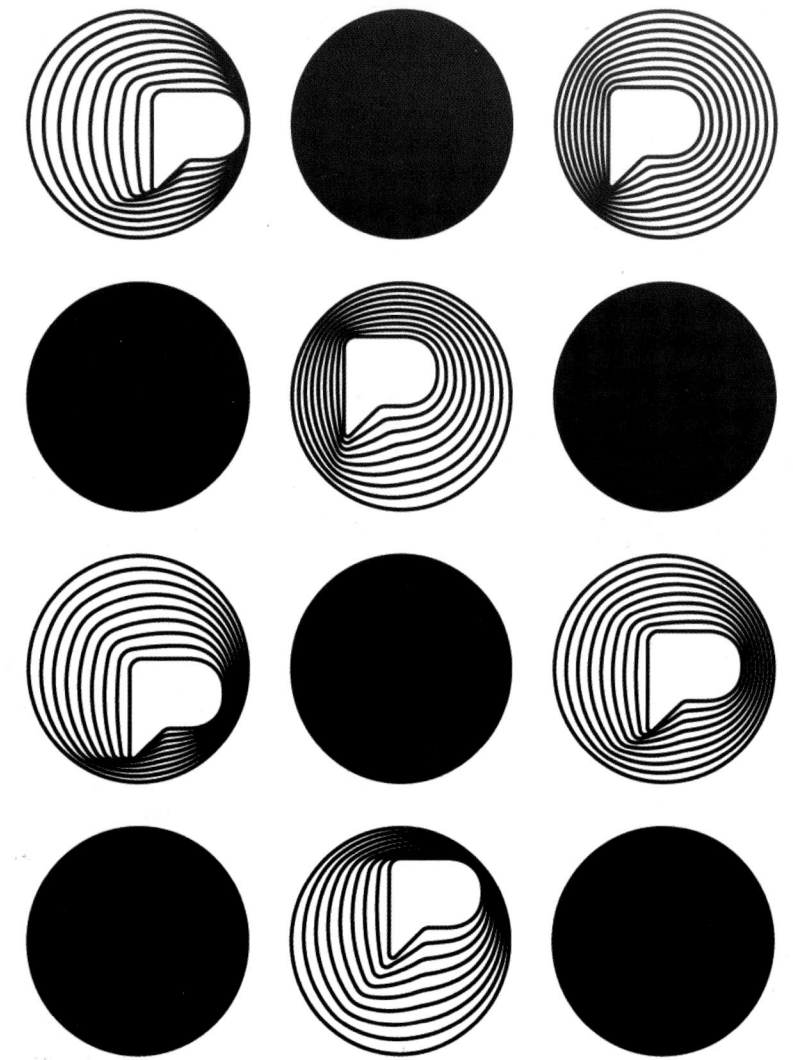

THE Po

114 N. 9TH ST. OMAHA NE, 68102

David Catherall
Dance and Music
402.312.0831

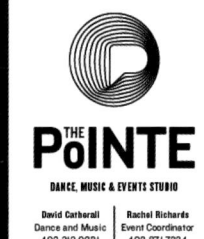

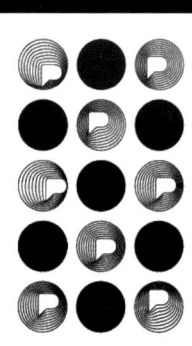

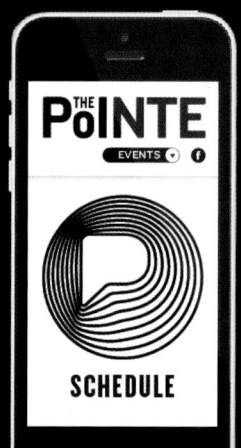

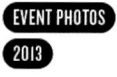

THE PoIN

THE PoINTE

114 N. 9TH ST. OMAHA NE, 68102

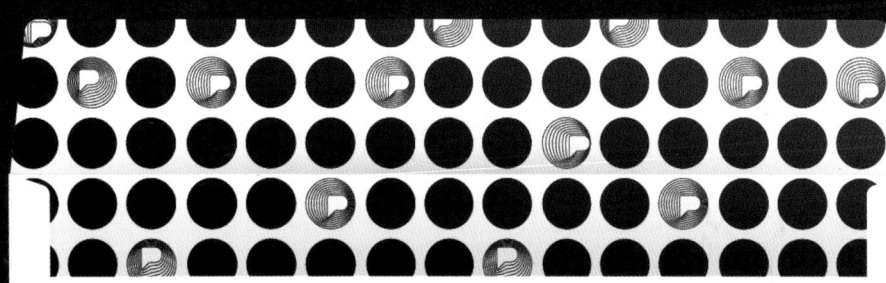

THE PoINTE

i Richards
Coordinator
871.7224

THEPOINTEDOWNTOWN.COM

THEPOINTEDOWNTOWN.COM

THE PoINTE

TE

E

70

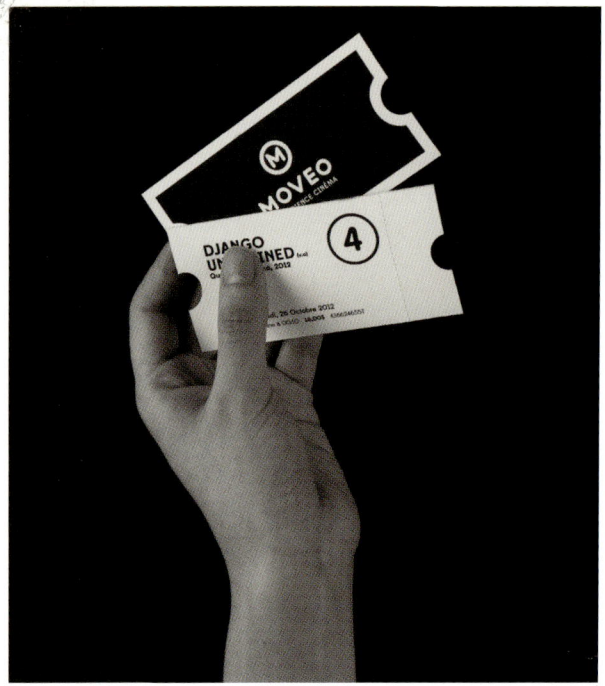

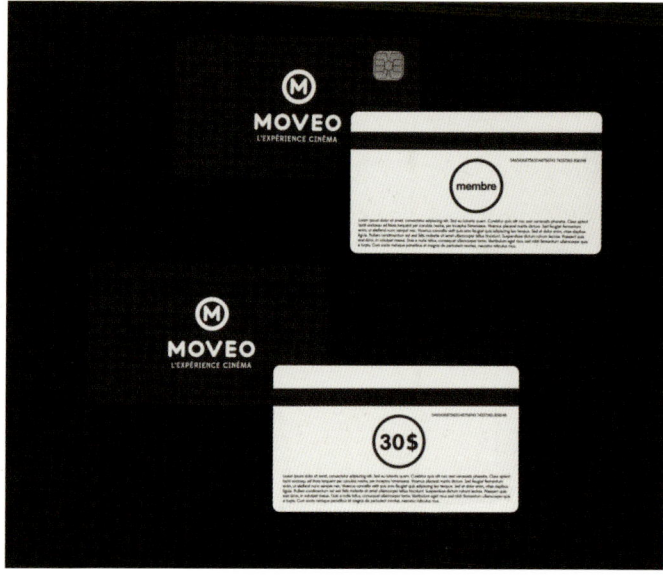

Moveo Cinema

Canada

Zorani Sanabria
Art Director

Antoine Proulx, David Lapointe-Gilbert
Designer

This is a branding for Moveo Cinema, aiming to revive its golden era to the cinema. The designer used the black and white palette, which was inspired by black and white films, to add a touch of nostalgia to the project.

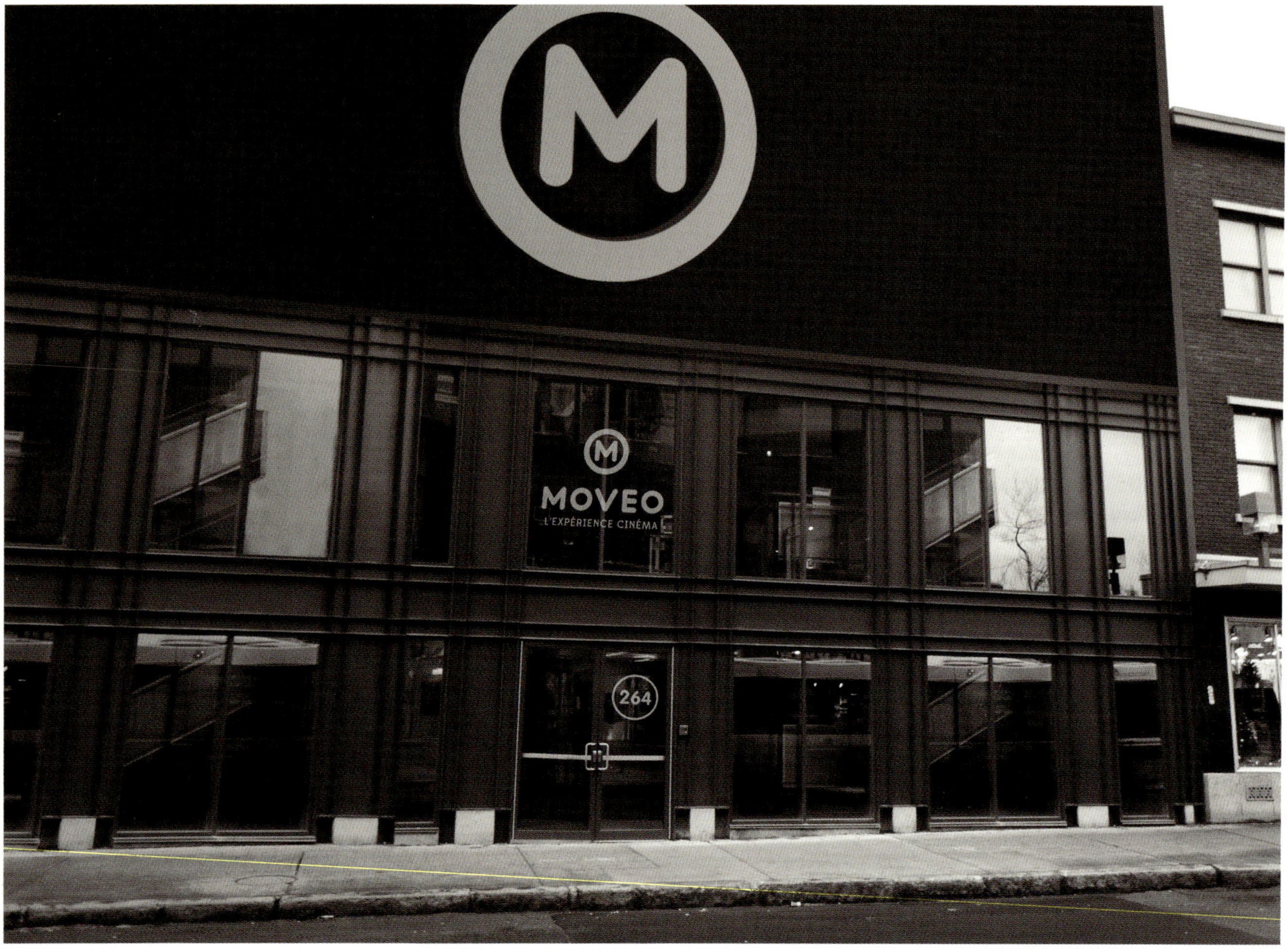

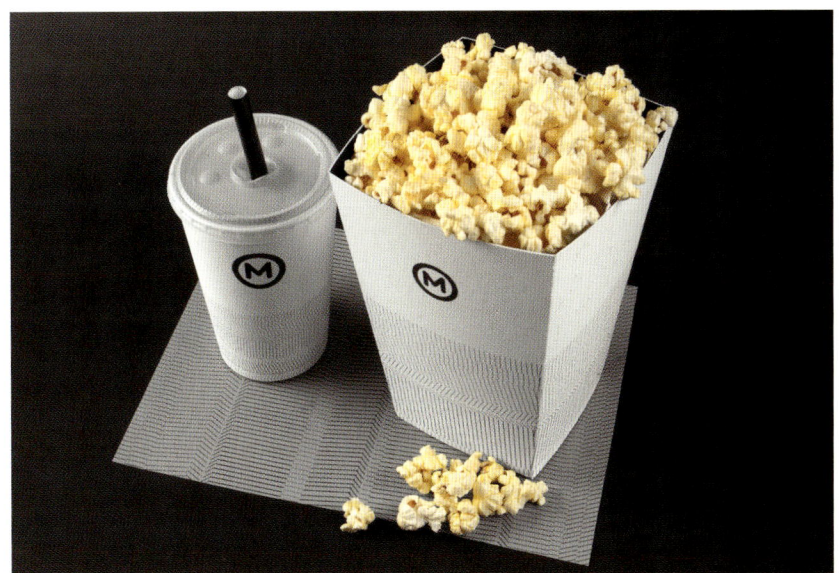

"Black and white are the most pure and inspiring colors. They are the base of any well-designed project and when we mix them, the gray appears to soften the two extremes."
—Antoine Proulx

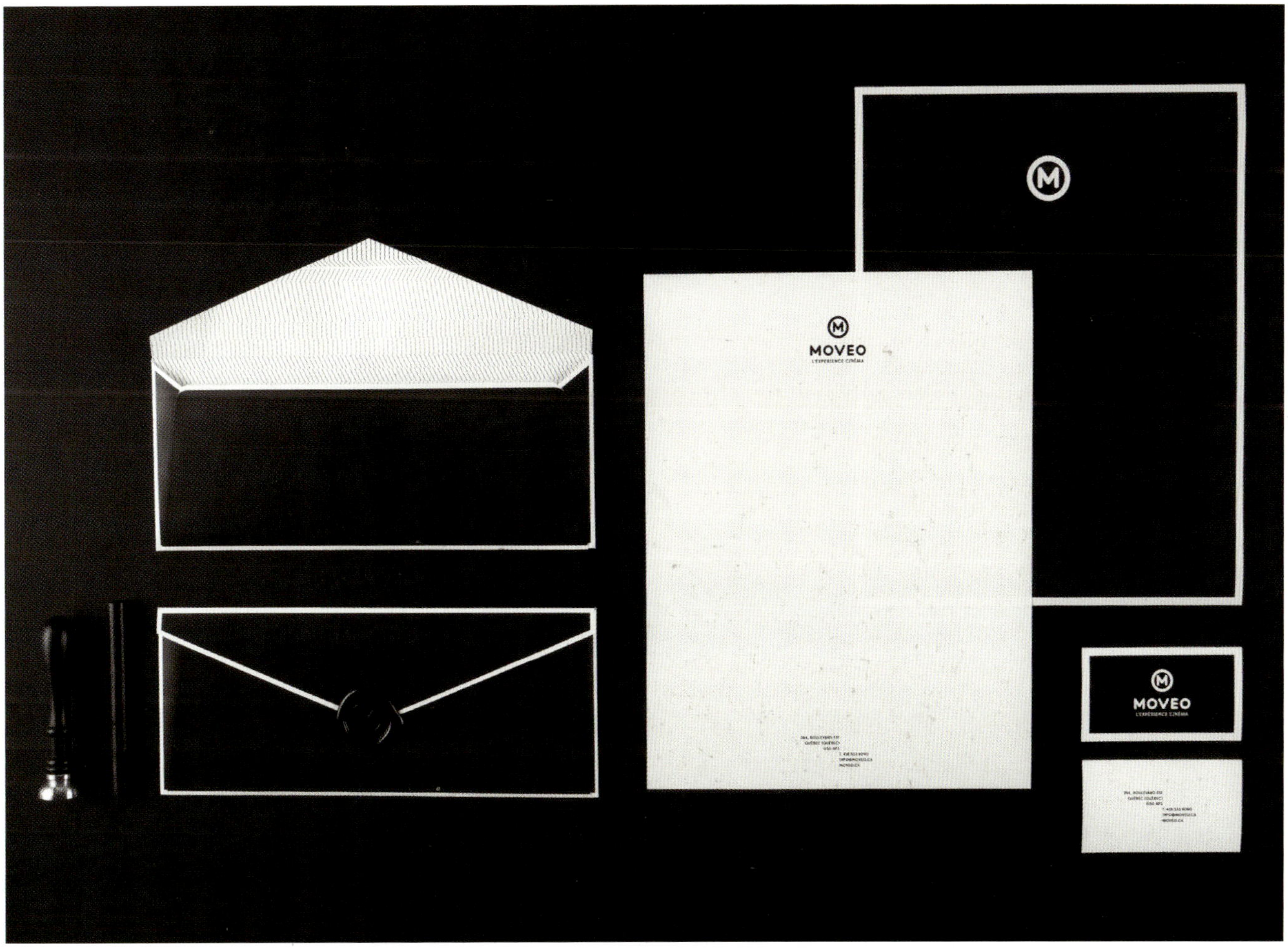

Misomber Nuan Look Book IV
Singapore

Somewhere Else
Design Agency

Yong
Creative Director

Misomber Nuan
Client

Misomber Nuan is a menswear designer whose collections focus on emptiness and voids. In this look book, the texture created was inspired by treated leathers present in Misomber Nuan's clothes. The various promotional literatures created for Misomber Nuan are all directed to express their experimental approach towards materials and fabrics.

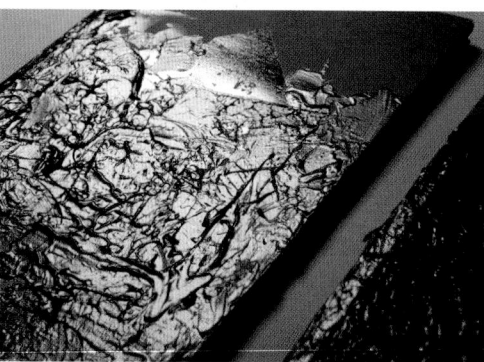
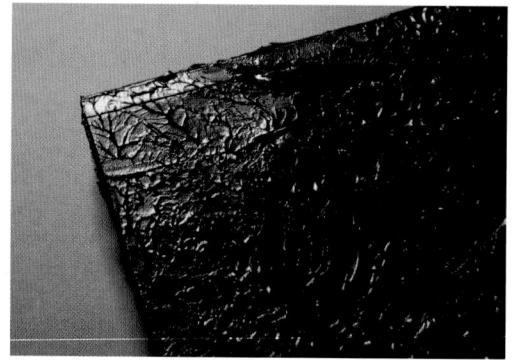

www.somewhere-else.info

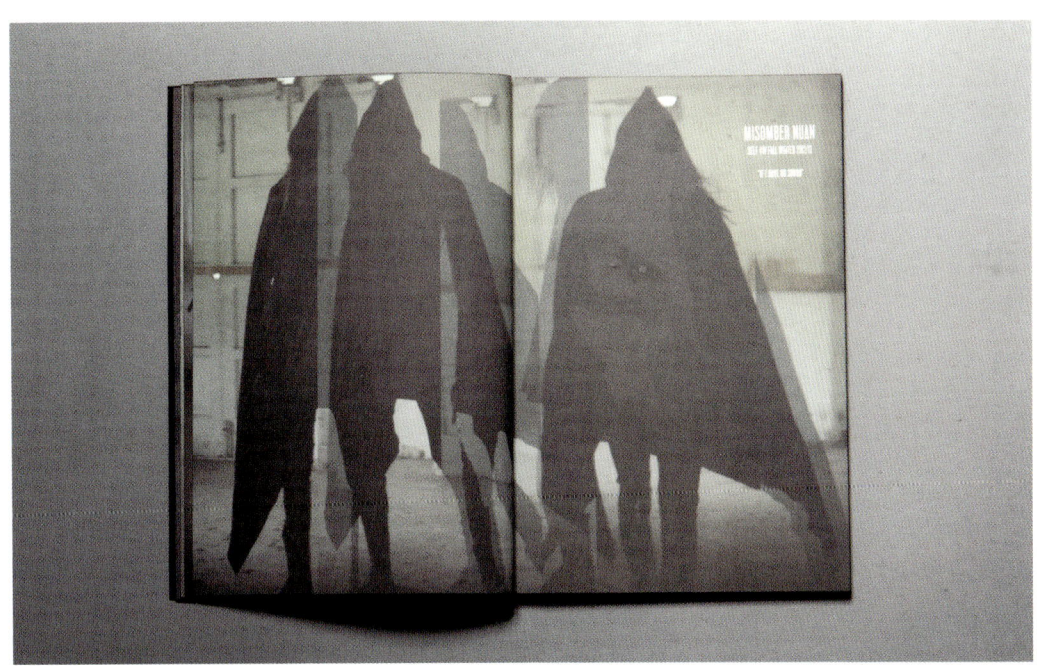

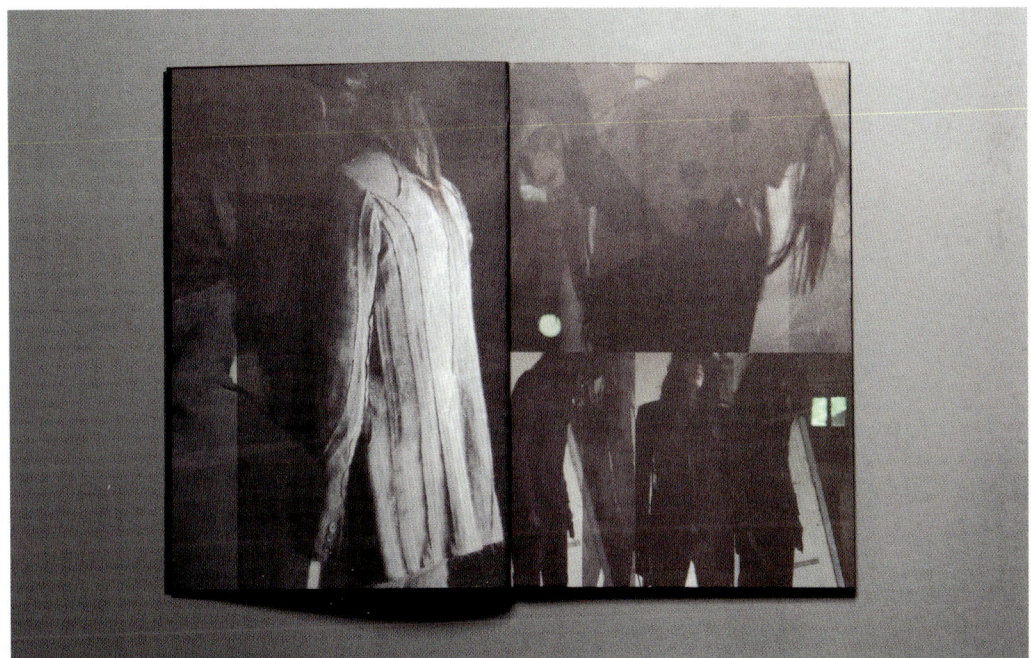

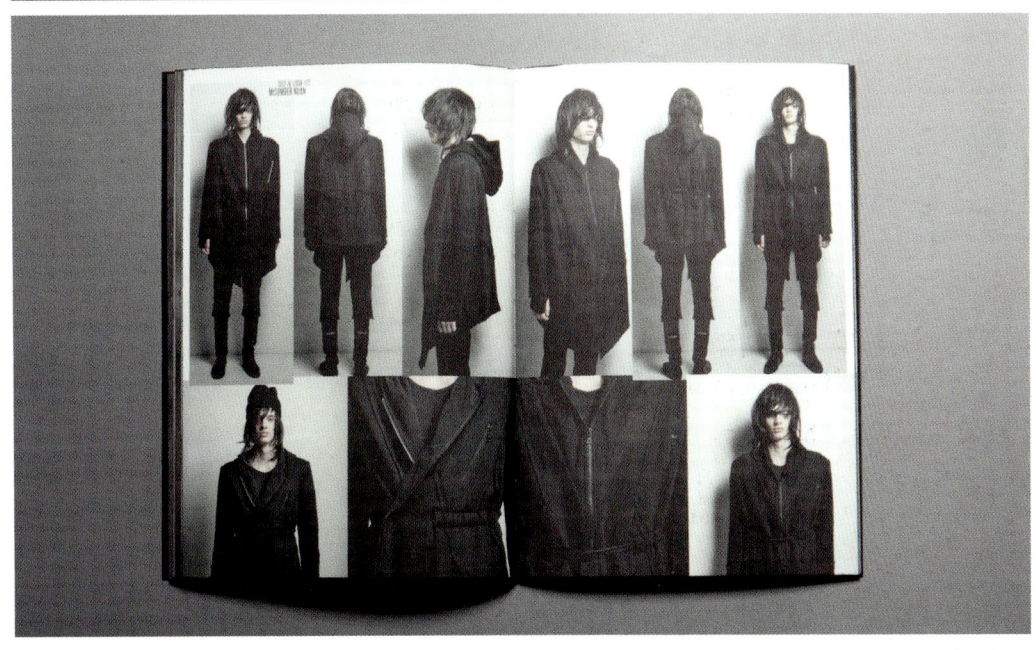

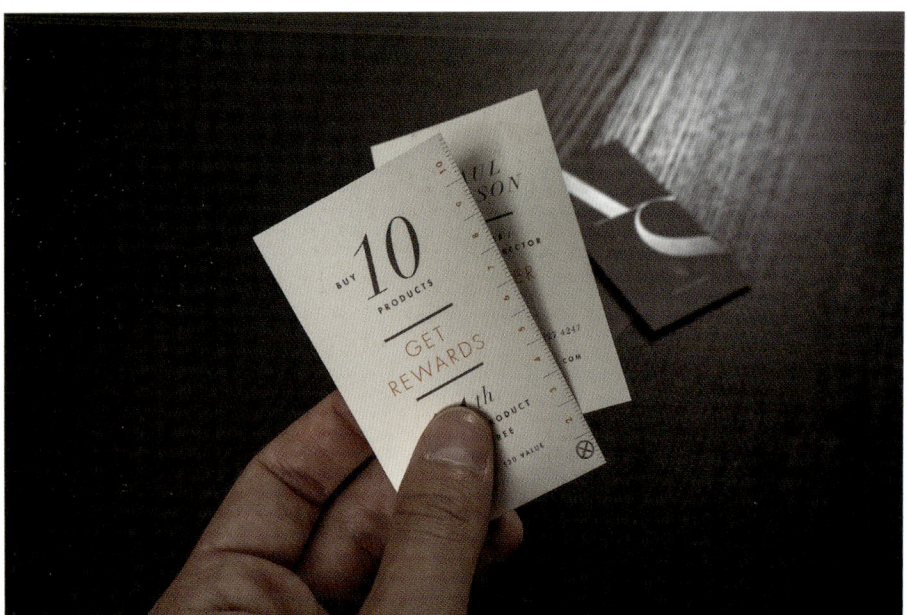

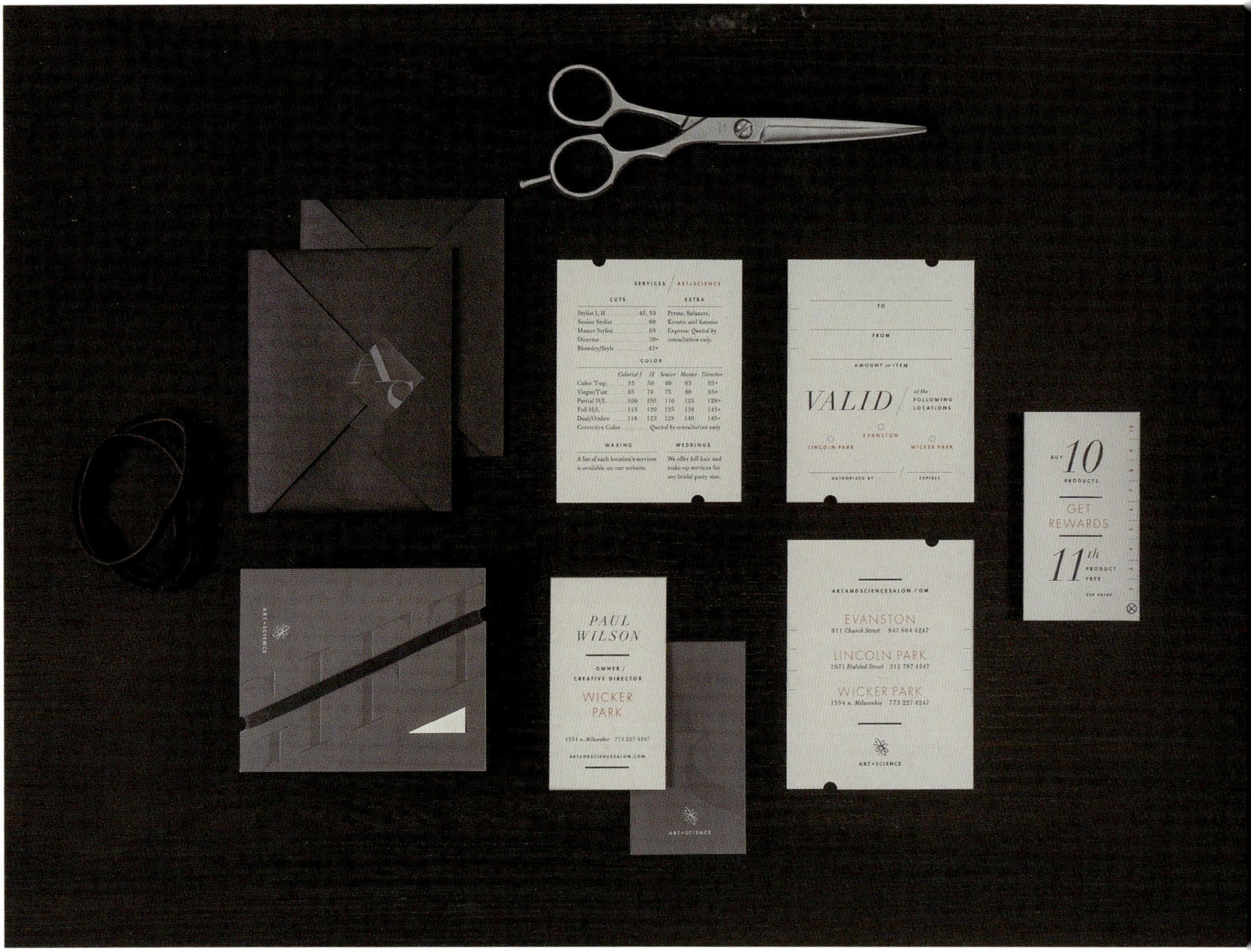

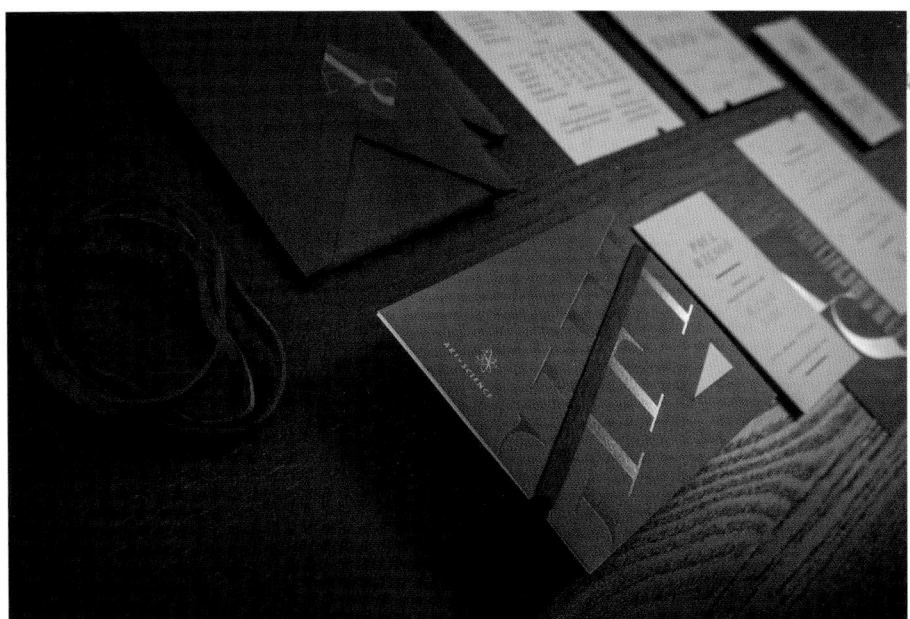

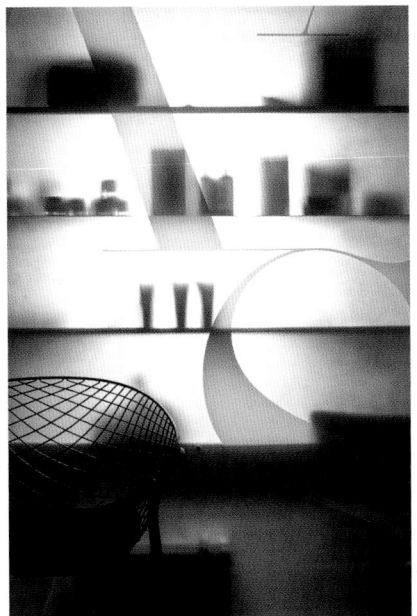

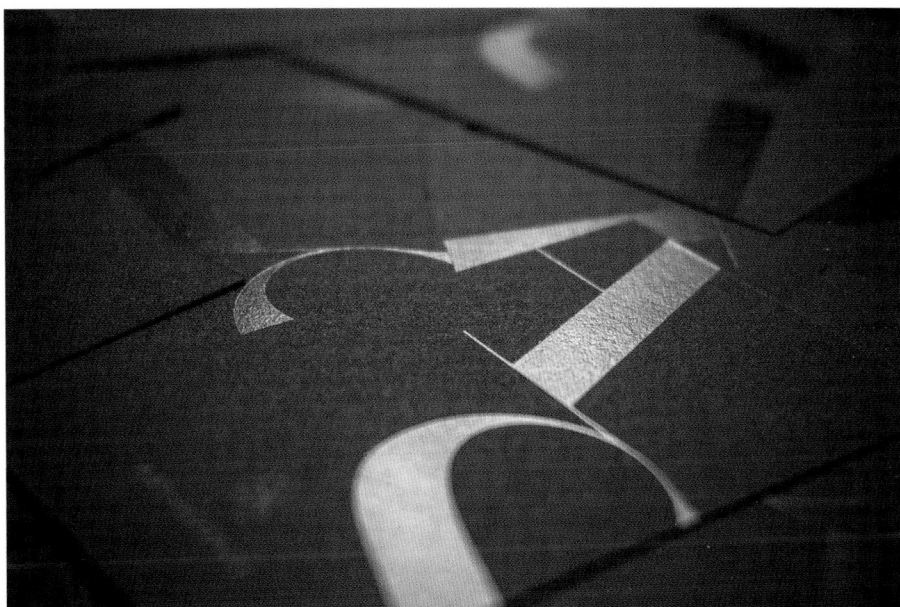

Art + Science Salon
United States

Firebelly Design
Design Agency

Will Miller
Designer

Art + Science Salon
Client

The rebranding for Chicago-based Art + Science salon explores a deeper meaning of a good haircut. The design manifests a skillful play of the black and white palette. The new identity covers print materials such as gift cards, interiors and signage.

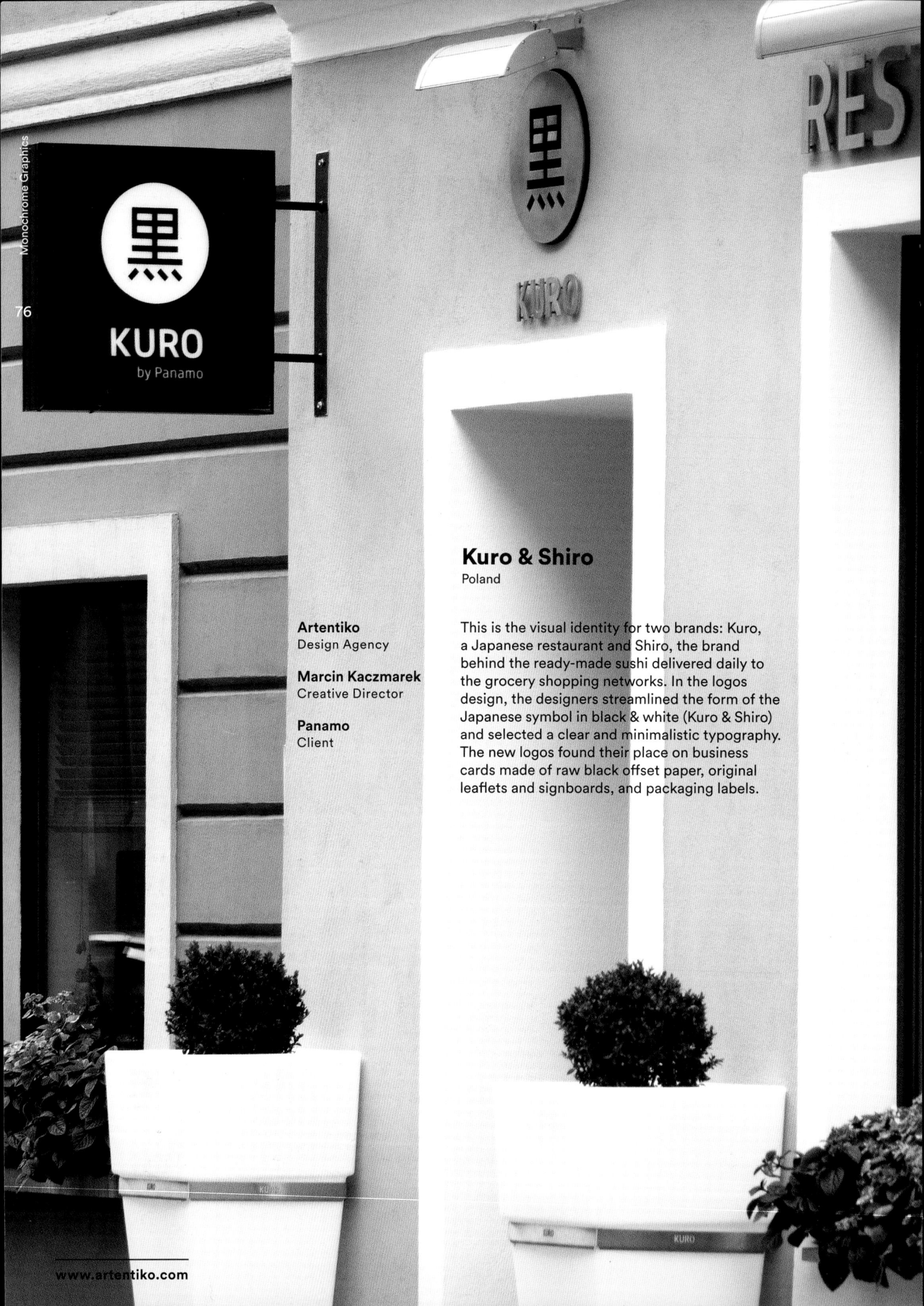

KURO
by Panamo

RES

Artentiko
Design Agency

Marcin Kaczmarek
Creative Director

Panamo
Client

Kuro & Shiro
Poland

This is the visual identity for two brands: Kuro, a Japanese restaurant and Shiro, the brand behind the ready-made sushi delivered daily to the grocery shopping networks. In the logos design, the designers streamlined the form of the Japanese symbol in black & white (Kuro & Shiro) and selected a clear and minimalistic typography. The new logos found their place on business cards made of raw black offset paper, original leaflets and signboards, and packaging labels.

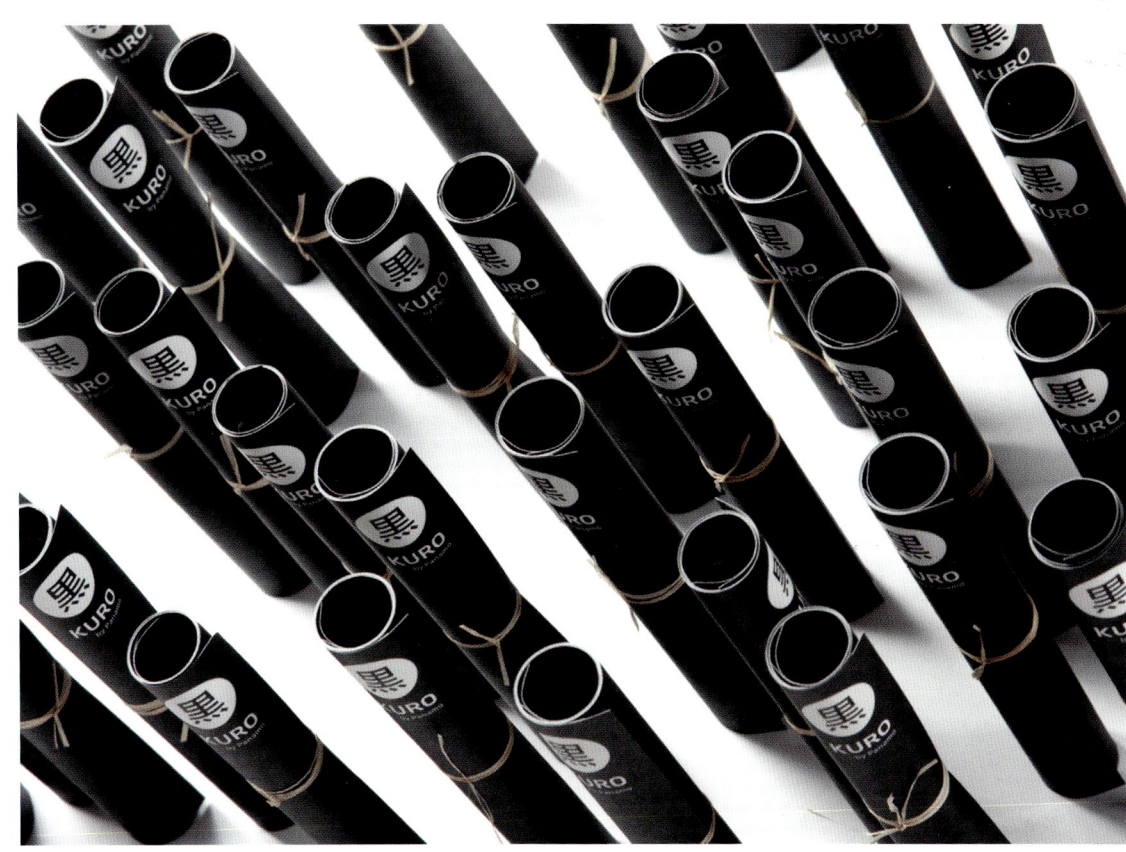

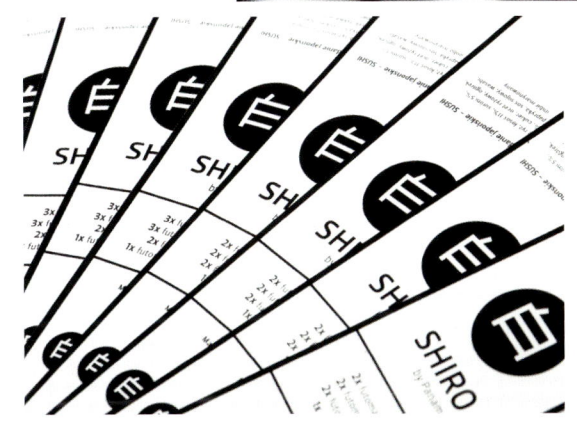

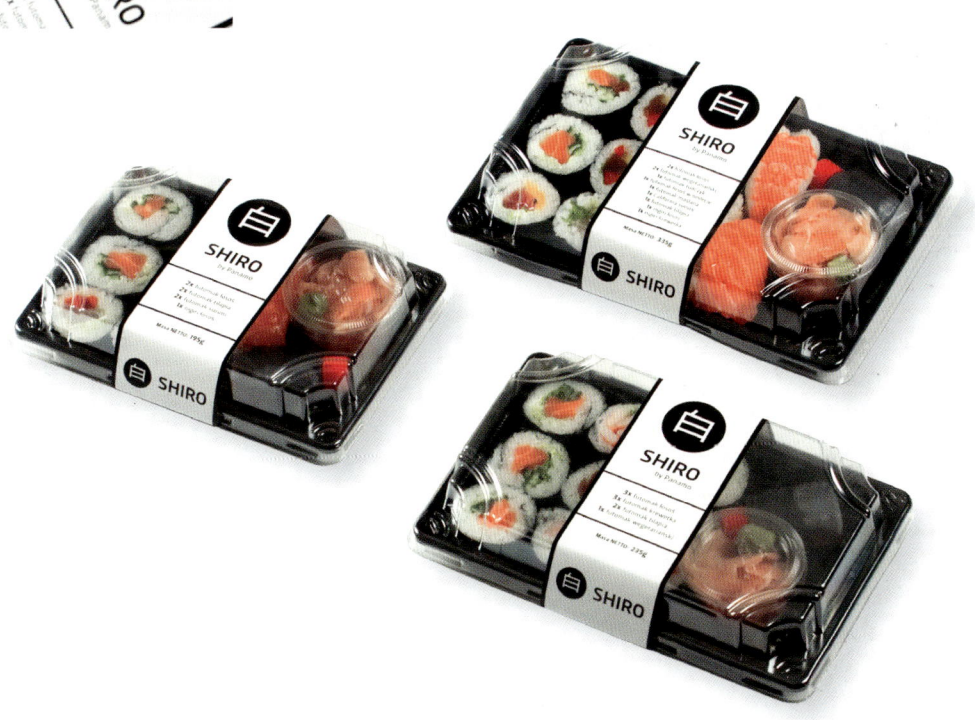

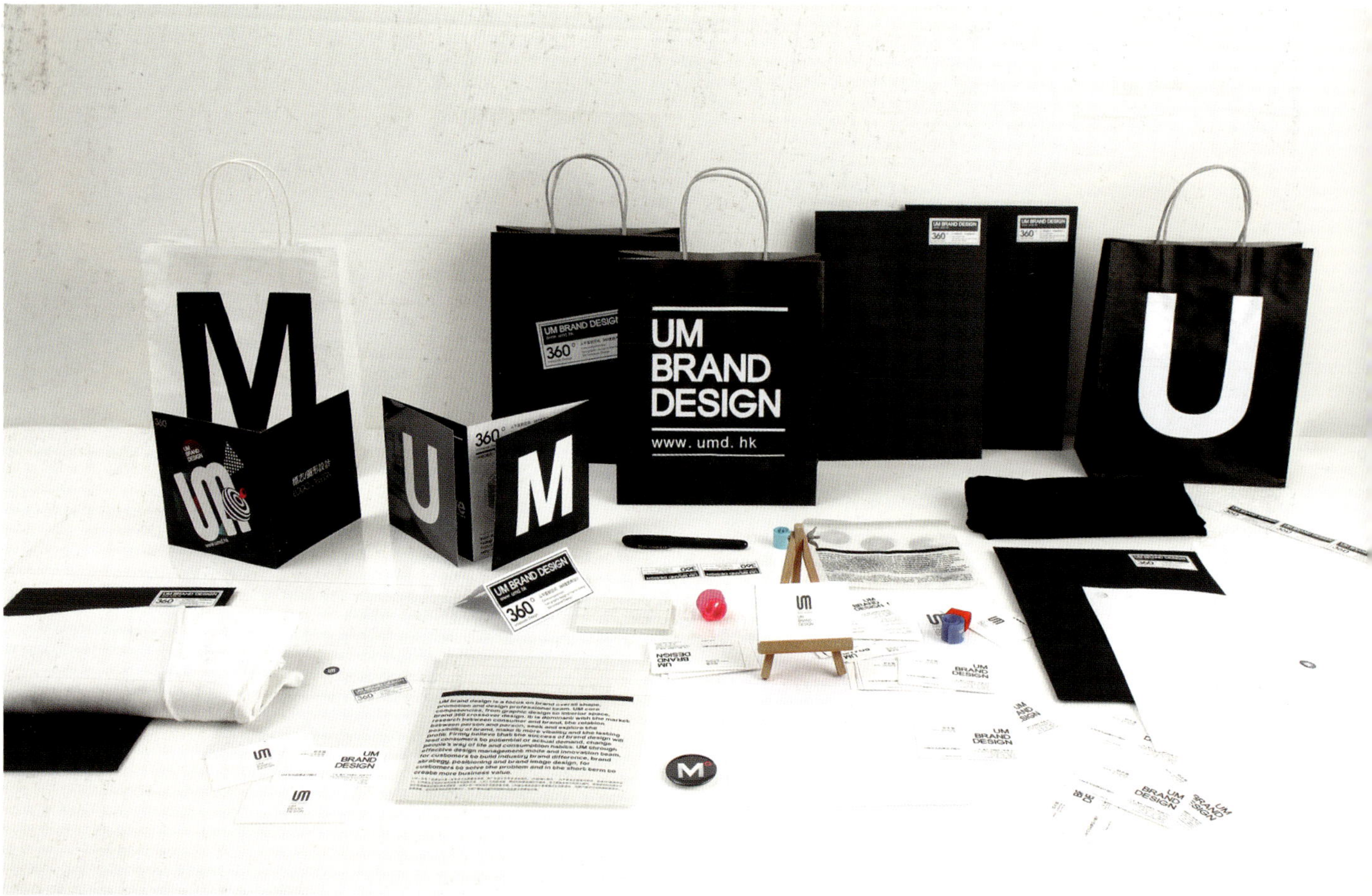

UM Brand Identity Design

China

UM Brand Design
Design Agency

**Zheng Zhiqiang,
He Guojie**
Designers

Xian Huaqiang
Photographer

The project expresses a simple yet strong visual identity by using black and white colors in the design while taking into account the need to emphasize the brand image and the studio's focus on variability and flexibility.

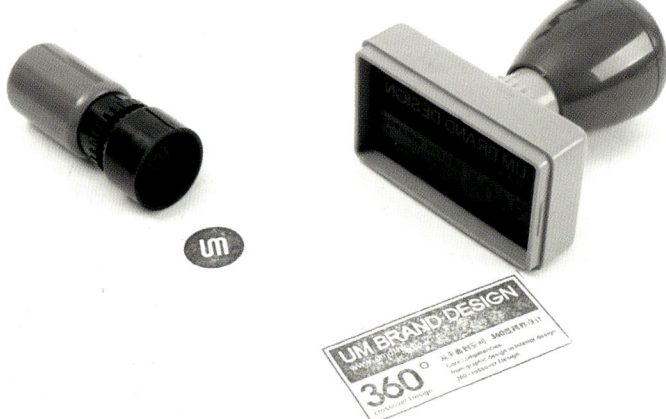

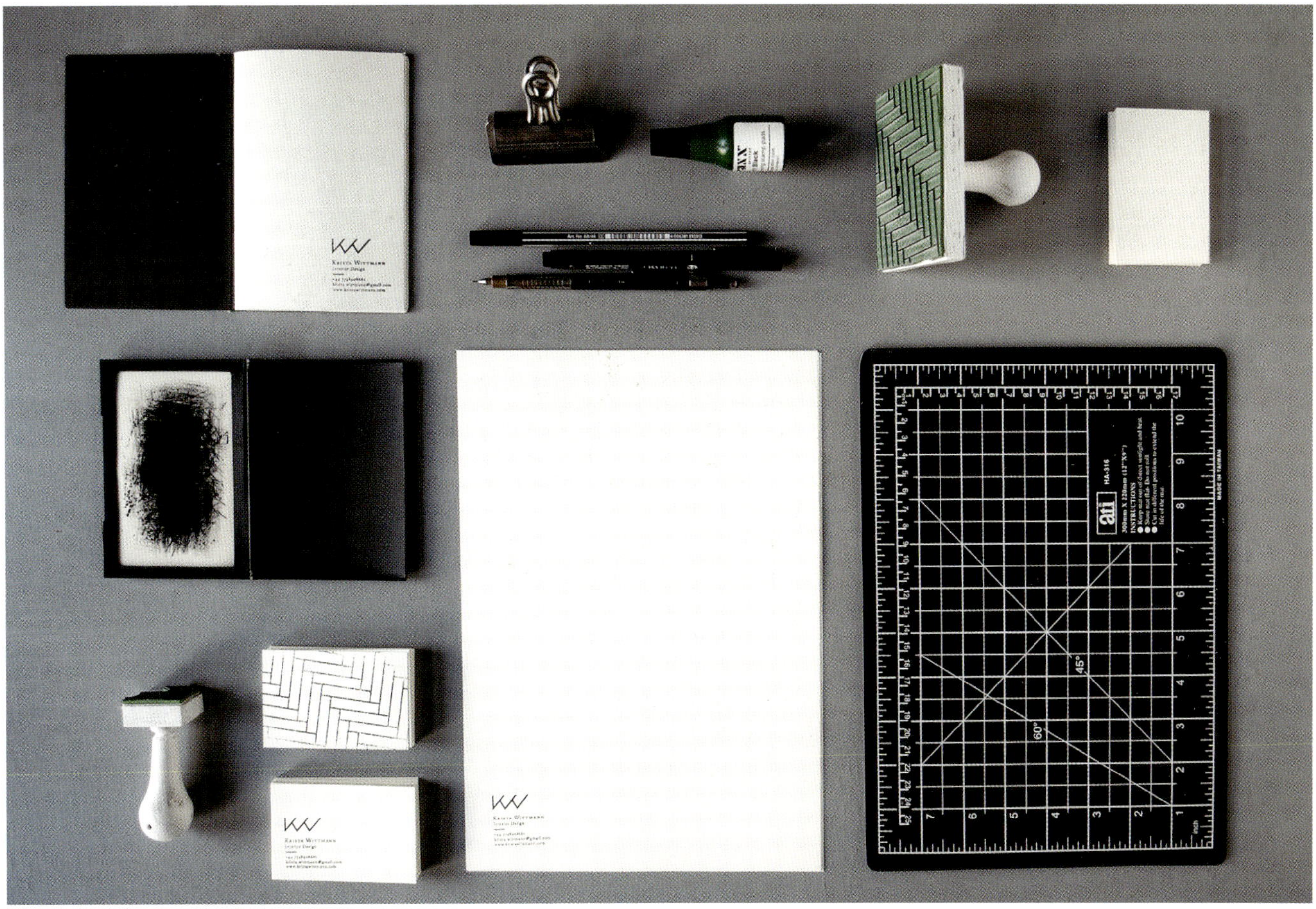

Krista Wittmann

Hungary

Eszter Laki
Designer

**Zsófi Dobos,
Eszter Laki**
Photographer

Krista Wittmann
Client

It is the identity designed for Krista Wittmann, a young interior designer from London. The designer Eszter preferred to use monochrome colors in the design, which was why eggshell-colored textures paper was chosen for the business cards and the letter. Eszter painted the wood-handle of the stamps white: in this way the vivid green rubber may present a more intense emotion.

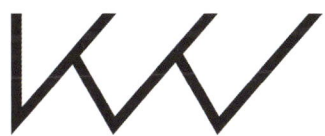

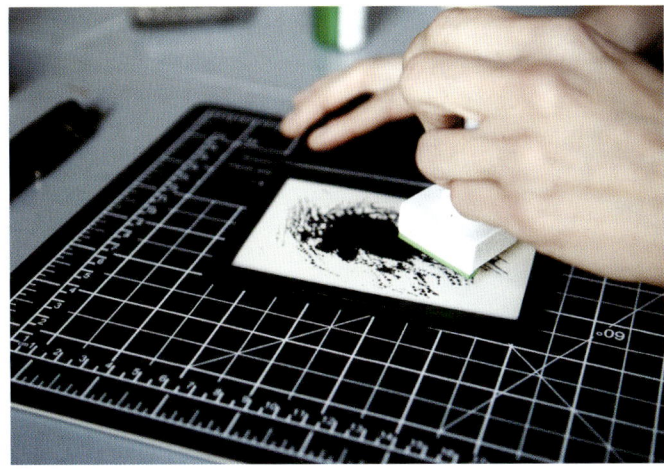

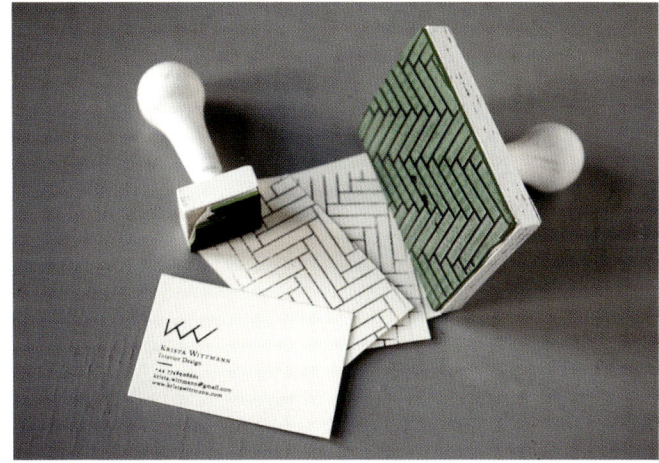

"There is nothing better in design than black & white & gray."

--Eskimo

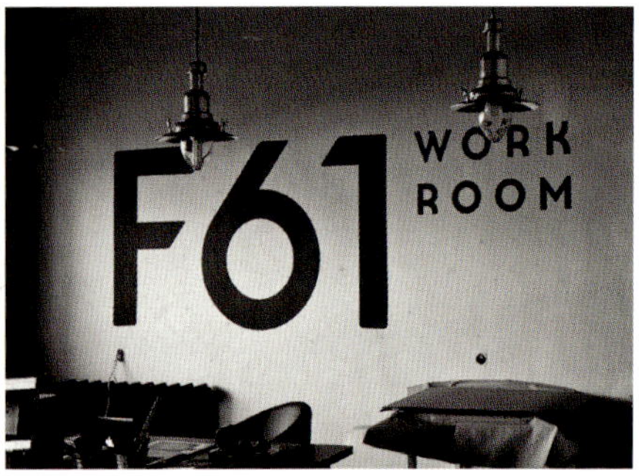

80

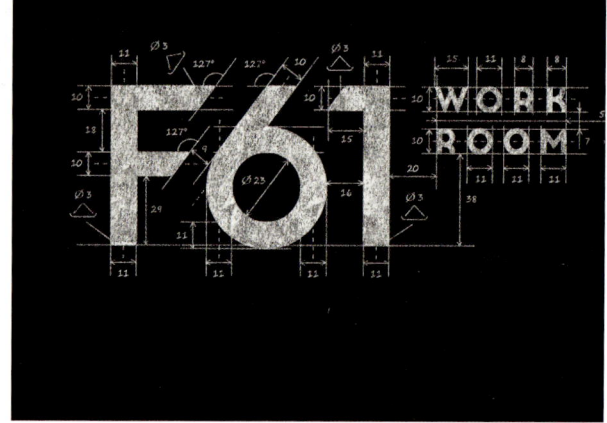

F61 Work Room

Russia

Eskimo
Design Agency

Pavel Emelyanov
Designer

F61 is a print studio in St. Petersburg. The identity was inspired by the print machines schemes: circles, cylinders, parallel lines, clear geometric shapes. The black-and-white color palette of the style gives it a finished strict look and stands out from other traditional printing companies. Tag line "EXELLENCE OF PRINT DESIGN" speaks for itself and reveals the philosophy of the studio.

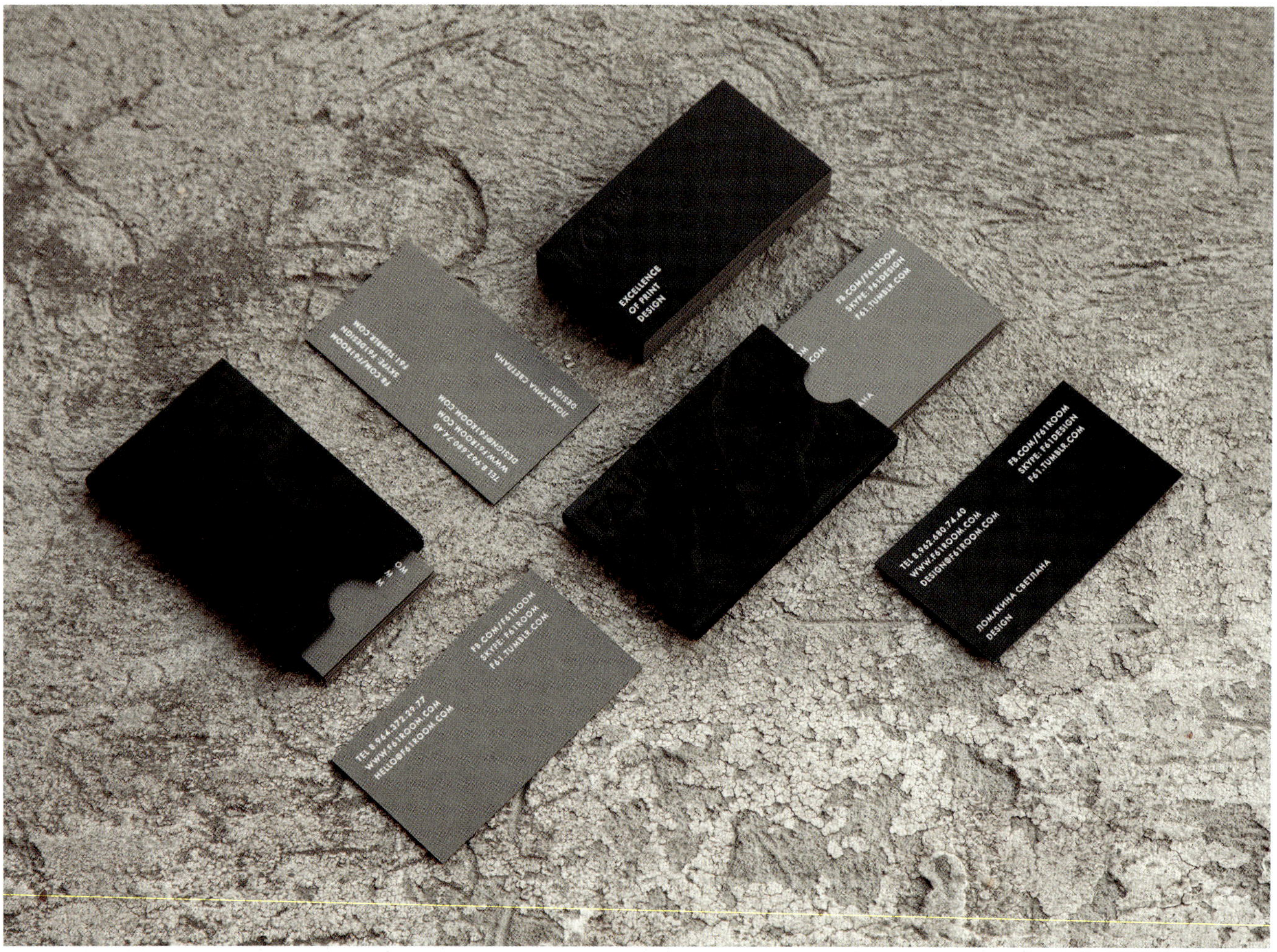

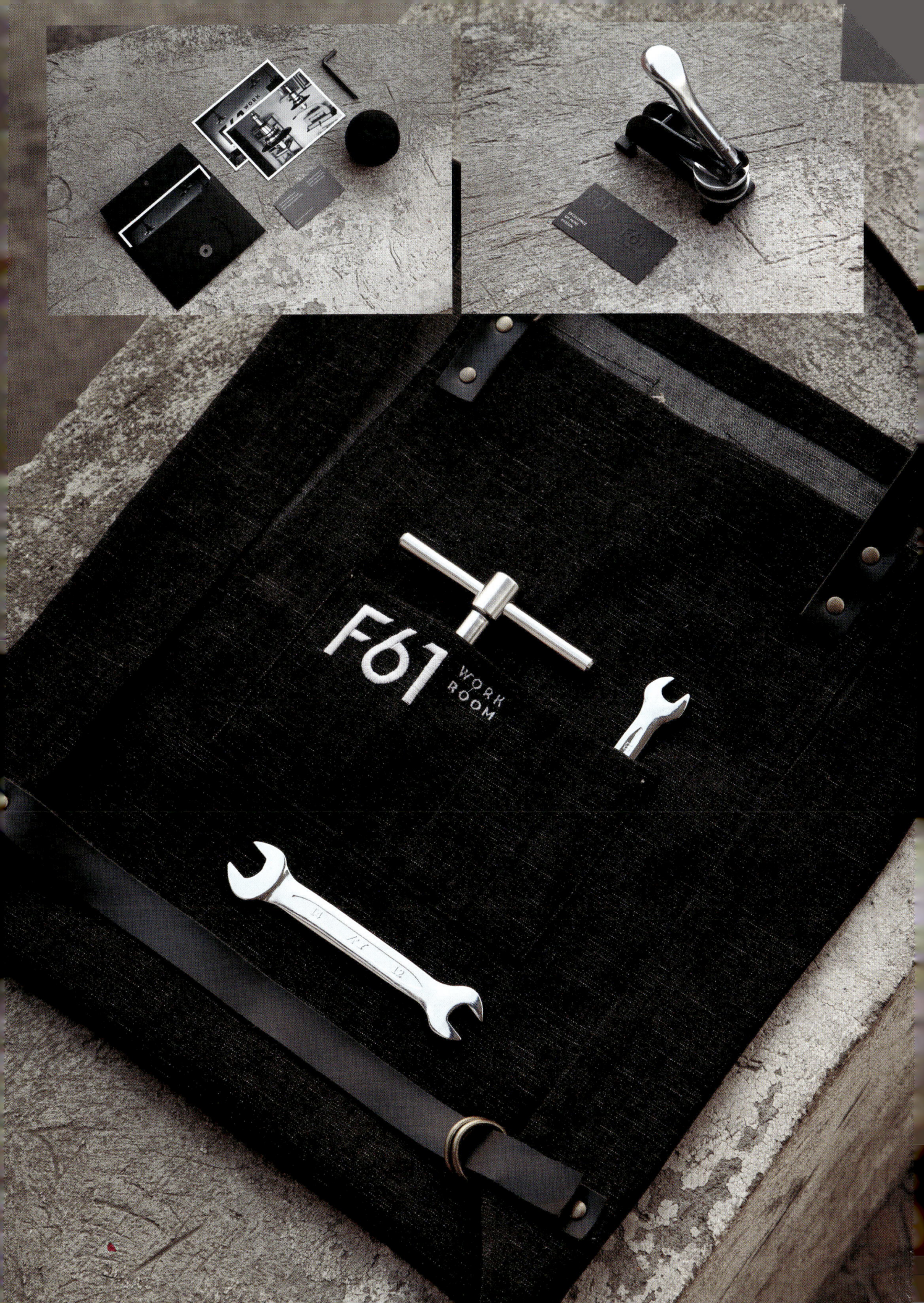

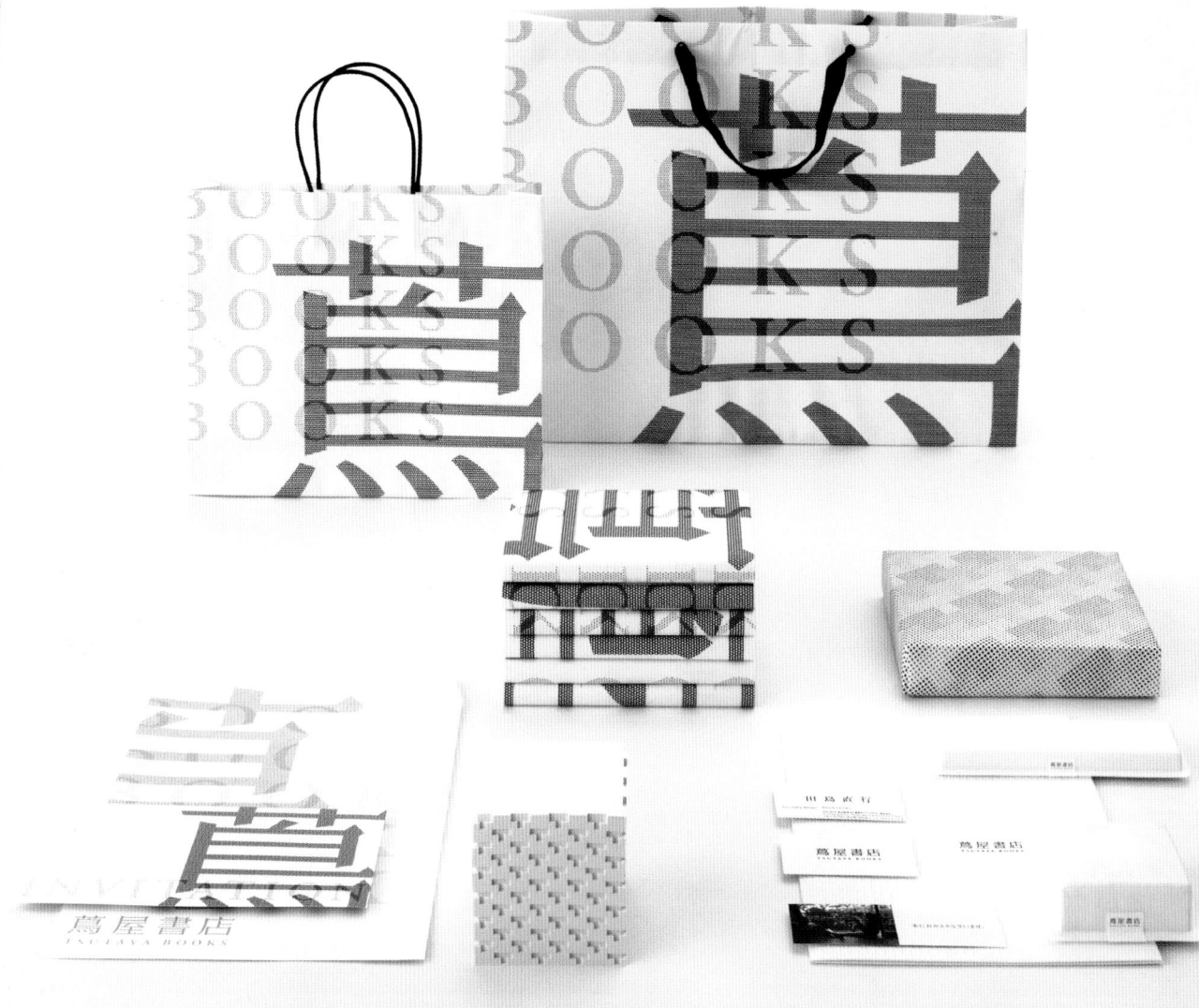

Tsutaya Shoten
Japan

Hara Design Institute, Nippon Design Center, Inc.
Design Agency

Kenya Hara
Art Director

Kaoru Matsuno, Haruka Misawa, Naoko Sasaki
Designer

Culture Convenience Club Co., Ltd.
Client

The Daikanyama's Tsutaya project is symbolized by the renovation of the logotype, turning the Roman-lettered TSUTAYA to the Kanji for Tsutaya Shoten. The new logotype is easy to read and straightforwardly expresses the beauty of Kanji. This thin, light permeable sign includes large letter that is clearly visible from both front and back.

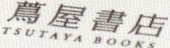

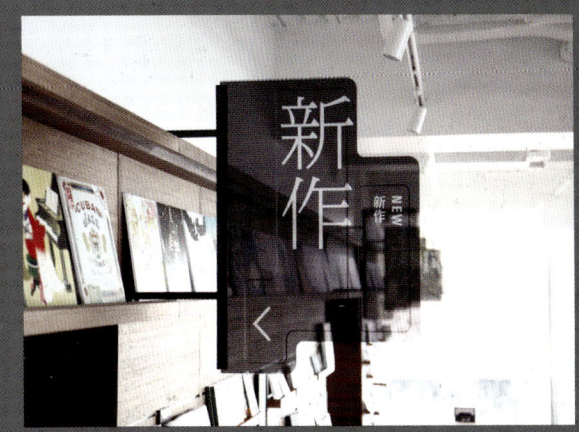

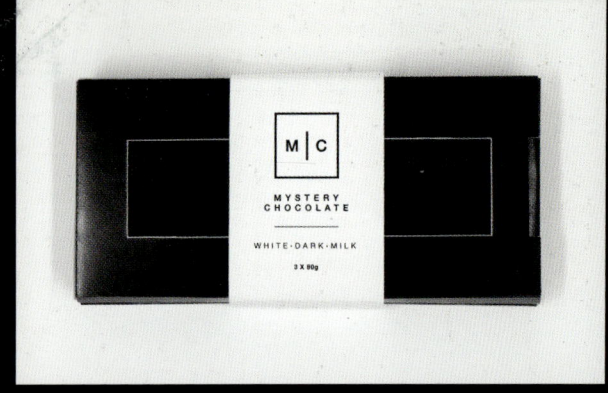

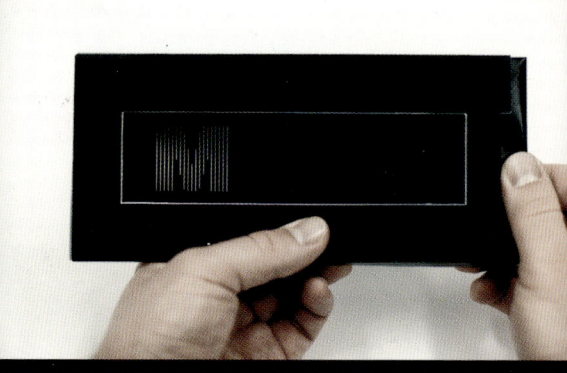

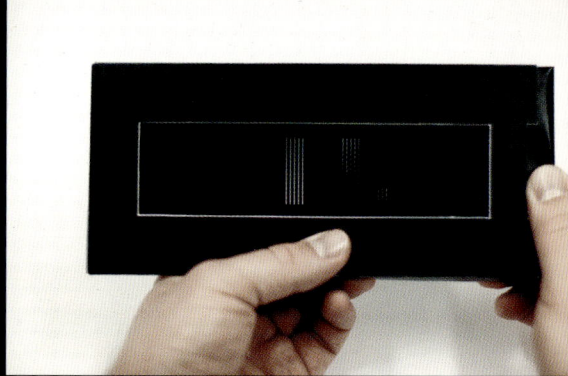

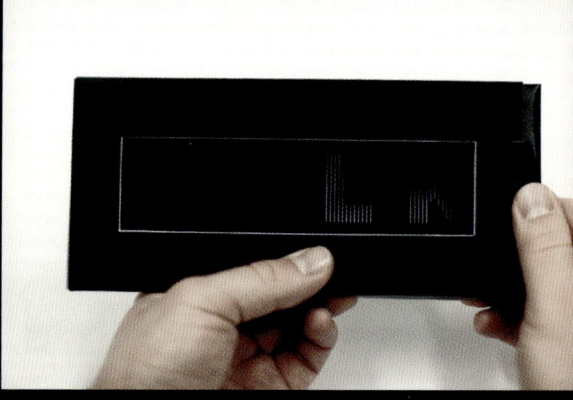

Mystery Chocolate
Hungary

Kevin Harald Campean
Designer & Photographer

The basis of this chocolate packaging concept is to be playful and distinct. The three small boxes for the white, black and milk chocolate are in black color and without any text. The ingredients information is on the white paper stipe wrapping the three together. The playfulness of the package resides in the fact that you will only find out which type the chocolate is when it is pulled out of the box. The letters appears and disappears one by one. The basic mechanism corresponds to the barrier grid animation technique that creates an optical illusion.

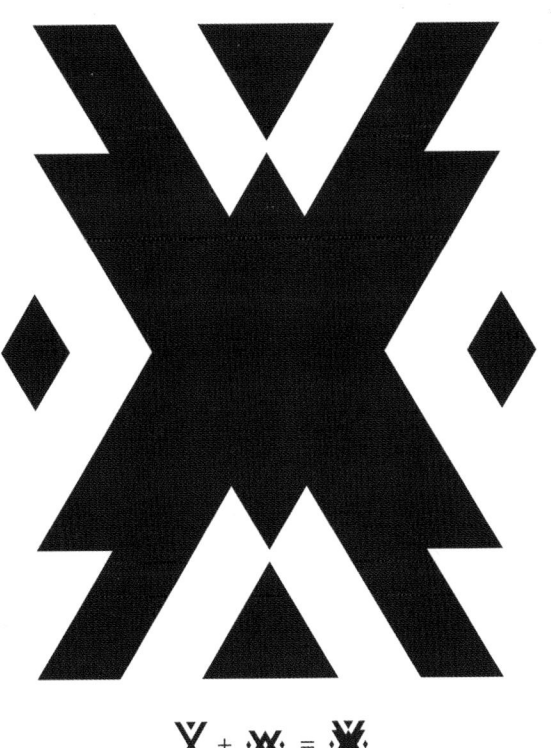

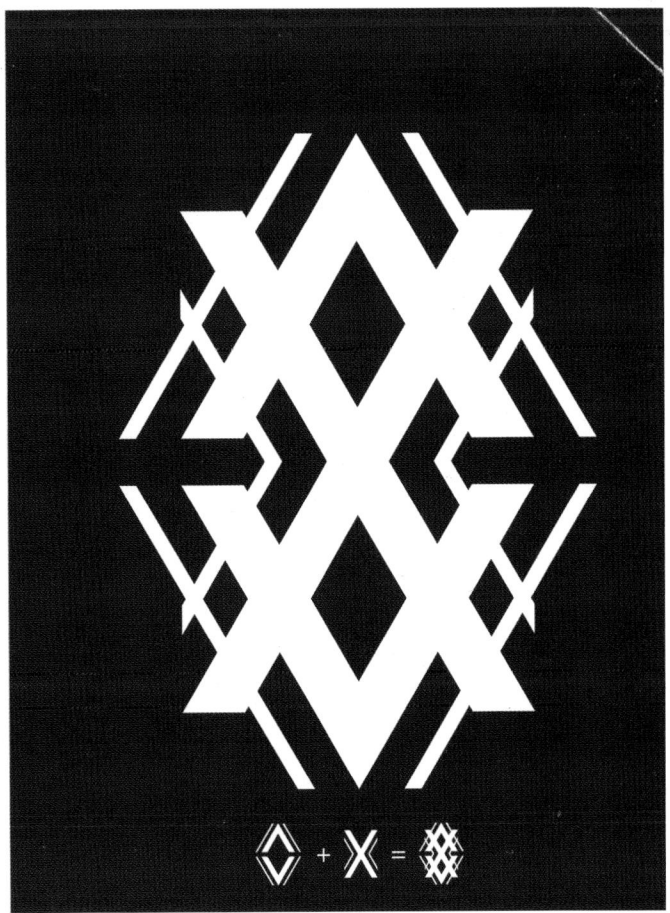

MVA Identity
Portugal

Un-staged
Design Agency

**Ana Pais,
Tiago Resende**
Designer

Manuel Ventura
Client

Manuel Ventura Architects is an architecture atelier based in Oporto, Portugal. The playing of the form "V" constitutes the essential of the brand identity and the official logotype which are used as the decoration of the stationery and space to reinforce the identity of the atelier.

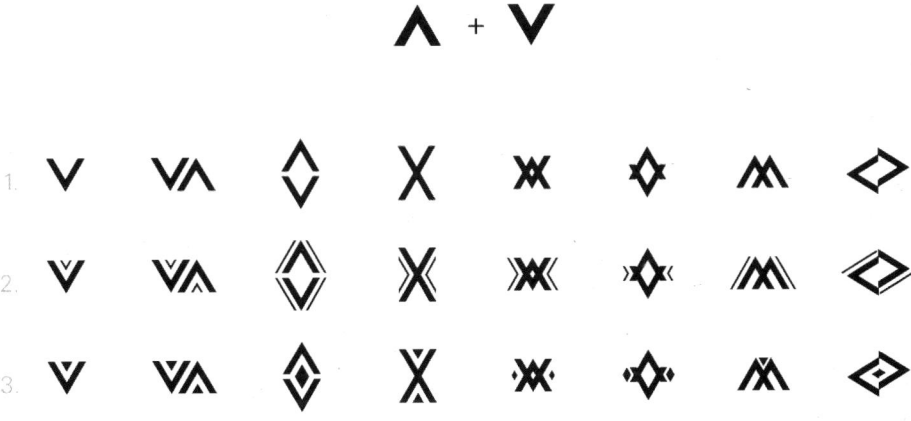

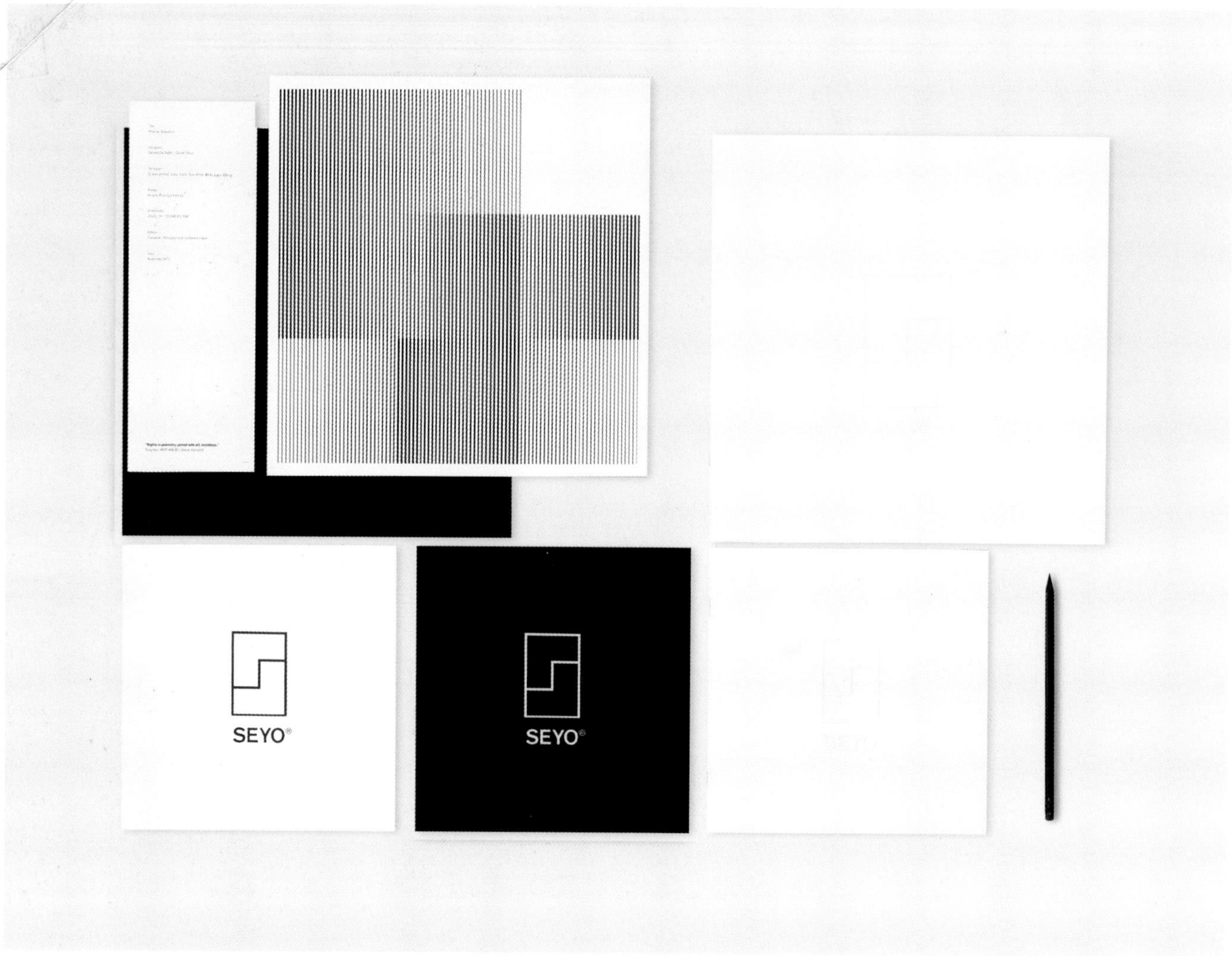

Seyo
Italy

Artiva Design
Design Agency

**Daniele De Batté
& Davide Sossi**
Designer

Seyo
Client

The name Seyo comes from ancient Greek, which means to push on. In this case it takes on a broader and more figurative sense. The design helps the company present a professional role of guiding and advising its clients at every step of their business journey.

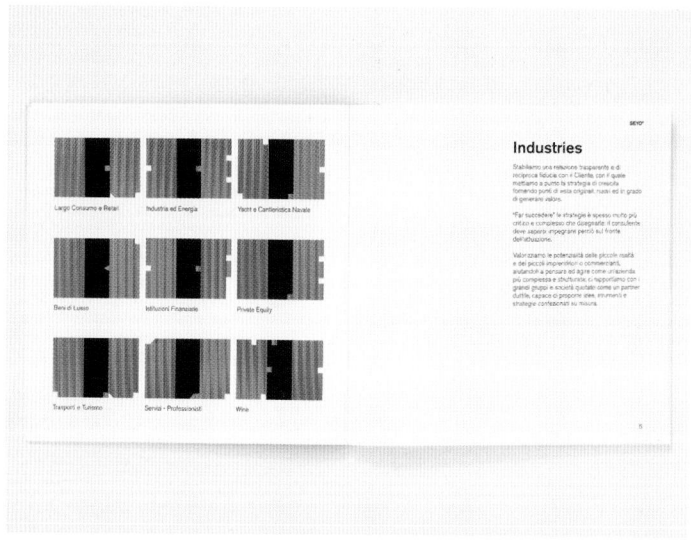

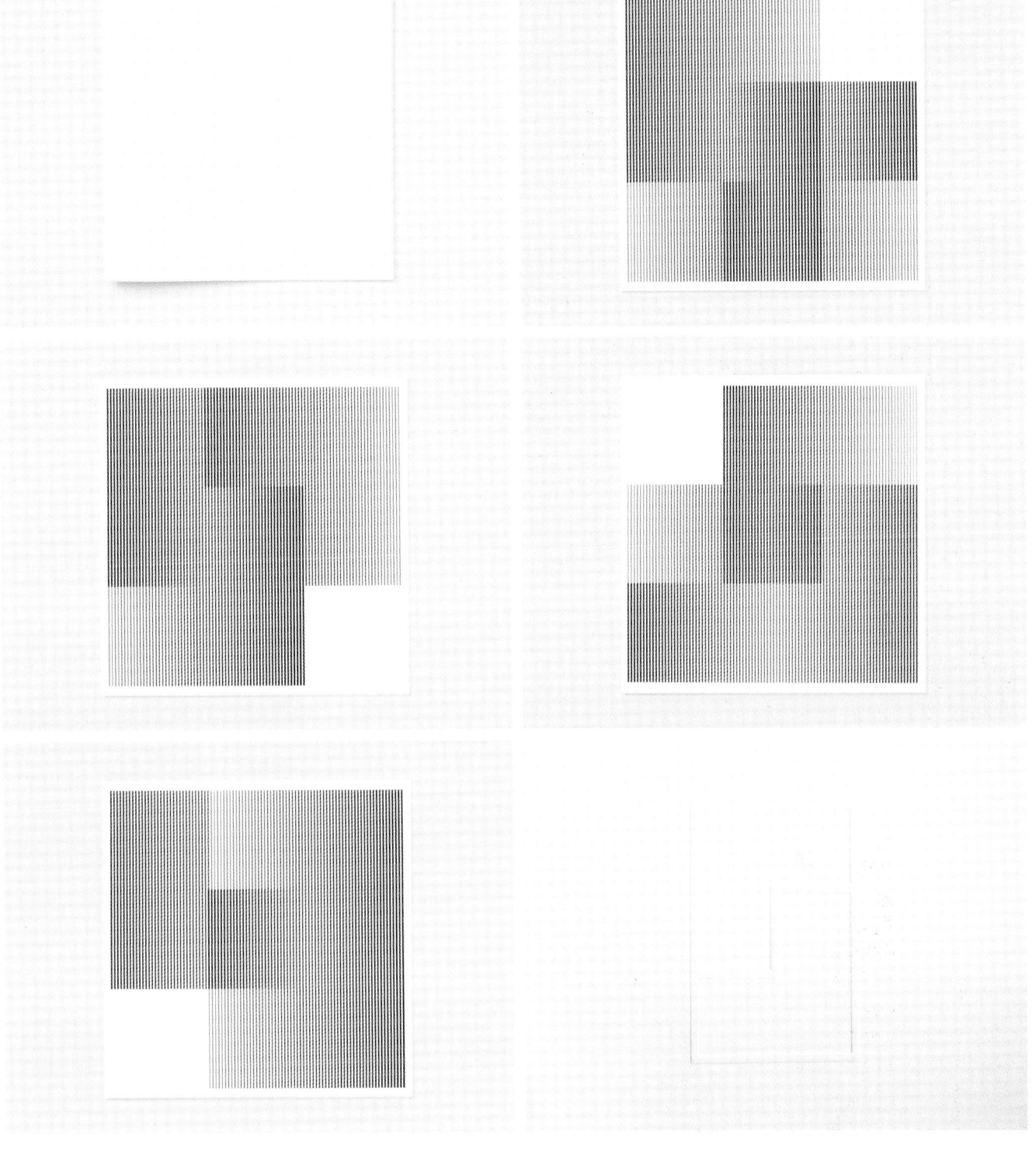

"The absence of color is a precious bound which doesn't enrich the work but reveals its essential shape. This is a rule that helps to keep the counterpoint between order and chaos, a tension that creates energy."
—Daniele De Batté (Artiva Design)

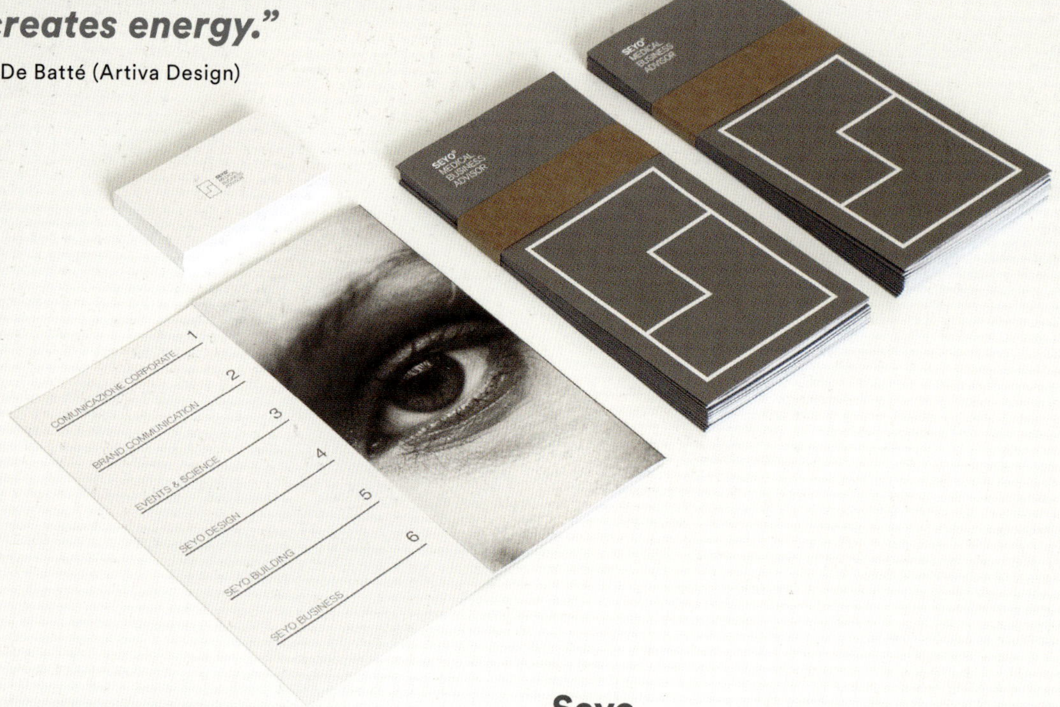

COMUNICAZIONE CORPORATE 1
BRAND COMMUNICATION 2
EVENTS & SCIENCE 3
SEYO DESIGN 4
SEYO BUILDING 5
SEYO BUSINESS 6

Seyo
Italy

Artiva Design
Design Agency

**Daniele De Batté,
Davide Sossi**
Designer

Seyo
Client

The logotype SEYO is a monogram consisting of two geometric modules that makes the type "S". These two shapes can be defined as "polyominoes" and voice two important concepts: "construction" and "synergy".

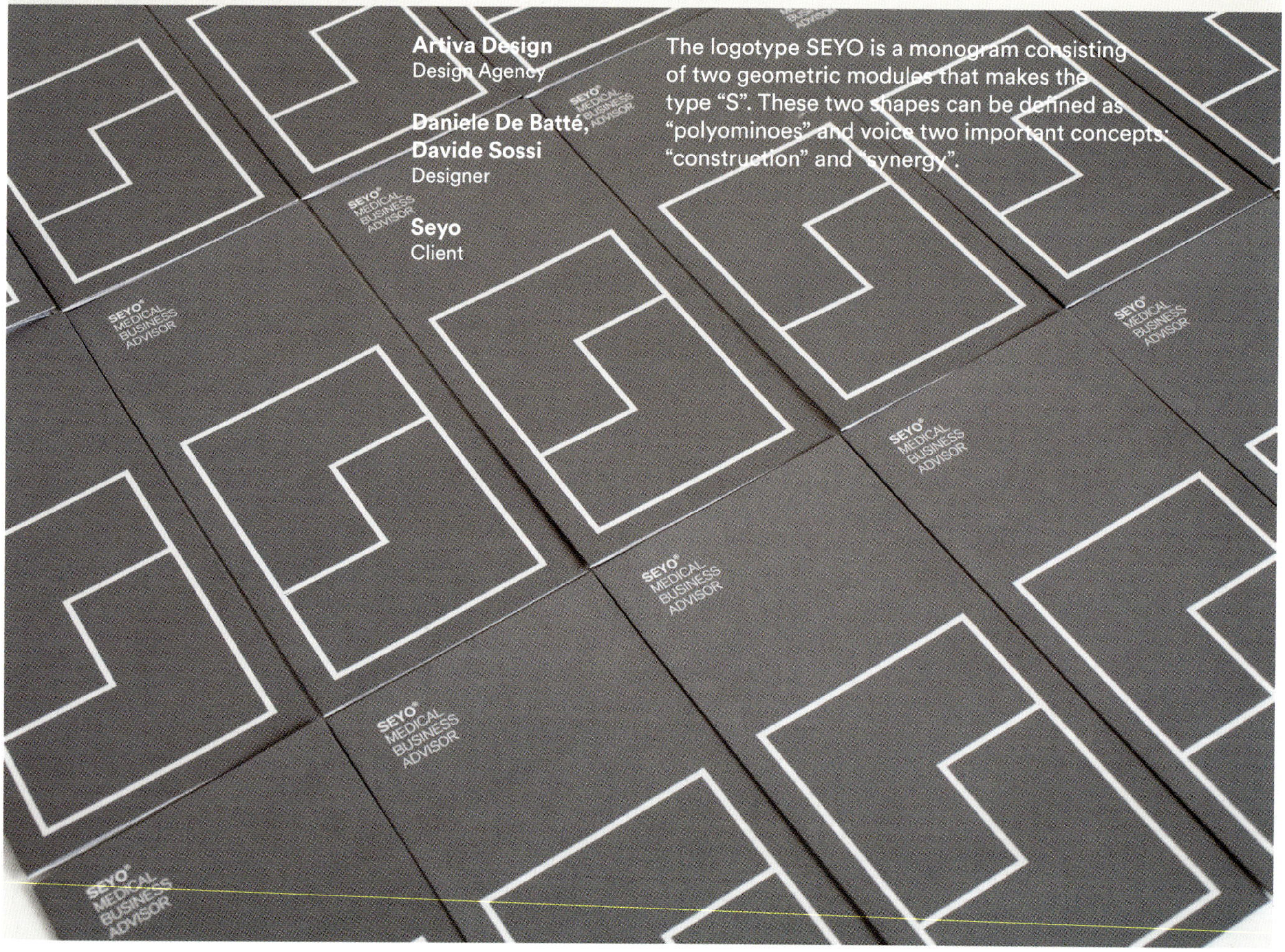

www.artiva.it

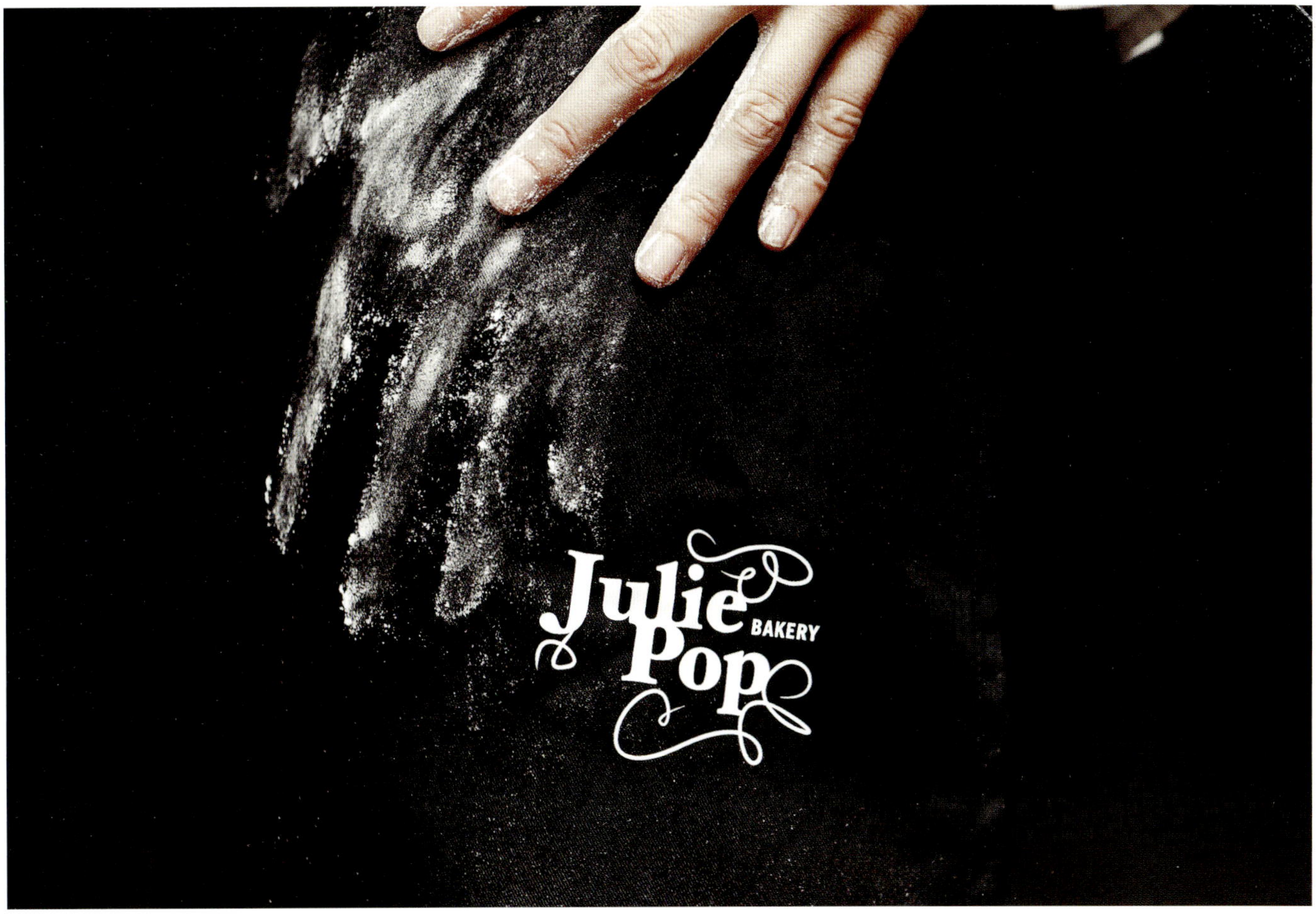

Julie Pop Bakery

Austria

Bureau Rabensteiner
Design Agency

Mike Rabensteiner
Art Director
& Photographer

Isabella Meischberger
Designer

Julia Wojta
Client

The Julie Pop Bakery is a new American style bakery based in Vienna. The identity design for their new online business uses a black background to better reflect the colorful variety of the bakery's handmade cake pops.

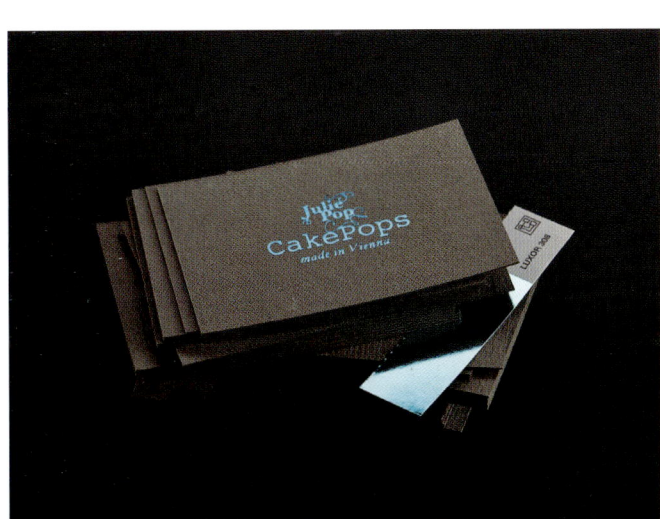

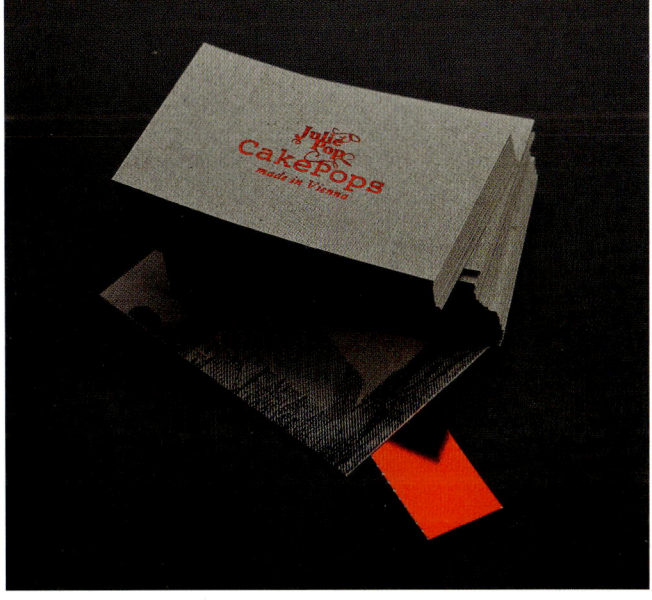

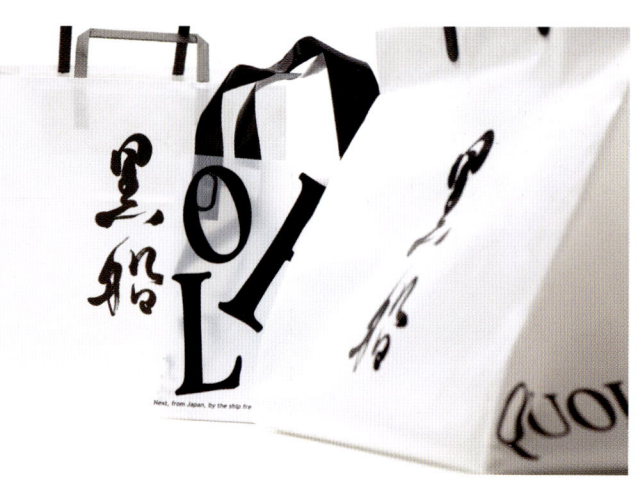
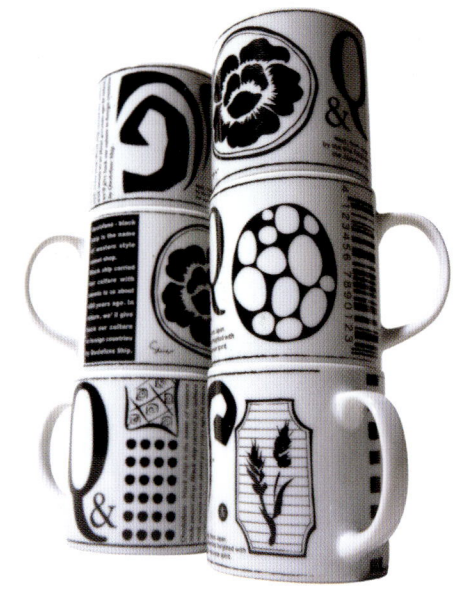

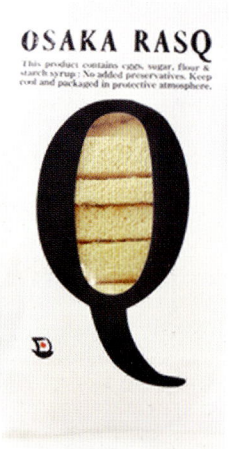

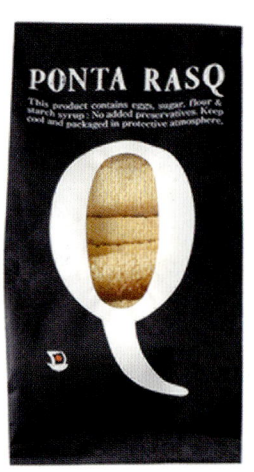
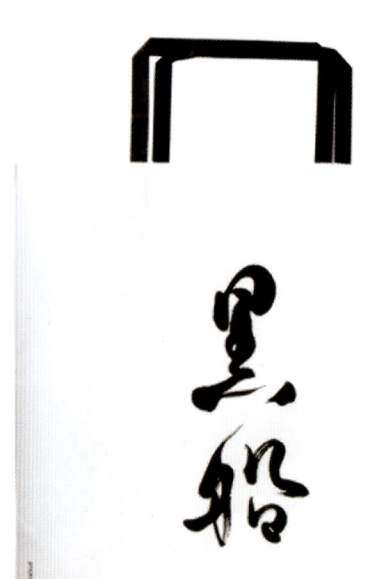
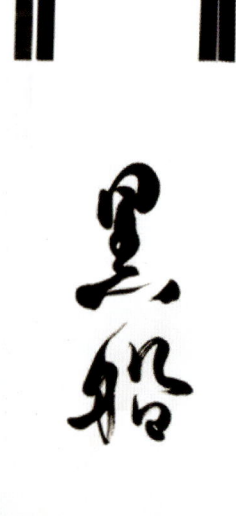
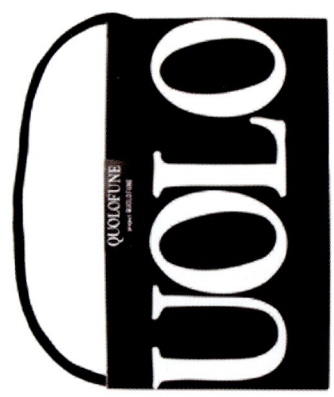
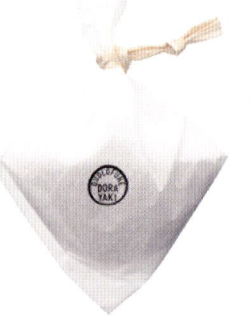

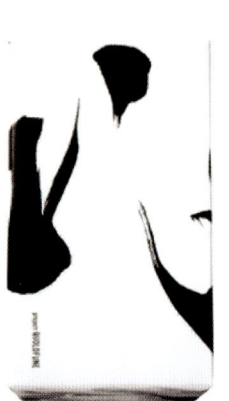
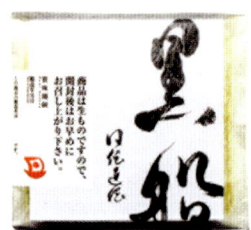

OSAKA RASQ

PONTA RASQ

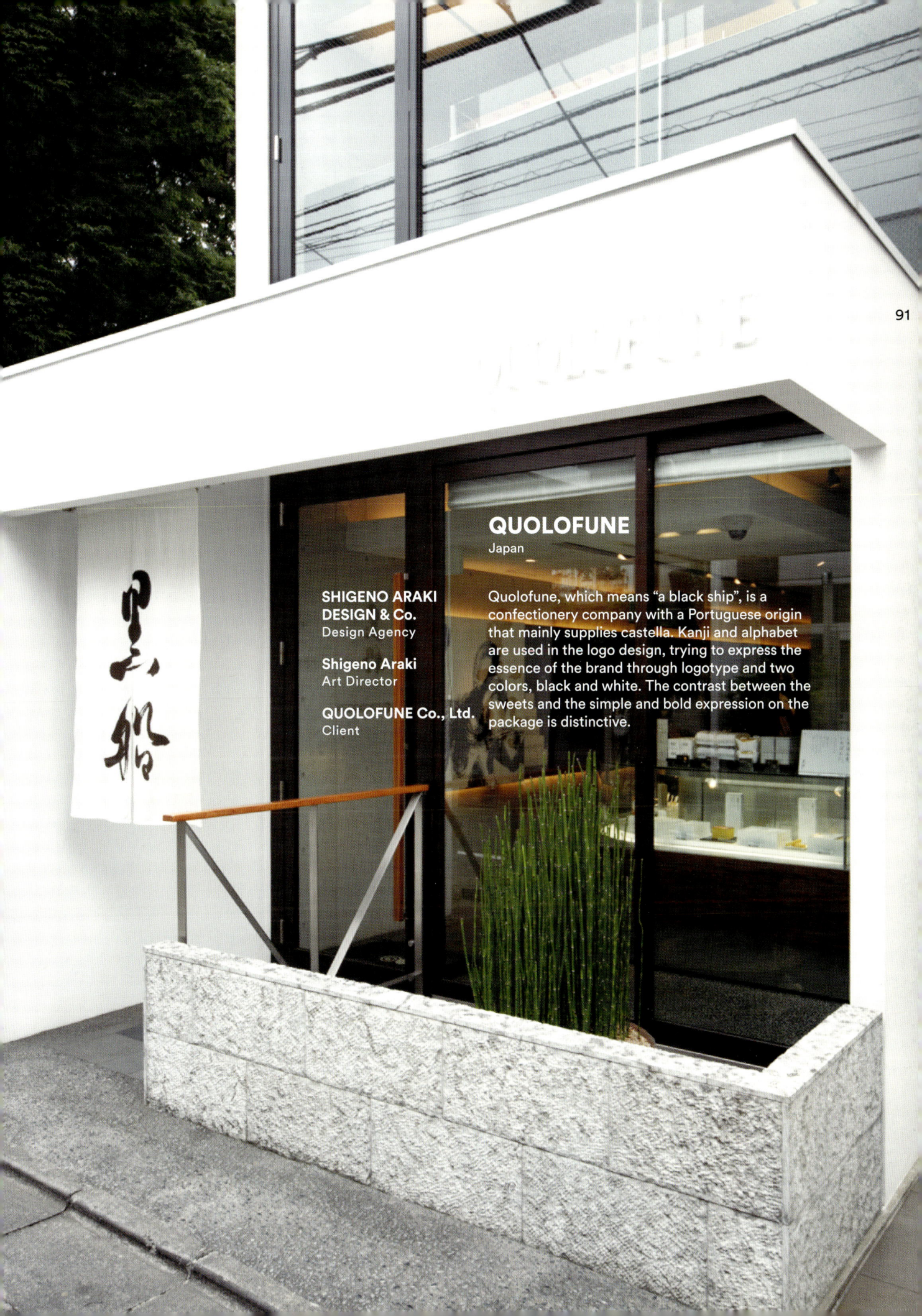

QUOLOFUNE
Japan

SHIGENO ARAKI DESIGN & Co.
Design Agency

Shigeno Araki
Art Director

QUOLOFUNE Co., Ltd.
Client

Quolofune, which means "a black ship", is a confectionery company with a Portuguese origin that mainly supplies castella. Kanji and alphabet are used in the logo design, trying to express the essence of the brand through logotype and two colors, black and white. The contrast between the sweets and the simple and bold expression on the package is distinctive.

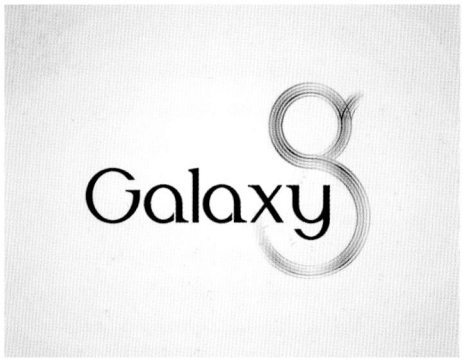

Hilton Athens Galaxy Bar
Italy

Sublimio – Unique Design Formula
Design Agency

Matteo Modica
Creative Director

Hilton Athens
Client

The Hilton Galaxy Bar enjoys a unique location that offers a wonderful view above Athens. The rebranding aims to mix the brand's past, present and future to give birth to a timeless identity and experience. The creative concept is based on the term definition of "galaxy": "any large and brilliant or impressive assemblage of persons or things: ex. A galaxy of the opera stars".

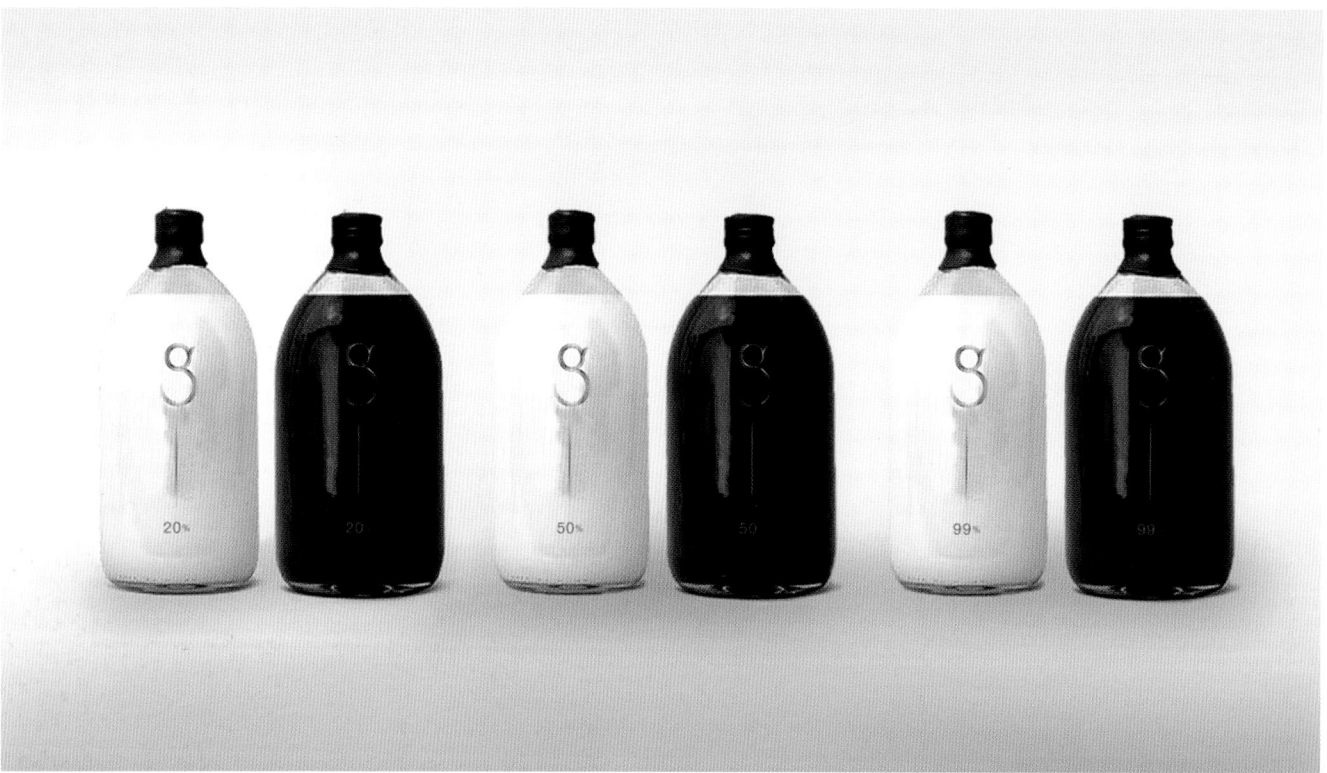

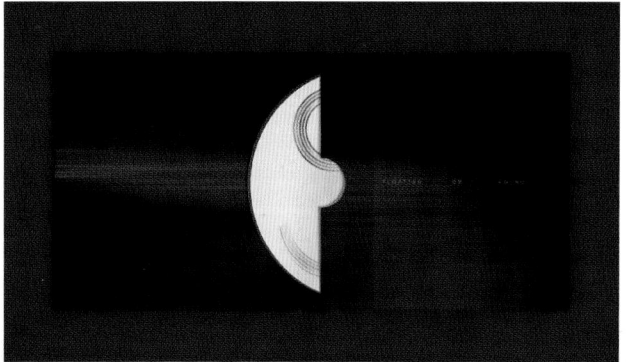

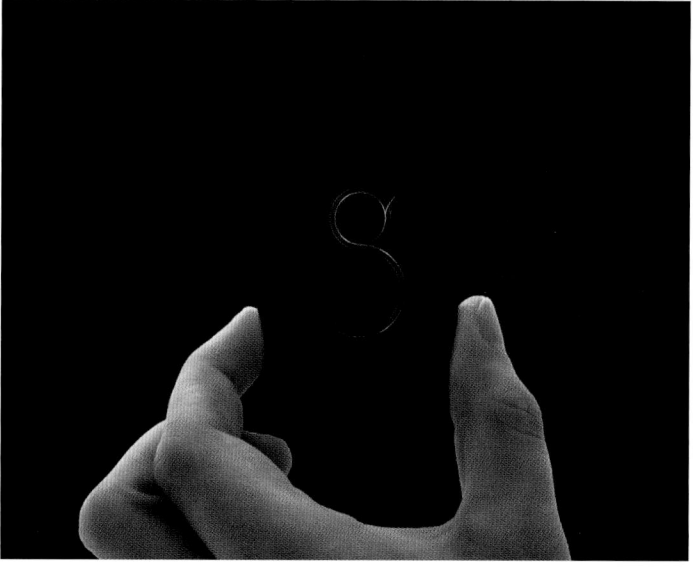

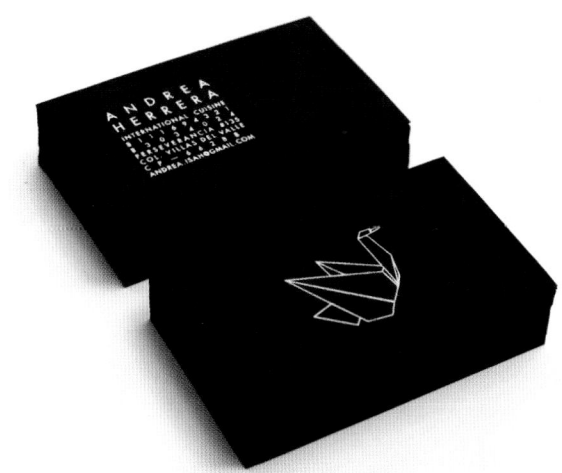

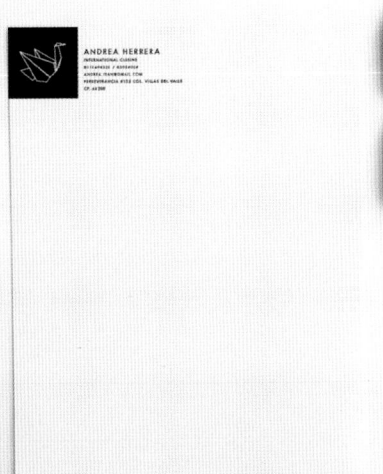

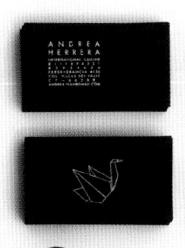
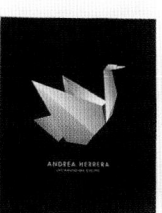
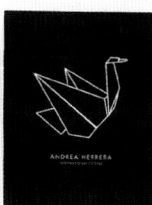
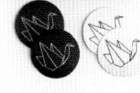
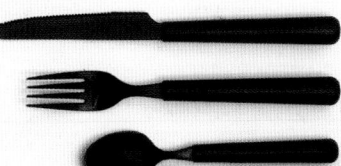

Andrea Herrera — International Cuisine
Mexico

Nation
Design Agency

**Juma Herrera,
Sergio Meade**
Creative Director

Chef. Andrea Herrera
Client

The black and white identity of Andrea Herrera communicates the complexity, time, effort and patience that are required to elaborate a dish and transform it into an elegant object of desire. The designer likens cooking to origami as they both require patience and should be perceived as an art form. The project is based on the shape of a swan, a long standing symbol for aesthetics and beauty.

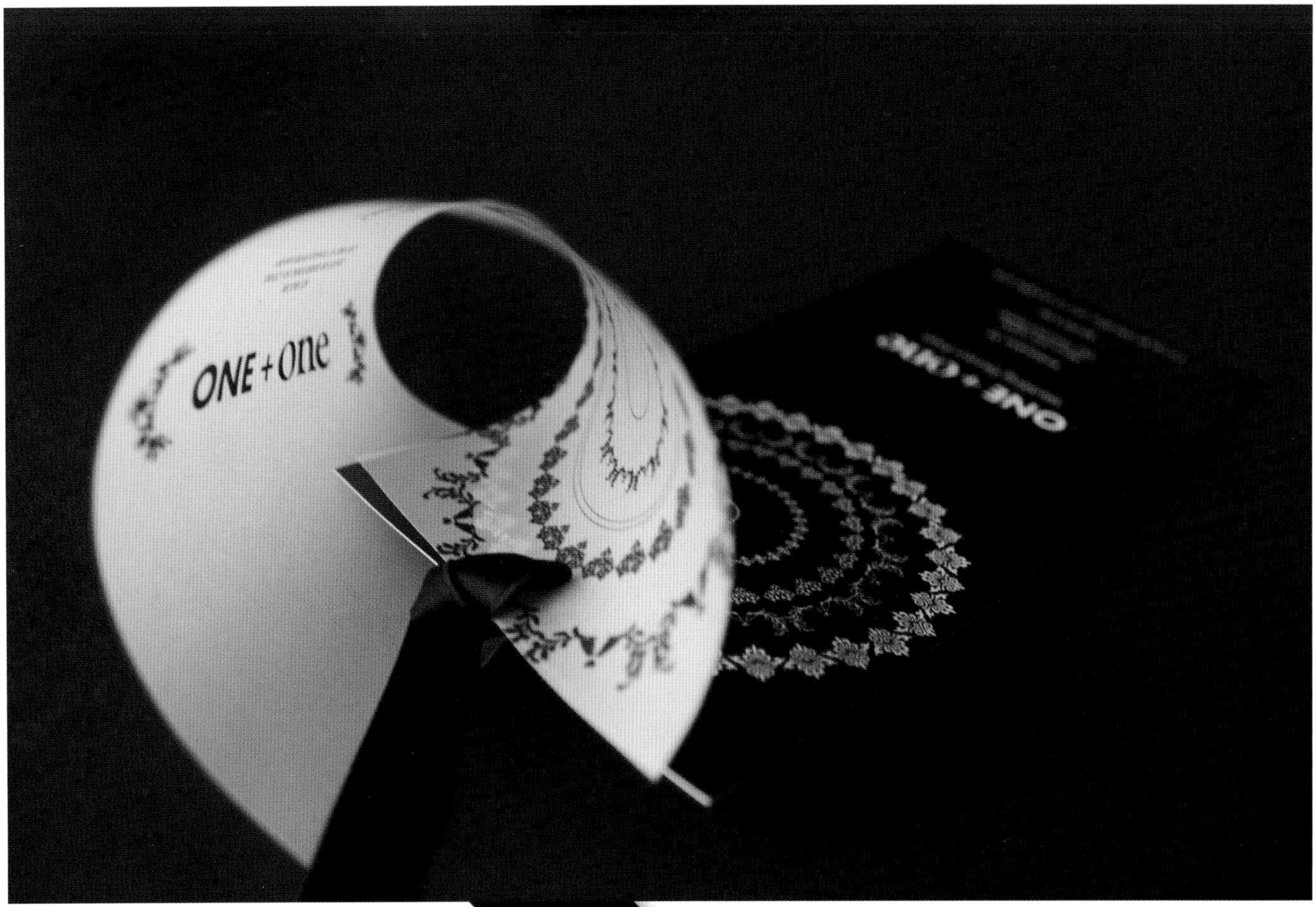

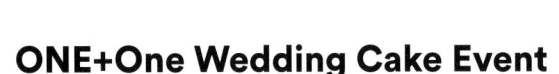

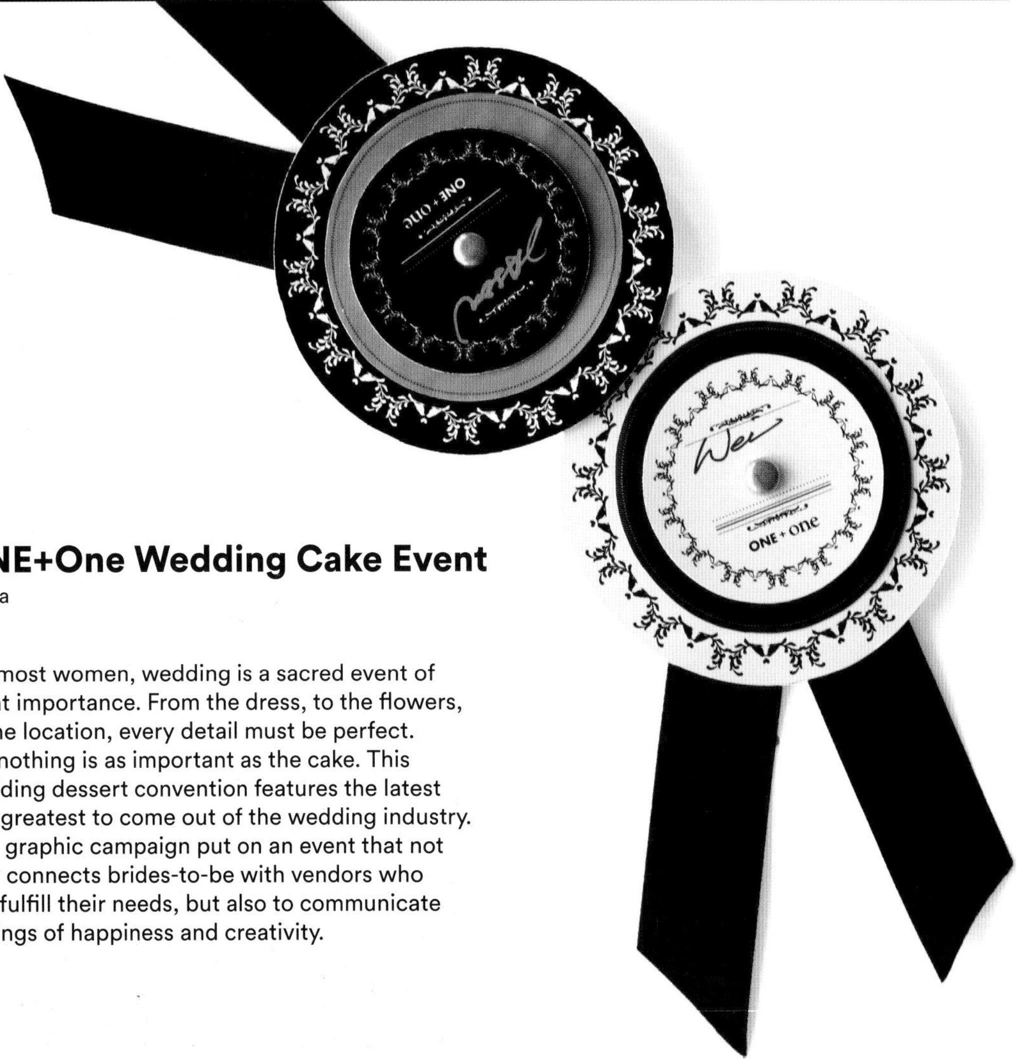

ONE+One Wedding Cake Event
China

Wei Sun
Designer

For most women, wedding is a sacred event of great importance. From the dress, to the flowers, to the location, every detail must be perfect. But nothing is as important as the cake. This wedding dessert convention features the latest and greatest to come out of the wedding industry. This graphic campaign put on an event that not only connects brides-to-be with vendors who can fulfill their needs, but also to communicate feelings of happiness and creativity.

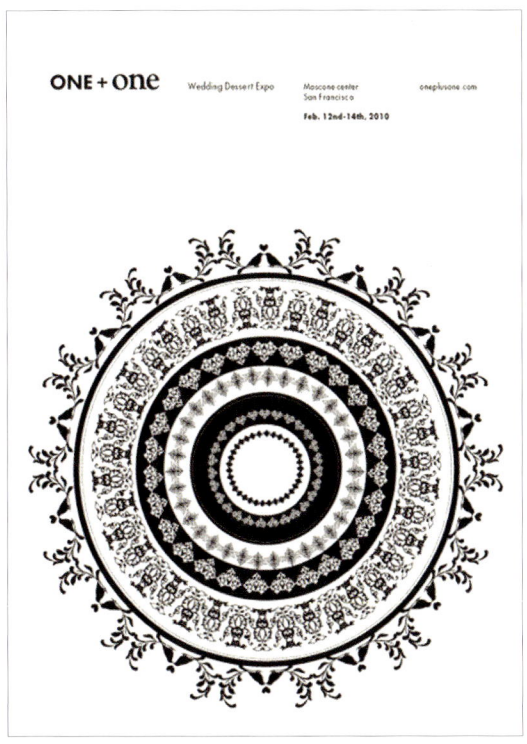

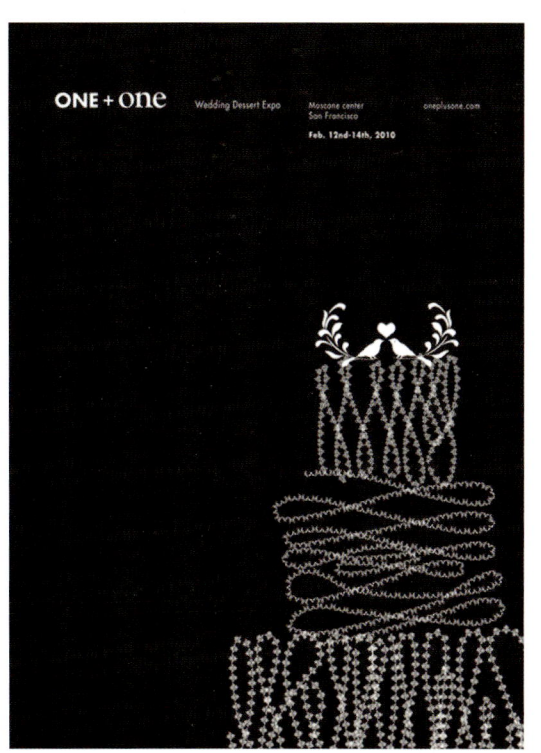

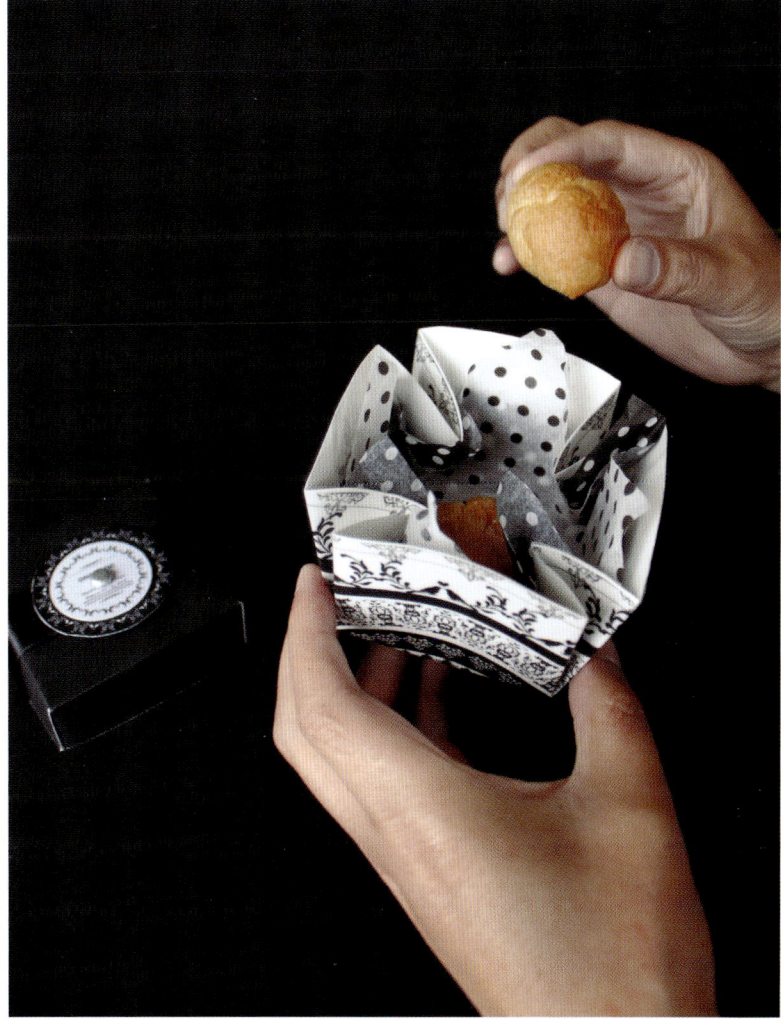

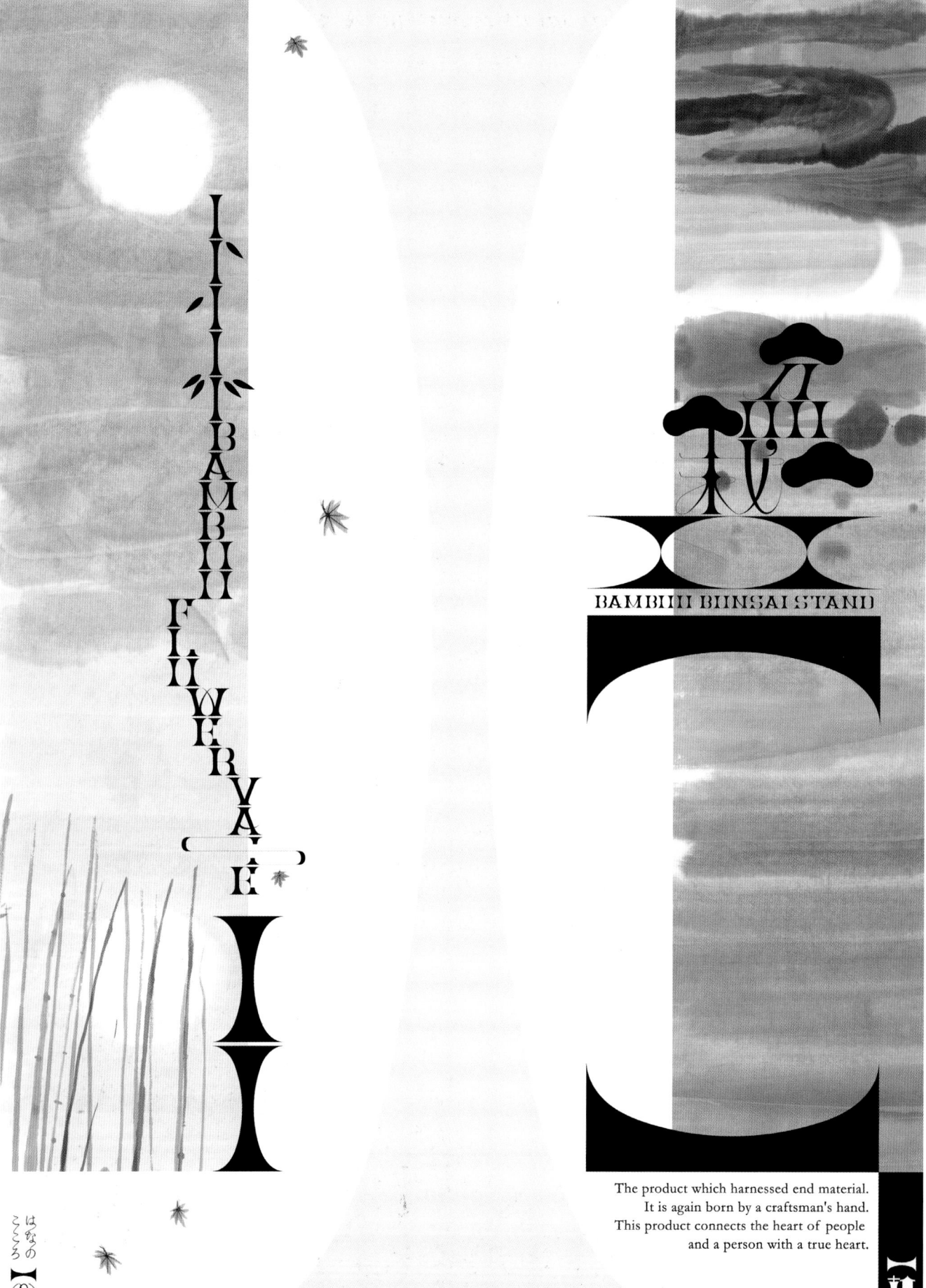

BAMBOO FLOWER VASE

はなのこころ
りん

BAMBOO BONSAI STAND

The product which harnessed end material.
It is again born by a craftsman's hand.
This product connects the heart of people
and a person with a true heart.

"Black and white has an effect of highlighting what really matters."
—Hajime Tsushima (Tsushima Design Office)

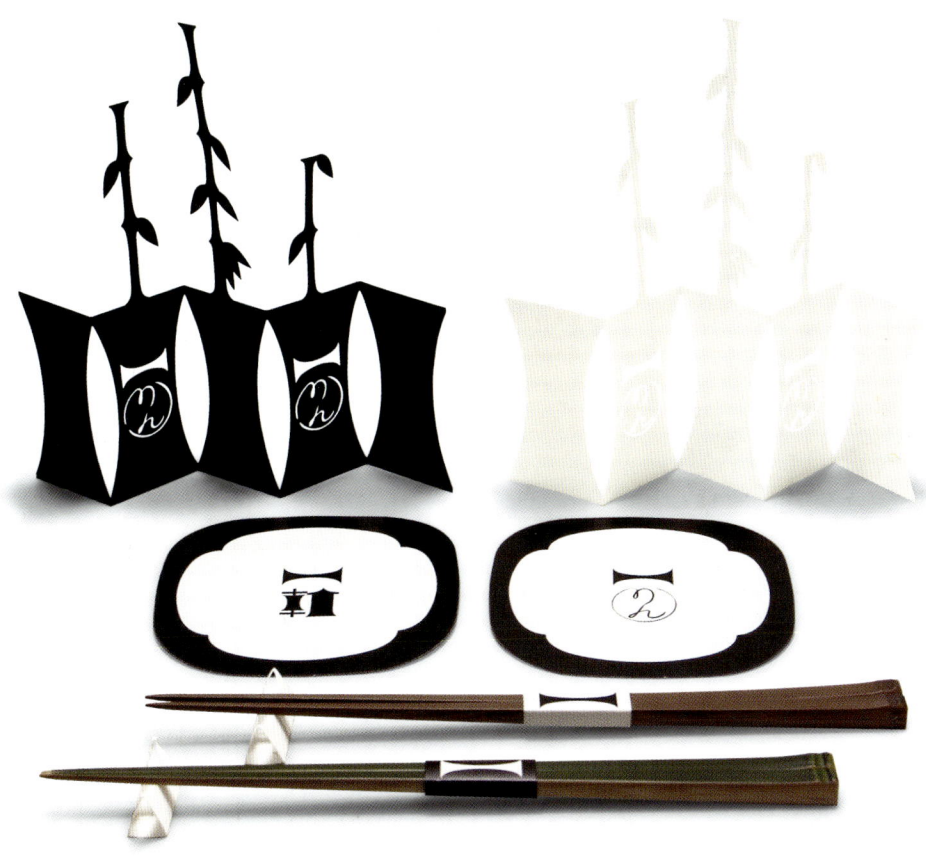

Ichirin
Japan

Tsushima Design Office
Design Agency

Hajime Tsushima, Yukiko Tsushima, Takasugi Noda, Seiji Fujimoto
Designer

Hokushin Factory
Client

This project began with an environmental idea: reuse its end material. Bamboo is used as the graphic motif for the bud vase Ichirin. Accordingly, other graphic elements were also developed from the very basic form. The wooden box is from a reused scaffolding board, which can be a package and a gift.

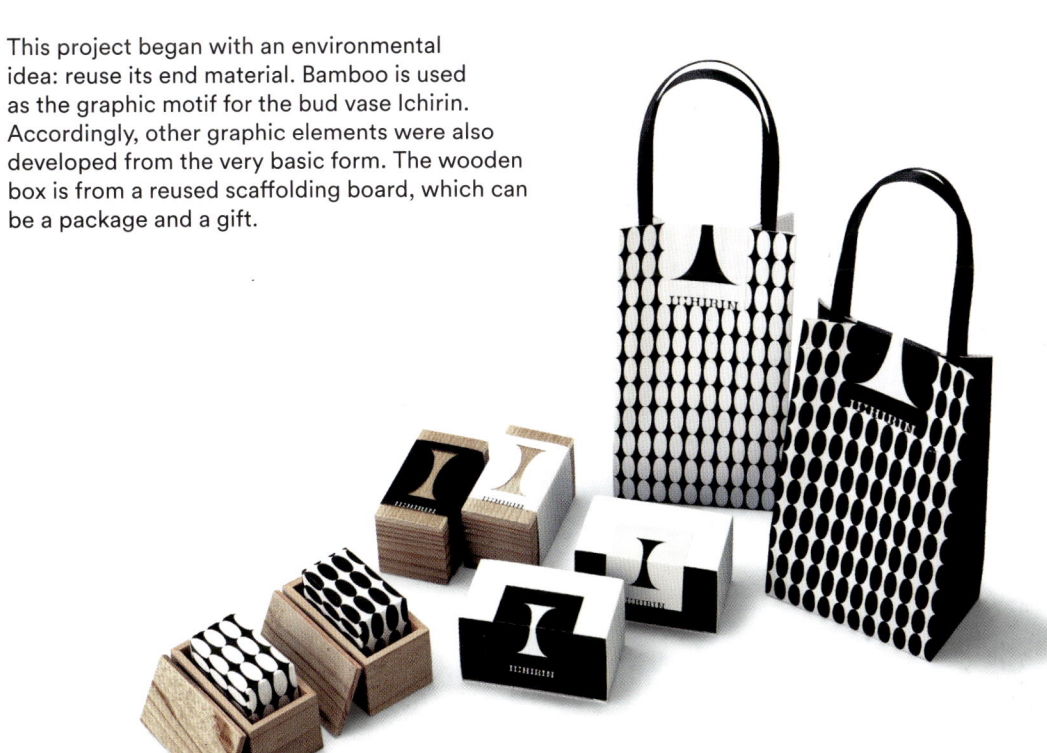

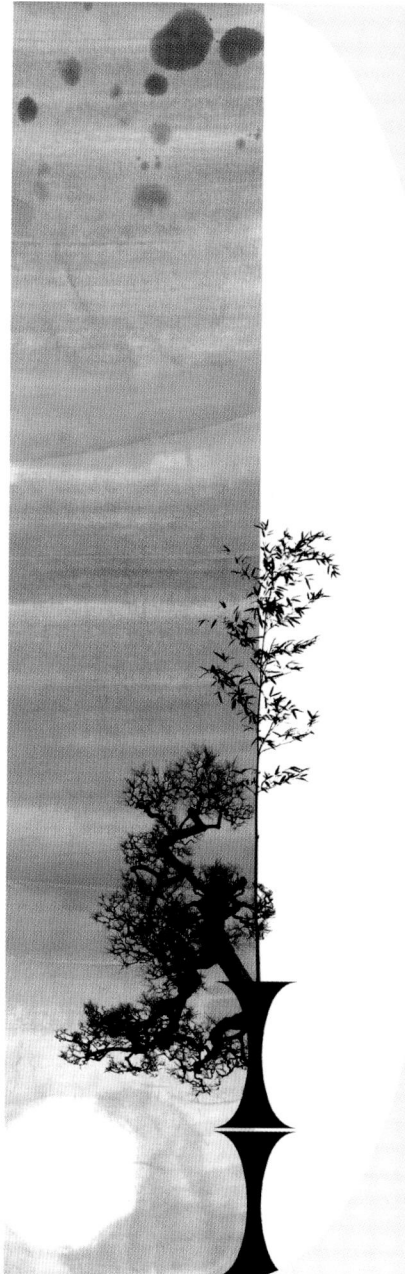

ICHIRIN

We think that the heart which values a thing is lost in this time of having been full of wealth.
There are also many things which can be used still more also into the thing thrown away simply.
The heart which values limited resources feels like the beginning of valuing the heart truly.
If I have the importance of resources noticed, I will think that it is happy.
Such a great product was done from the end material which was always being thrown away.

BLACK & WHITE

はなの
こころ

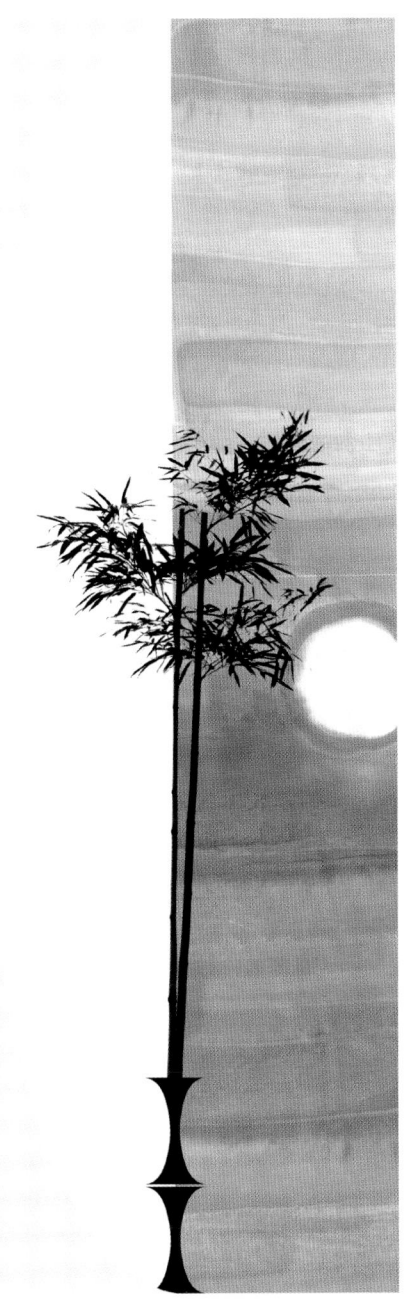

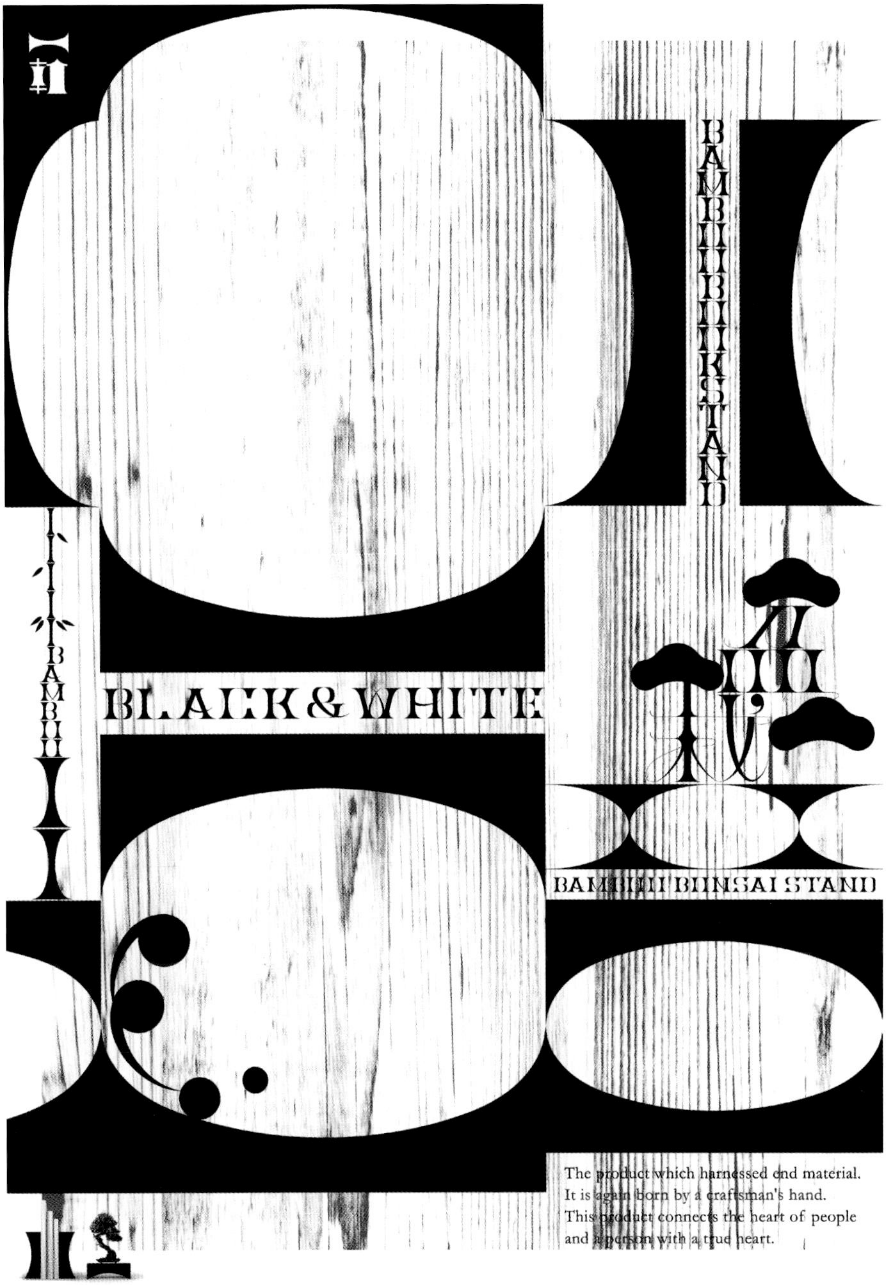

BAMBOO BONSAI STAND

BAMBOO

BLACK & WHITE

BAMBOO BONSAI STAND

The product which harnessed end material.
It is again born by a craftsman's hand.
This product connects the heart of people
and a person with a true heart.

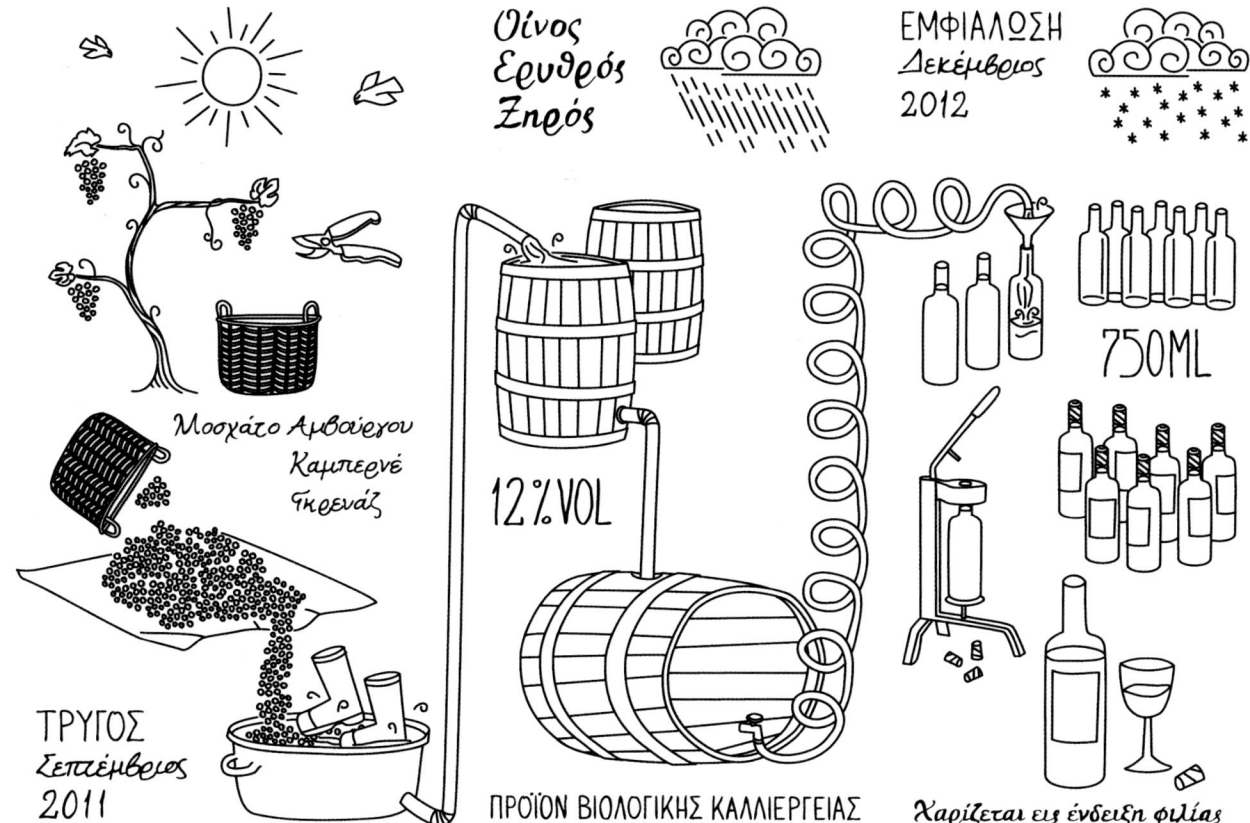

Filirea Gi

Greece

Zafeiriadis Christos
Designer

Zafeiriadis Paschalis
Client

The packaging design is for a limited edition homemade wine. The illustration depicts the process of wine-making from the harvest to the bottling. The bottle is wrapped with silk-screen printed paper to add a handmade touch to the design.

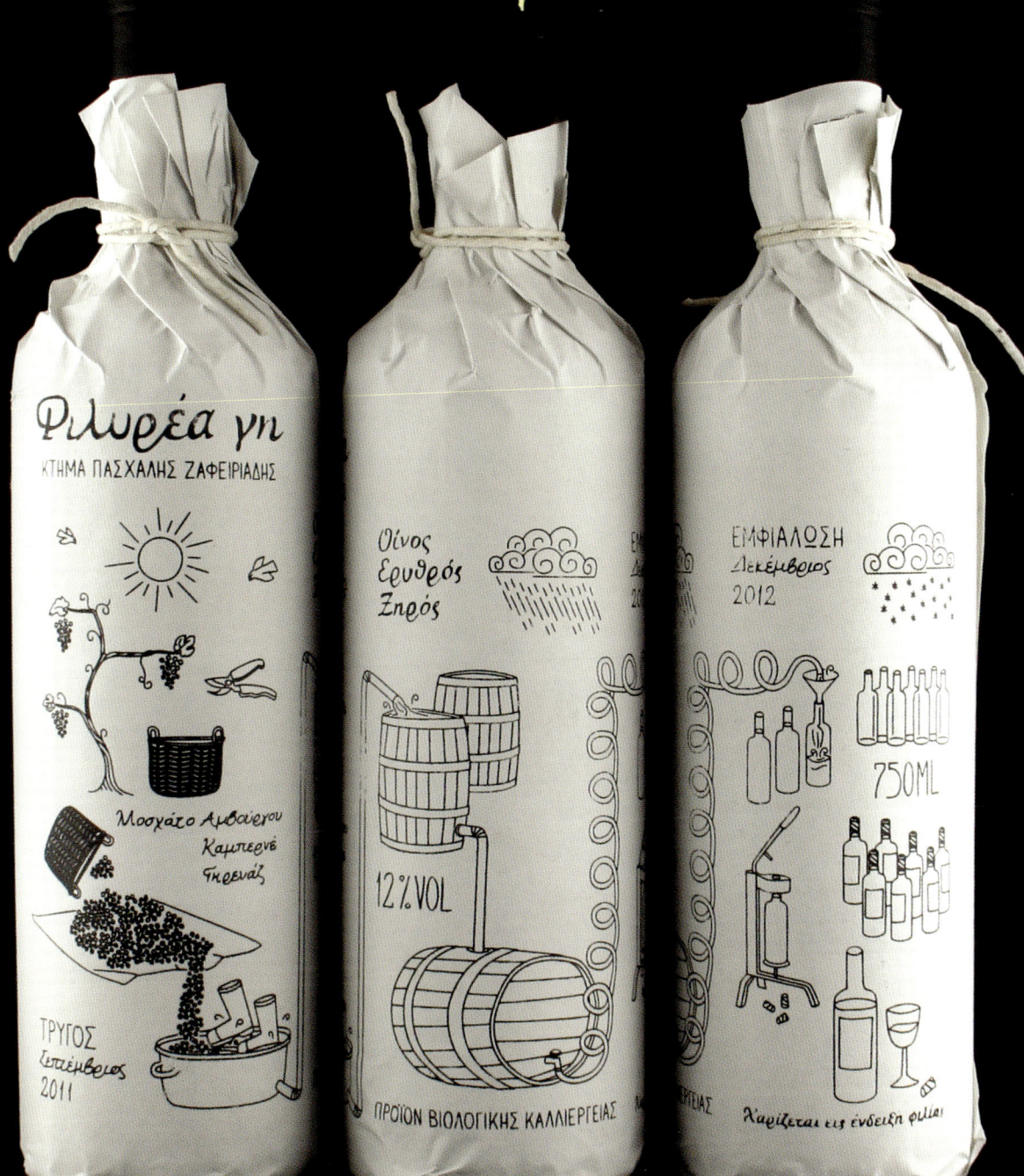

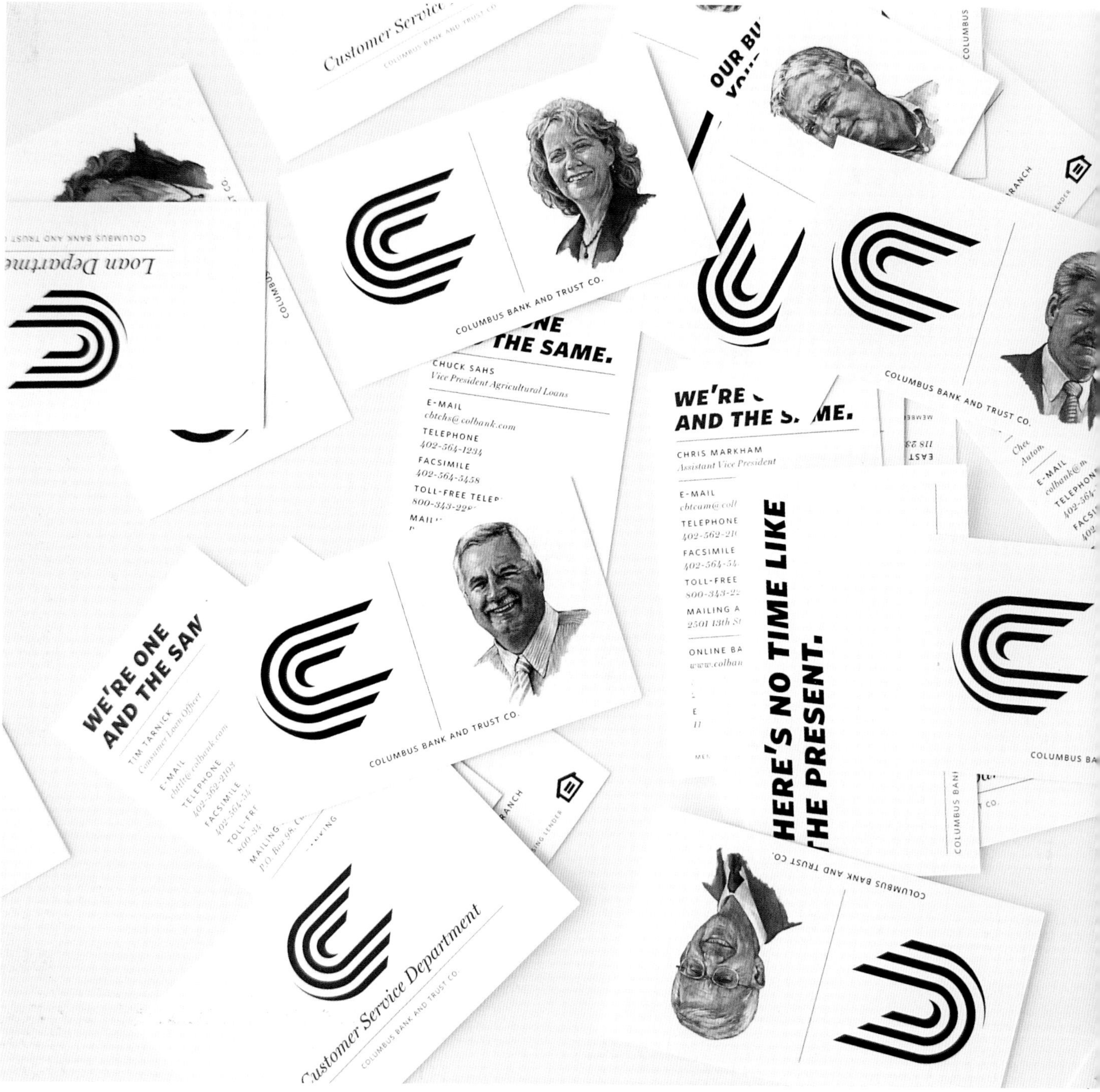

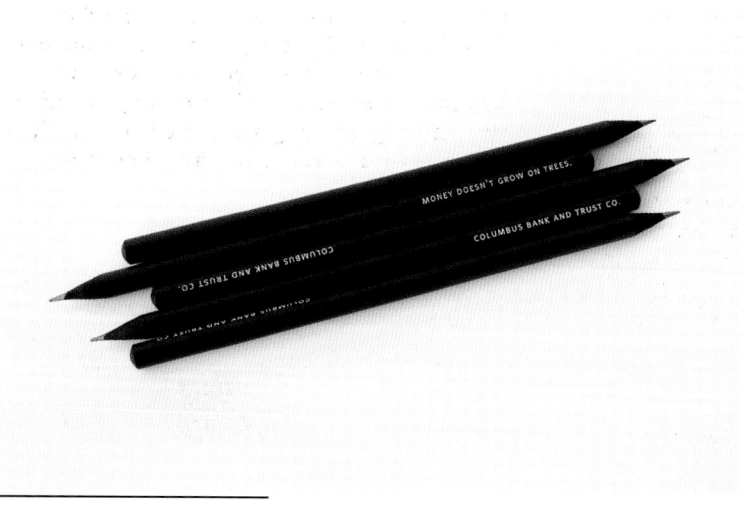

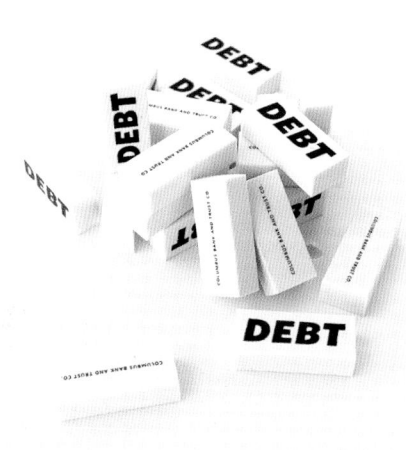

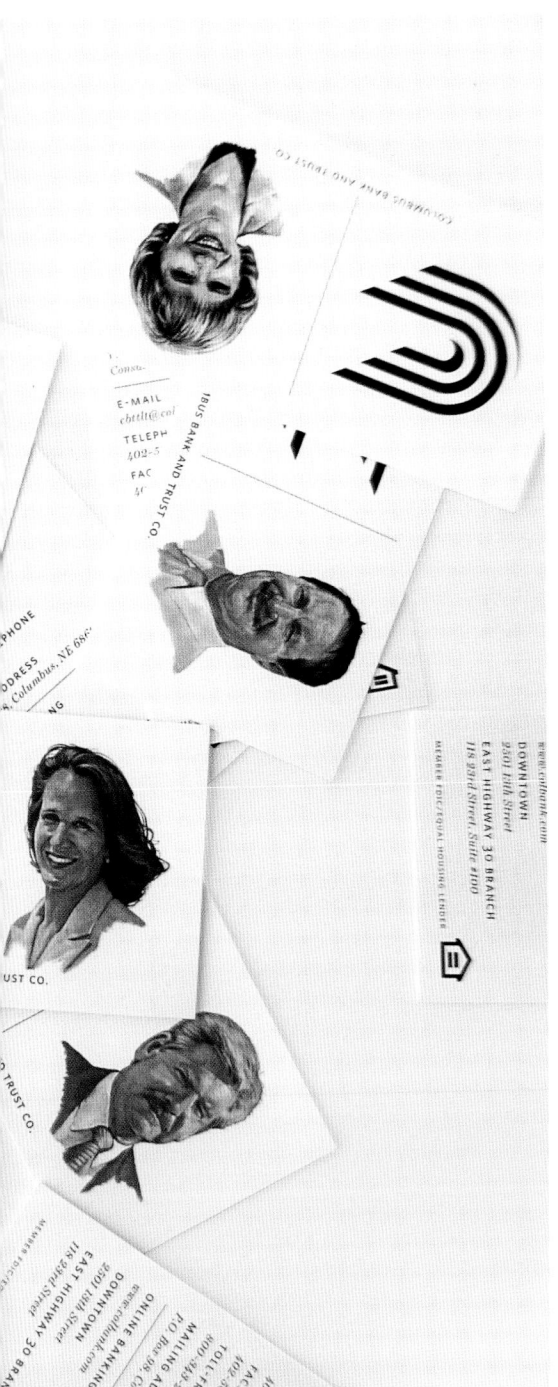

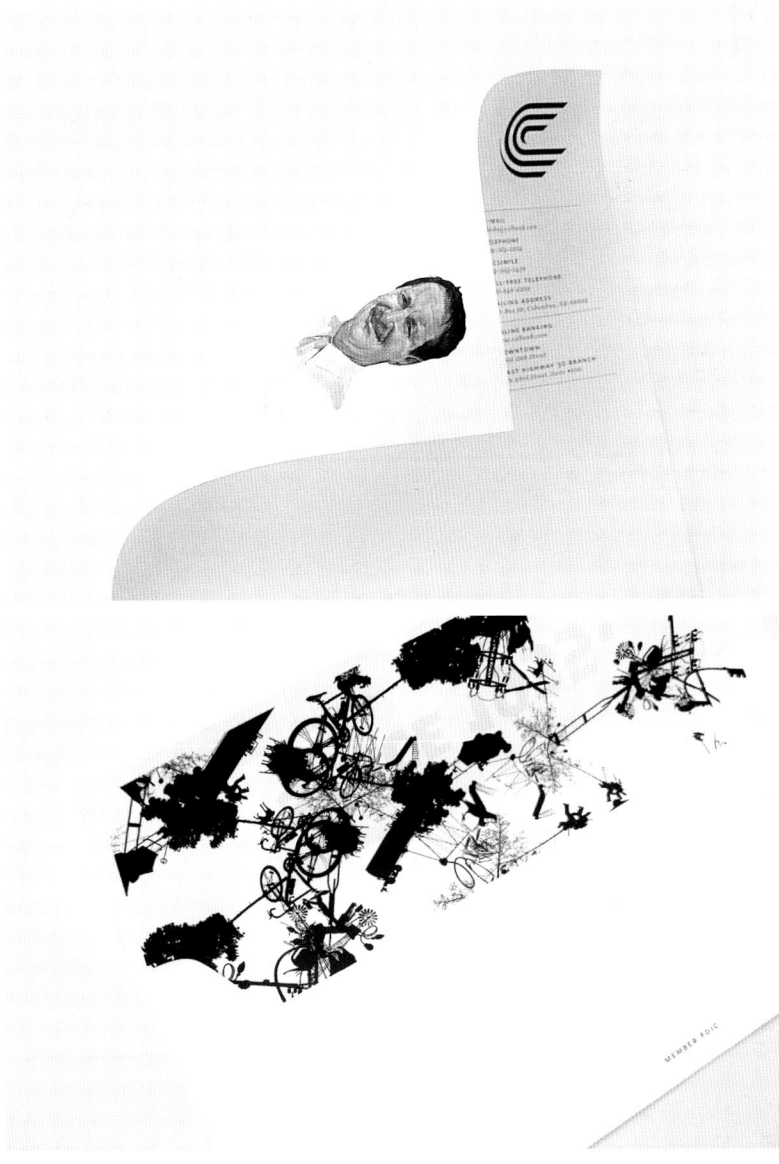

Columbus Bank and Trust Co.

United States

Topos Graphics
Design Agency

**Seth Labenz,
Roy Rub**
Designers

Seth Labenz
Photographer

**Columbus Bank and
Trust Co.**
Client

The rebranding for the Columbus Bank and
Trust Company stands out with its contrasting
colors. Locally owned and the only one of its
kind in town, the bank has been around since
1935. Coupling this history with its contemporary
business practices, the designers intended to
fashion them as arbiters of the new by way of the
old—keeping their original 1935 black-and-white
palette while paying extreme attention to the
detail.

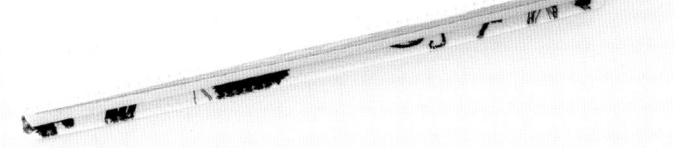

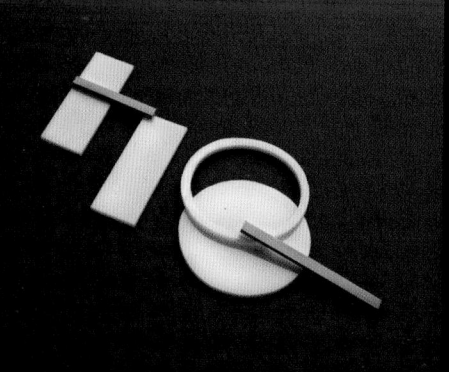

Manifiesto Futura
Design Agency

Tiqo
Client

Tiqo
Mexico

Tiqo is a tequila based beverage. Inspired by the moonlight hitting the slim figure on a quiet night at the beach, the project, including the brand identity, label and package design, was created for those who enjoy mixing romance, beaches with alcohol.

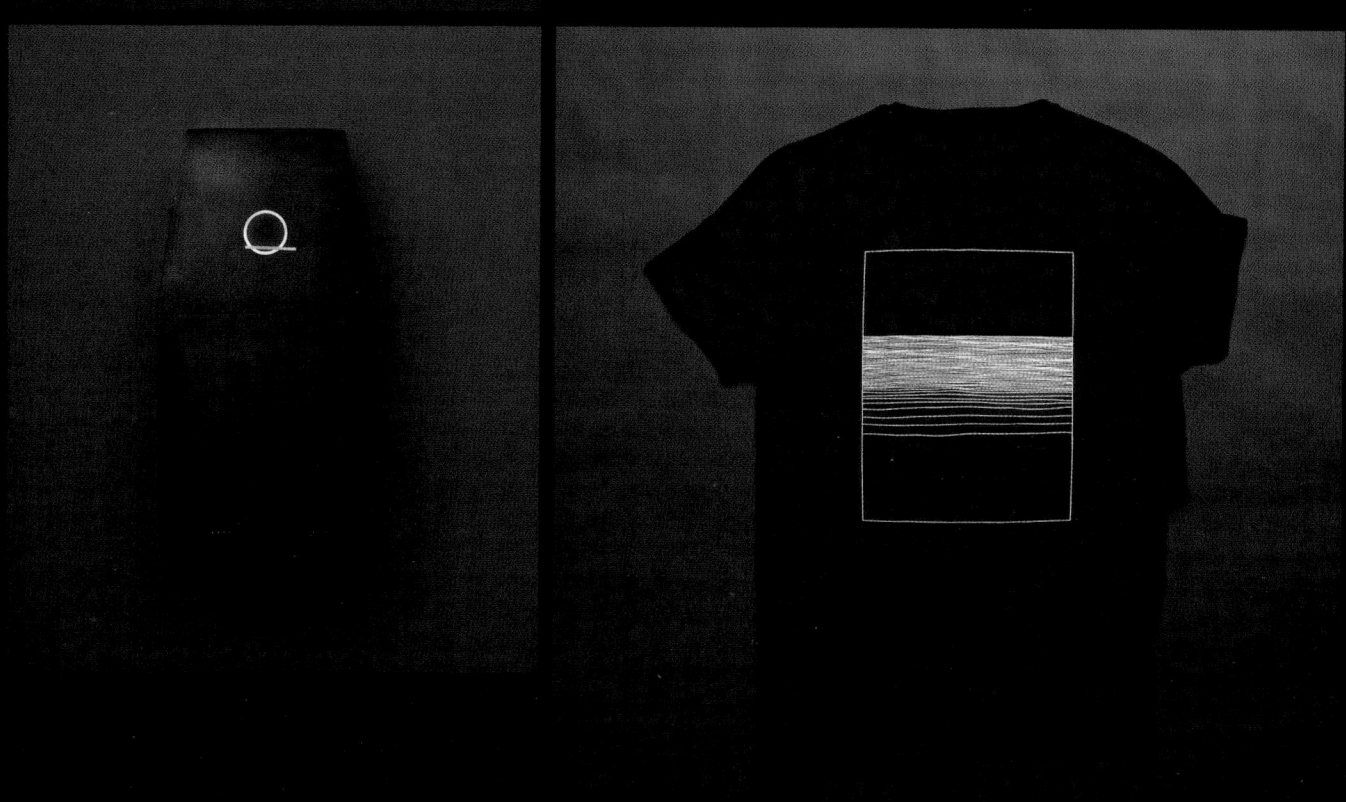

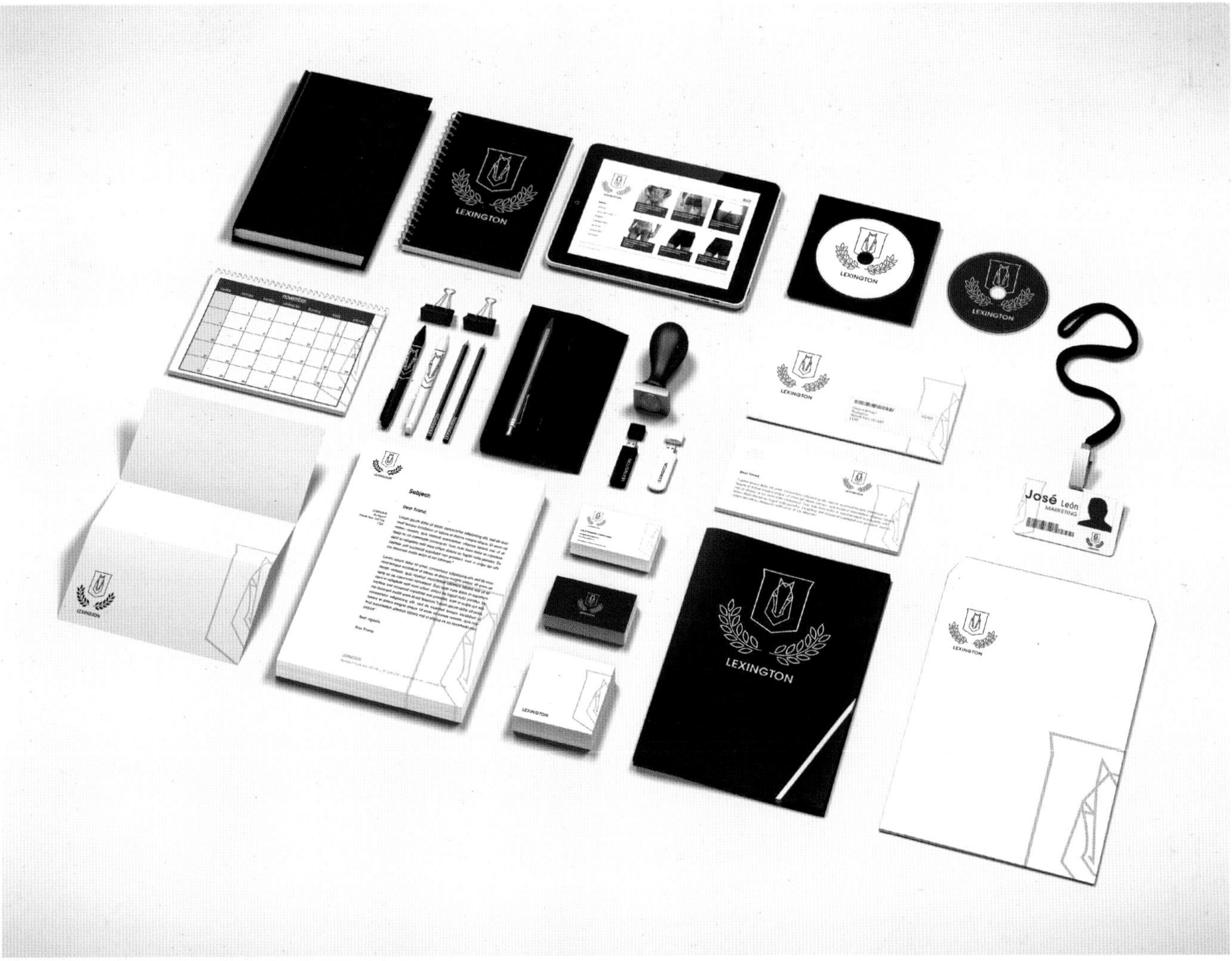

Lexington
Mexico

Citrus
Design Agency

Violeta Velasco
Creative Director

César Armando Reyes Aguilar
Art Director

LEXINGTON
Client

The Lexington is a men's underwear brand. The logo demonstrates virility and men's seeking of the dominant of nature. The horse and the English shield were chosen to give exaltation of the glamorous side of men.

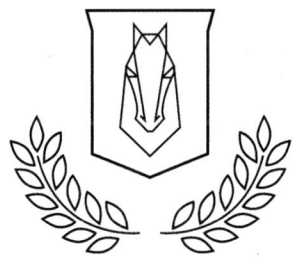

LEXINGTON

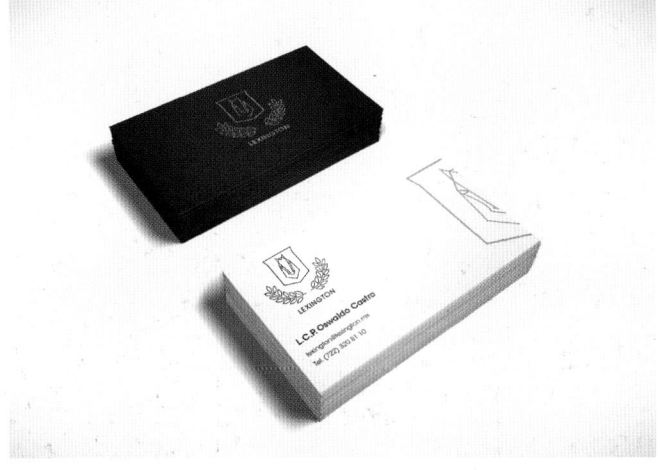

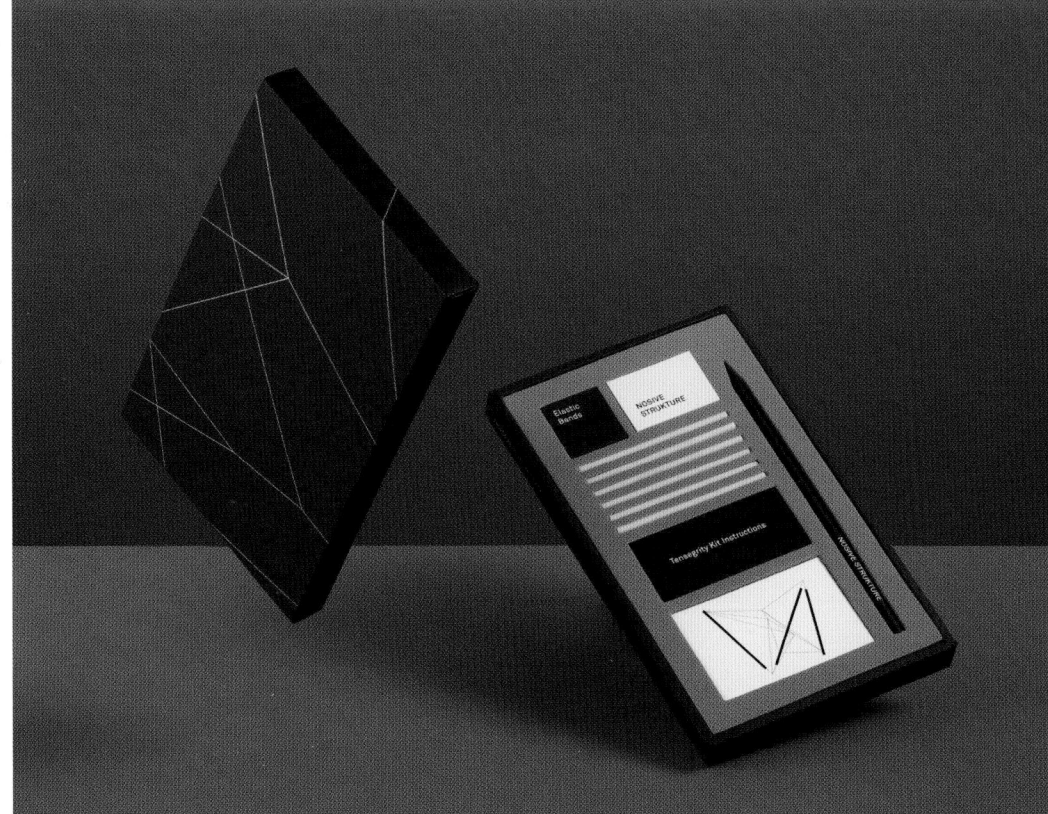

Nosive Strukture
United Kingdom

Bunch
Design Agency

Denis Kovac
Creative Director

Nosive Strukture
Client

Nosive Strukture is a structural engineering studio with an unconventional attitude towards business, working environments and life itself. Equally inspired by their unique approach and their studio space, Bunch developed a stark, technical identity based on tensegrity structures and a black and white palette, which was applied to its stationery, signage, website and various other applications, including triplex business cards, cardboard file folders with die cuts and a direct mailer featuring a custom made, laser cut, tensegrity model.

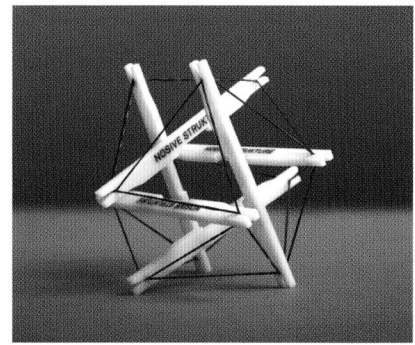

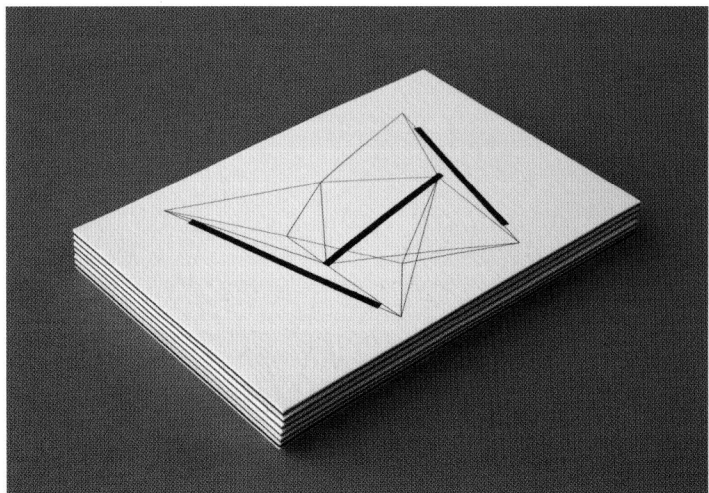

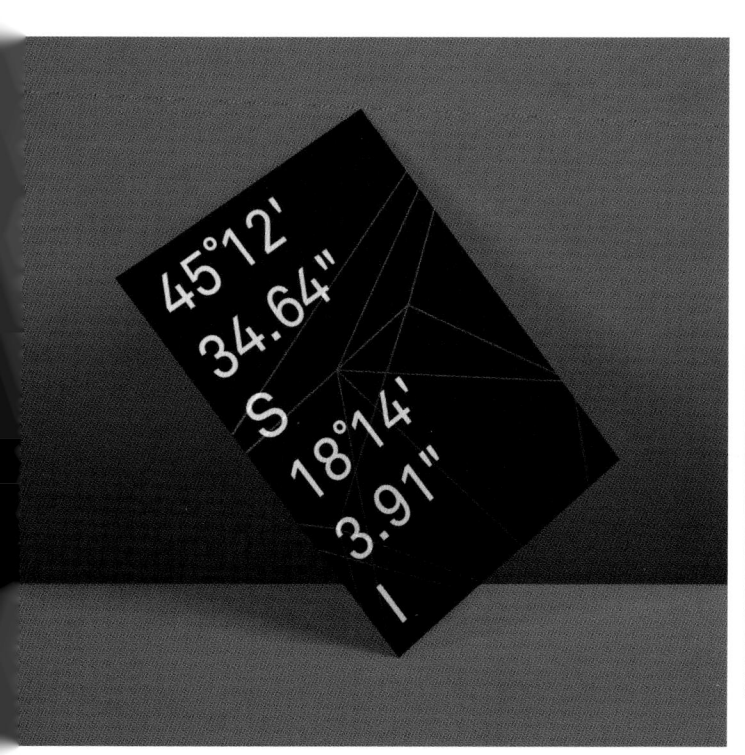

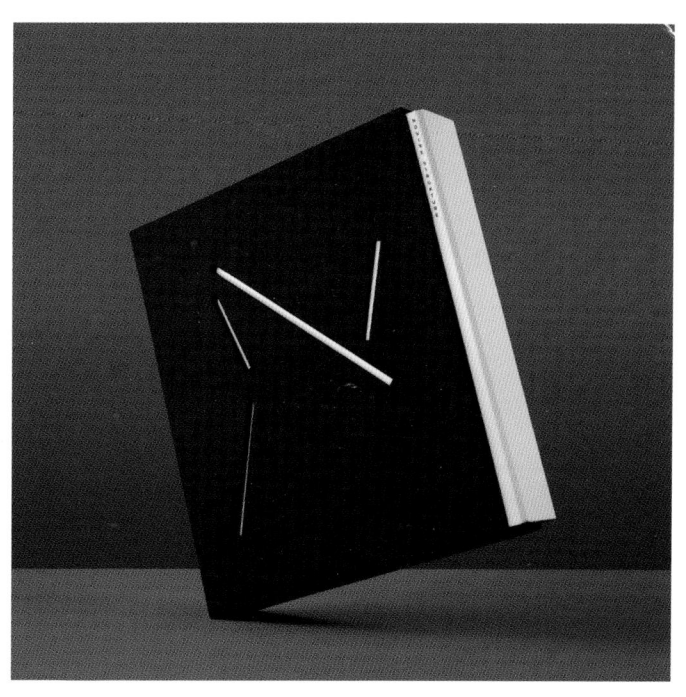

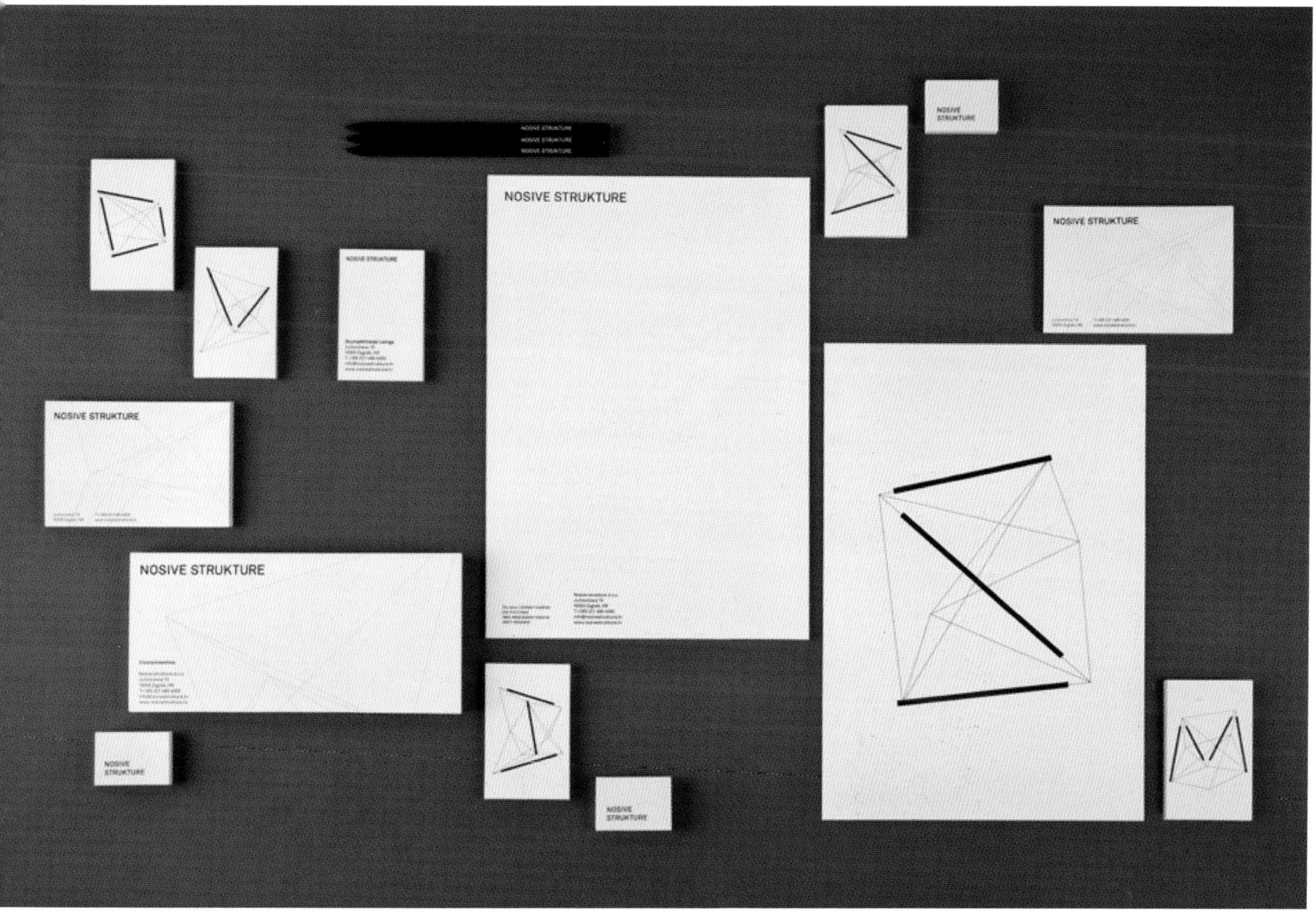

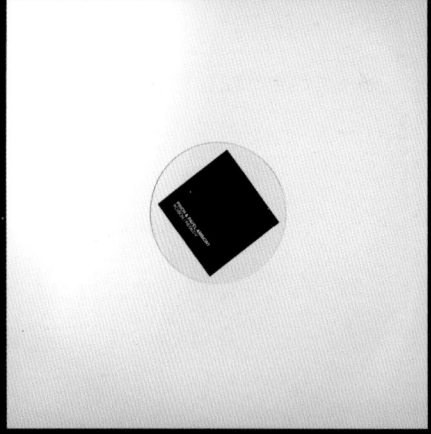
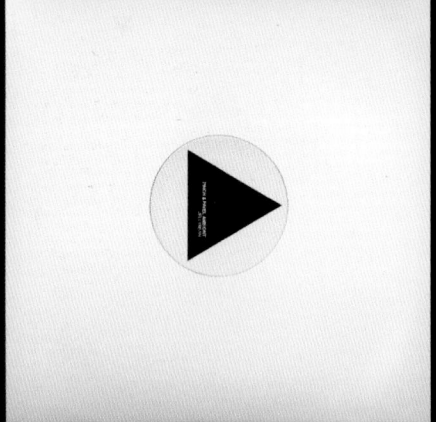

P&P 12' Vinyl Record Design
Czech Republic

Creasence
Design Agency

Alexander Nevolin
Creative Director

P&P Recording
Client

The 12 inches vinyl limited edition record design showcased the two tracks of deep dark techno Dubstep, transforming the concepts behind the music into a simple but striking design for the label artwork that really stand out from the shelves of record shops.

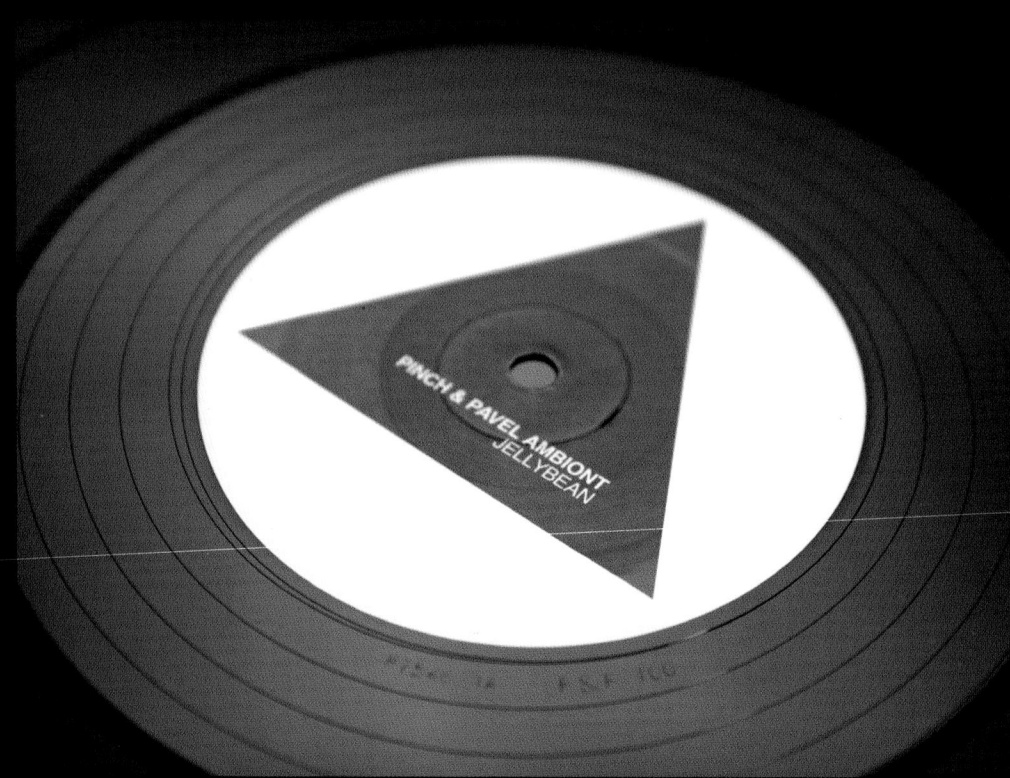

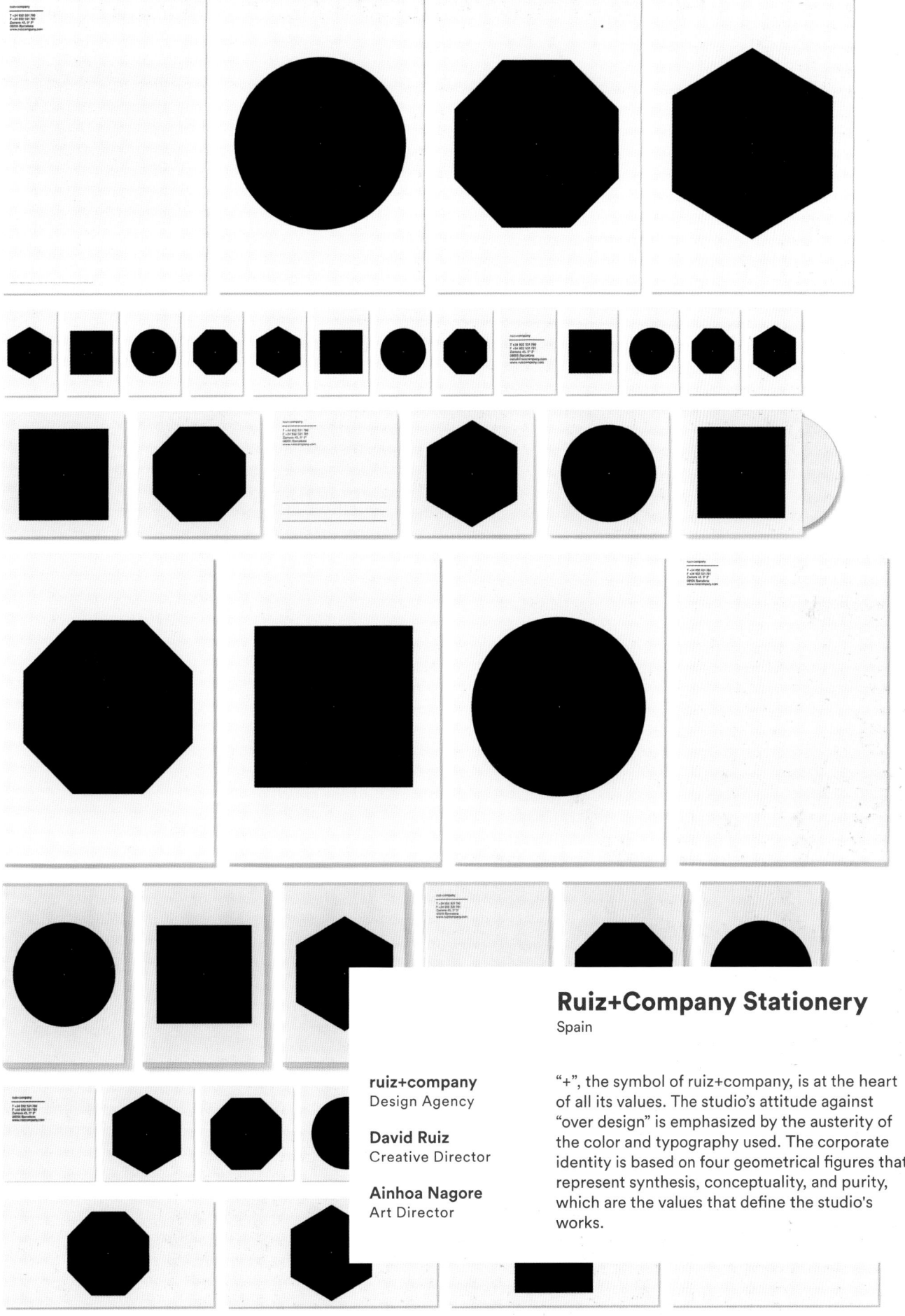

Ruiz+Company Stationery
Spain

ruiz+company
Design Agency

David Ruiz
Creative Director

Ainhoa Nagore
Art Director

"+", the symbol of ruiz+company, is at the heart of all its values. The studio's attitude against "over design" is emphasized by the austerity of the color and typography used. The corporate identity is based on four geometrical figures that represent synthesis, conceptuality, and purity, which are the values that define the studio's works.

Appointment
Japan

OUWN
Design Agency

Atsushi Ishiguro
Designer

MUSHROOM
Client

110

The poster was created for a concert held at a French restaurant in Tokyo. As the client requested not to use the image of the restaurant directly, the designer used a dynamic graphic design with the black color to mimic the concert's atmosphere.

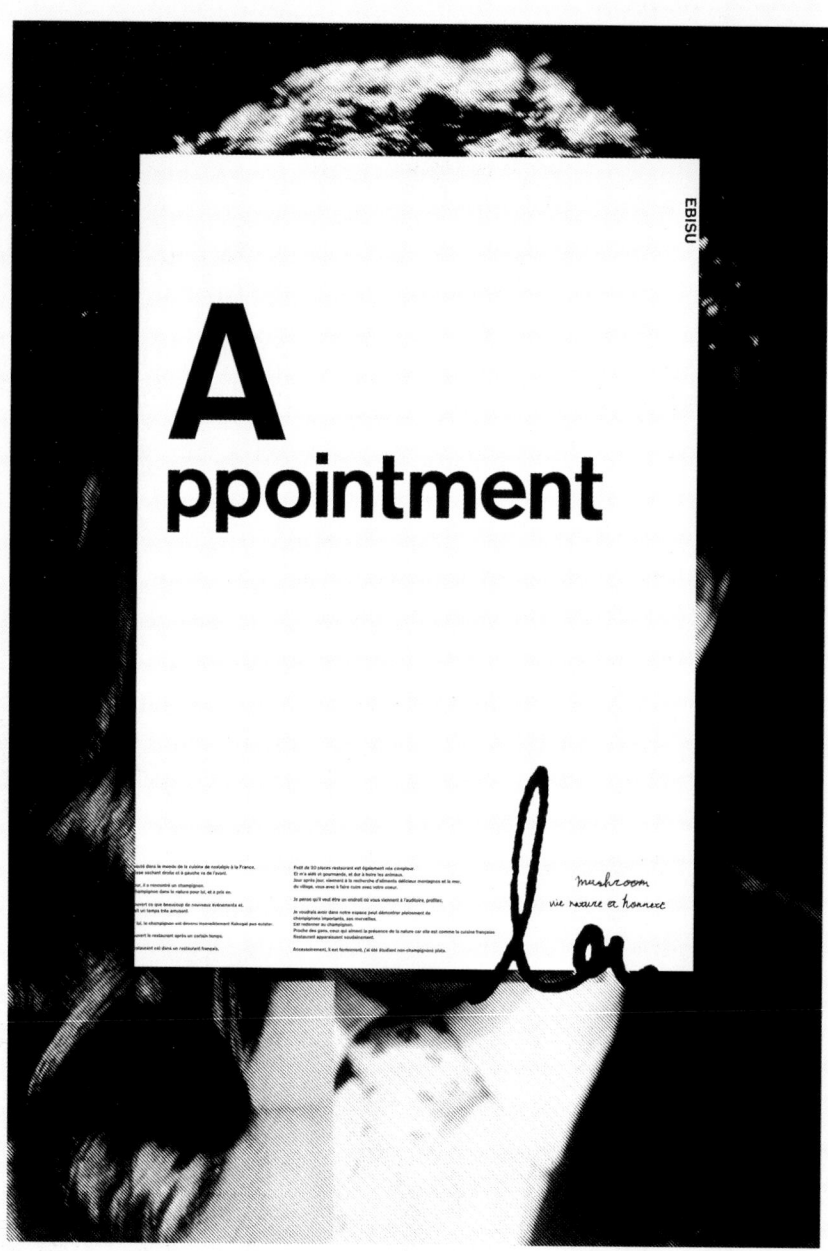

EBISU

A

ppointment

seuté dans le monde de la cuisine de nostalgie à la France, laisse sachant droite et à gauche va de l'avant.

Petit de 20 places restaurant est également mis compteur.
Et m'a aidé et gourmande, et dur à boire les animaux.
Jour après jour, viennent à la recherche d'aliments délicieux montagnes et la mer, du village, vous avez à faire cuire avec votre coeur.

pour, il a rencontré un champignon.
champignon dans la nature pour lui, et a pris en.

Je pense qu'il veut être un endroit où vous viennent à l'auditoire, profitez,

rouvert ce que beaucoup de nouveaux événements et, uel un temps très amusant.

Je voudrais avoir dans notre espace peut démontrer pleinement de champignons importants, ses merveilles.
Est redonner au champignon.
Proche des gens, ceux qui aiment la présence de la nature car elle est comme la cuisine française
Restaurant apparaissent soudainement.

r lui, le champignon est devenu insensiblement Kakegai pas exister.

uvert le restaurant après un certain temps.

Accassicrement, il est fermement, j'ai été étudiant non-champignons plats.

restaurant est dans un restaurant français.

mushroom
vie nature et honnete

"*A black and white design simplifes the focus of your vision, clearing your mind and prioritizing what is right or wrong, like life.*"
—Lucas Nasson Kim

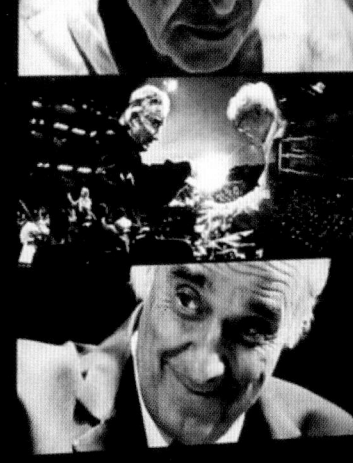

Dave Brubeck and João Carlos Martins
United States

Lucasnasson
Design Agency

Lucas Kim
Art Director

Jay K Hoffman
Client

For the promotional materials for a concert of the two musicians Dave Brubeck and João Carlos Martins, the designer used piano as a common ground to embody the different traits of the two. The beauty and elegance of the black and white piano keys and the simplicity of the music sheet highlight the essence of the concert.

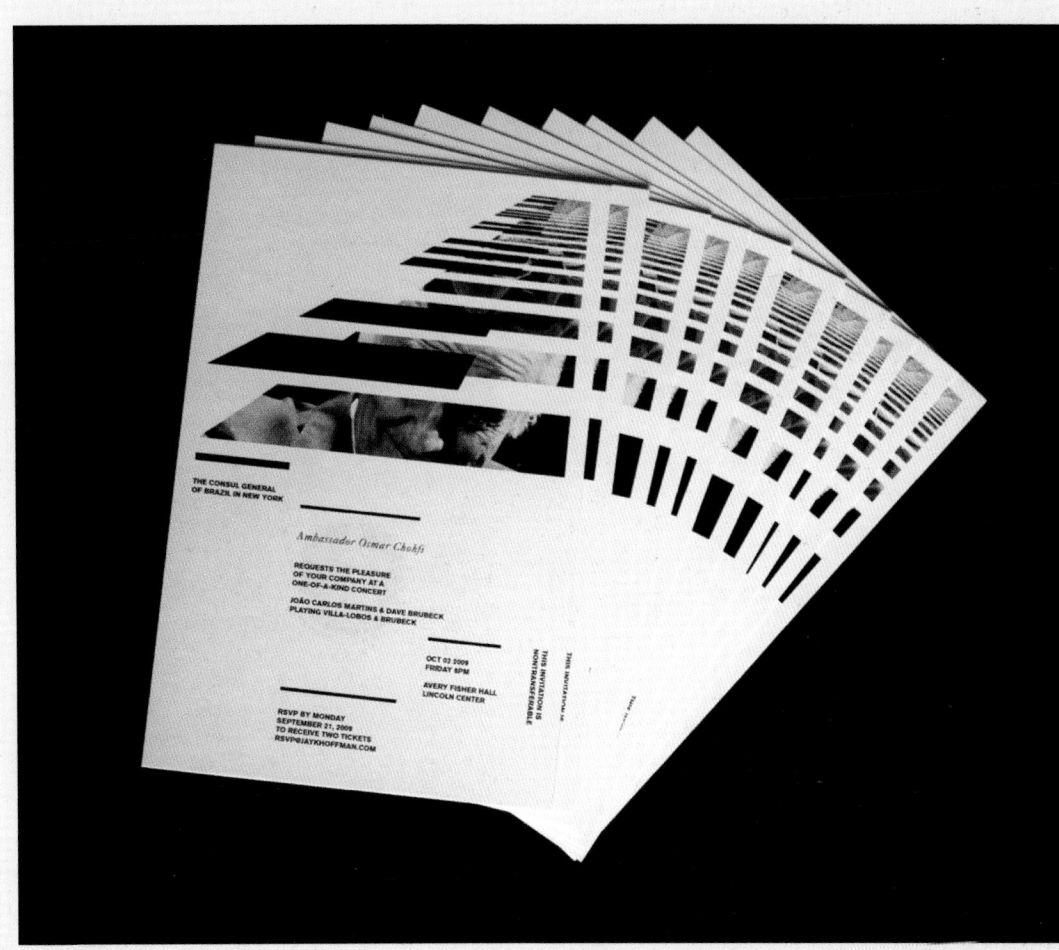

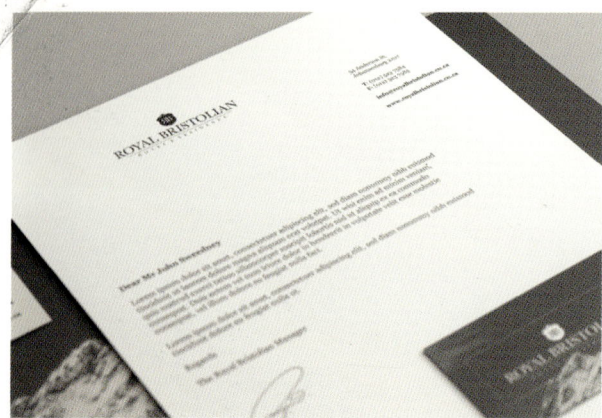

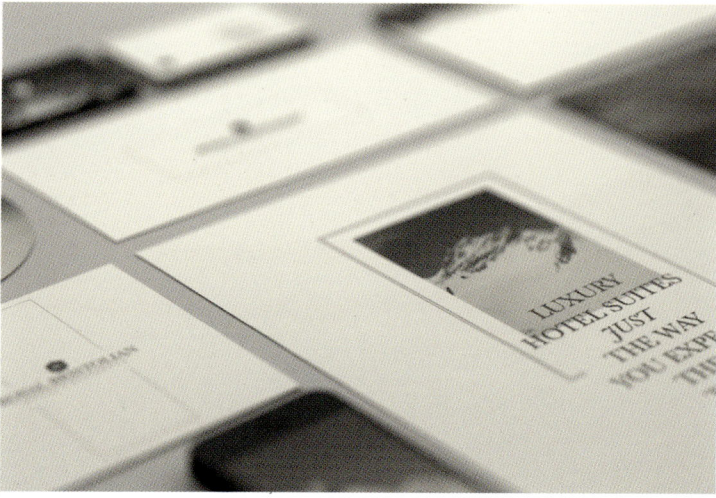

114

The Royal Bristolian
South Africa

Stefan Mostert
Designer
& Photographer

Personal Portfolio Work
Client

The corporate identity for a luxury hotel aims to create a timeless brand image. The use of monotone colors is the best way to illustrate elegance and luxury along with the sense of timelessness. The strong serif typeface creates a feel of craftsmanship while the black and white grainy photography of the mountains adds a touch of nostalgia.

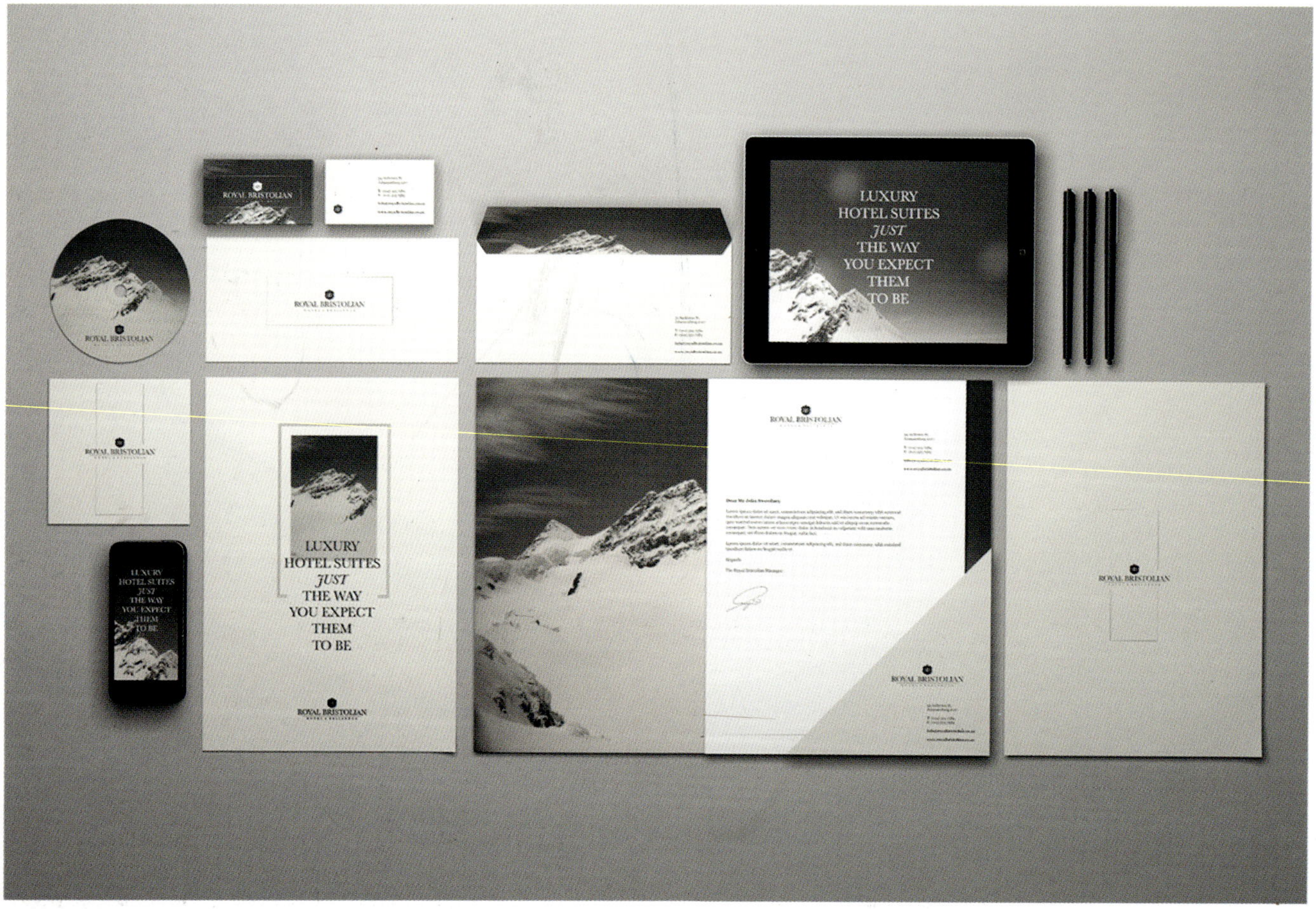

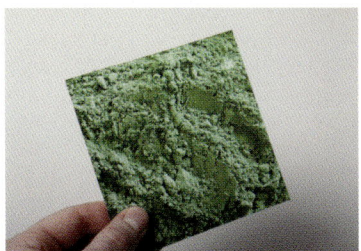

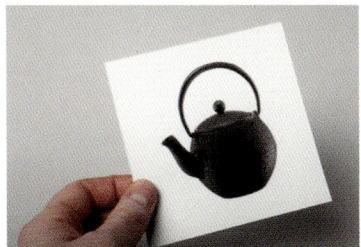

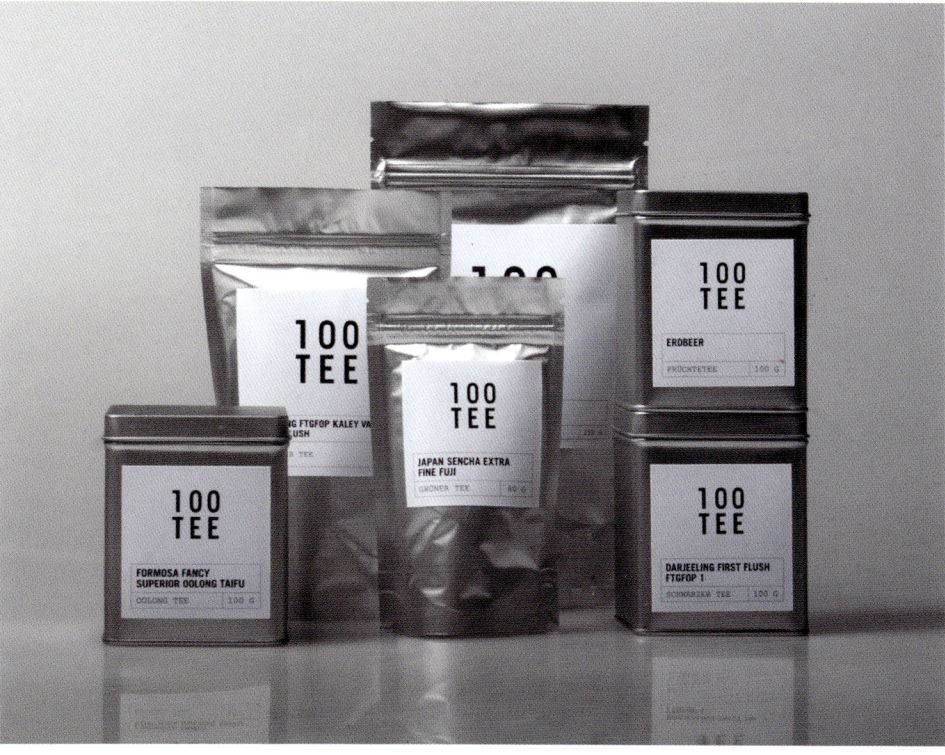

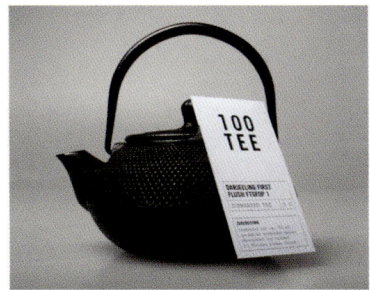

100TEE
Germany

Jann de Vries
Designer

100TEE
Client

The minimalist color scheme is modern and classy, pushing the tea products onto the foreground of the viewer's perspective. In that case the new identity gets an authentic and unique look which is untypical for similar products in regional and international tea markets.

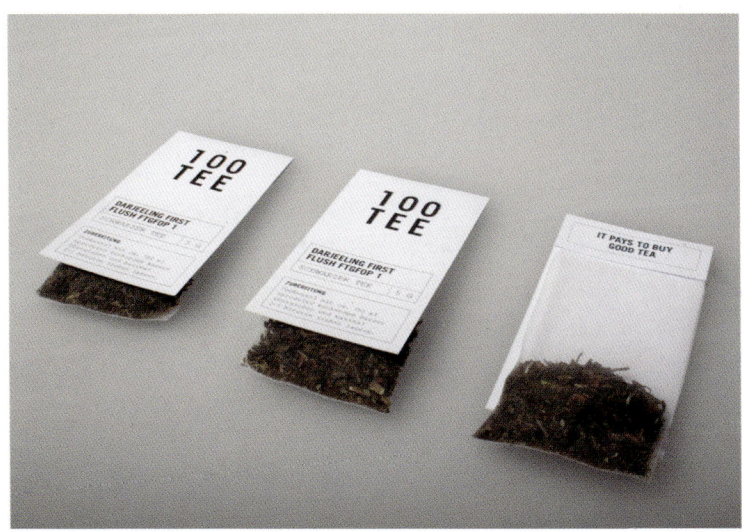

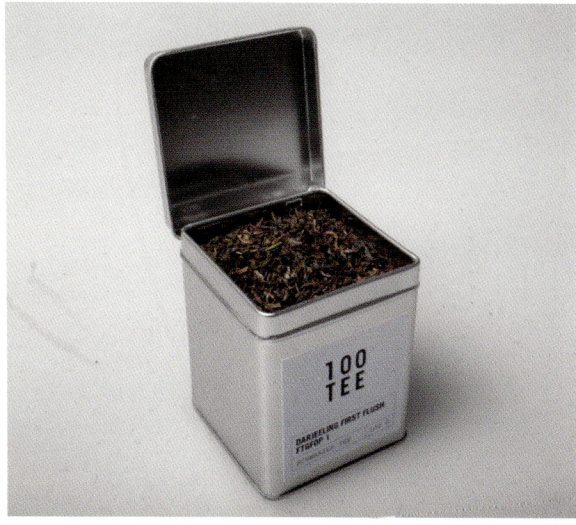

www.min-style.de

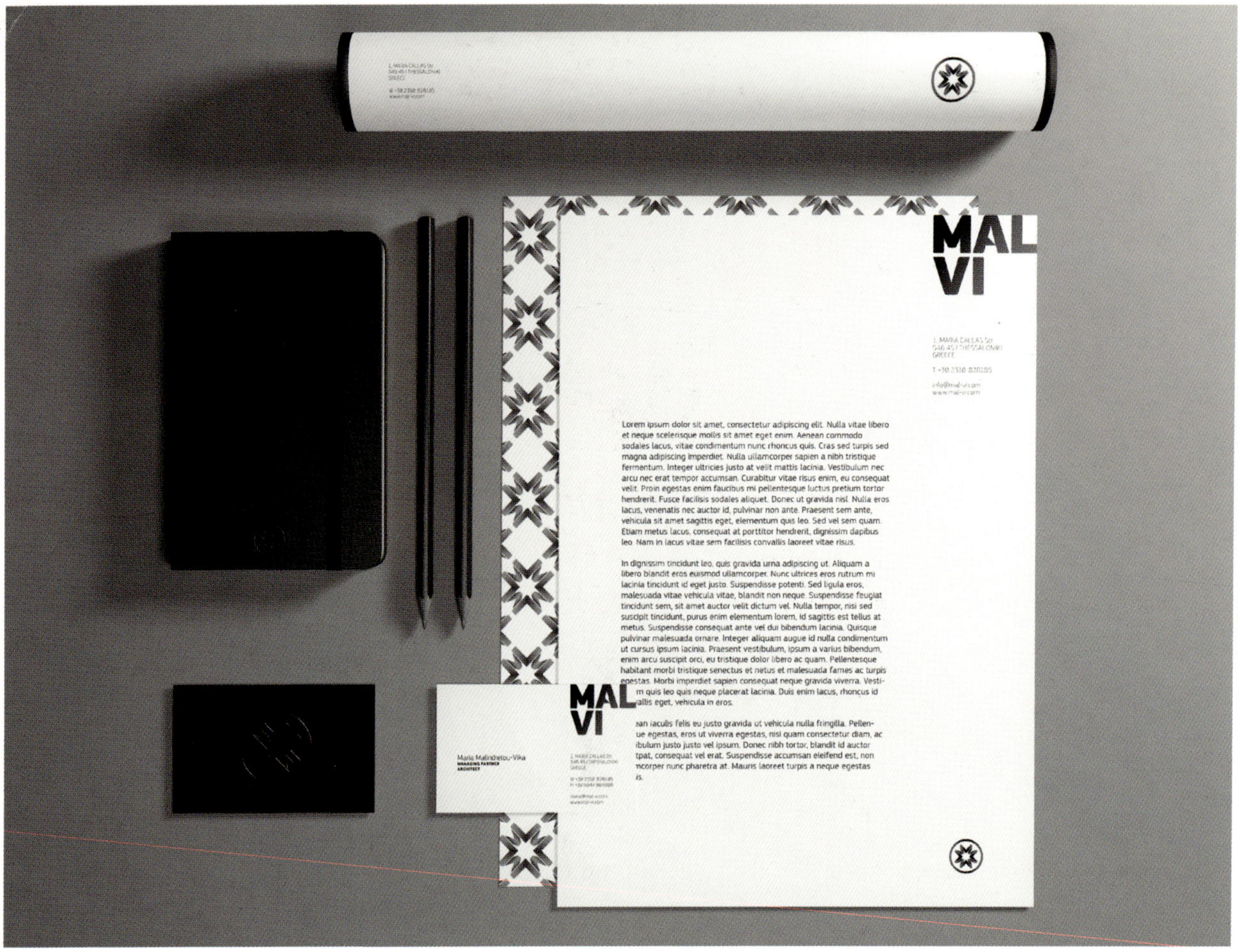

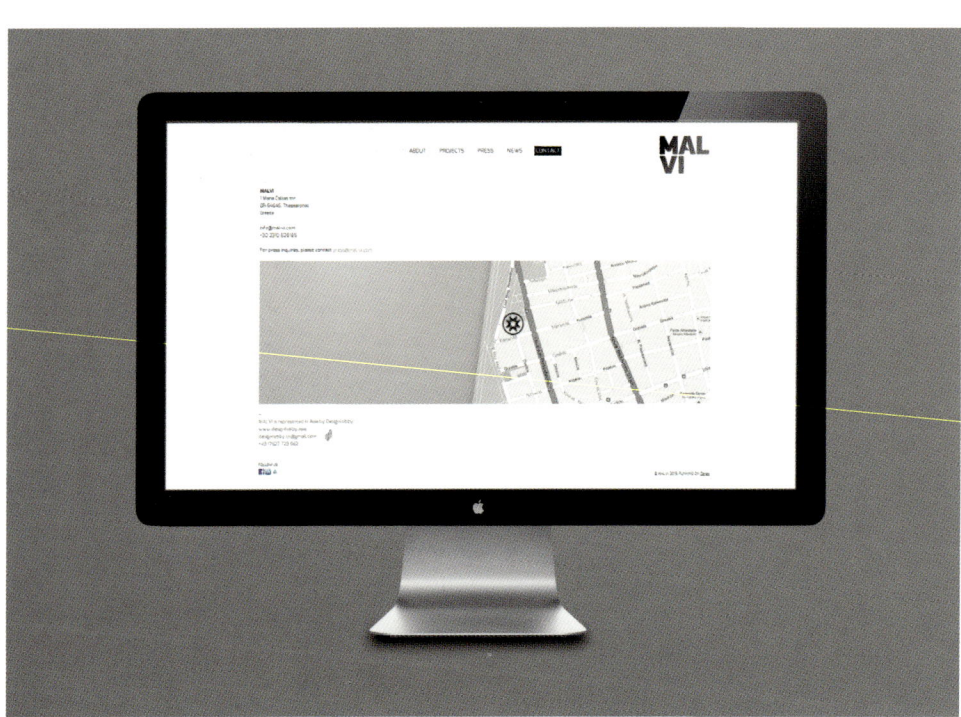

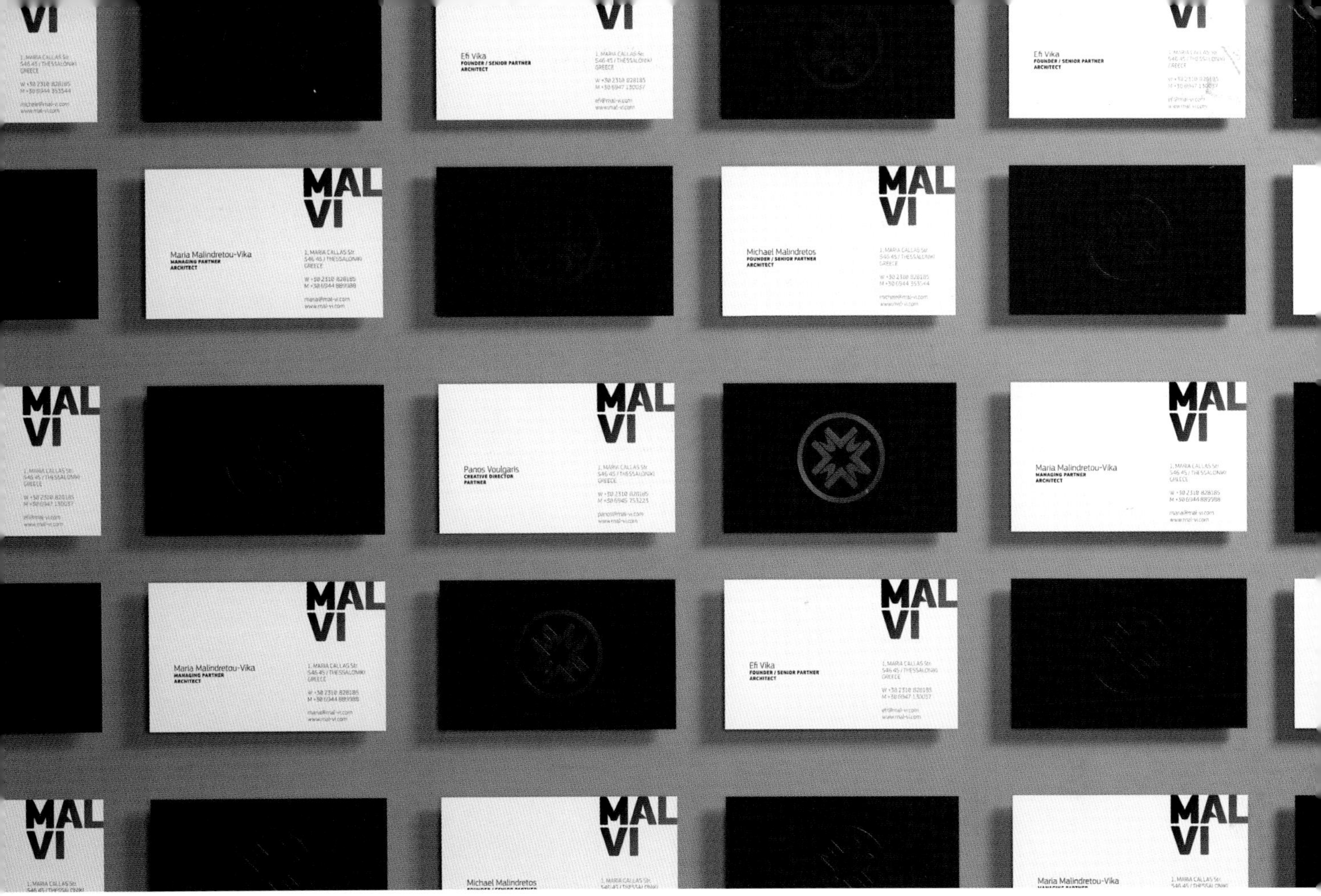

MALVI
Greece

Panos Voulgaris
Creative Director

**Panos Voulgaris,
Maria Malindretou-
Vika**
Designer

MALVI
Client

A new logo, a consistent brand identity and a redesigned website were launched for the MALVI studio that recently expanded its field from architecture to industrial design and branding. The most recent and important projects of the studio are presented in a clear and comprehensive manner.

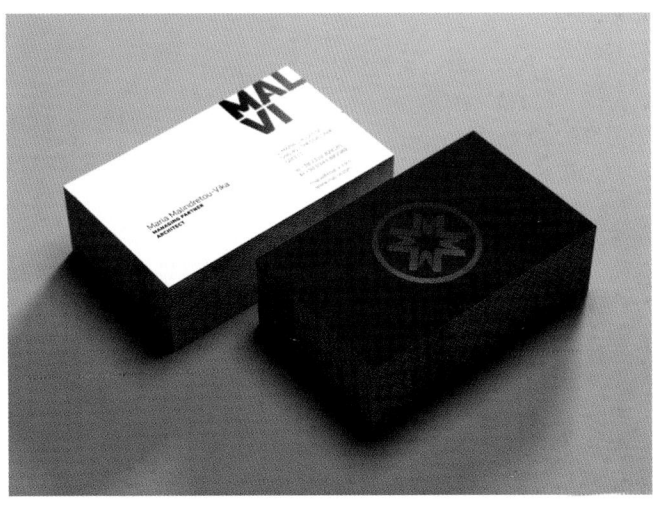

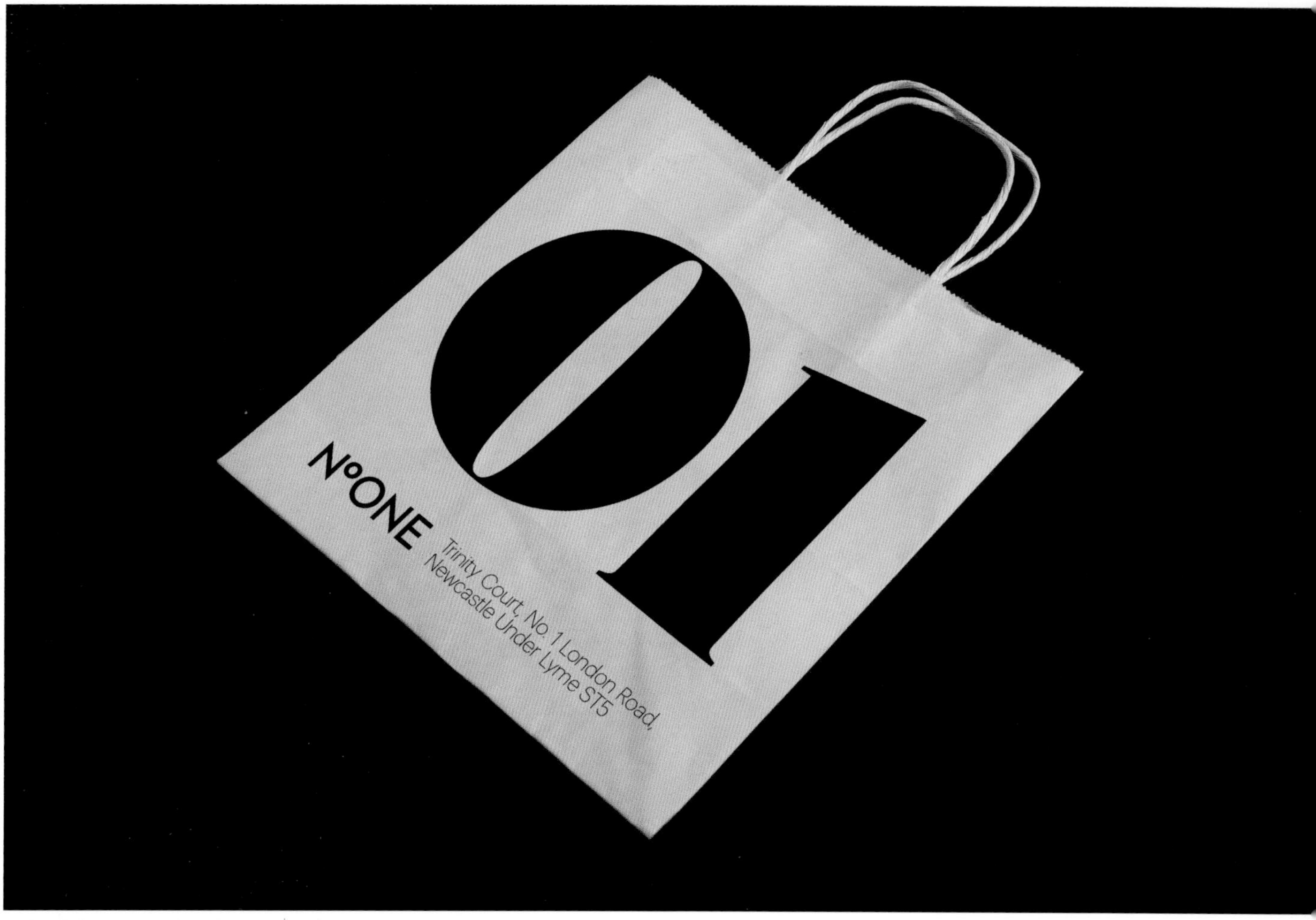
01
NºONE
Trinity Court, No. 1 London Road,
Newcastle Under Lyme ST5

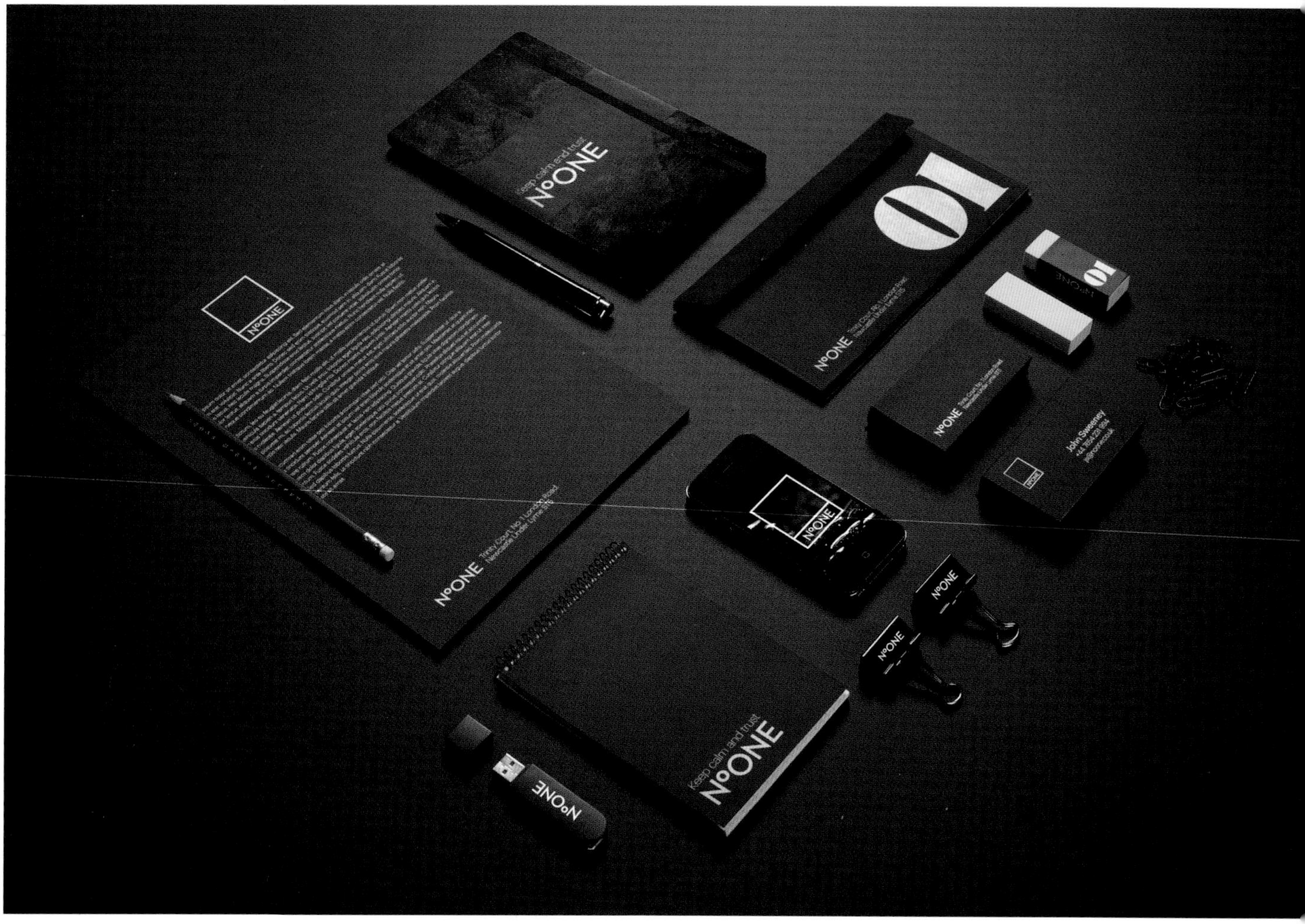
Keep calm and trust
NºONE
01
NºONE
NºONE
NºONE
John Sweeney
Keep calm and trust
NºONE
NºONE

"Design only in monochrome focuses more on shapes and ideas. Of course I love vibrant colors, but the simplicity in black and white is always my favorite."
—emptypage design studio

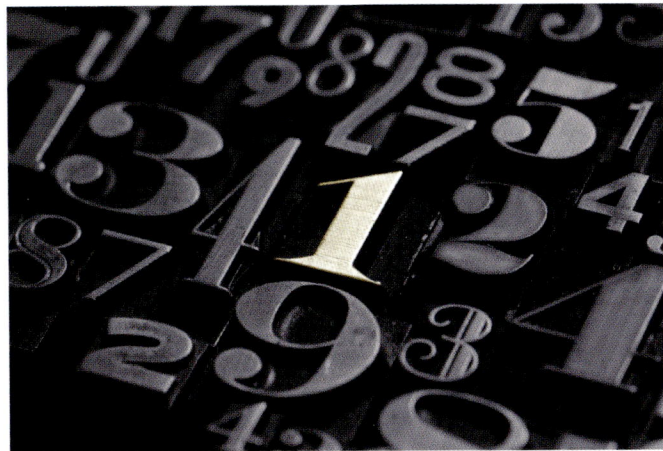

No.One Gallery Branding
Ireland

emptypage design studio
Design Agency

Lukasz Kulakowski
Designer

The branding is for an independent commercial art gallery specializing in photography, illustration and fine art. Using pure black and white gives more flexibility to the presentation of a classy space.

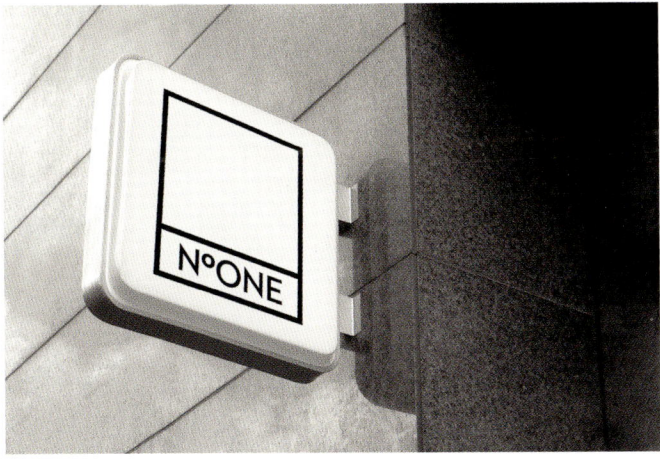

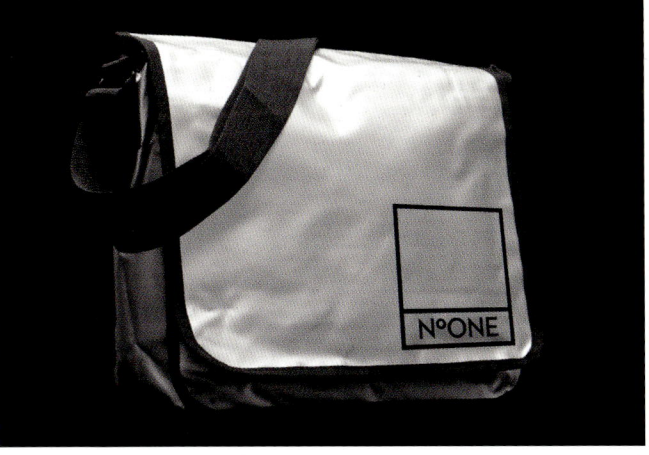

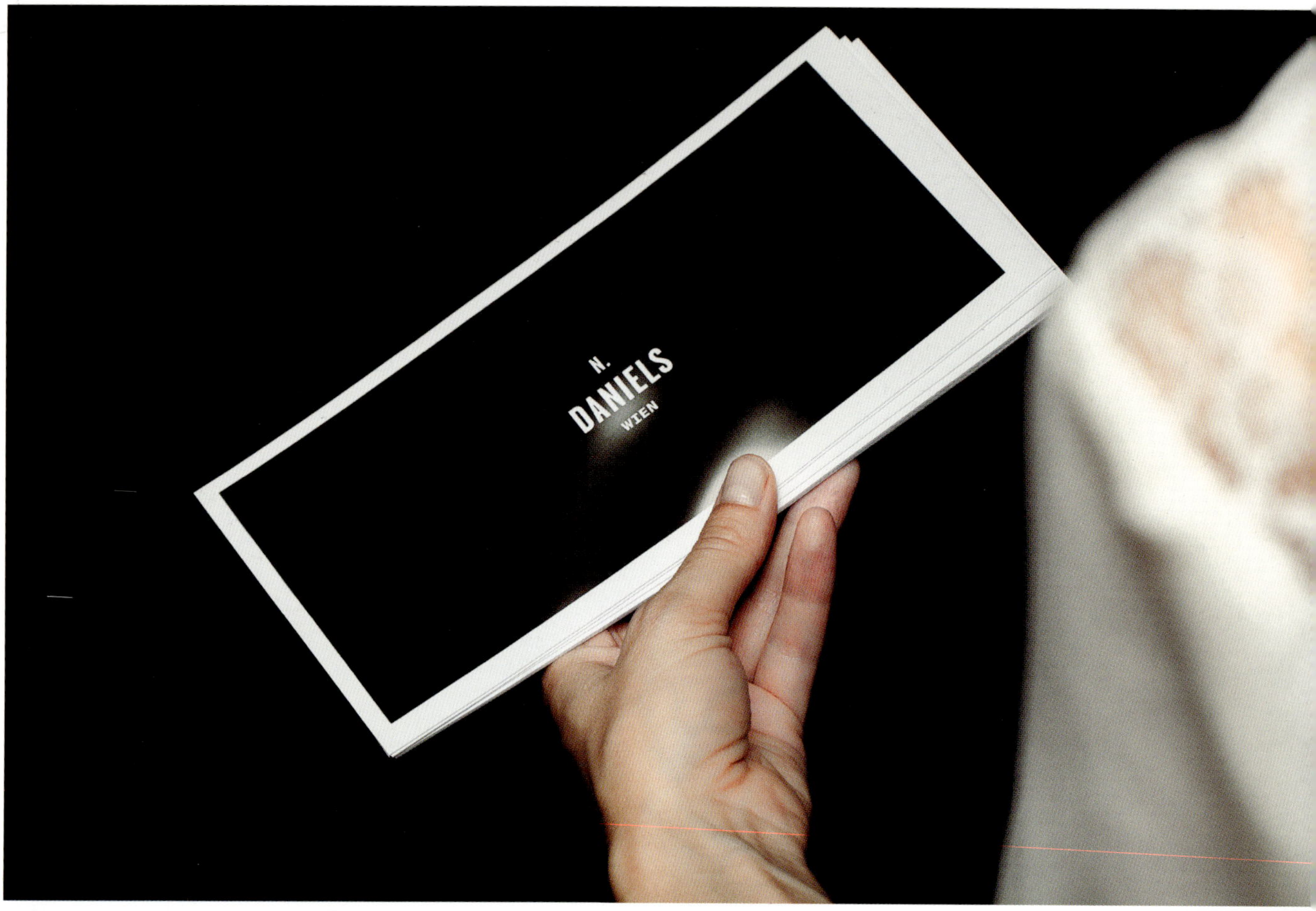
N.
DANIELS
WIEN

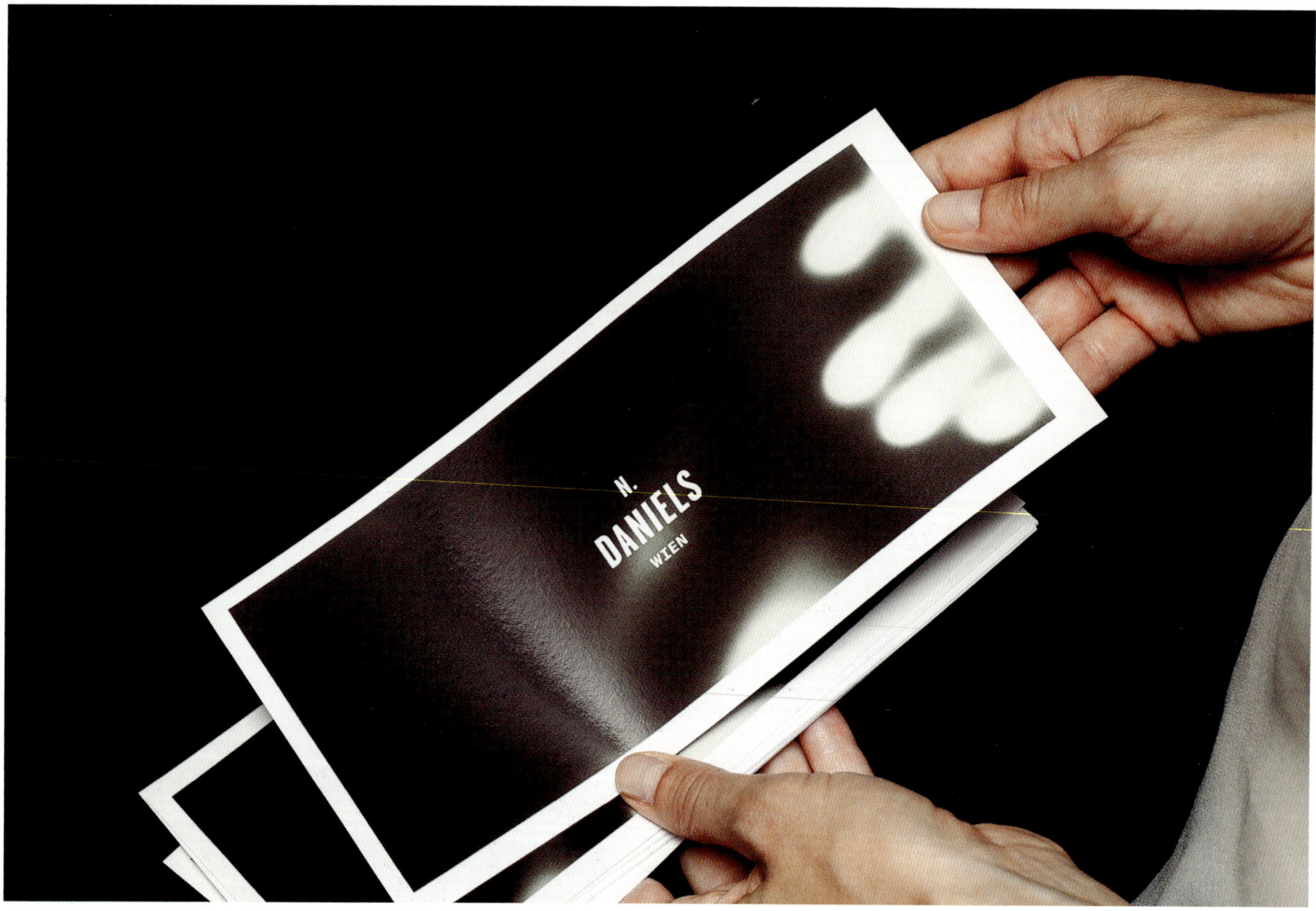
N.
DANIELS
WIEN

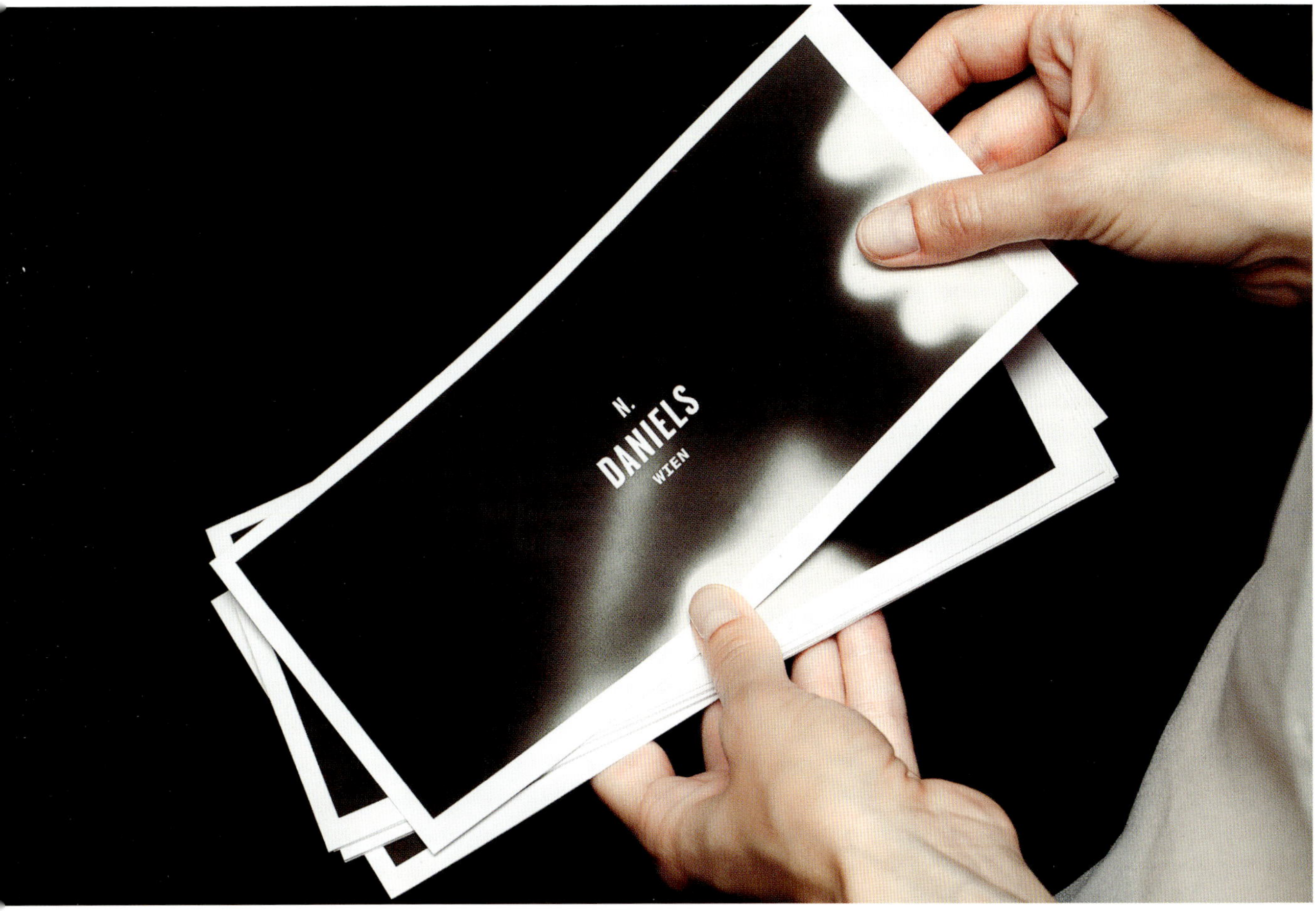
N.
DANIELS
WIEN

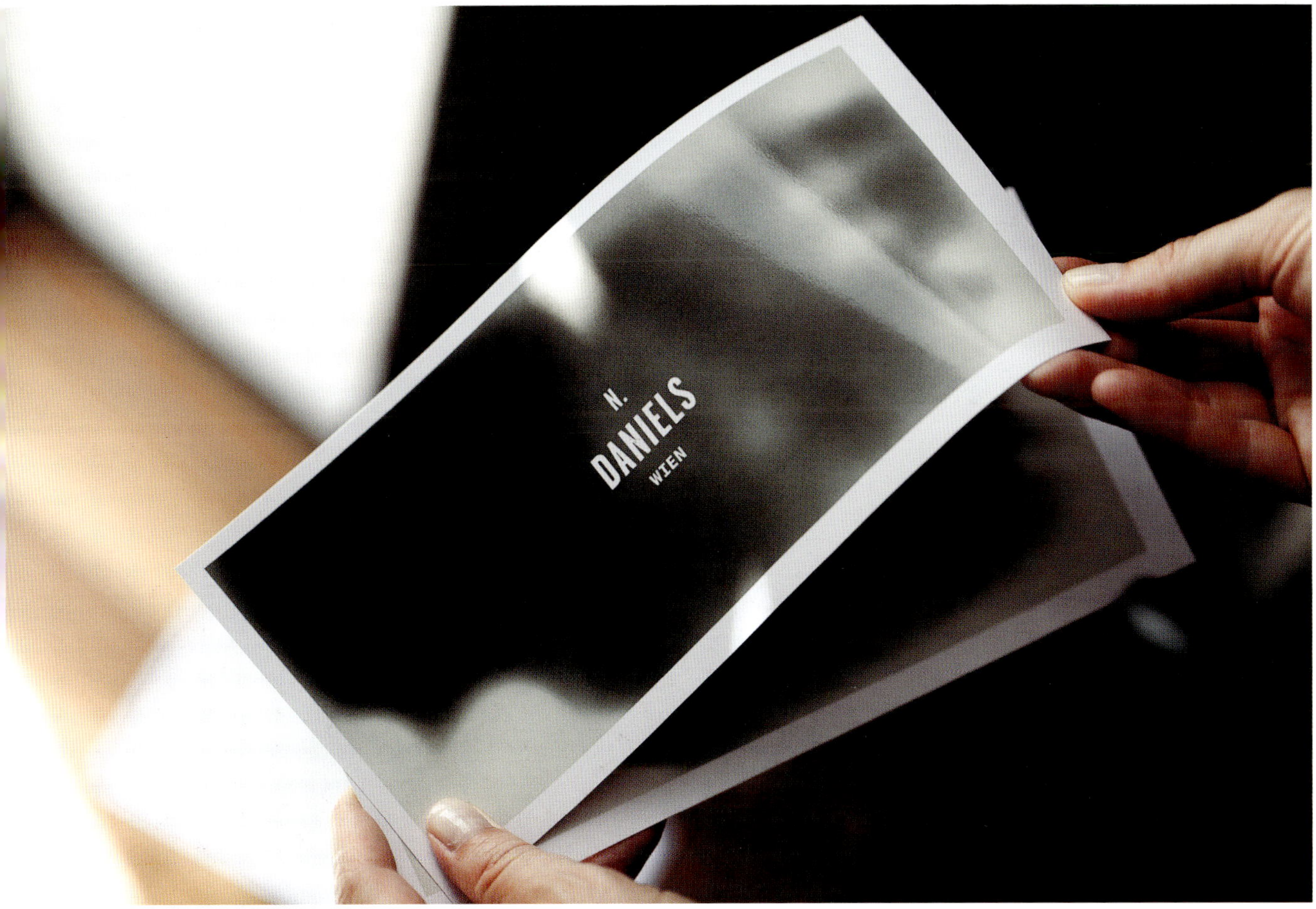
N.
DANIELS
WIEN

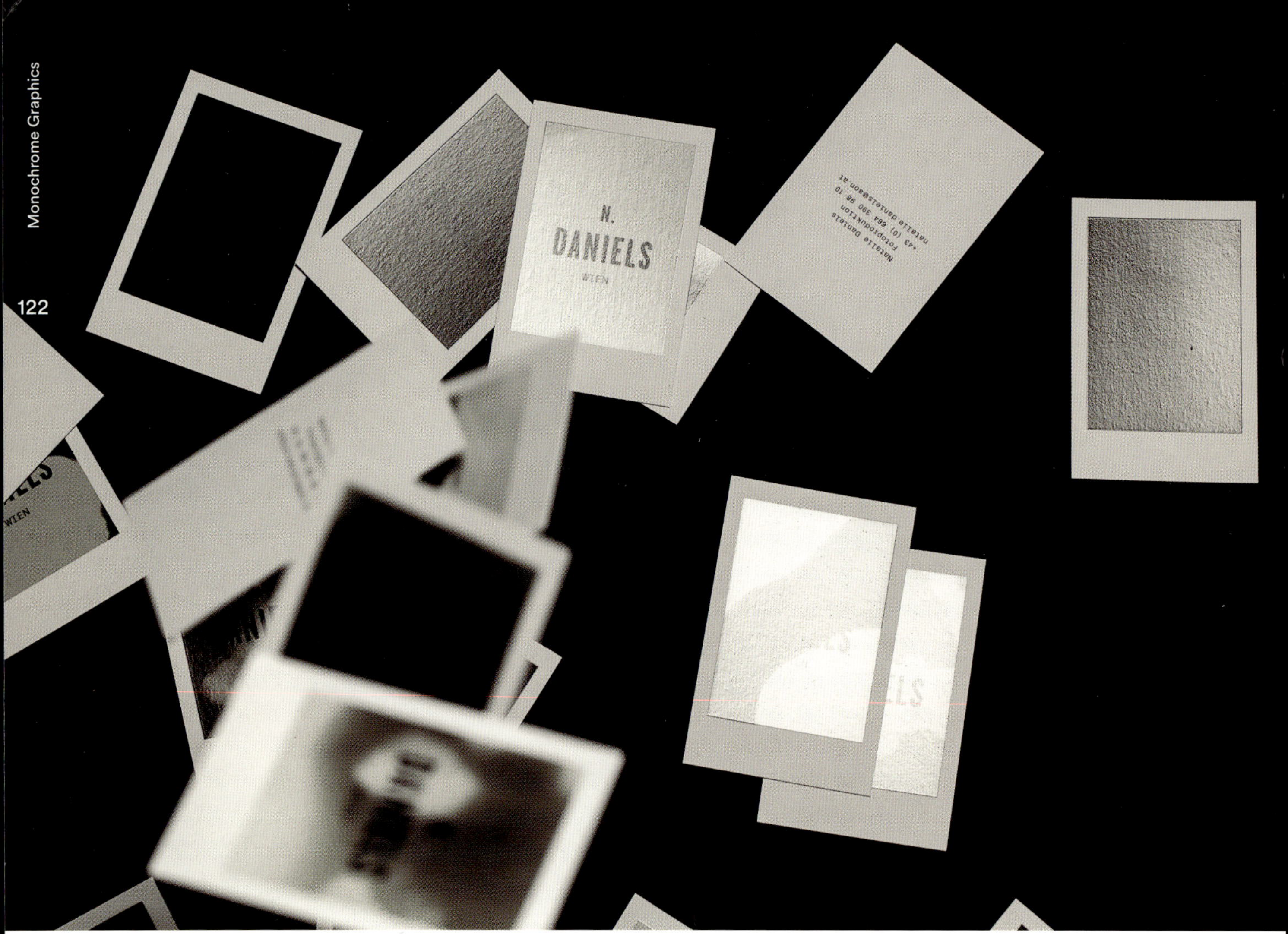

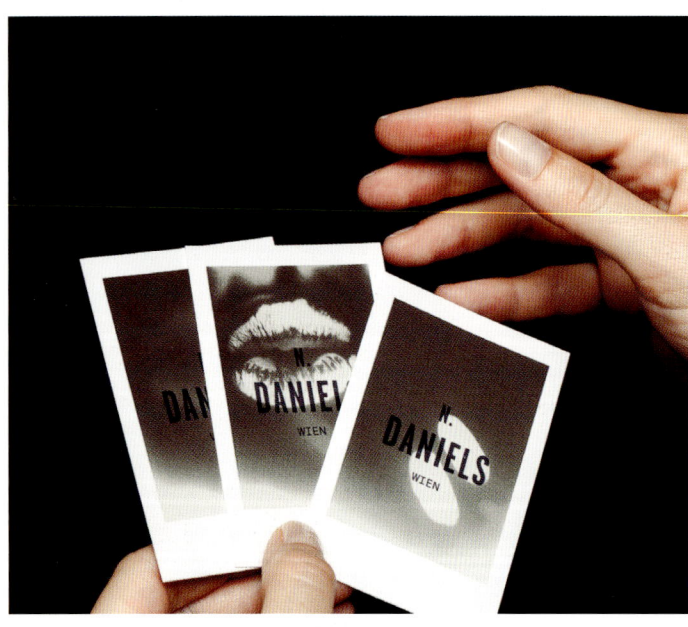

N. Daniels Wien Stationery Set

Austria

Bureau Rabensteiner
Design Agency

Mike Rabensteiner
Art Director
& Photographer

Isabella Meischberger
Designer

Natalie Daniels
Client

This brilliant stationery set was created for Vienna based photo producer Natalie Daniels. The black color of the heat-sensitive black varnish fades at body temperature. Different images will appear on it as people hold it on their hands. The business cards with a constantly changing surface make a dynamic and lively design.

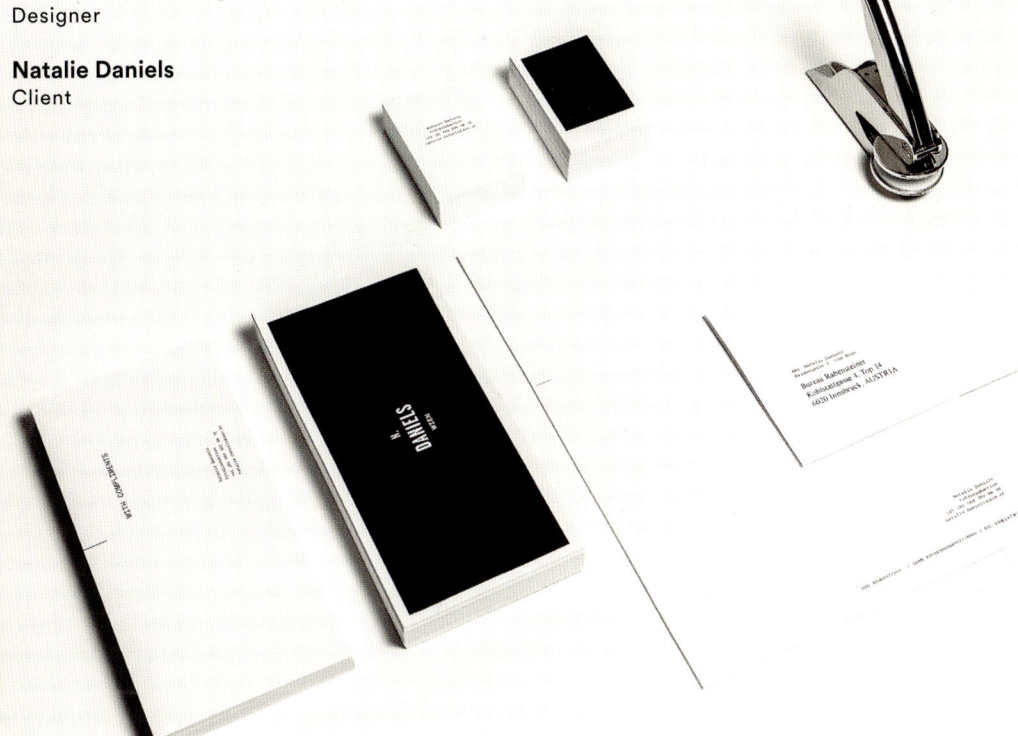

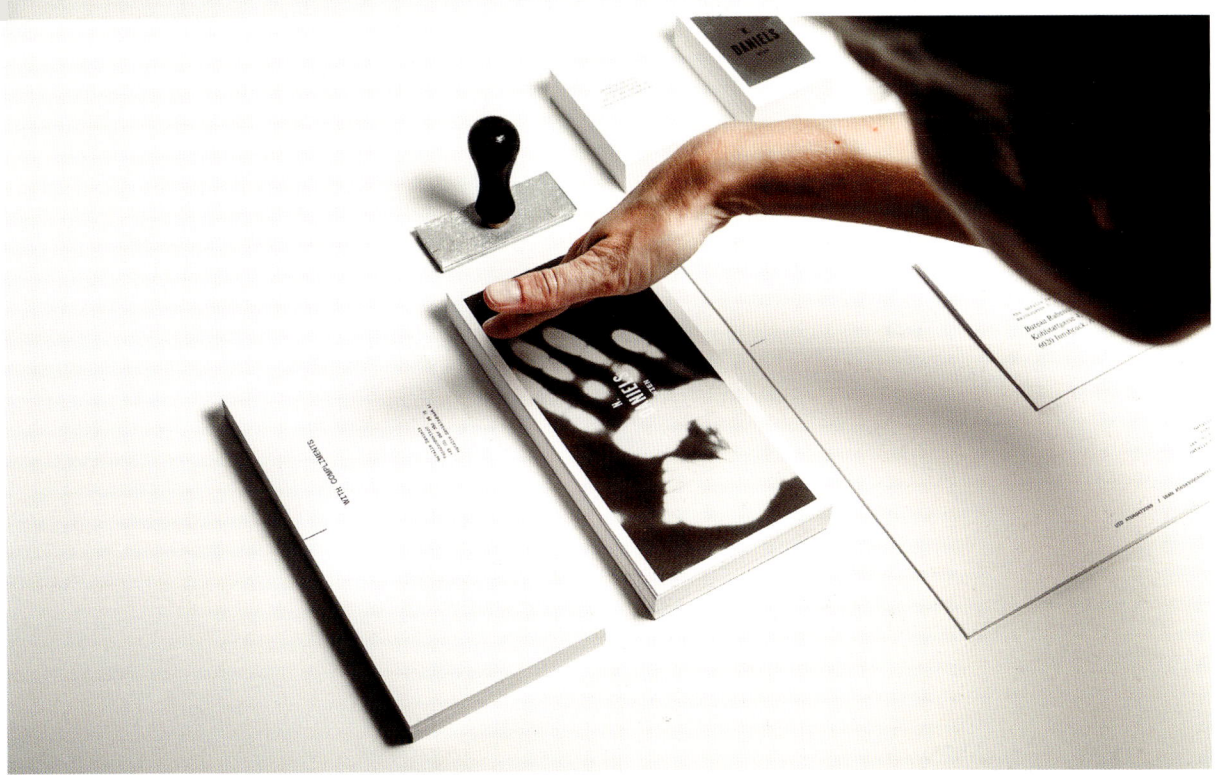

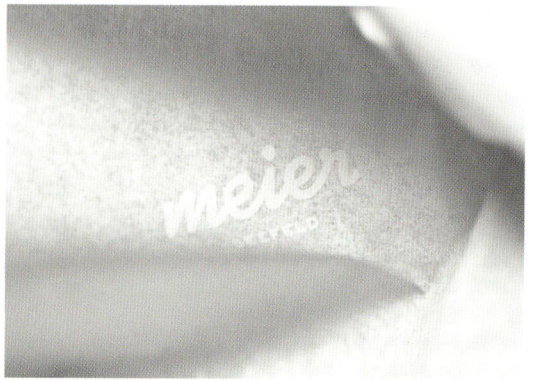

124

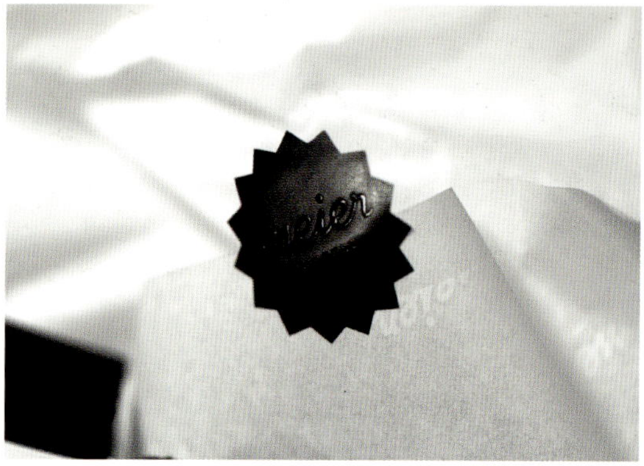

Meier Seefeld
Austria

Bureau Rabensteiner
Design Agency

Mike Rabensteiner
Art Director
& Photographer

Isabella Meischberger
Designer

Ernst Meier
Client

Meier Seefeld is a women clothing boutique. The black and white identity conveys understated luxury in a comfortable atmosphere to both visitors and locals. An extensive line of stationery was printed on high quality paper stock. The identity set covers the wrapping paper, shopping bags, folders for receipts, the signage and detailed accessories, such as postcards and individually produced portable light boxes for displays.

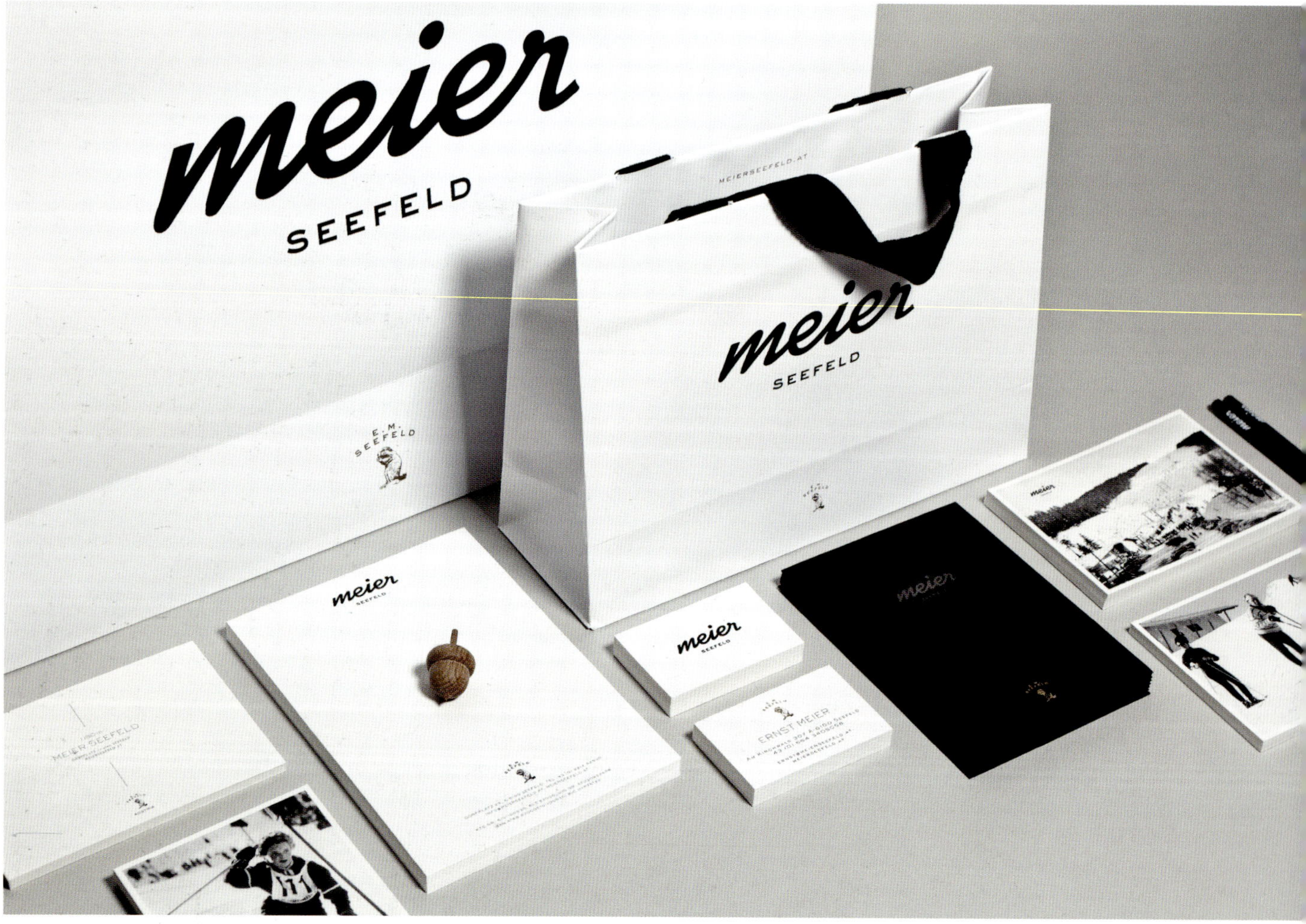

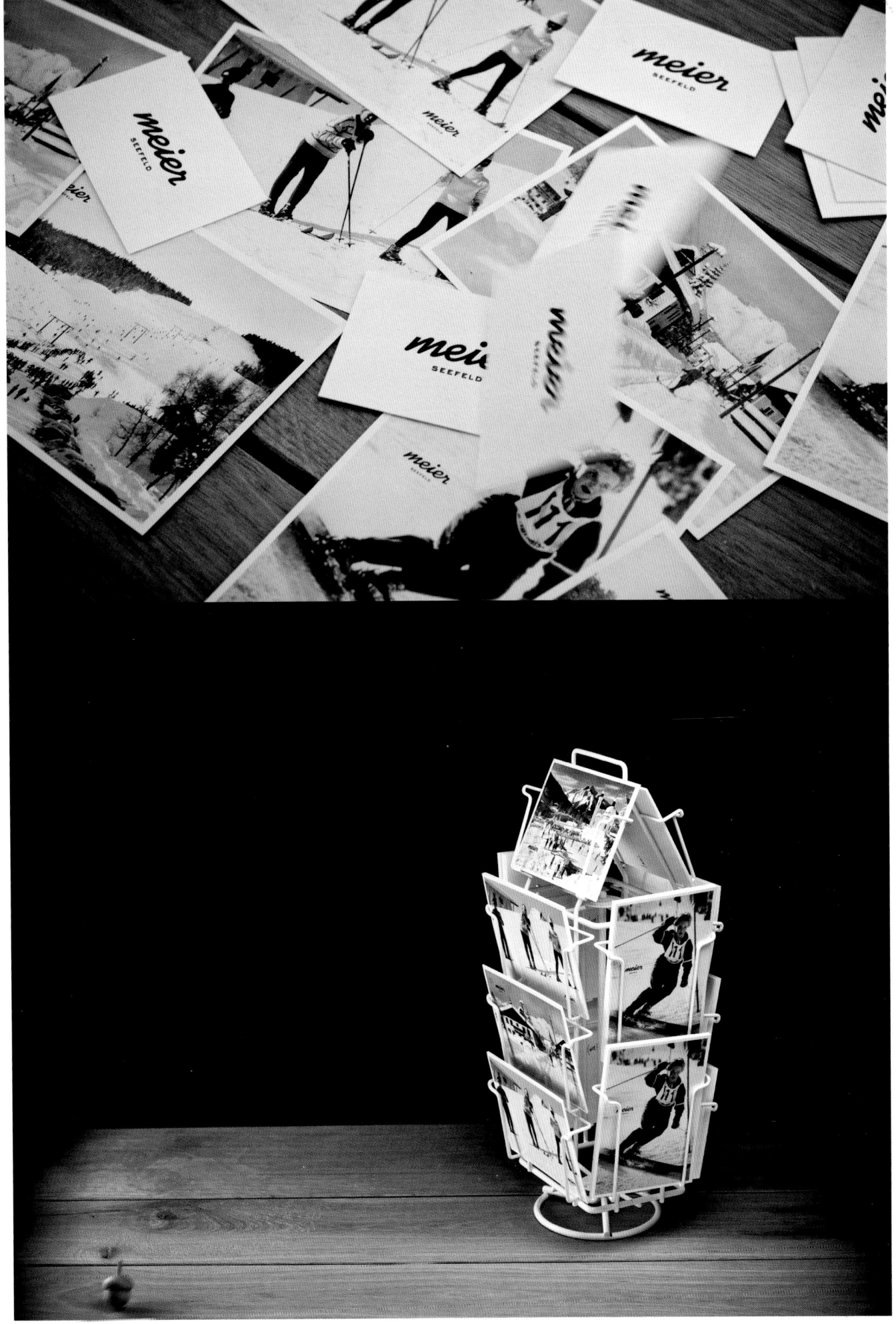

left.

Dirección
Línea de dirección simbólica #06
Col. Lorem ipsum dolor sit amet,
CP: 59687. Mx.

Teléfonos
Tel. 55 78063432
Tel. 55 78063413

Web
contacto@leftstore.com.mx
leftstore.com.mx

—

Left

Mexico

Icono Seis
Design Agency

**Sergio Vichique,
Adriana Monroy**
Designer

Left Store
Client

Left is a small casual clothing store and gallery in Mexico City. In the corporate identity, the black ink on white background emphasizes a contrast and provides a strong visual impact. The result is a clean and friendly identity that accurately represents the vision and character of the store without being dominant over the different brands that are sold in the store.

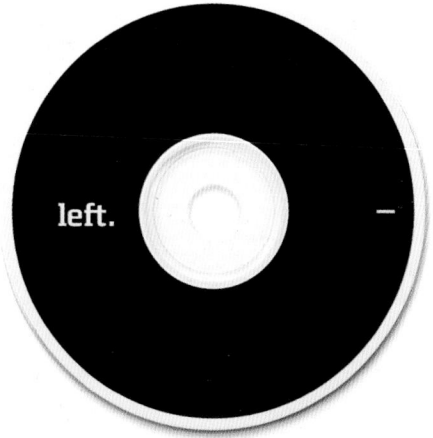

left. —

left Store
Línea de dirección simbólica #06
Col. Lorem ipsum dolor sit amet,
CP: 59687. Mx.
Tel. 556789012
Web. insthink.com

Manuel Nájera García
Gerente General
E-mail. manuel@leftstore.com.mx
Tel. 556789012
Cel. 044 5588679601

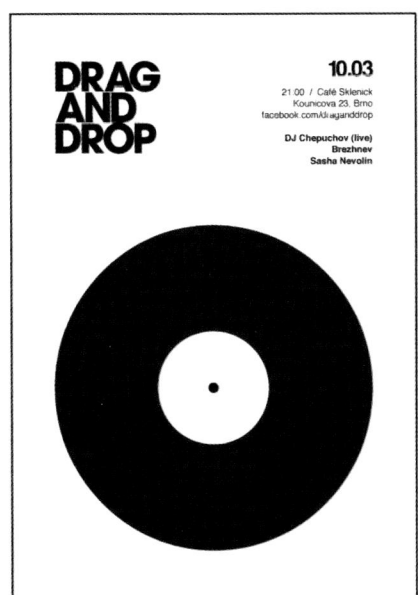

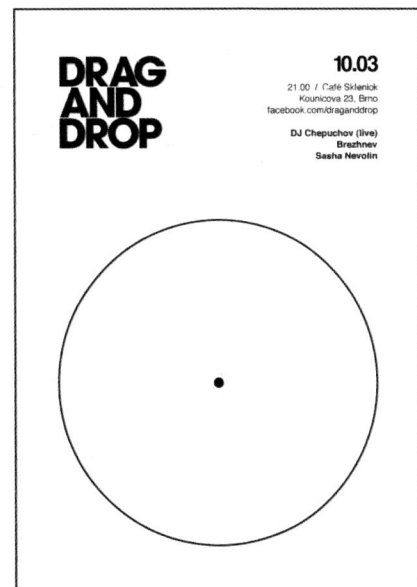

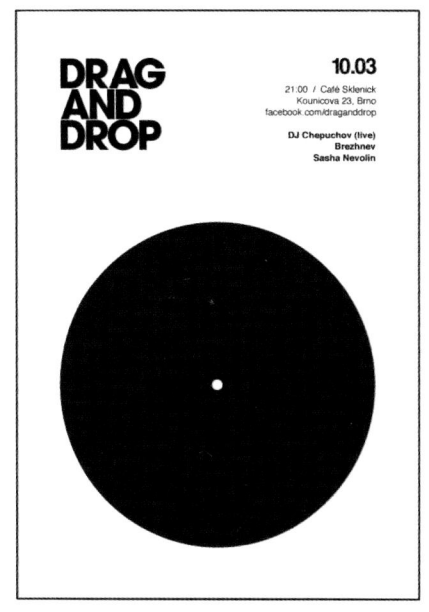

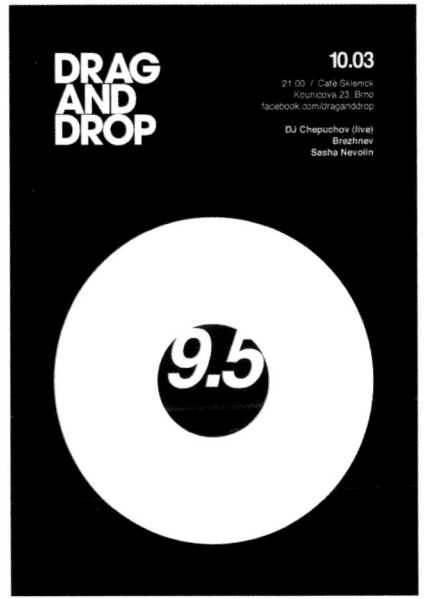

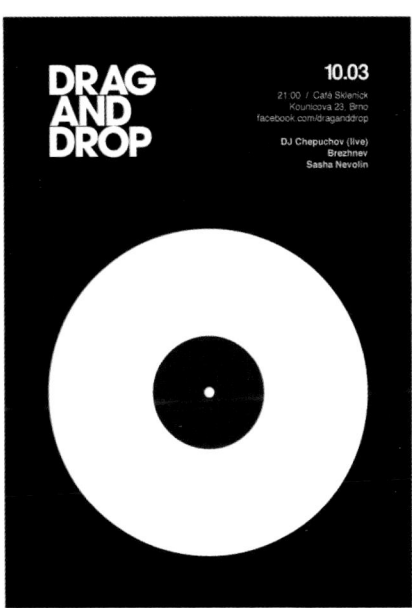

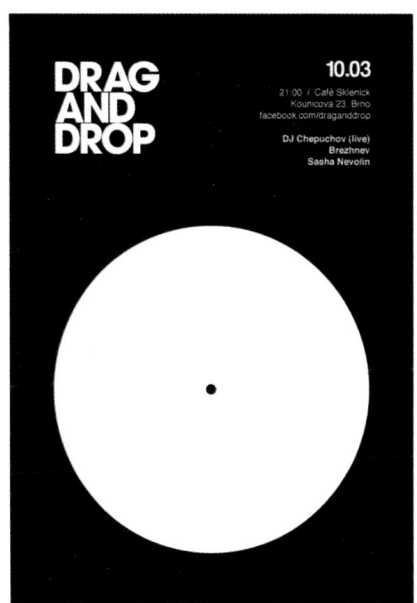

Drag and Drop
Czech Republic

Creasence
Design Agency

Alexander Nevolin
Creative Director

DRAG AND DROP
Client

Drag and Drop is a series of new electronic music events based in Prague, Czech Republic. The events have underground and minimal techno music format. The simple and minimalist design in black and white includes naming, brand identity, promotion, original promo posters and flyers.

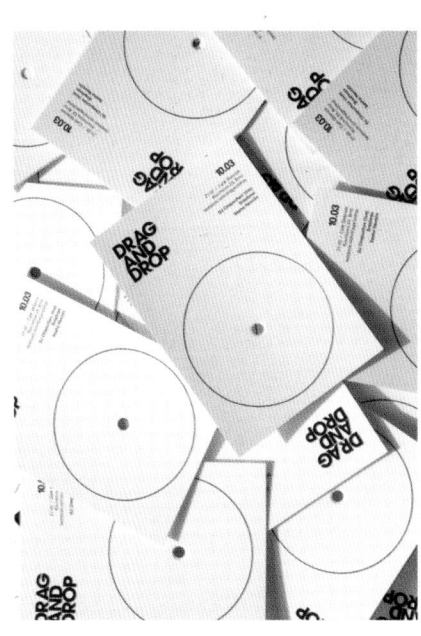

128

ruiz+company
Design Agency

David Ruiz
Creative Director

Ainhoa Nagore
Art Director

Trossos del Priorat
Client

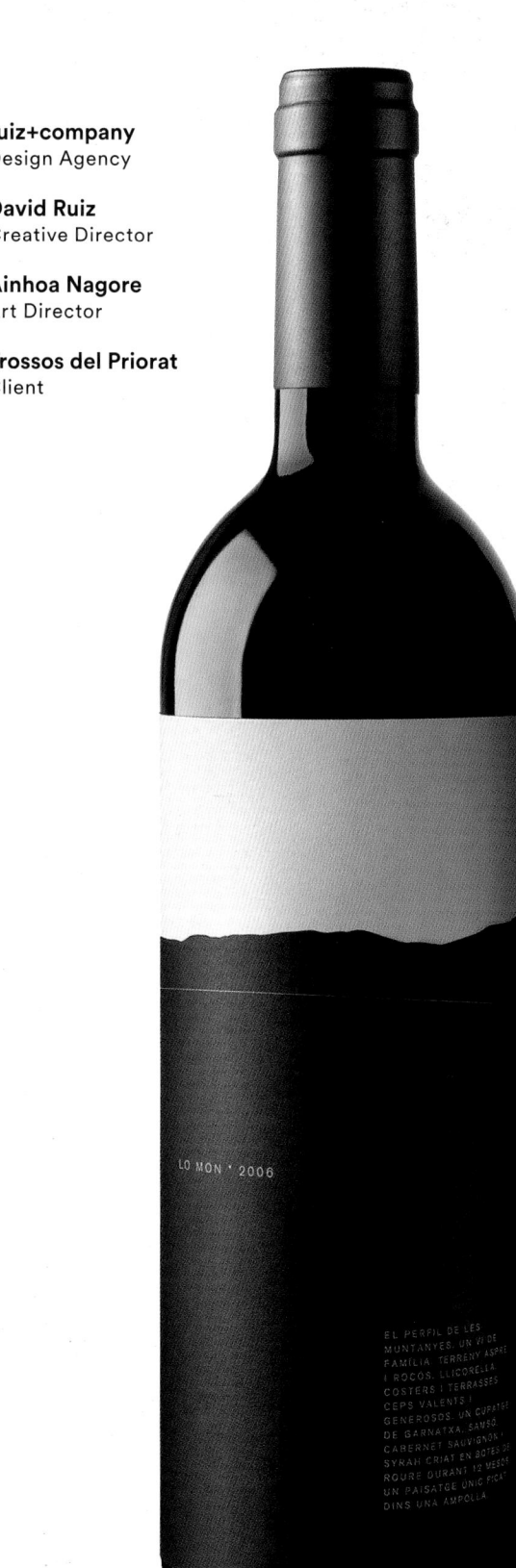

LO MON • 2006

EL PERFIL DE LES
MUNTANYES, UN VI DE
FAMÍLIA, TERRENY ASPRE
I ROCÓS, LLICORELLA
COSTERS I TERRASSES
CEPS VALENTS I
GENEROSOS, UN CUPATGE
DE GARNATXA, SAMSÓ,
CABERNET SAUVIGNON I
SYRAH CRIAT EN BOTES DE
ROURE DURANT 12 MESOS
UN PAISATGE ÚNIC FICAT
DINS UNA AMPOLLA

Lo Mon

Spain

Lo Mon is the first wine produced by the "Trossos del Priorat" winery. The main characteristic of wines from this area is the earth in which the vines are grown. That's why the "Lo Mon" label has broadened its format as much as possible, turning into a large landscape that wraps around the bottle. The front and back have been deconstructed, becoming a single label where the tasting notes take center stage. The use of color and typography is a departure from the codes normally used by the wine industry.

Skunk Anansie, Smashes & Trashes
United Kingdom

Shotopop
Design Agency

**Carin Standford
& Casper Franken**
Designers

Skunk Anansie
Client

The limited edition box set put all Skunk Anansie's history for their hardcore fans. Weighing in at almost 3kg, this little black box is packed with all kinds of goodies: 2 DVD's, 2 CD's, 4 Vinyls, 16 posters, 36 photo-cards, 9 panoramic cards and a 44 pages book. The color pallet is simple and elegant.

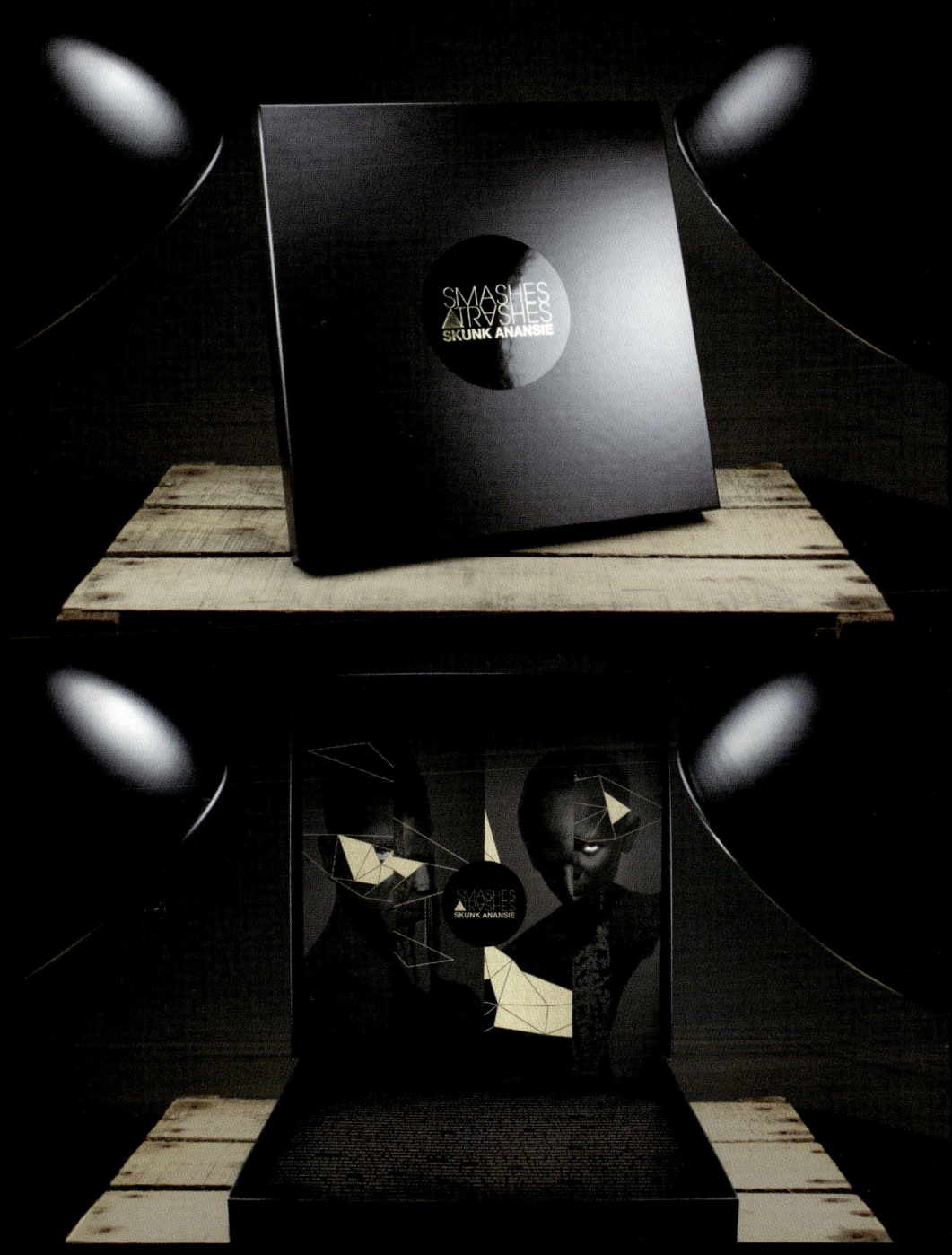

Simon Says
Hungary

Simon Says
Design Agency

José Simon
Designer

This project mainly focuses on making visual identities, building brands, coordinating and managing design and production processes. The name Simon Says came from classical children's game and also associated with the designer's name; the designer used black and white in the design to define his less is more attitude towards graphic design.

130

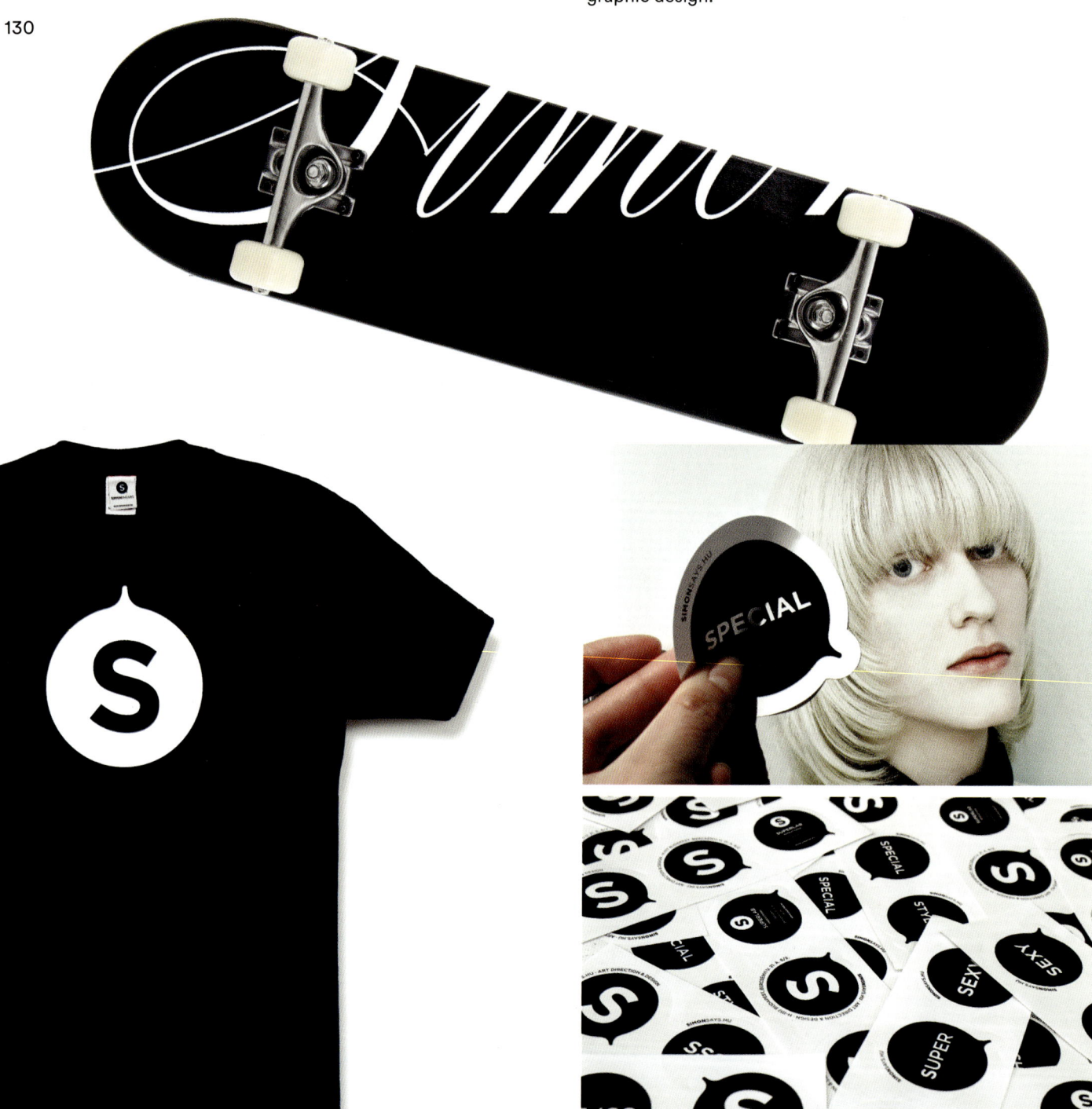

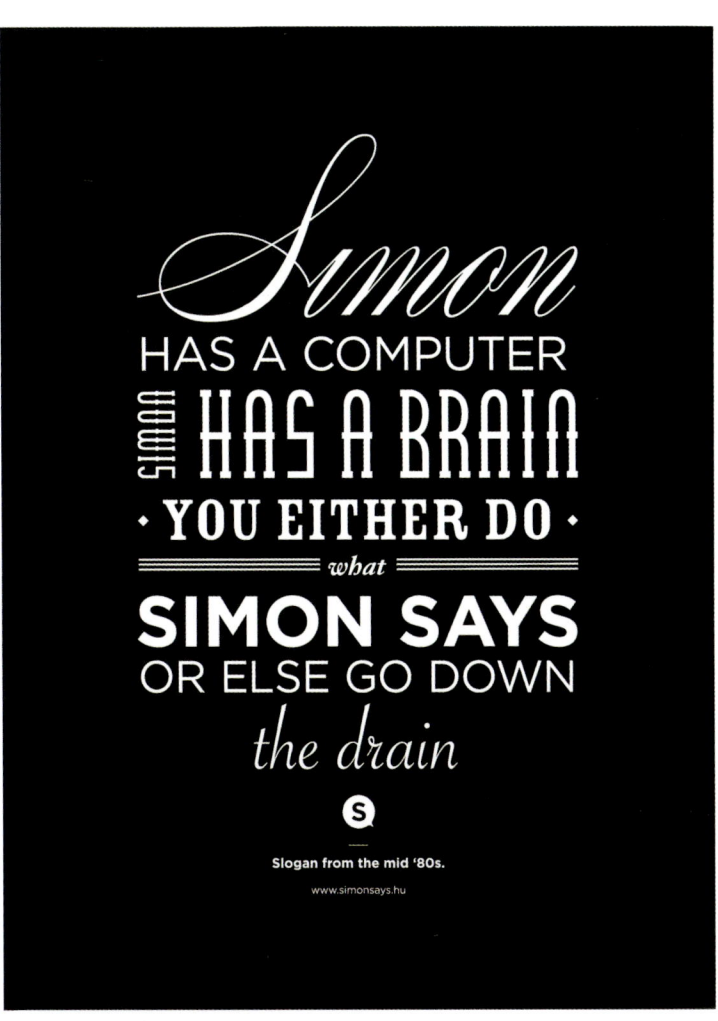

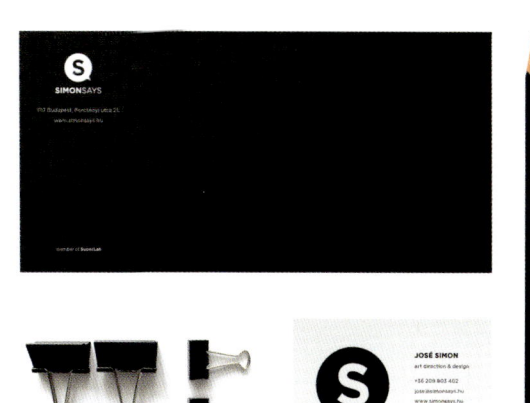

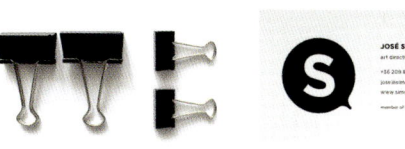

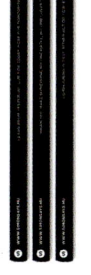

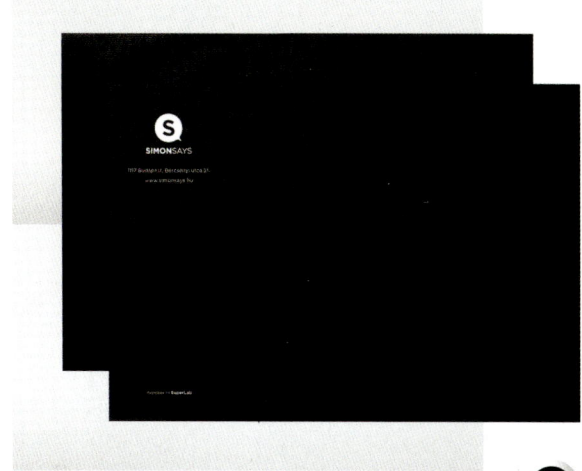

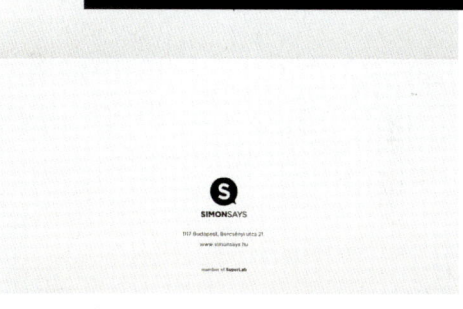

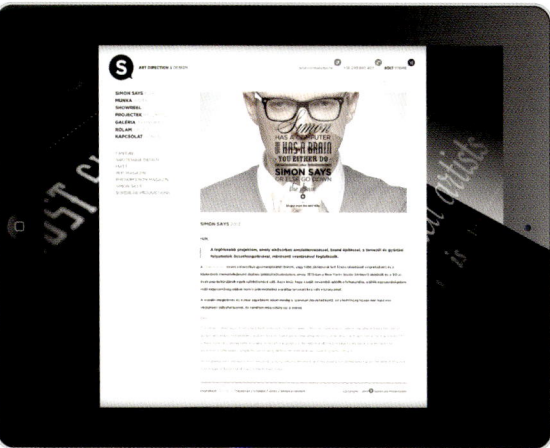

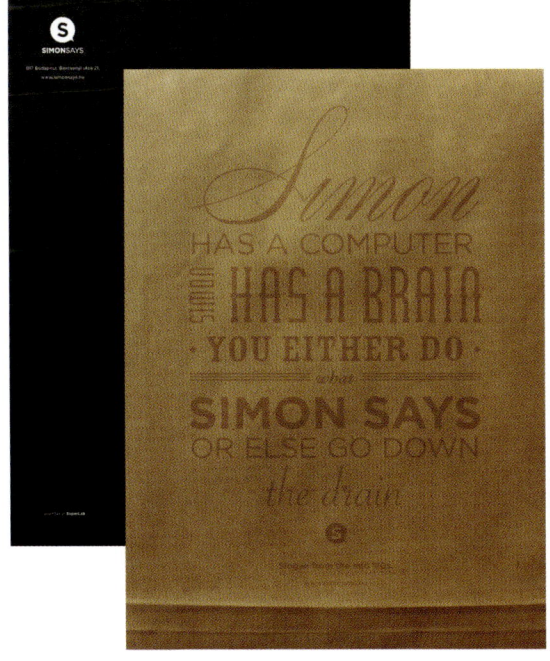

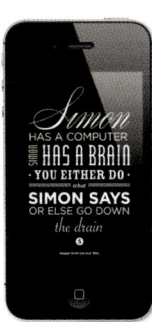

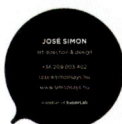

> *"Black and white is absolute – every other color is relative to them."*
> —Raphael Fritz (Pfeffersack & Soehne)

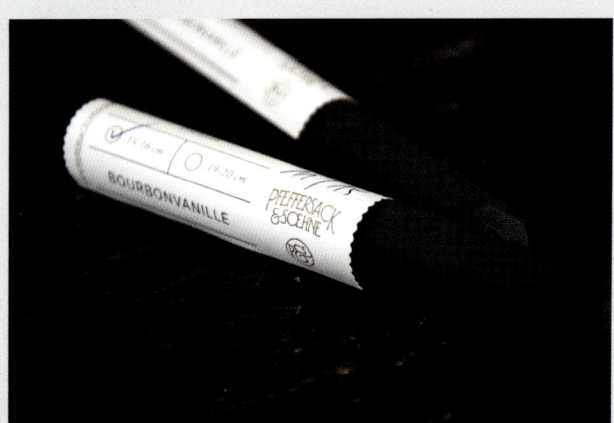

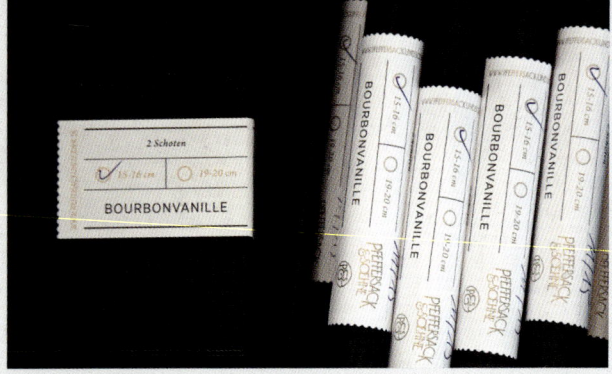

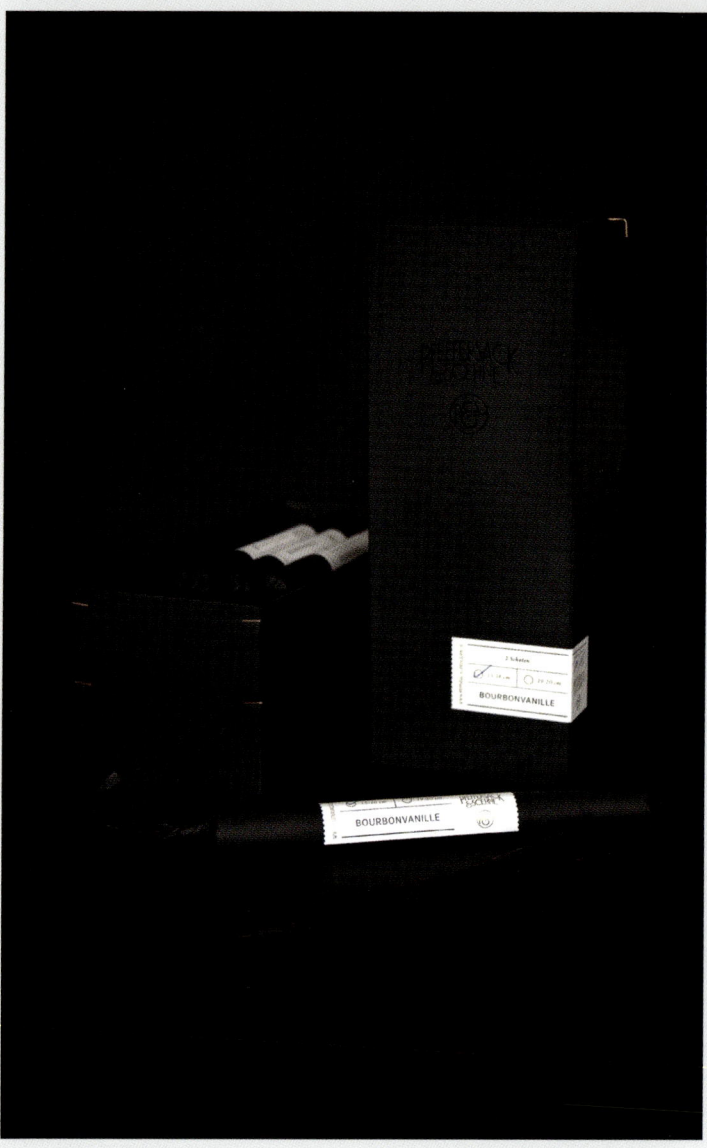

Pfeffersack & Soehne Vanilla Packaging
Germany

Pfeffersack & Soehne
Design Agency

**Raphael Fritz,
Christian Ganser,
Stefan Ternes,
Thomas Winkler**
Designer

Pfeffersack & Soehue
Client

The delicately packed spices achieve perfect flavor preservation. The discreet design has a timeless appeal, yet is humorously reminiscent of the old days, when Hanseatic spice traders were mocked "Pfeffersaecke". The premium vanilla from Madagascar in corked glass tubes ennobled with a black wrapping, featuring hand finished labels and a retail packaging made of stapled cardboard.

Omega Gi

United States

Thomas McNulty
Art Director

Tran Huynh
Designer

Omega SA
Client

Omega Gi is a line of skin care products. The
design creates a compelling packaging for its
retail markets and cohesive product extensions
with an in-store display. The clean lines and
color scheme manifest a feeling of serenity and
elegance.

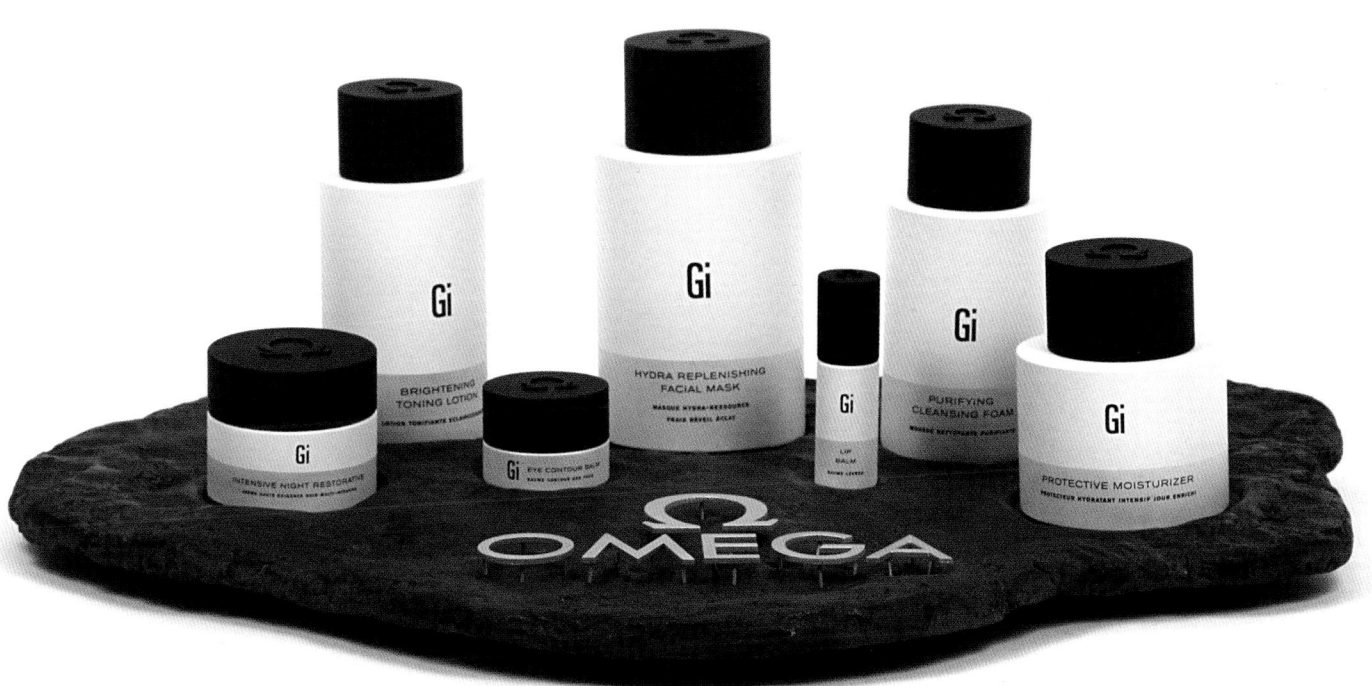

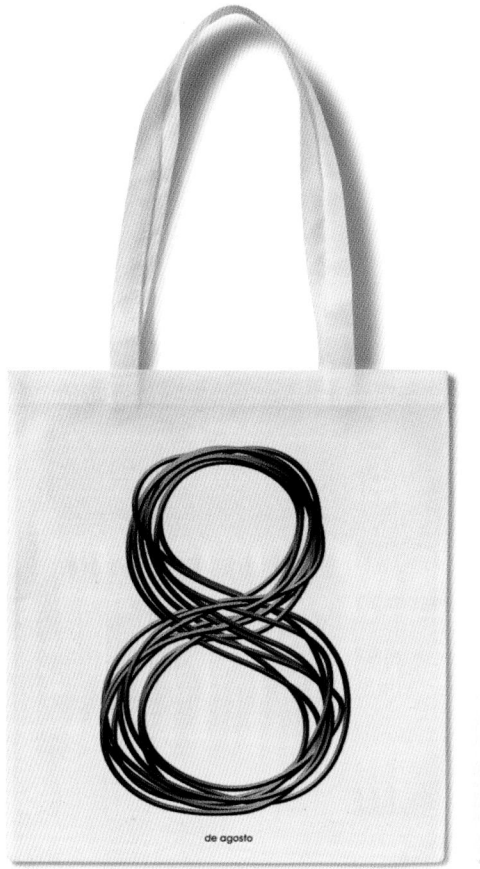
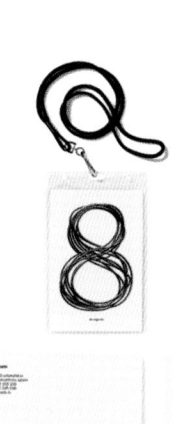

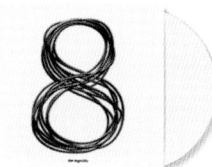
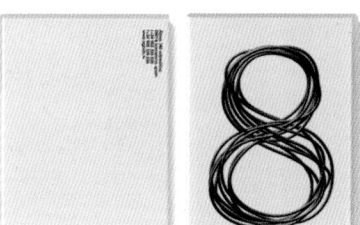

8 de agosto

Spain

ruiz+company
Design Agency

David Ruiz
Creative Director

Ainhoa Nagore
Art Director

Vicente Ruiz
Designer

8 de agosto
Client

A dynamic number eight created from multiple filaments as the symbol for "8 de agosto" (8 August), the new division of the production house, Agosto, specializing in animation and motion graphics. Its abstract, almost unreal treatment makes it resemble the symbol for infinity and brings it closer to Agosto's world of experimentation.

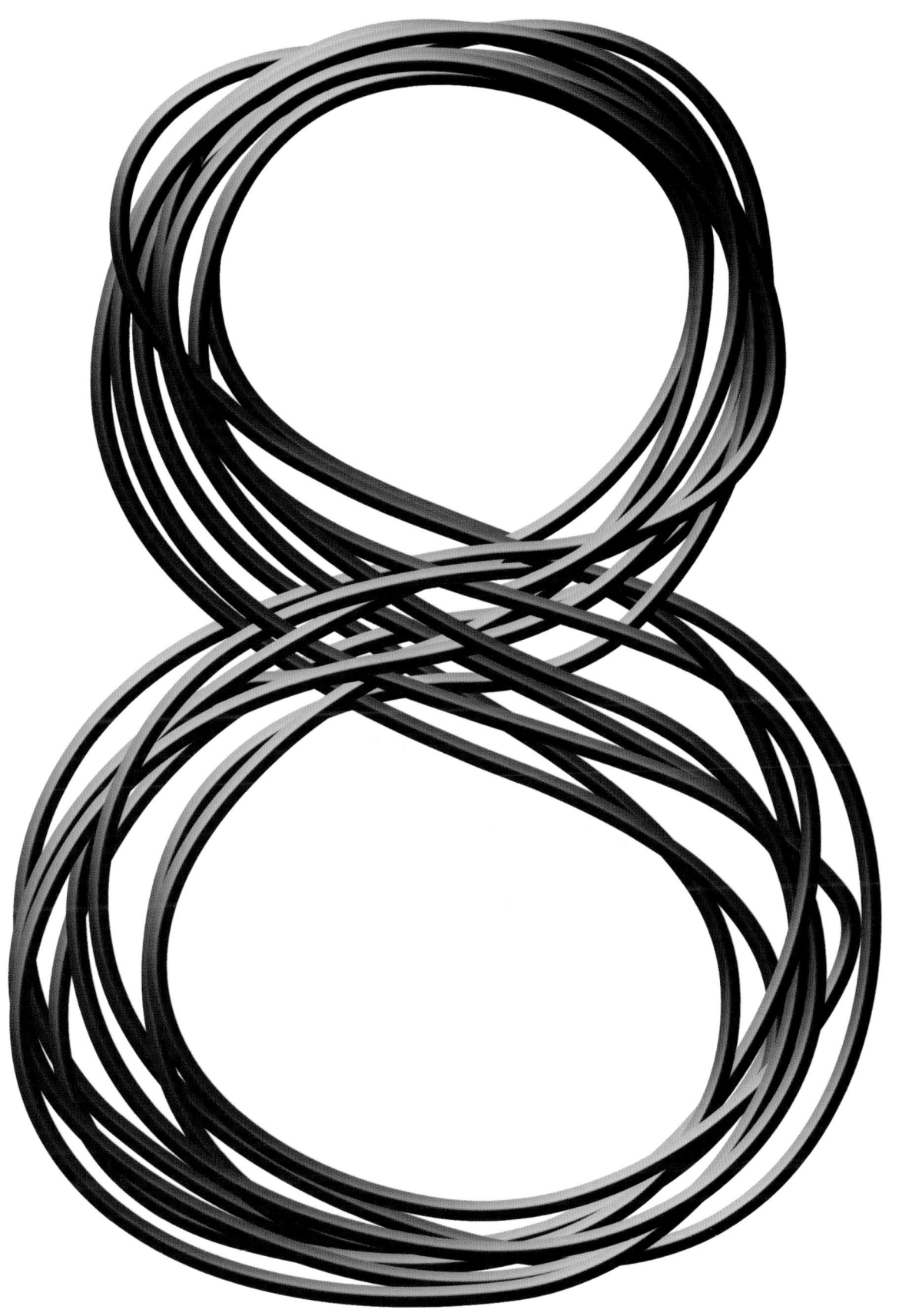

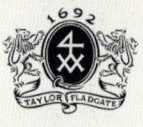

TAYLOR'S²¹ PORT WINE

ABCDEFGHI
JKLMNOPQ
RSTUVWXYZ

Taylor's 21 Port Wine
Portugal

MAAN Design Studio
Design Agency

Vitor Claro
Designer

The typography and the correspondent communication code system in black and white was created for Taylor's 21's new products that seek to attract a new generation of consumers in defining a new way of looking at Port Wine.

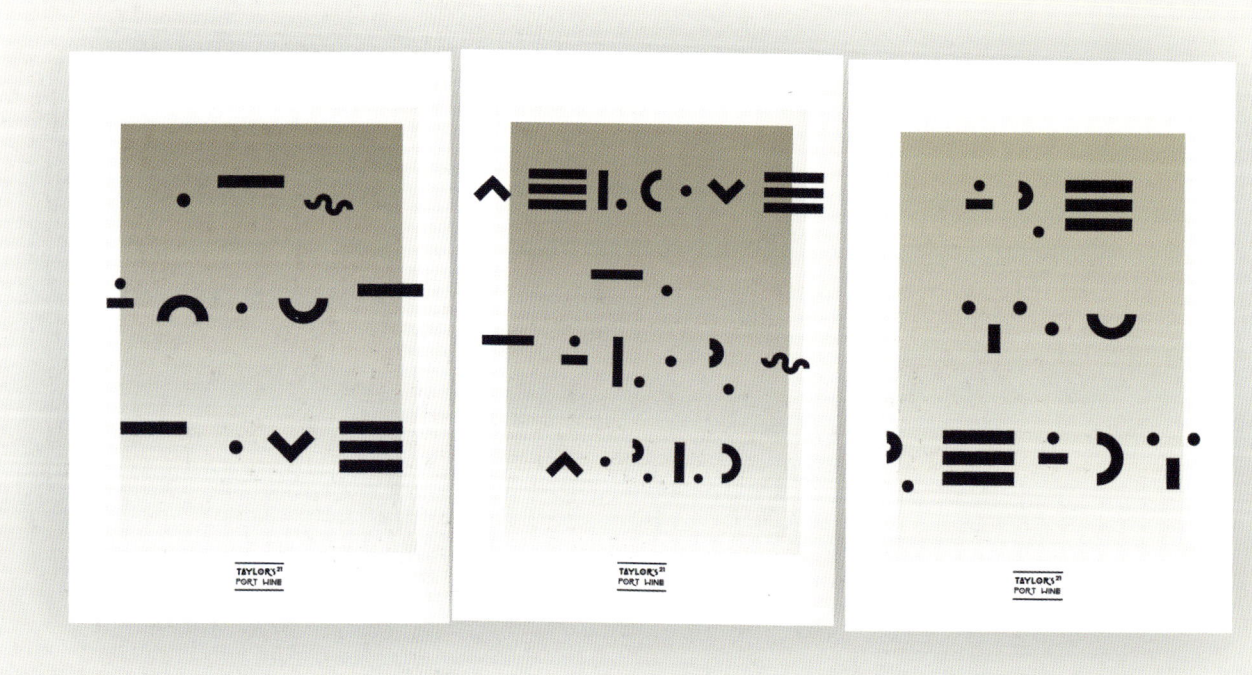

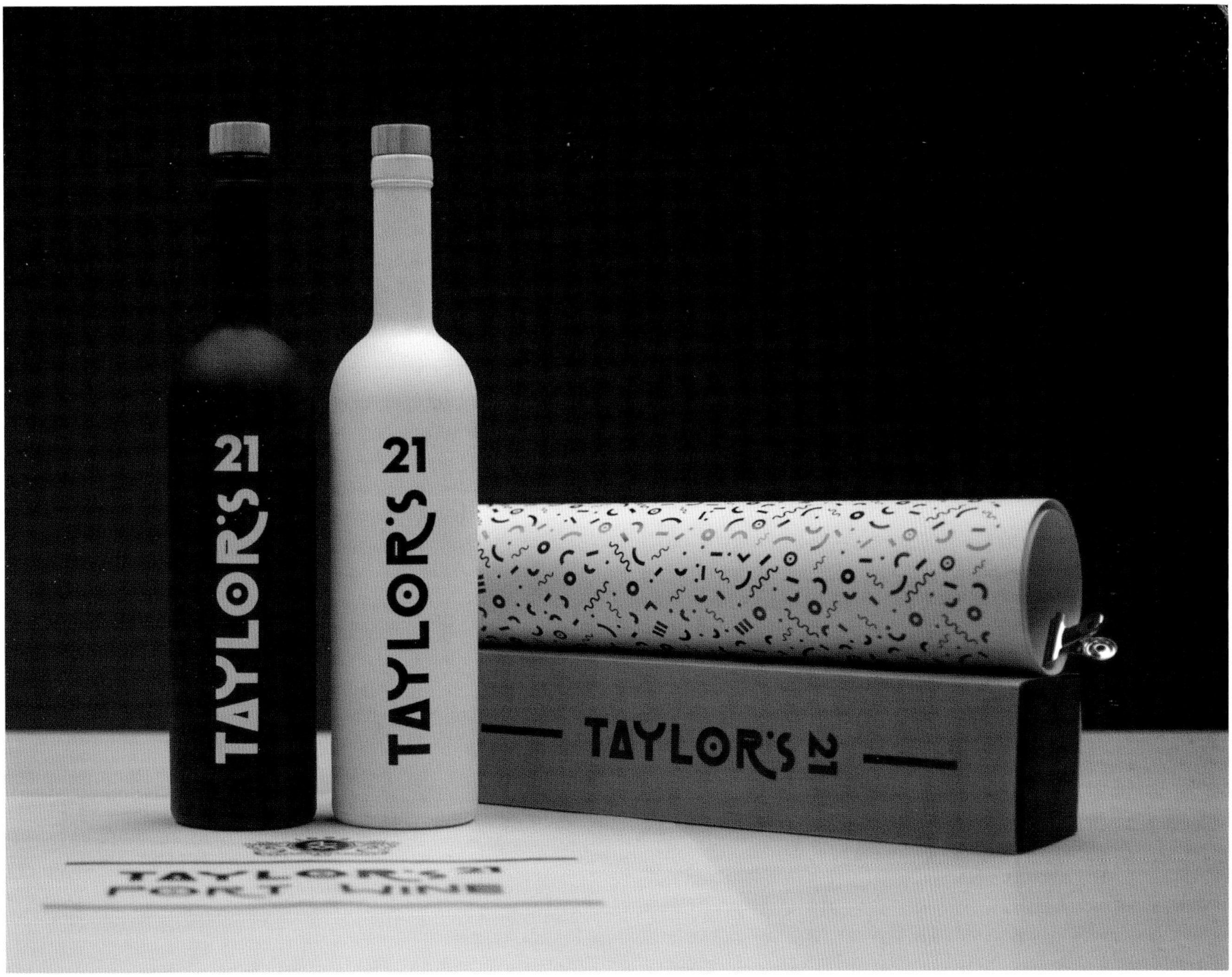

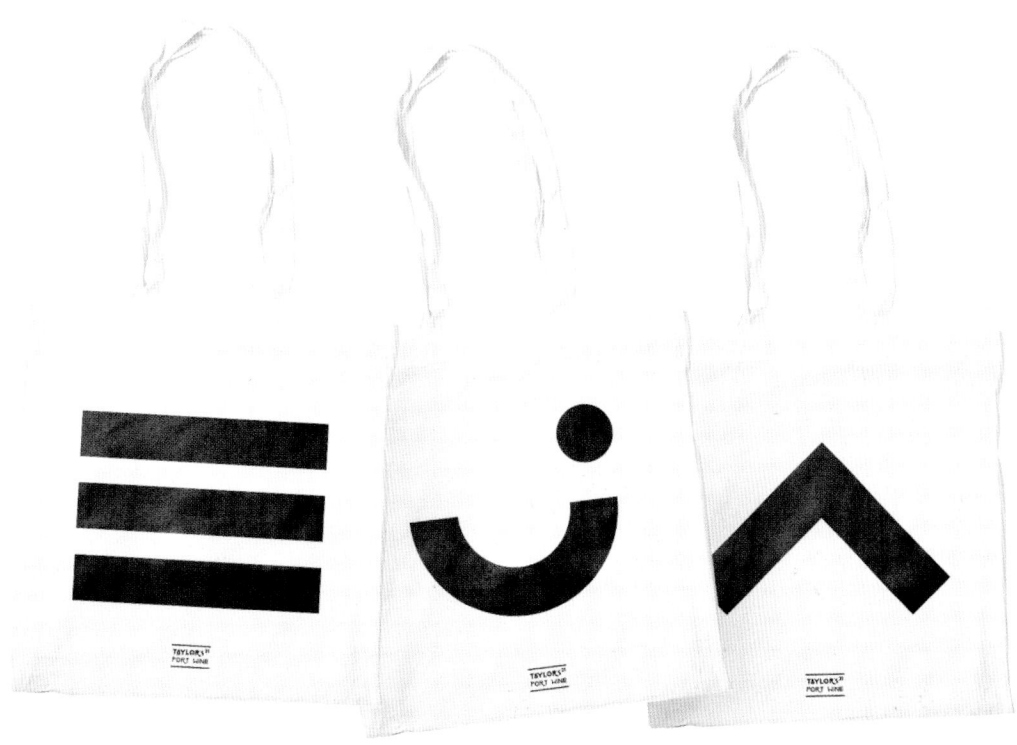

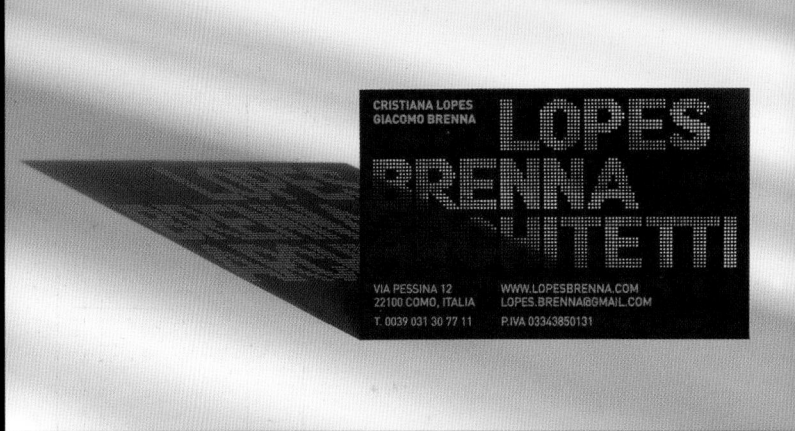

Lopes Brenna Architetti
Business Card

Portugal

**FEB Design &
FIBA Design**
Design Agency
& Photographer

**Marta Fragata,
Miguel Batista**
Designers

Lopes Brenna Architetti
Client

The business card design for Lopes Brenna Architetti stands out with its high contrast between black and white and the effect of light coming through the laser cut, which creates a stereoscopic feel that echoes the architecture theme.

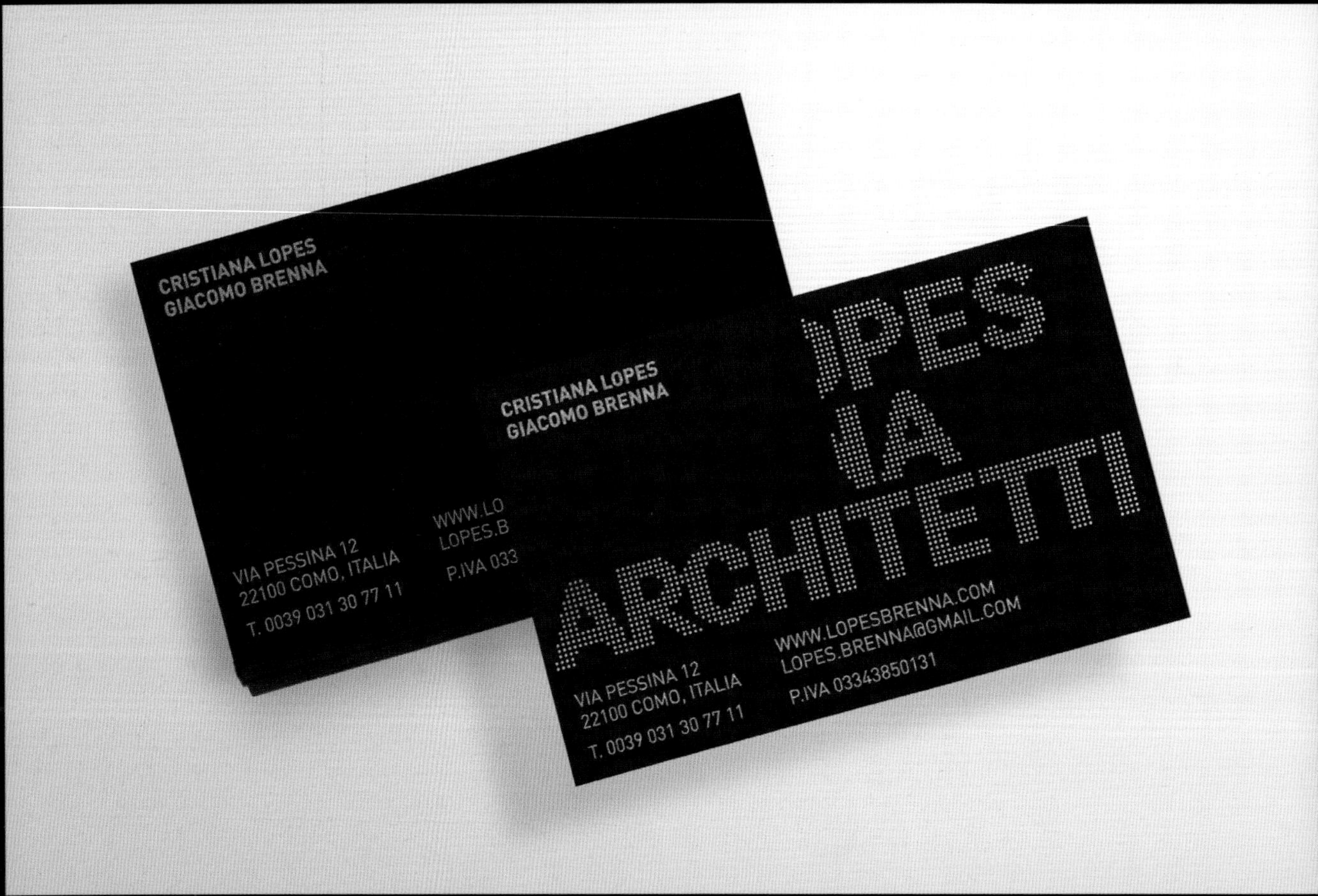

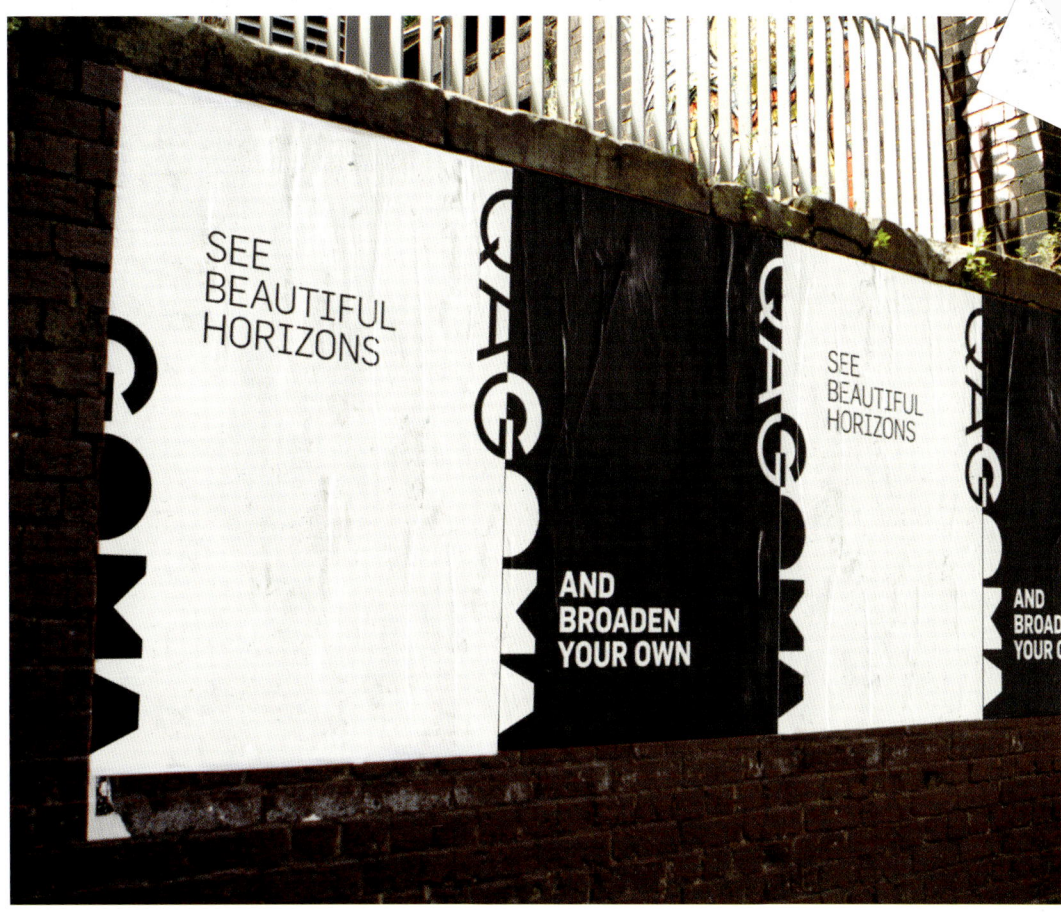

QAGOMA
Australia

Interbrand
Design Agency

**Eric Ng,
Charl Laubscher,
Drew Coughlin,
Sue Mould,
Diana Chirilas**
Designers

**Queensland Art
Gallery, Gallery of
Modern Art**
Client

The challenge was to reposition the two sites: the Queensland Art Gallery (QAG) and Gallery of Modern Art (GOMA) into a single QAGOMA brand. Inspired by the Chinese Yin Yang philosophy, the designers created a strikingly simple visual and verbal system that pulls the two brands together while celebrates their differences. The Yin Yang concept indicates a black and white approach. This color choice plays up the differences between the two galleries, while the typographic style and two weights of the same font hint their similar origin.

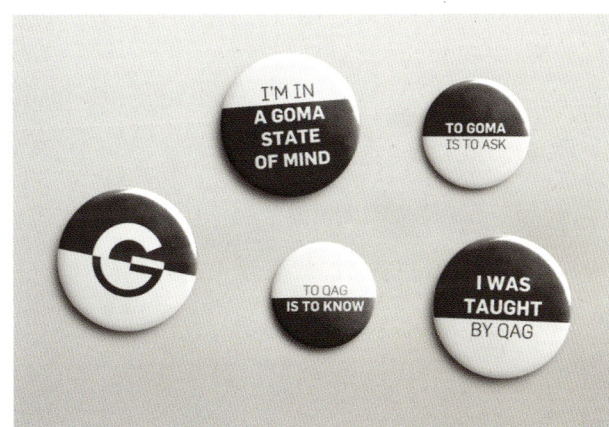

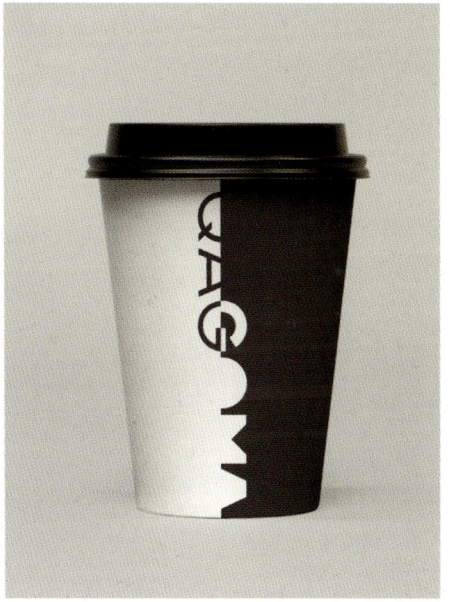

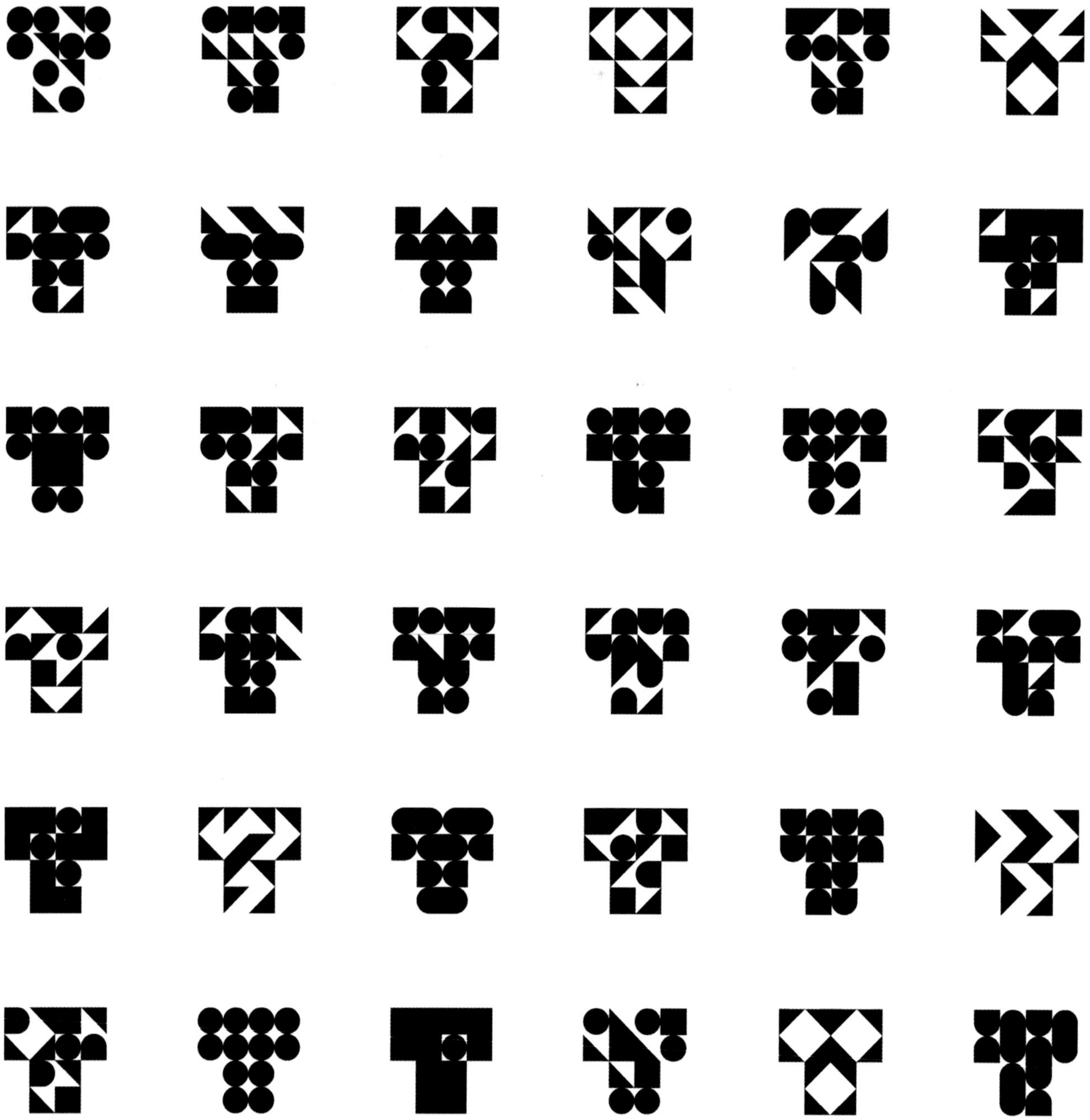

T-Platforms
Russia

Tomatdesign
Design Agency

Andrey Tarakanov
Creative Director

**Denis Bashev,
Marina Vlasova,
Anton Krivulya**
Designers

T-Platforms
Client

The cluster system is a base for any supercomputer, and it also became the basic idea for a logo, forming letter "T". Resembling computer languages, the module of the logo has four basic geometric figures in a free order, thus generating unlimited variations of the logo to relate to the brand's image of a high-end IT company.

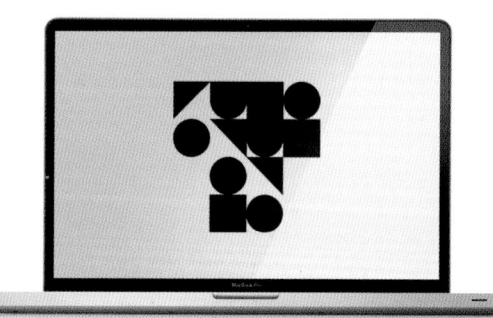

www.tomatdesign.ru

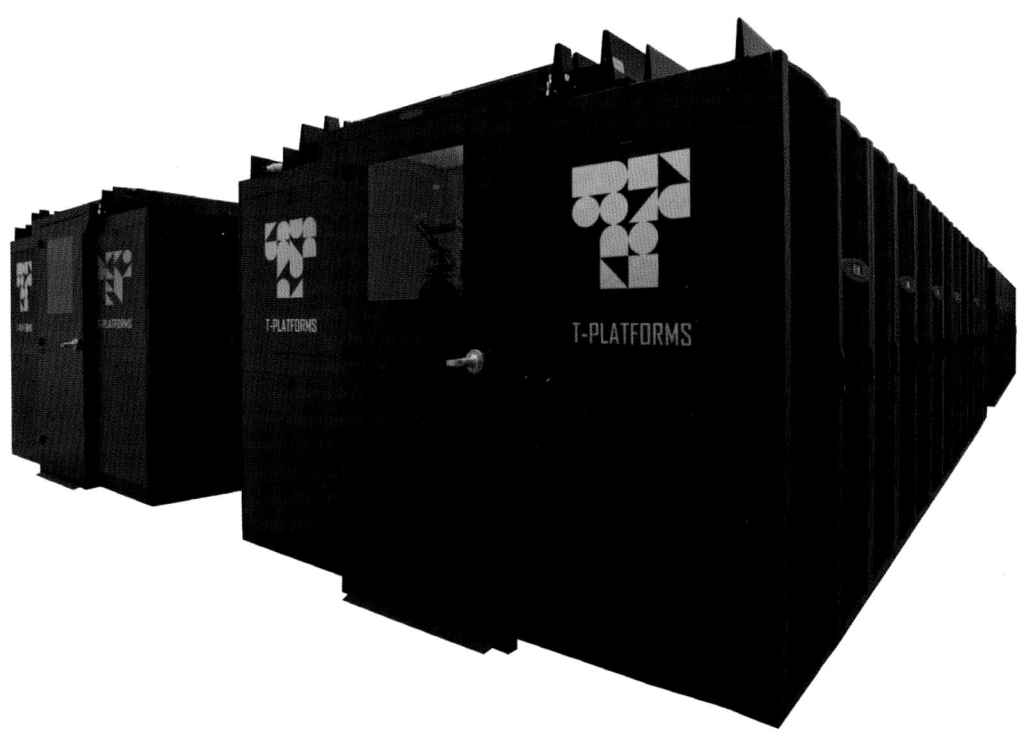

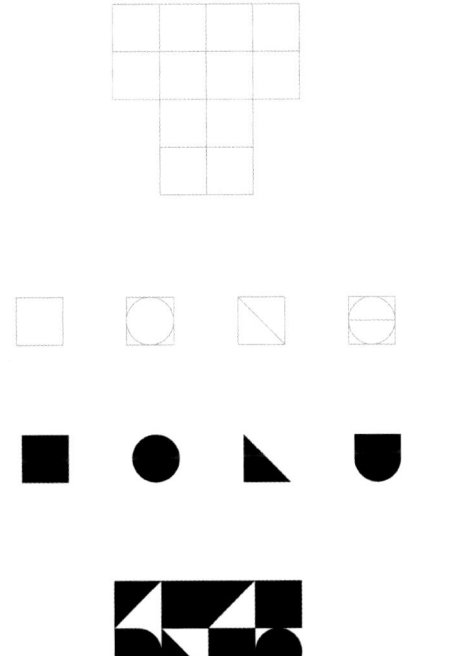

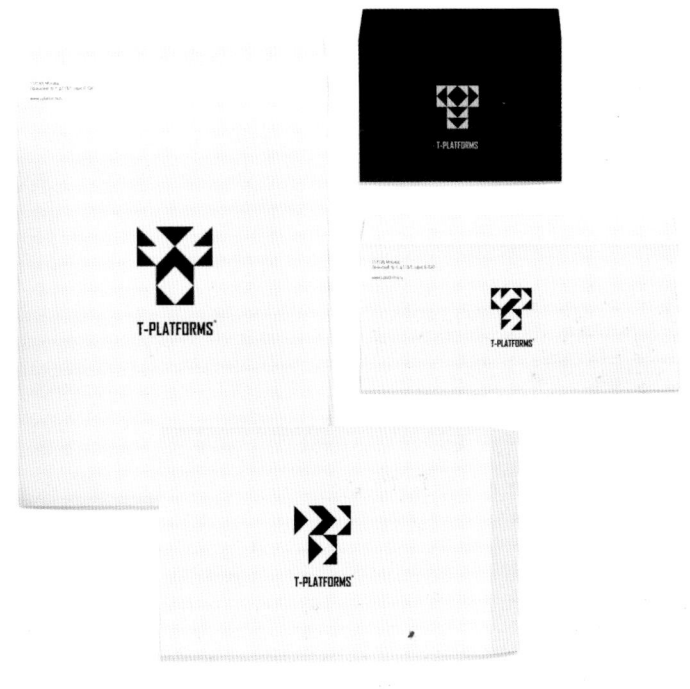

$$10^{12}$$

**ДЕСЯТЬ ТРИЛЛИОНОВ
ВАРИАНТОВ ЗНАКА**

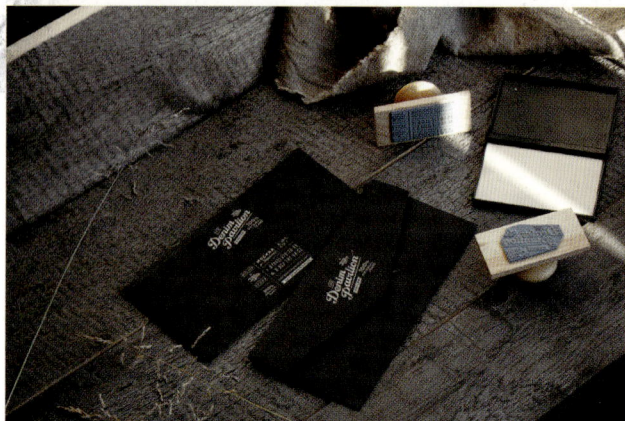
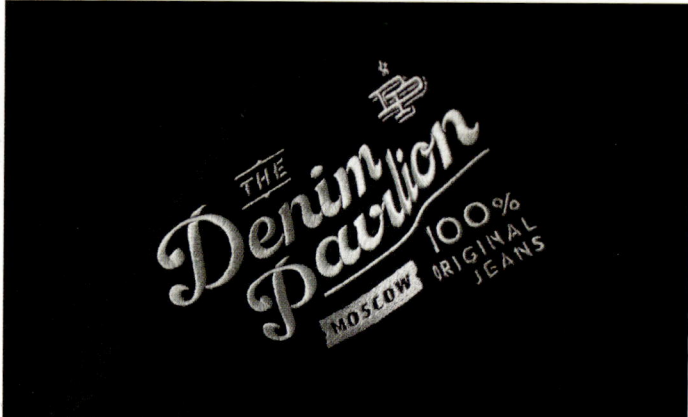

142

Denim Pavilion
Russia

Eskimo design studio
Design Agency

Emelyanov Pavel
Designer

Denim Pavilion
Client

For online jeans store Denim Pavilion that sells only quality original jeans from the USA and Japan, an identity based on typography and careful selection of materials came to life. The color choice was inspired by the styles of the jeans while the black textures paper resembles jeans texture. The wood color associated with the materials creates a more natural effect.

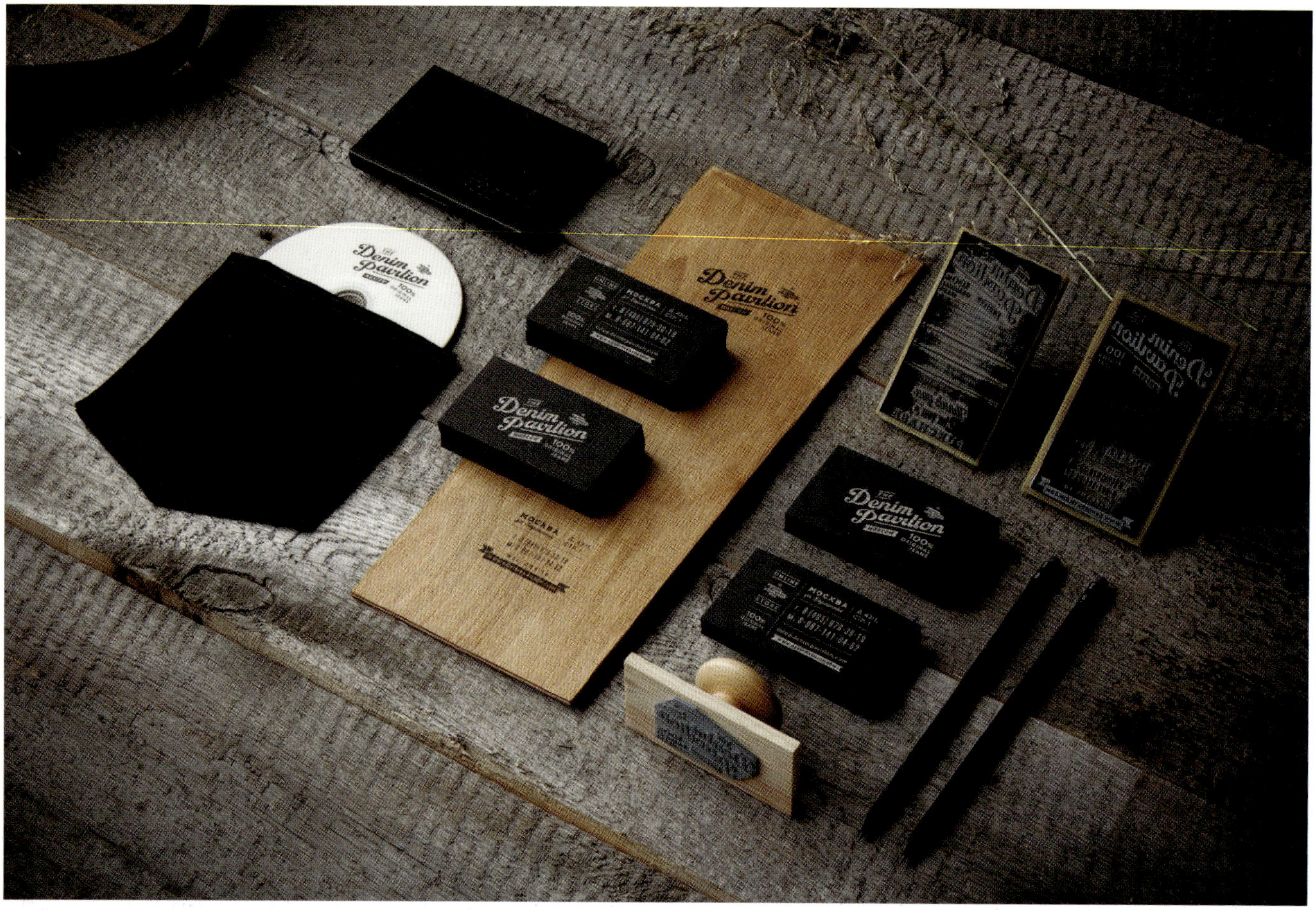

*"Black and white is such a dependable combination
that it takes discipline not to let it become a shtick."*
—Karen Huang (Manic Design)

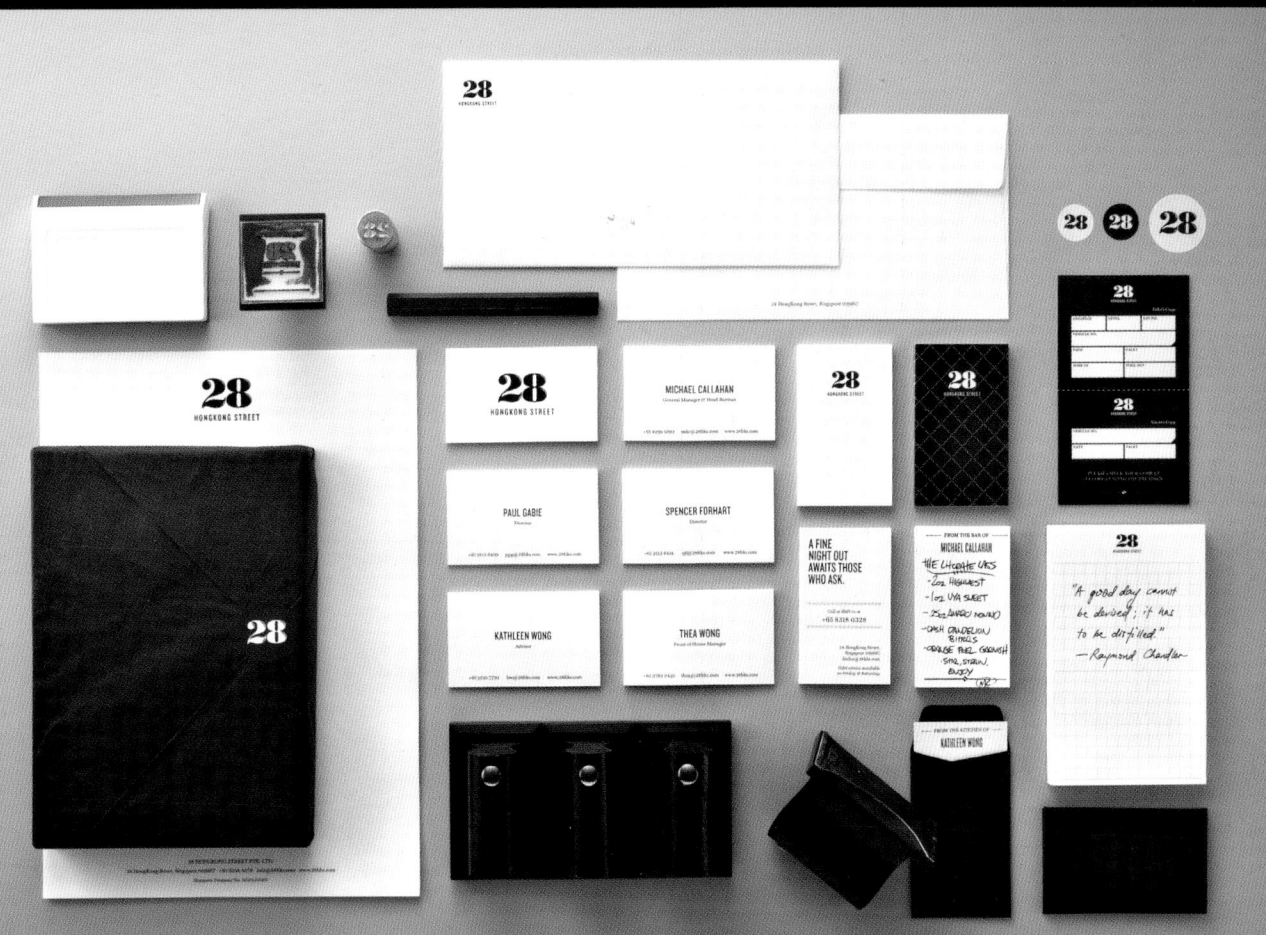

> *"If black is the darkest and white the brightest,
> then gray would be everything in between."*
> —Leon Dijkstra (Cooee)

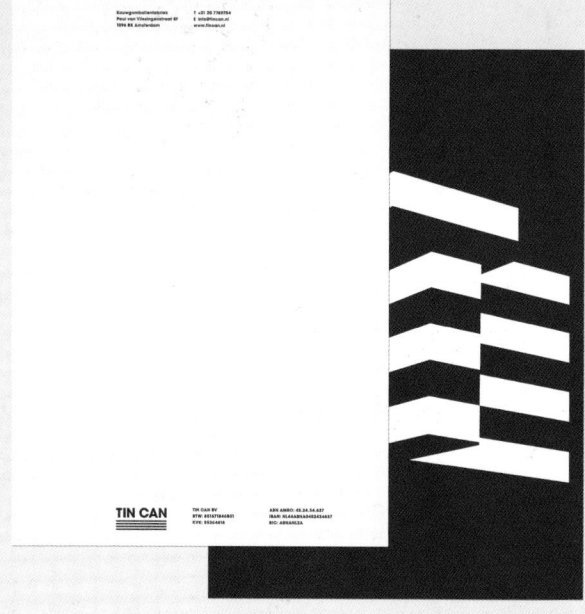
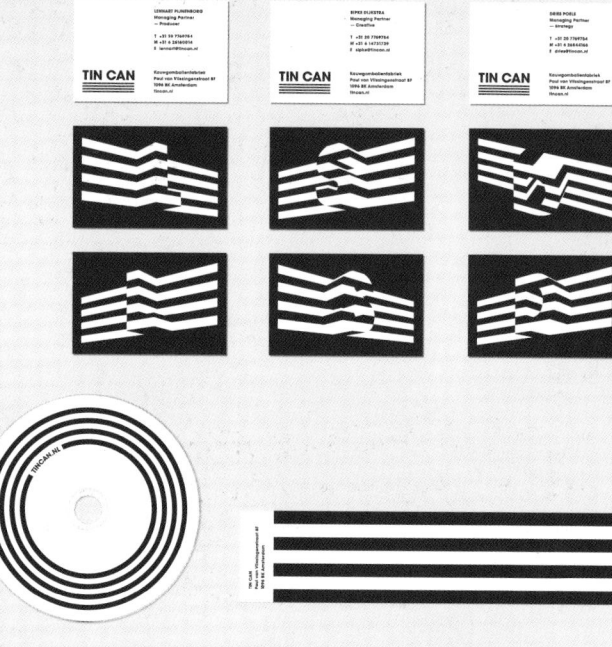
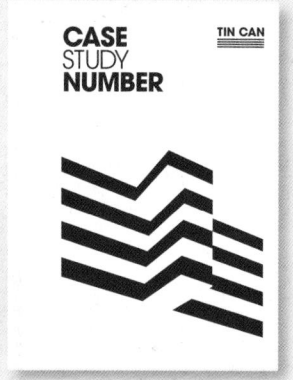
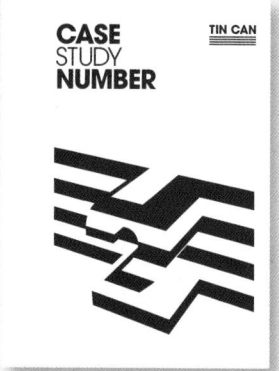
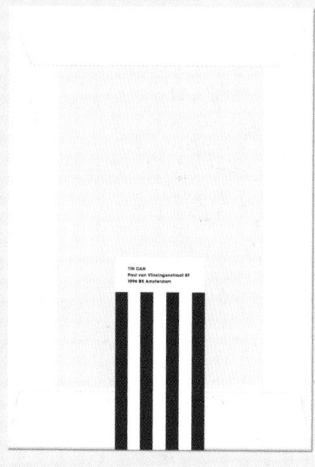
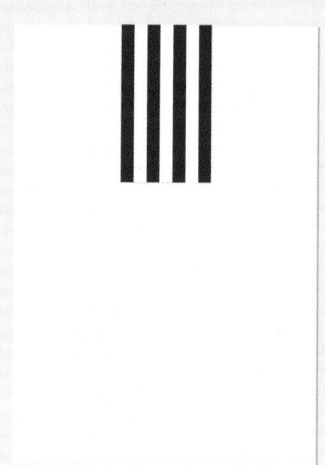

TIN CAN
The Netherlands

COOEE
Design Agency

Leon Dijkstra
Designer

TIN CAN
Client

Tin Can is a Dutch production company that focuses on the development and production of formats in the field of television, branding, online promotion and events. The entire identity consists of two basic elements that constitute the logo, namely a basic typography and four basic lines. Each line refers to one of the four disciplines of their profession. The refined gray lines are the main 'format' for the entire identity and are adaptable to different types of content and applications.

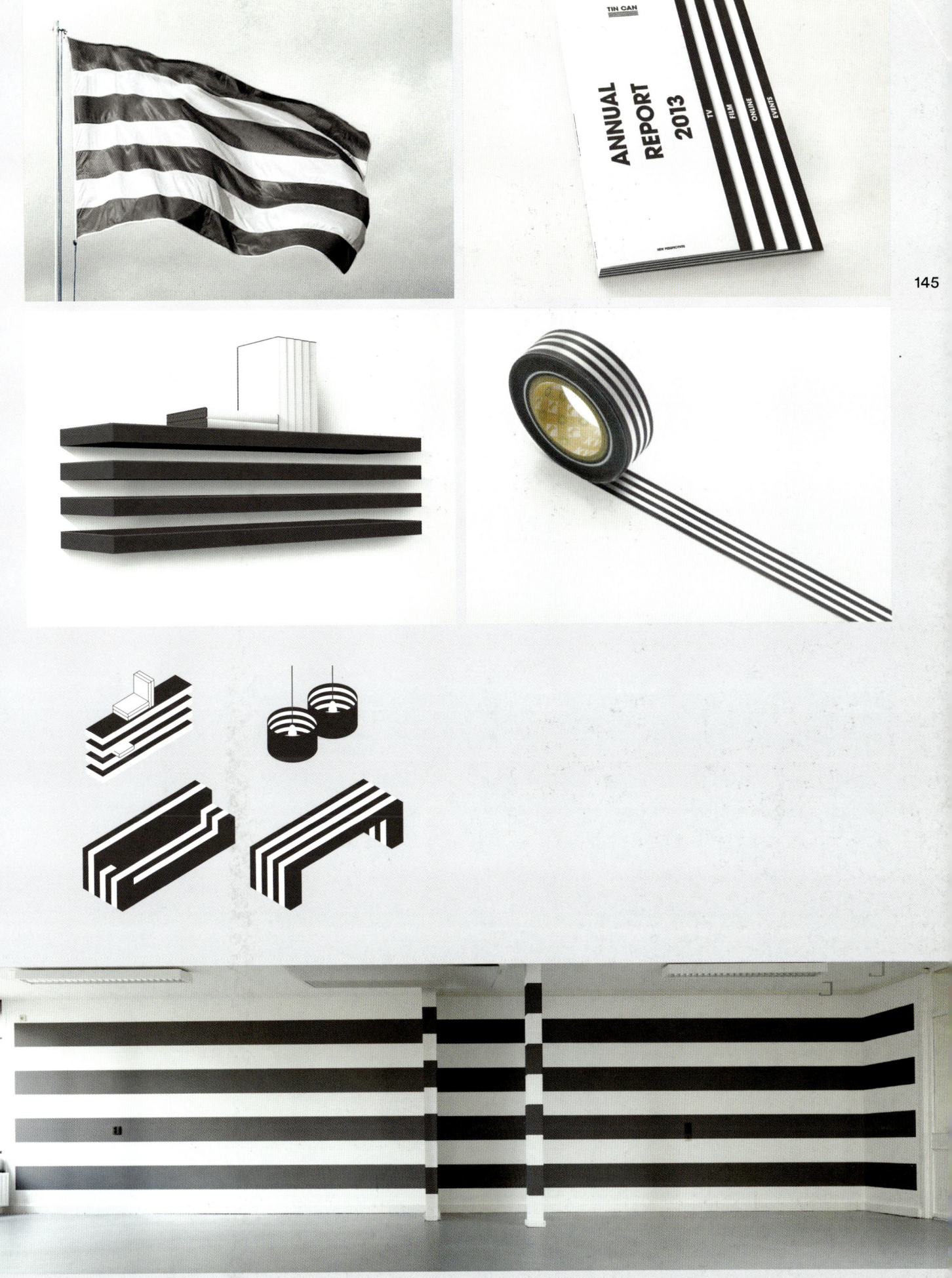

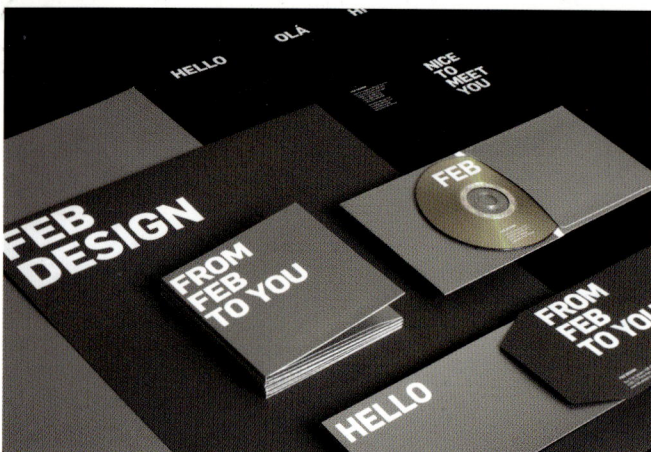 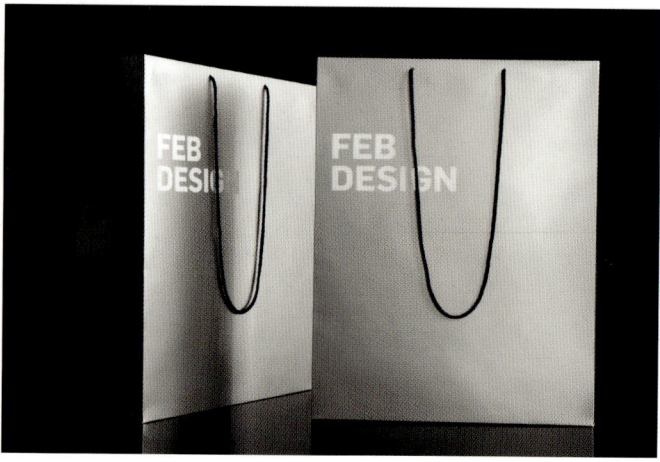

FEB Design
Portugal

**FEB Design
& FIBA Design**
Design Agency
& Photographer

**Marta Fragata,
Miguel Batista**
Designers

This is the identity for FEB Design that exemplifies the cohesiveness in design and how different materials in different sizes with different functions can go well together. The media becomes the message and the central character of this project. The tone of the selected sentences reflects the close relationship between the studio and their clients.

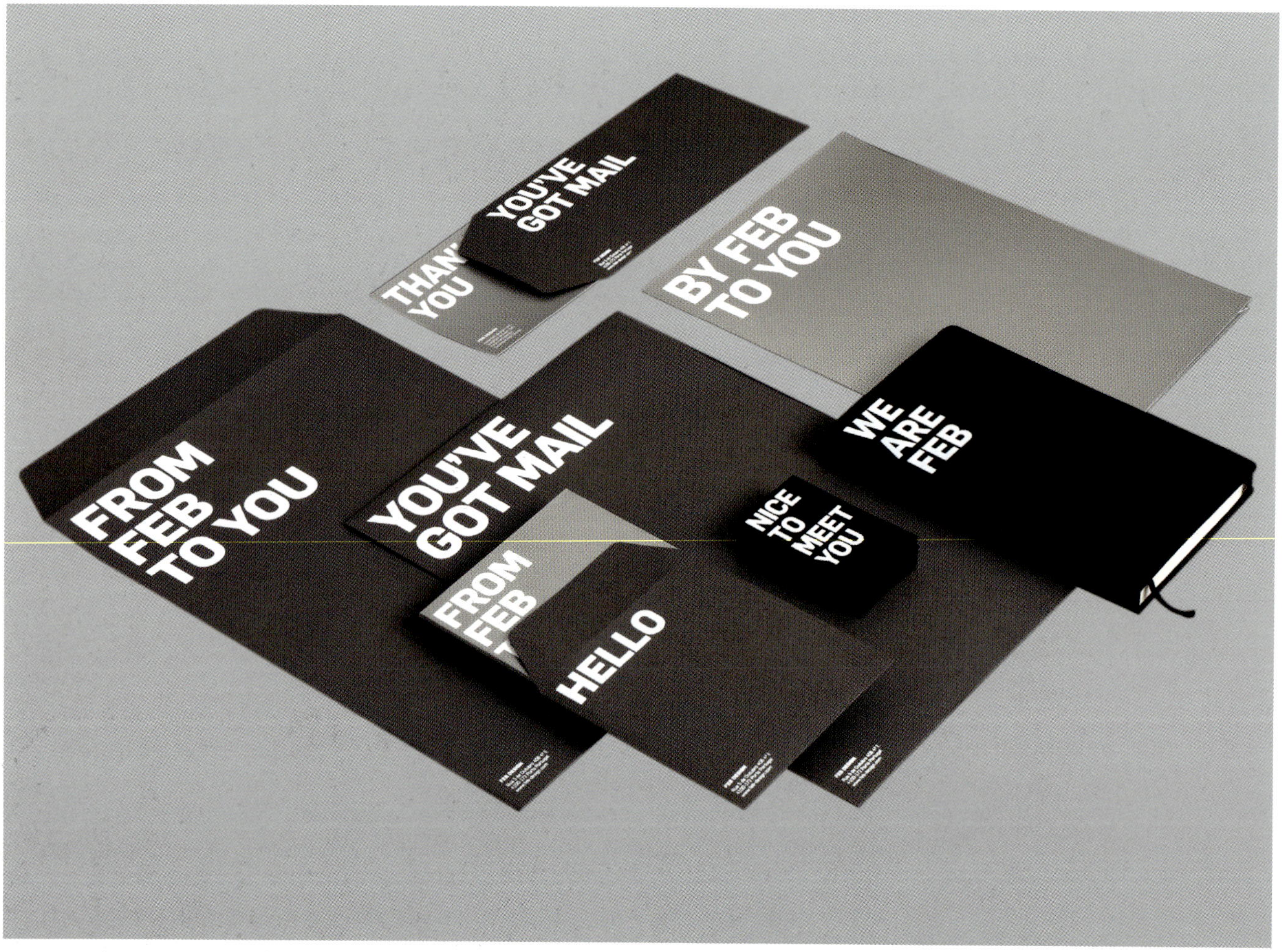

www.feb-design.com   www.fibadesign.com

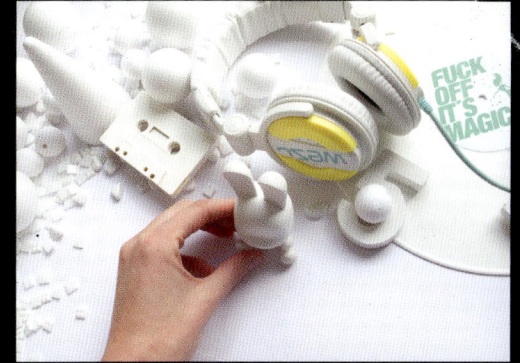

Hell.yes!

Every Thursday & Saturday

DÜSSELDORF // WWW.D-3001.DE   3001

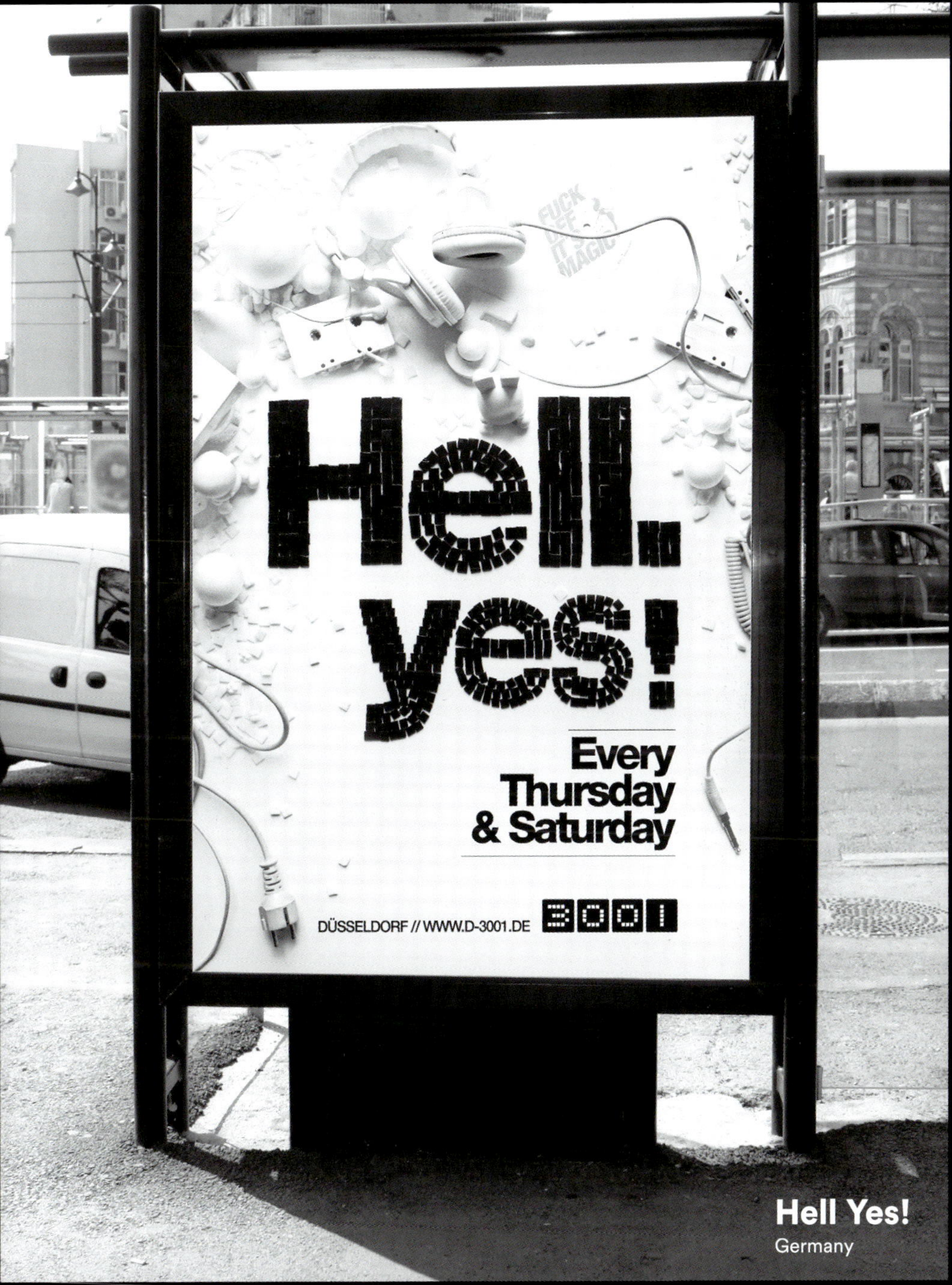

Hell Yes!
Germany

Denise Franke
Designer & Photographer

3001, Düsseldorf
Client

Hell Yes! is a poster campaign for 3001, a club for electronic music in Düsseldorf, Germany. The use of black and white narrows the design down to the basics, emphasizing the stark contrast between night and day, light and darkness in a club.

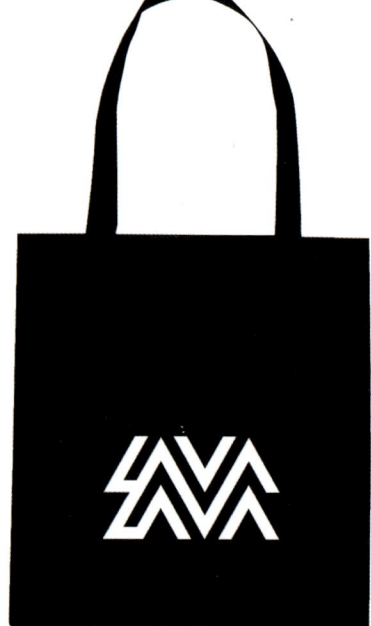

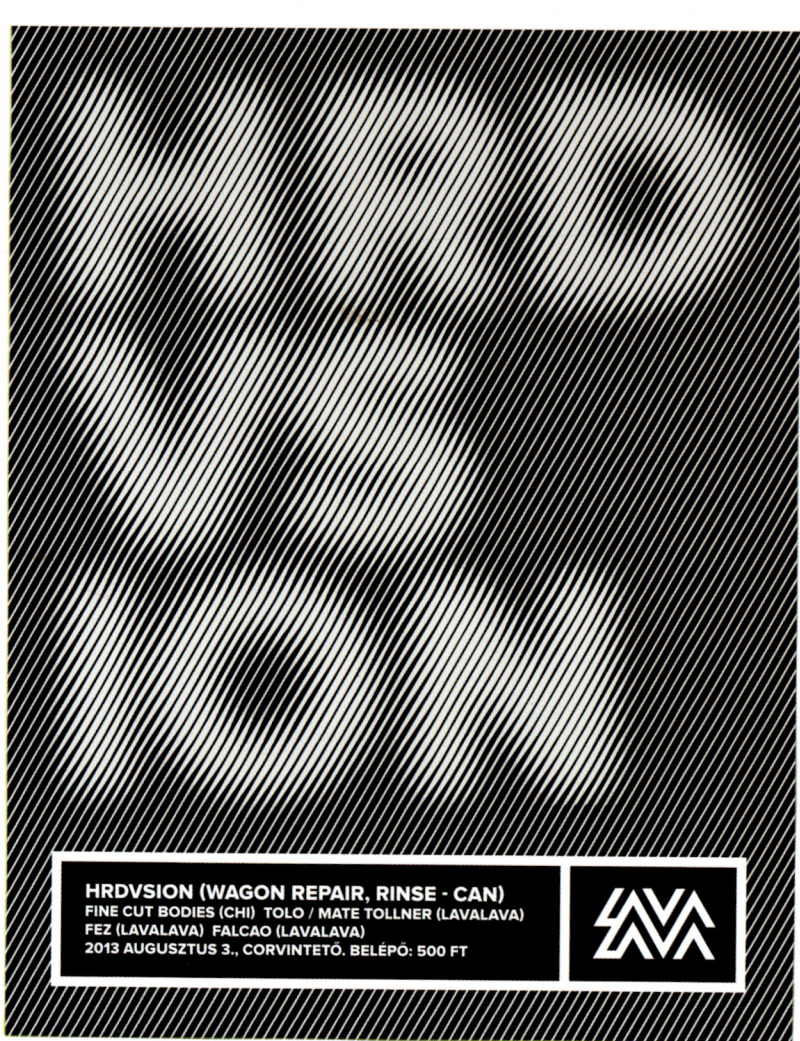

HRDVSION (WAGON REPAIR, RINSE - CAN)
FINE CUT BODIES (CHI) TOLO / MATE TOLLNER (LAVALAVA)
FEZ (LAVALAVA) FALCAO (LAVALAVA)
2013 AUGUSZTUS 3., CORVINTETŐ. BELÉPŐ: 500 FT

LavaLava
Hungary

Csaba Bernáth
Designer

LavaLava
Client

This is a logo redesigned for one of Hungary's leading underground house party series/event organizer group Lavalava. The playing of fonts and visuals in the design, along with the cool black and white tone speaks of the dark of the night and the fun Lavalava promises.

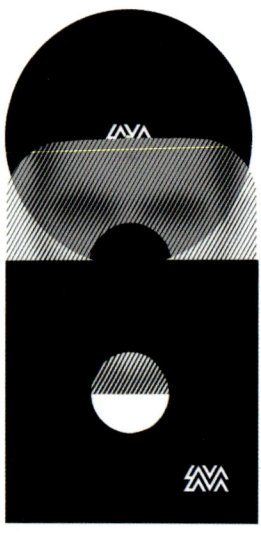

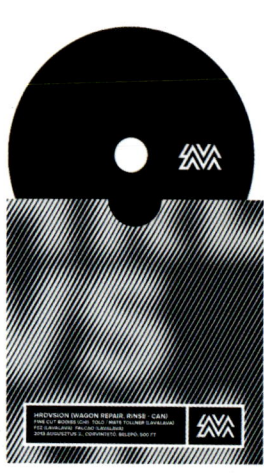

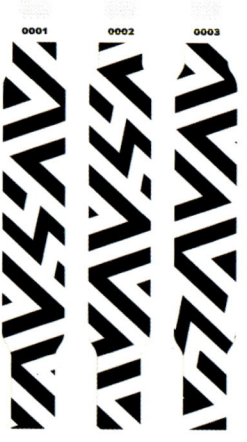

Oyster

Portugal

Rafael Fagulha
Designer

Restaurant
Client

The designer created this branding for a seafood restaurant, Oyster. The black and white oyster silhouettes make an eye-catching icon for the brand while the lines communicate the movement of the sea and the mystery in the dark of the oceans.

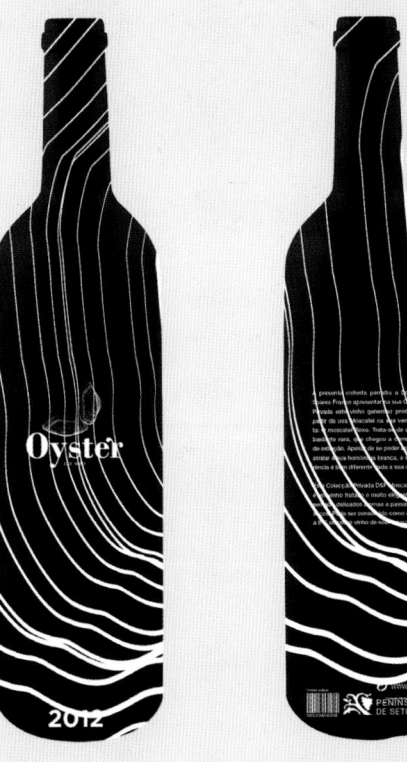

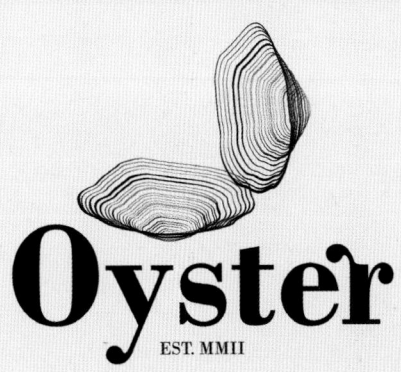

Oyster
EST. MMII

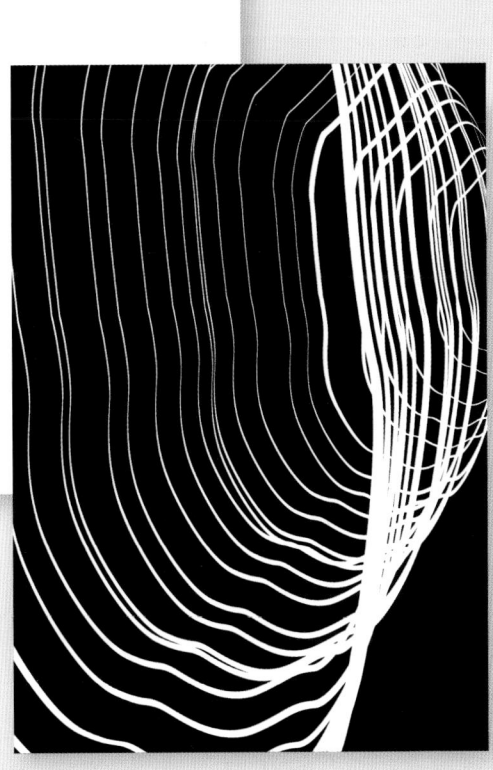

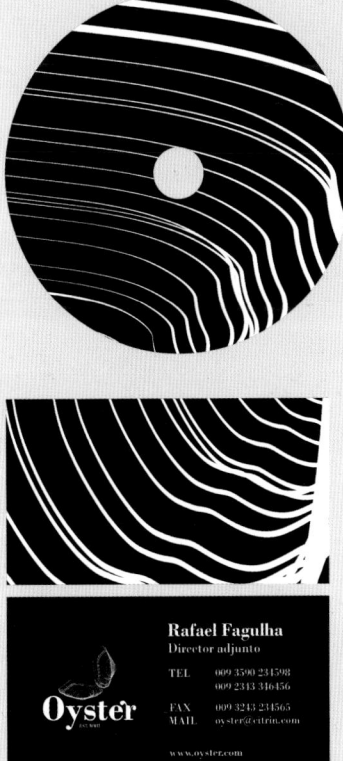

"All colors are in between black and white. And the sense of beauty which we Japanese have always cherished is also in the depth between these two colors."

—NOSIGNER

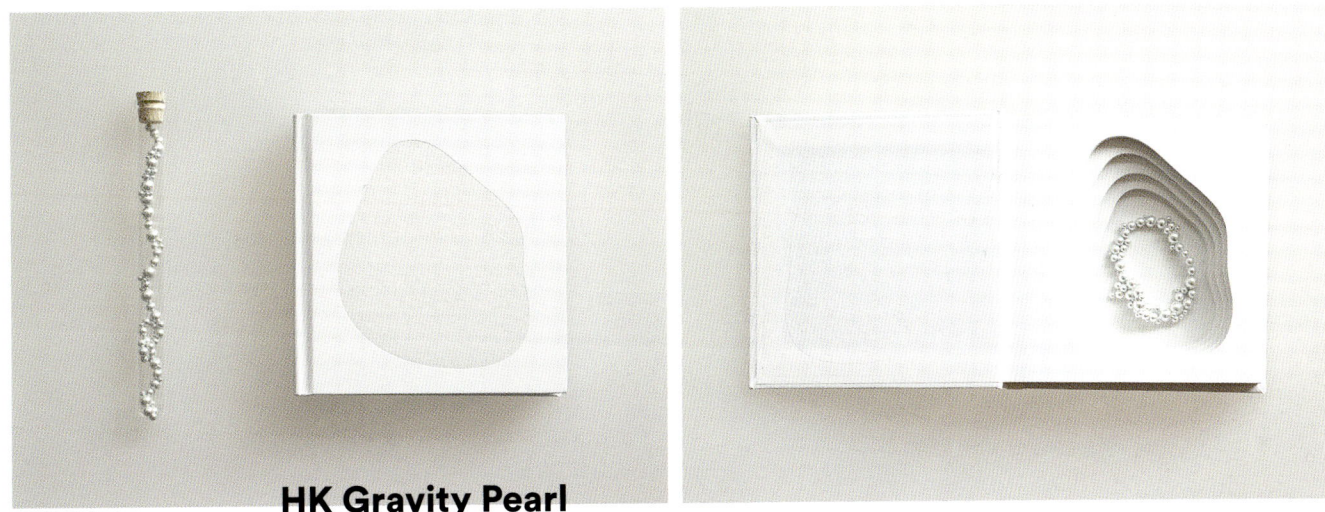

HK Gravity Pearl
Japan

NOSIGNER
Design Agency

Eisuke Tachikawa
Designer

JAPAN IMITATION PEARL & GLASS ARTICLE'S ASSOCIATION
Client

Taking advantage of the collective wealth of knowledge of the artisans of Izumi – the group who first created artificial pearls in Japan – Gravity Pearls for HK (pronounced as haku). The magnets embedded within the artificial pearls allow it to transform from a necklace to an earring, to a ring and to a broach. Coming together to resemble a cluster of bubbles, the pearls stand alone, not as copies, but as a unique product, proud of its artificiality.

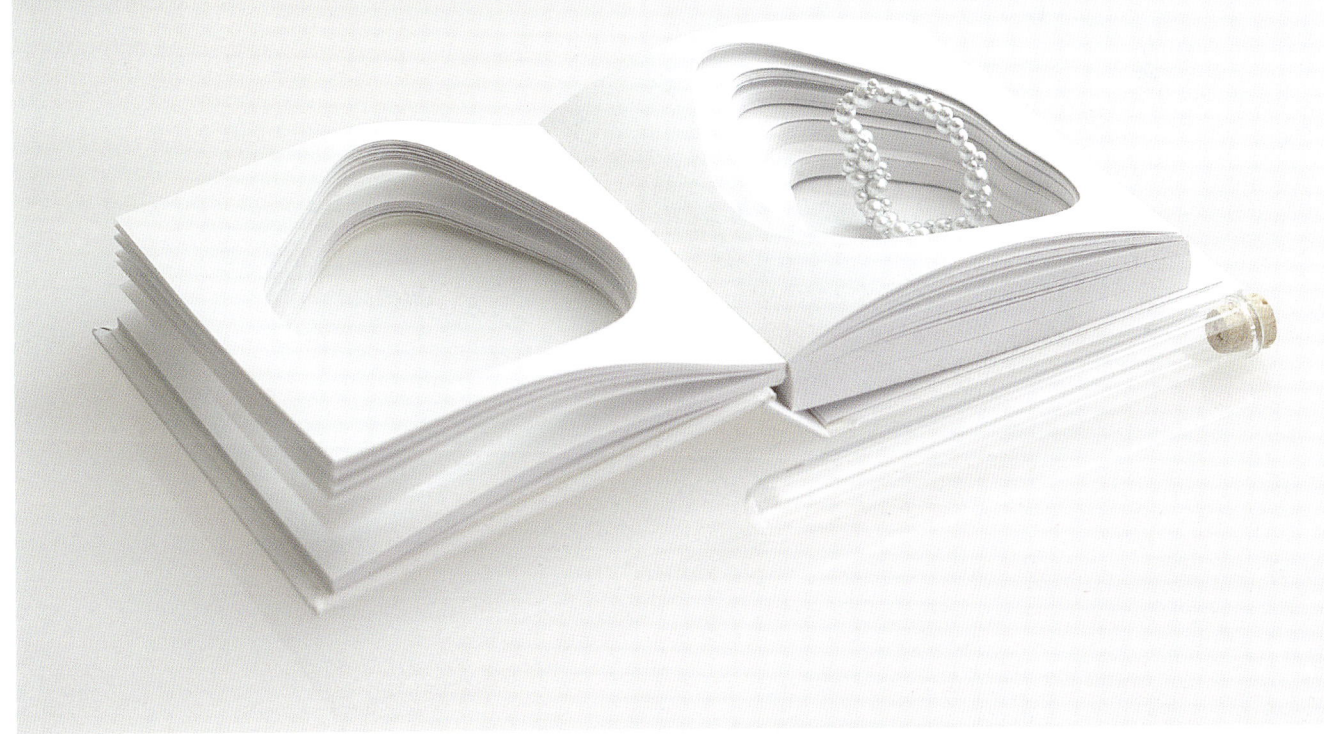

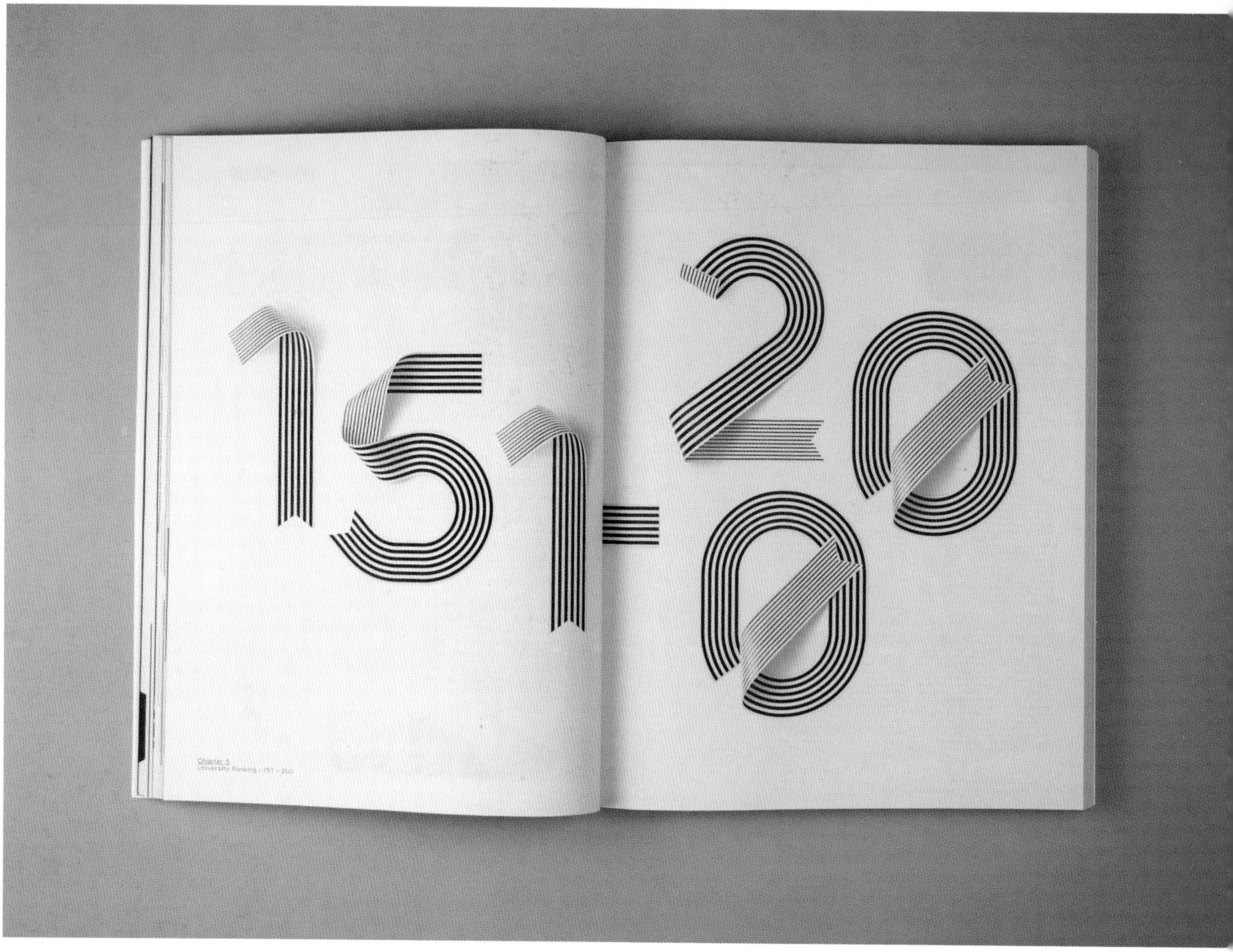

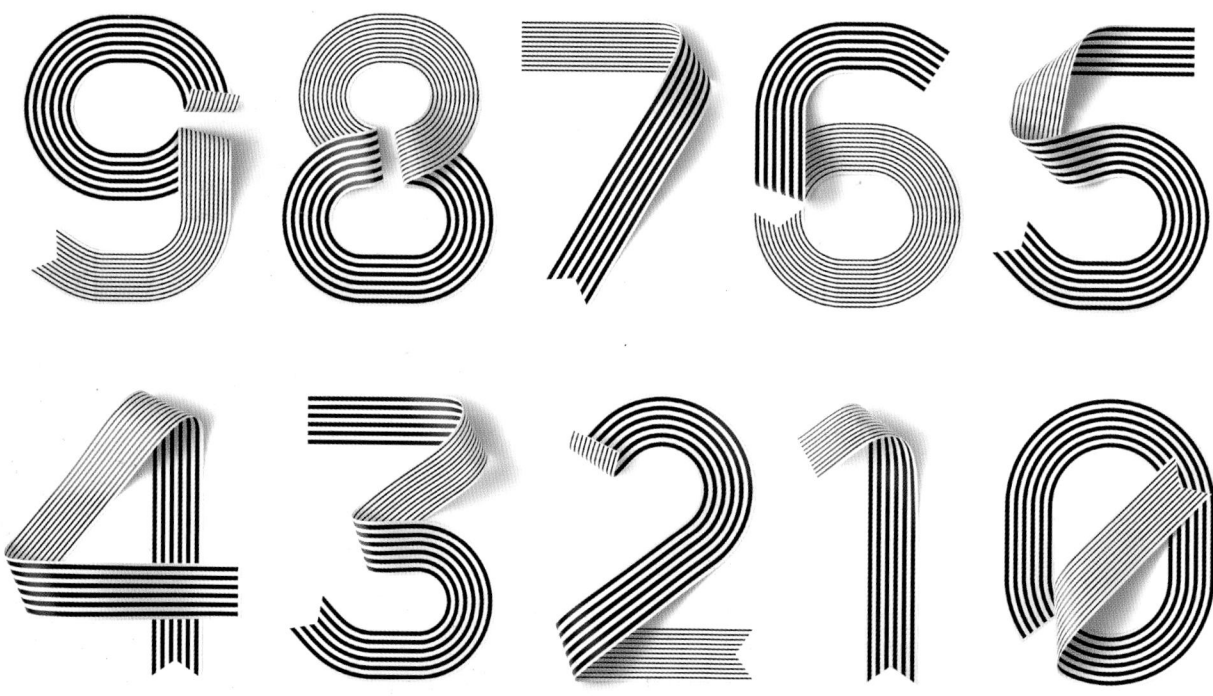

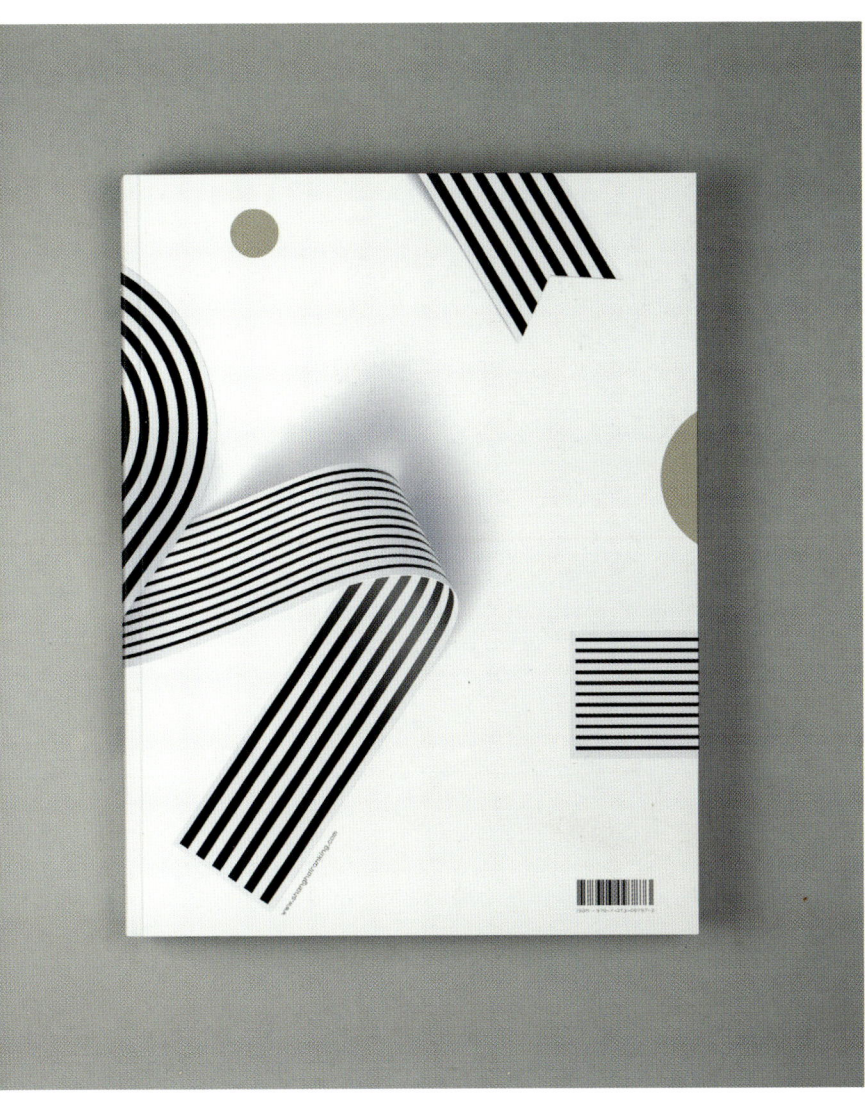

Shanghai Ranking
United Kingdom

Sawdust
Design Agency

**Rob Gonzalez
& Jonathan Quainton**
Designers

Shanghai Ranking
Client

This is the book design and art direction for a pioneering global university guide entitled Shanghai Jiao Tong Top 200 Research Universities Encyclopedia. Working closely with research developer Alisdair Jones, the designer realized his ambitious vision for the book with a sheer black and white color tone dancing on the pages.

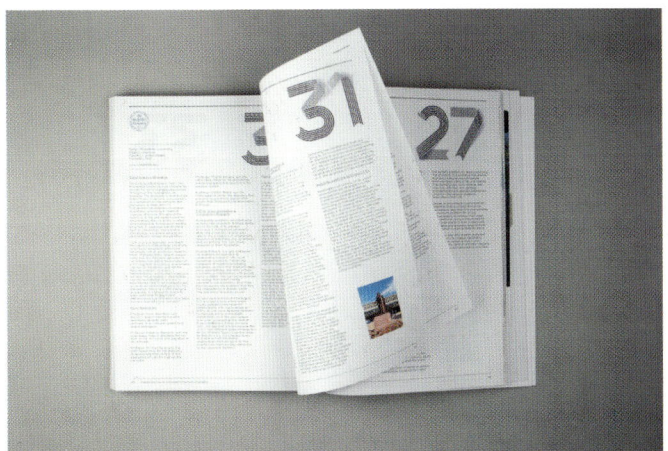

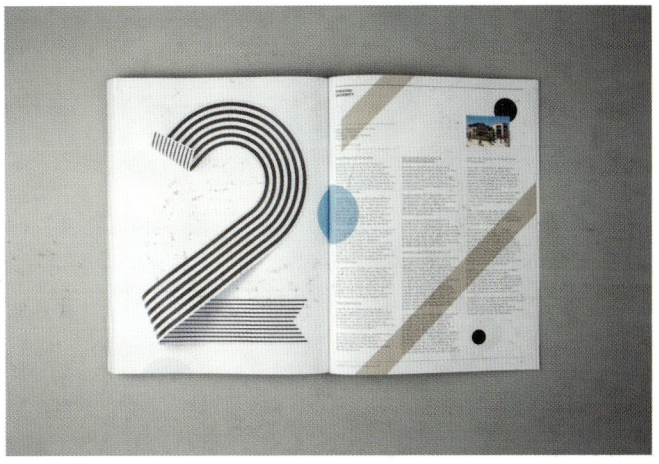

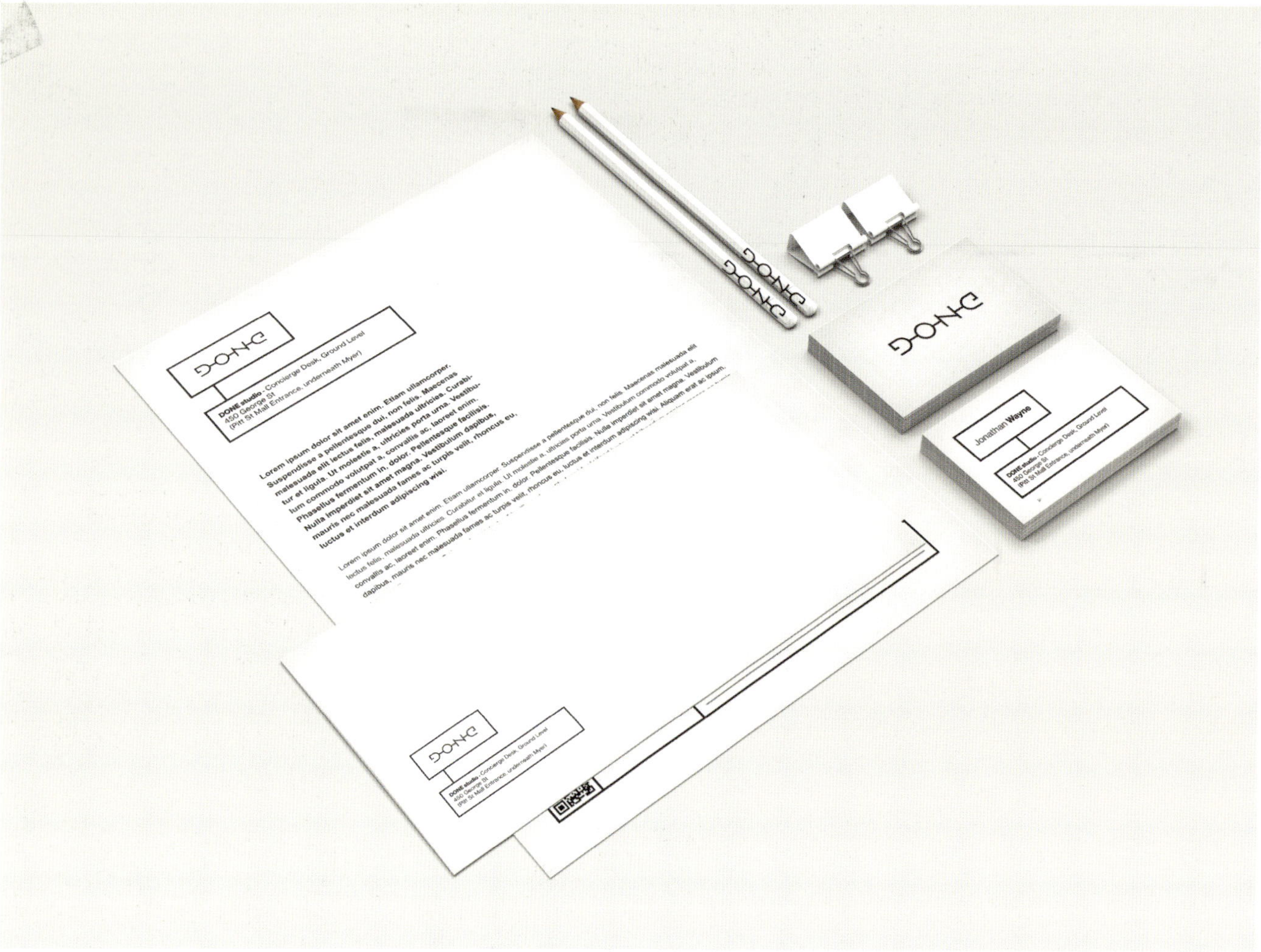

DONE

Poland

Jacek Janiczak
Designer

DONE
Client

DONE is a new creative studio from Sydney,
Australia, specializing in architecture and design.
The thin lines and minimalist palette give the
studio a refreshingly exquisite debut.

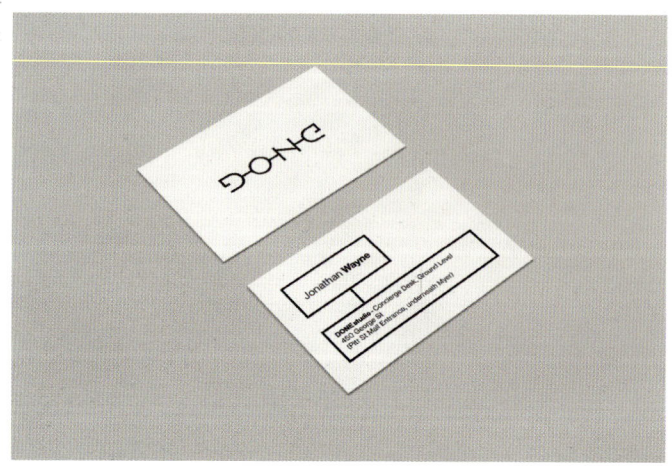

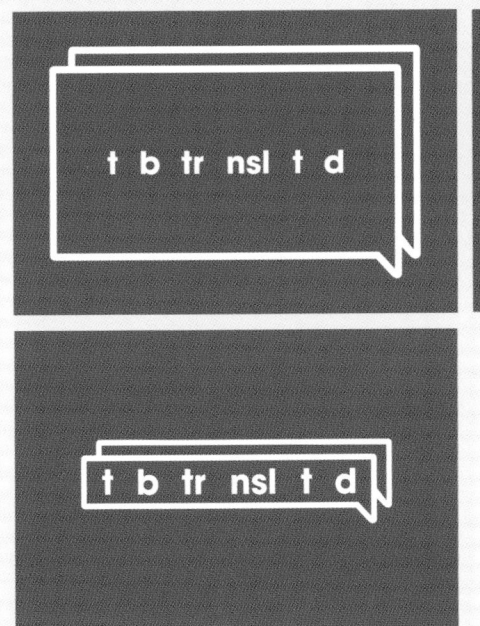

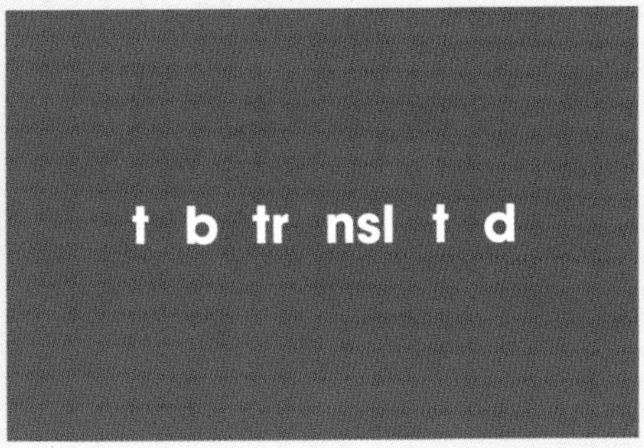

To be translated
Spain

Nueve Studio
Designer

To be translated
Client

To be translated, a translation and interpretation company based in Madrid needed a visual identity to refresh their brand image and communication means. The designers focused on typography, as translation involves converting one language to another, which led to the idea of enhancing an active changing process to facilitate communication.

t b tr nsl t d

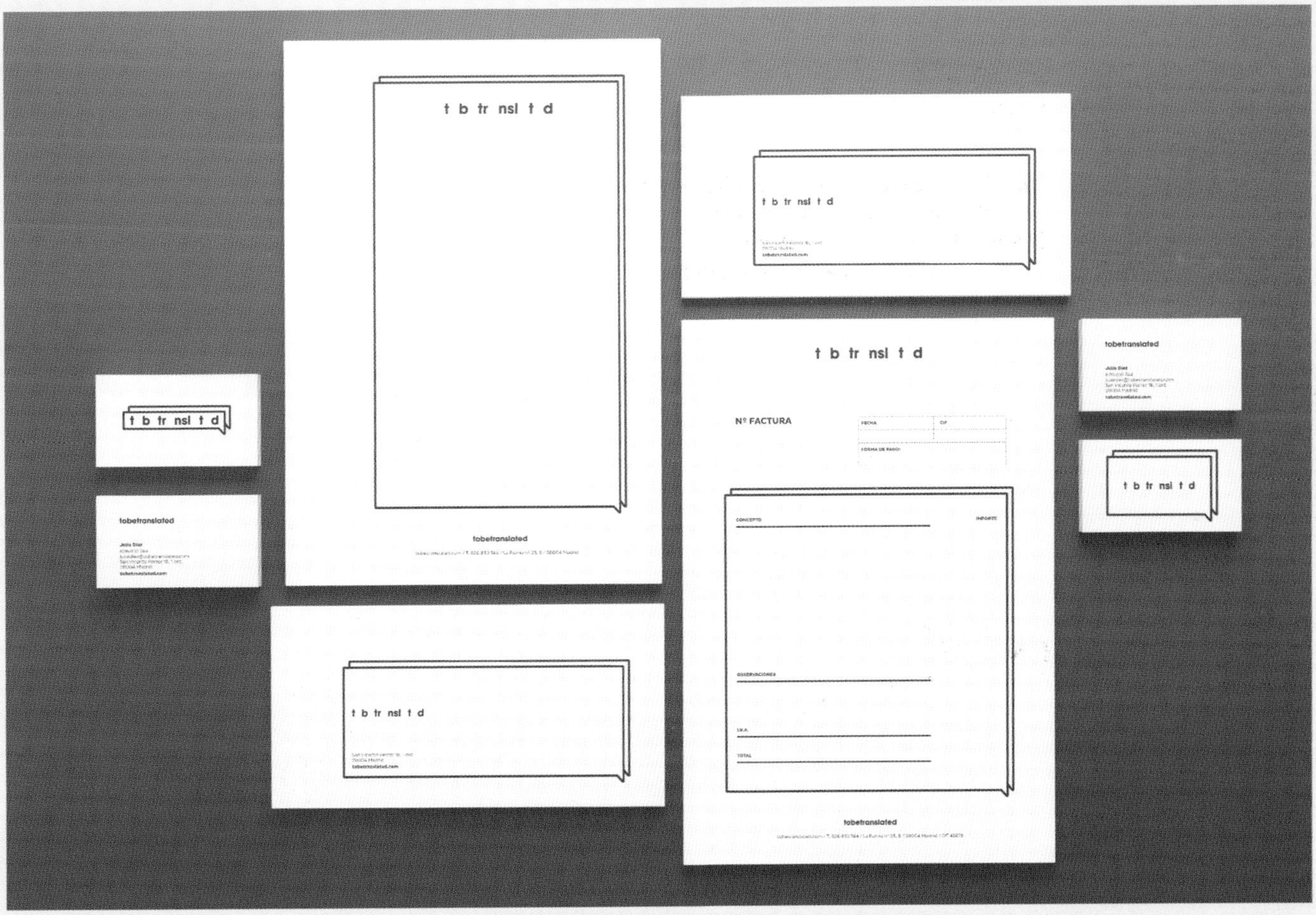

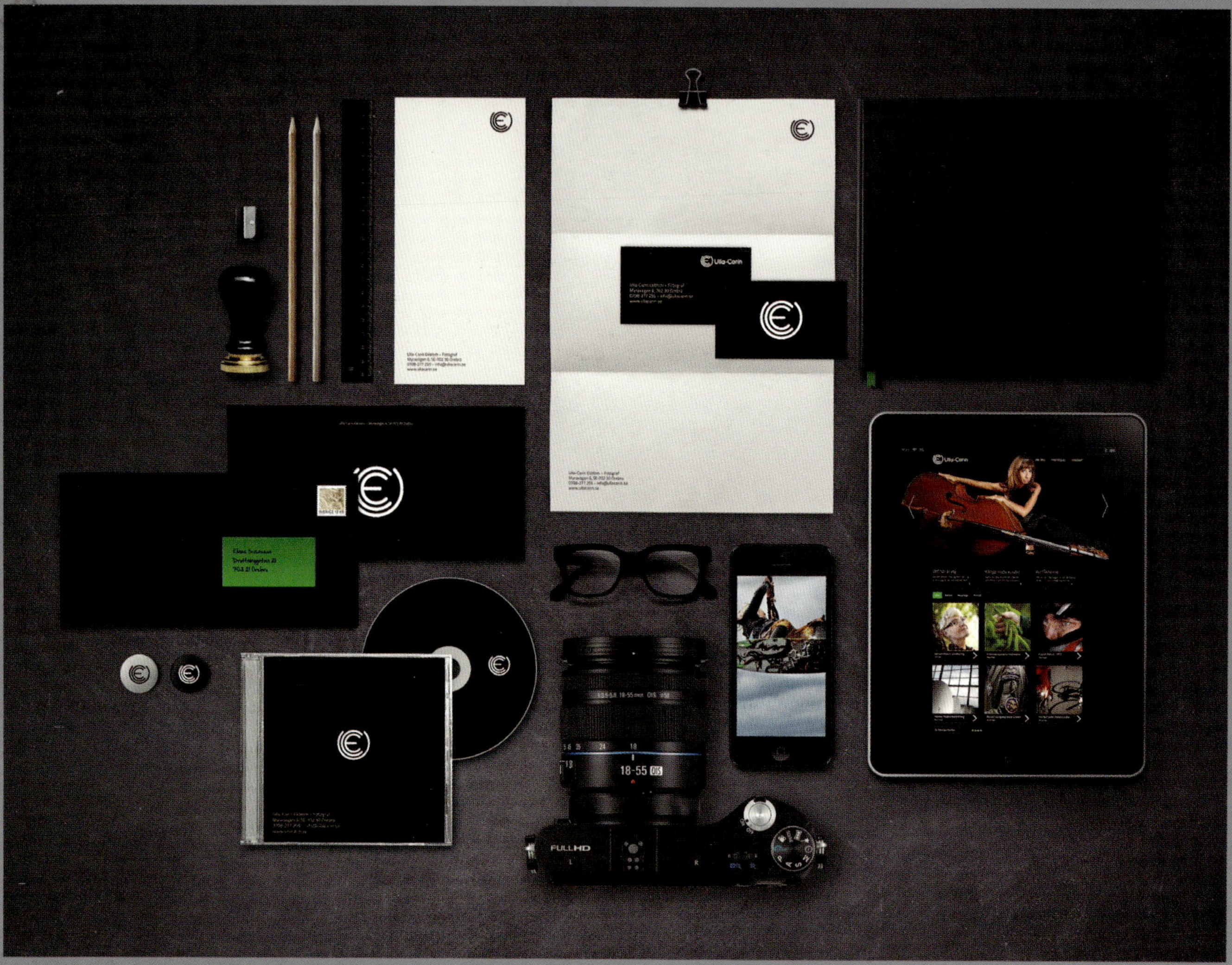

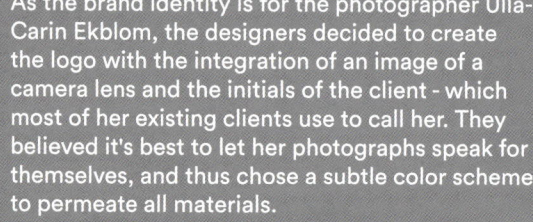

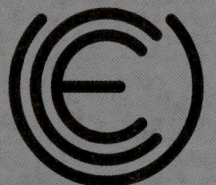

Ulla-Carin Ekblom
Sweden

**Filip Annerblom,
Miran A. Leander**
Designers

Ulla-Carin Ekblom
Client

As the brand identity is for the photographer Ulla-Carin Ekblom, the designers decided to create the logo with the integration of an image of a camera lens and the initials of the client - which most of her existing clients use to call her. They believed it's best to let her photographs speak for themselves, and thus chose a subtle color scheme to permeate all materials.

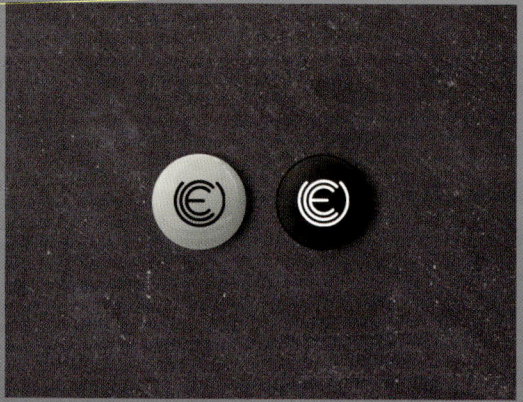

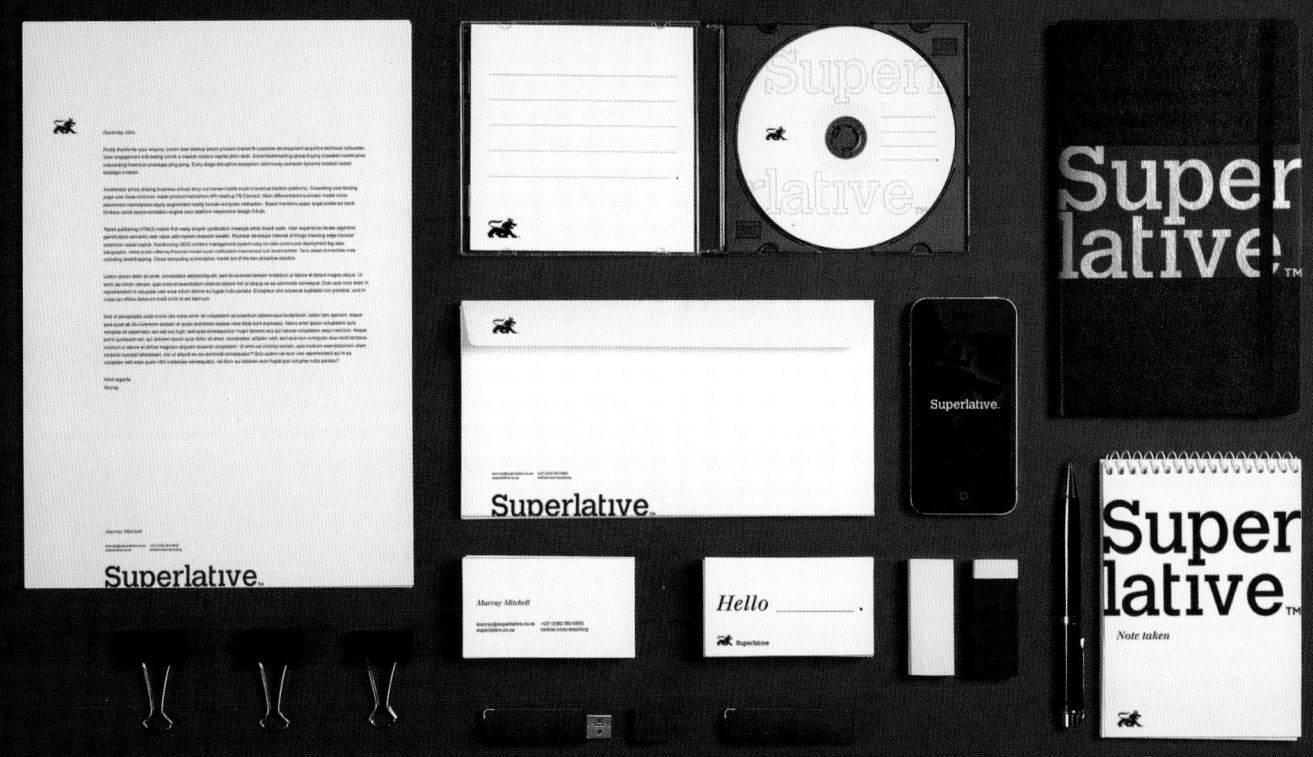

Superlative
South Africa

Erwin Bindeman
Designer

Murray Mitchell
Client

Superlative is a digital consultancy based in Cape Town, South Africa with a focus on user-experience design. By using the previous logo as visual reference and creating a series of geometrical guidelines, the designer kept things simple and vivid. The lion was turned to face reader's right, opposite to its previous orientation to suggest future and forward thinking. The stance of the lion implies power, authority and eagerness. The colors are rich black and stark white that help emphasize the clean, bold use of typography.

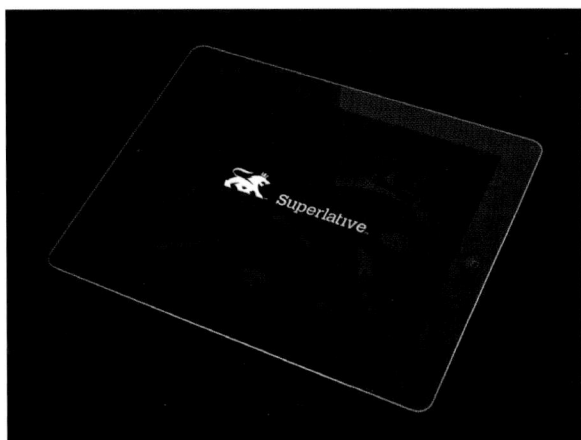

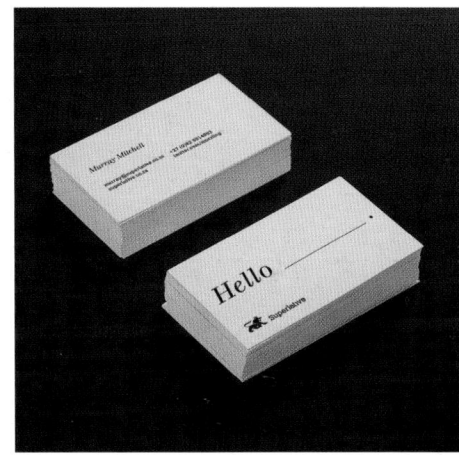

www.erwin.co.za

International Theatre Festival

Poland

Prograffic
Design Agency

Michał Stróż
Designer

Cultural Foundation Yakiza
Client

This is the labelling of the International Theatre Festival. The project includes logo, poster, postcard, bill and badge designing. The minimalist layout and the black and white color scheme create a clear graphic language.

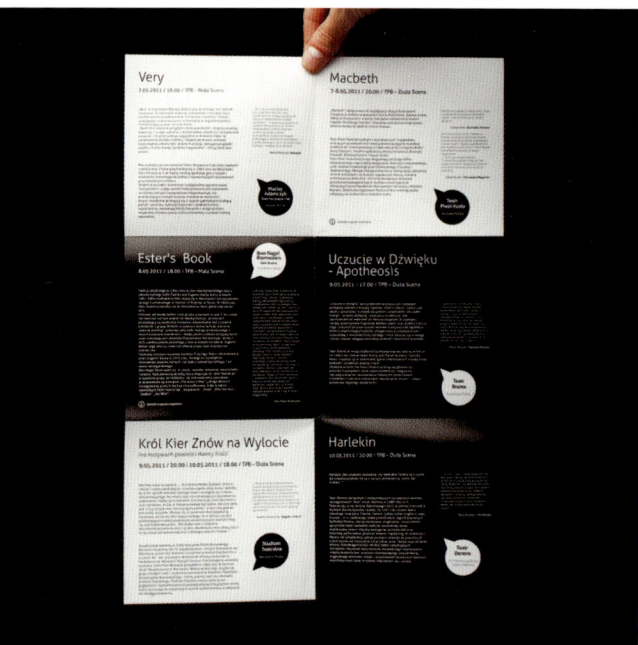

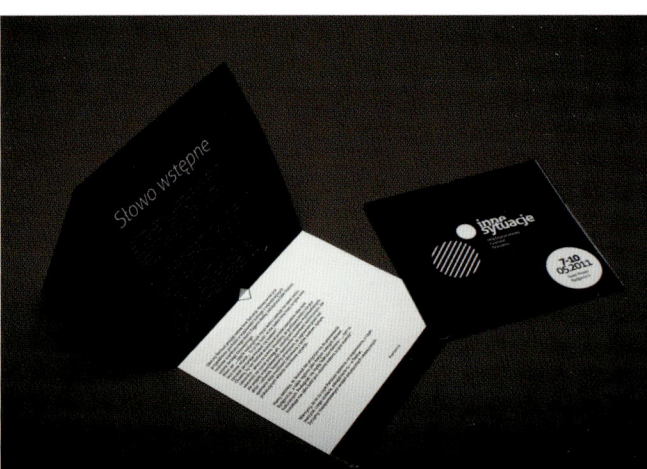

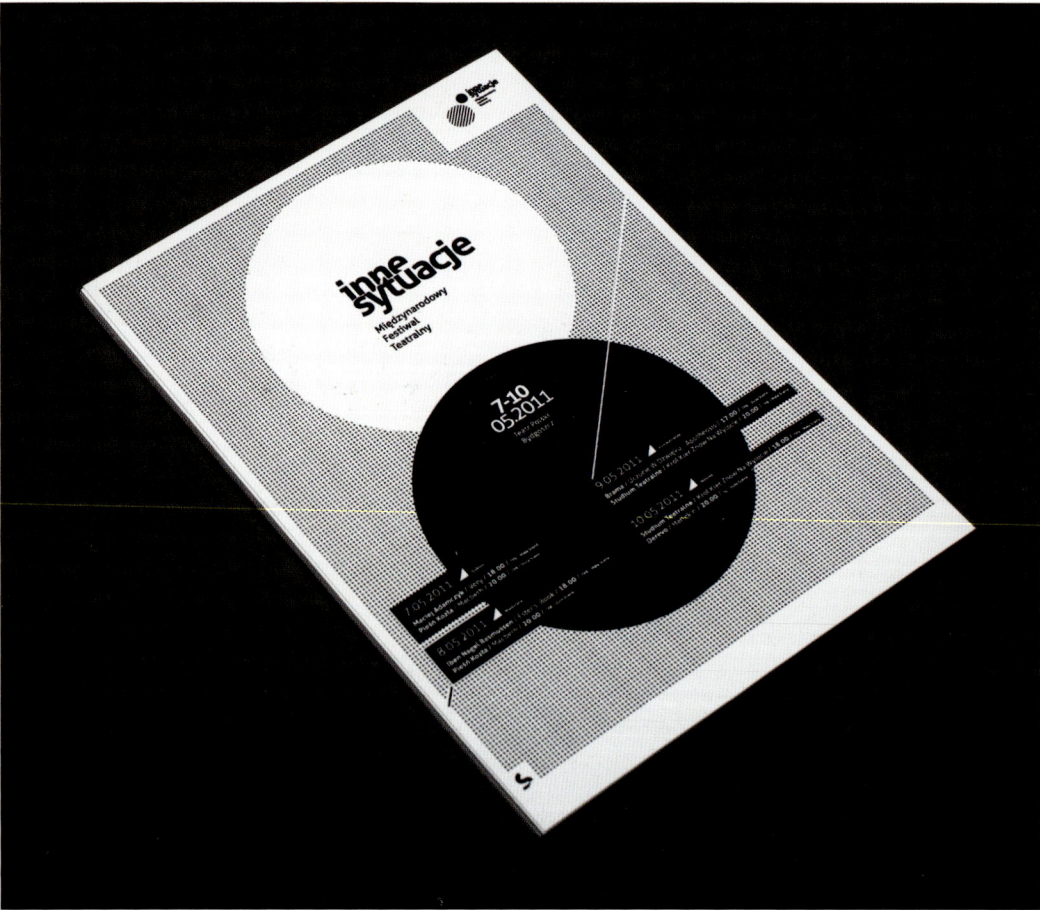

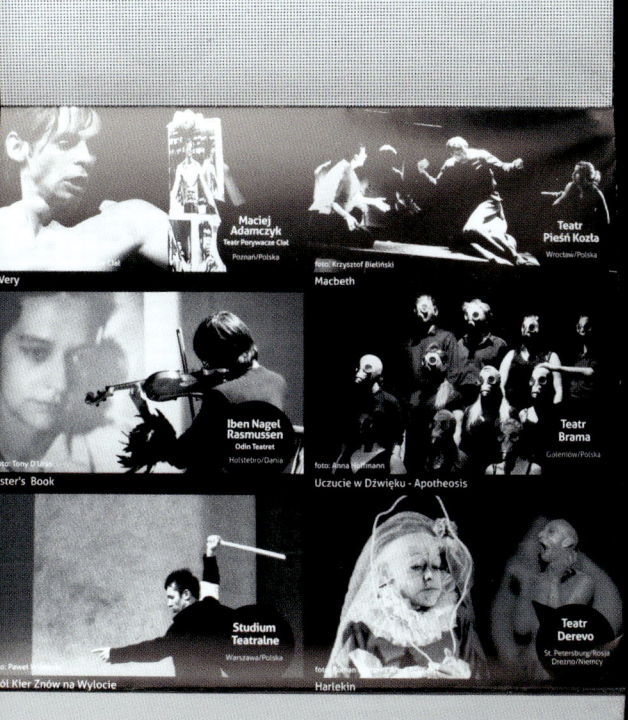

Very

Maciej Adamczyk
Teatr Porywacze Ciał
Poznań/Polska

foto: Krzysztof Bieliński

Teatr Pieśń Kozła
Wrocław/Polska

Macbeth

foto: Tony D'Urso

Iben Nagel Rasmussen
Odin Teatret
Holstebro/Dania

Ester's Book

foto: Anna Horbmann

Teatr Brama
Goleniów/Polska

Uczucie w Dźwięku - Apotheosis

foto: Paweł

Studium Teatralne
Warszawa/Polska

Król Kier Znów na Wylocie

foto:

Teatr Derevo
St. Petersburg/Rosja
Drezno/Niemcy

Harlekin

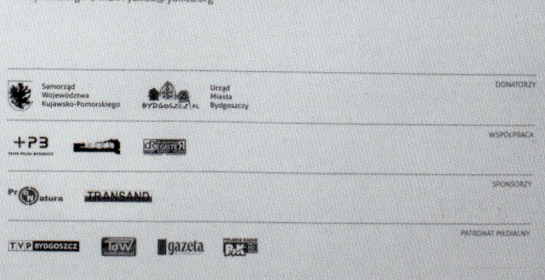

ORGANIZATOR

ORGANIZACJA POŻYTKU PUBLICZNEGO
FUNDACJA KULTURY YAKIZA

Biuro Fundacji
Wyższa Szkoła Gospodarki
ul. Garbary 2
85-229 Bydgoszcz
TEL +48 517949427
KR S-00001166603 * NIP: 967-11-56-165 * REGON: 09310774
KONTO : NORDEA BANK POLSKA S.A. 07 1440 1215 0000 0000 0383 3356
www.yakiza.org / e-mail : yakiza@yakiza.org

DONATORZY

Samorząd Województwa Kujawsko-Pomorskiego

BYDGOSZCZ.PL

Urząd Miasta Bydgoszczy

WSPÓŁPRACA

+P3

SPONSORZY

ProNatura   TRANSAND

PATRONAT MEDIALNY

T.V.P BYDGOSZCZ   idW   gazeta

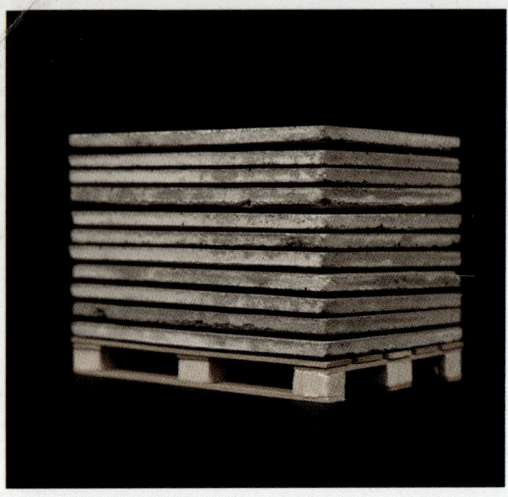

"The use of black and white makes it possible to evidence other essential aspects of design as the volume and area."

—Paul Ressencourt (Murmure agency)

Concrete

France

Murmure Agency
Design Agency

Paul Ressencourt
Creative Director

Julien Alirol
Art Director

Playing with the notion of scales, Murmure created a set of business cards made of concrete. The use of such a material in graphic design was enhanced by using the smallest and the most refined communication support and color. The refinement and the technique required for the typography highlight the harshness and the roughness of the material used.

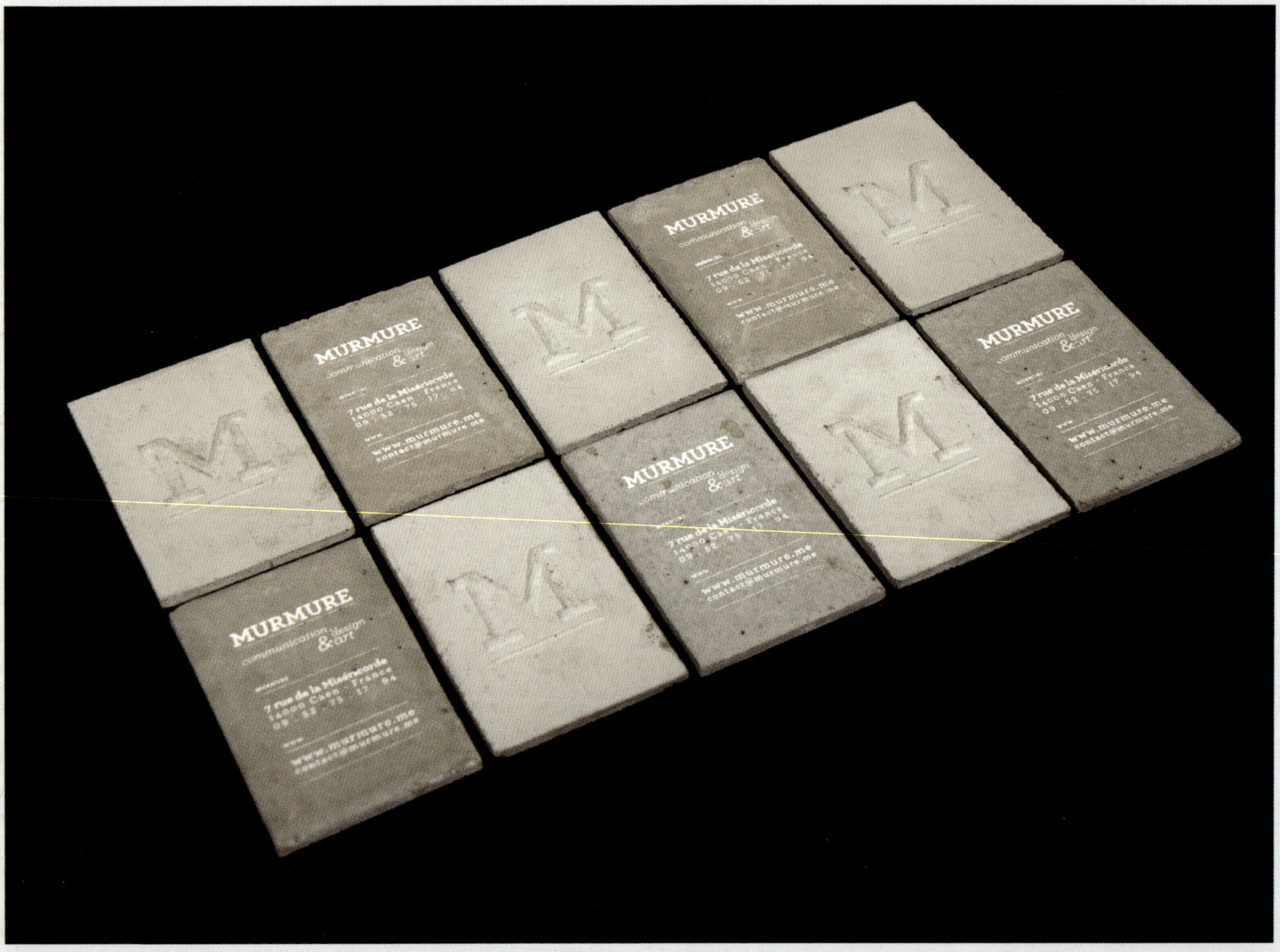

www.murmure.me

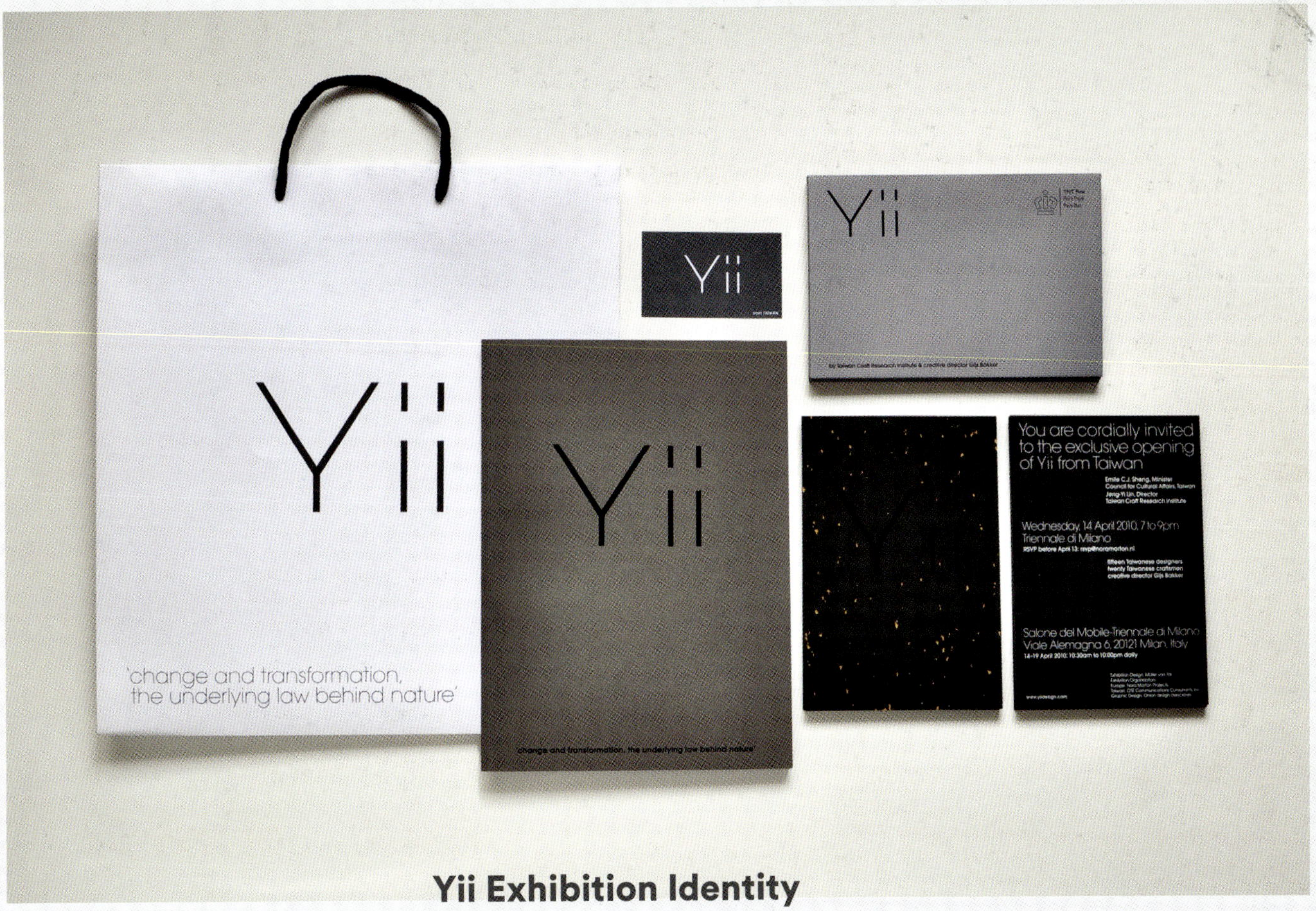

Yii Exhibition Identity

Taipei, P.R.C.

Onion Design Associates
Design Agency

Janett Wang
Creative Director

Andrew Wong
Art Director

Karen Tsai
Designer

National Taiwan Craft Research and Development Institute
Client

"Yii", pronounced as the letter E, is taken from the classic text I-Ching, the Book of Changes. The typeface "Avant Garde Extra Light" used in the logo design was selected for its geometrical simplicity. The strokes and spacing were modified as a subtly reference to a Trigram figure marking from the baguà symbol; mimicking one of the eight possible trigrams of the I-Ching. The solid line represents yang while the open line represents yin, two interdependent forces.

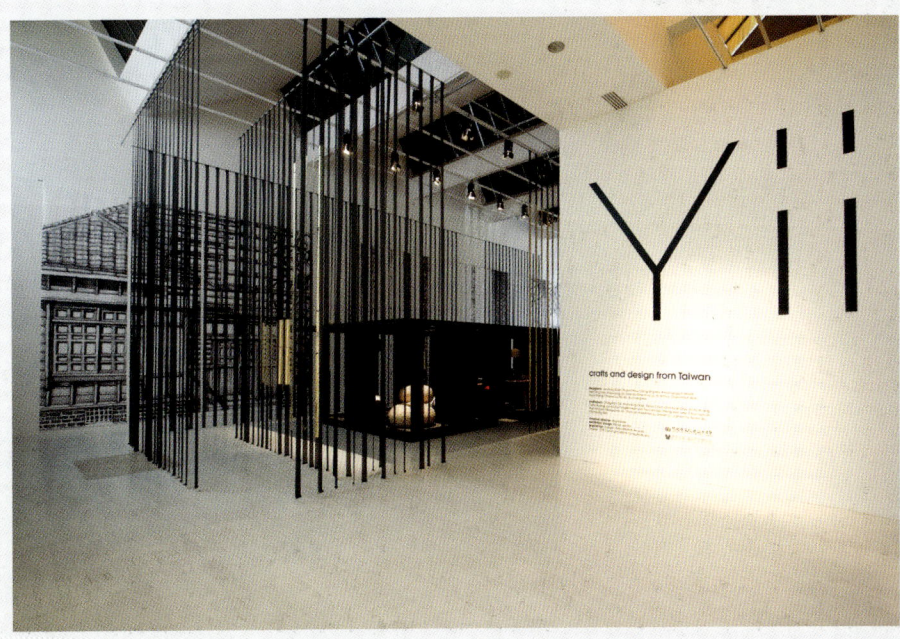

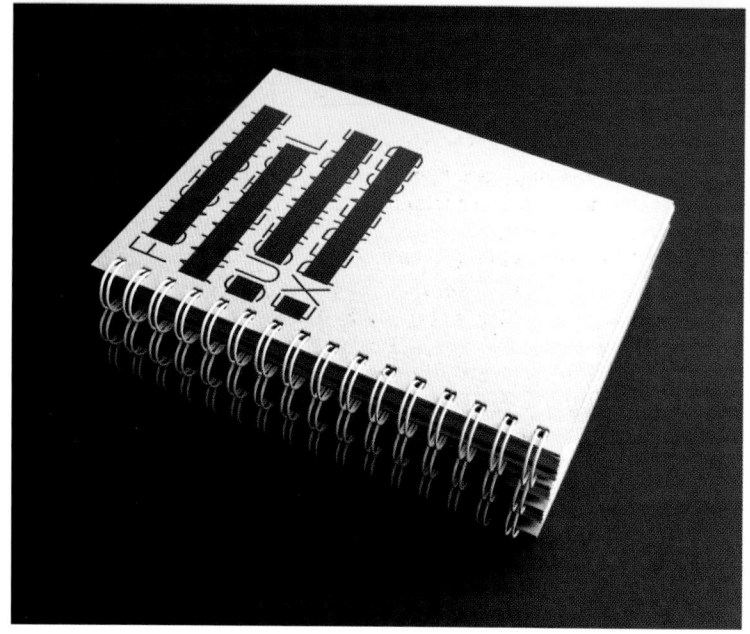

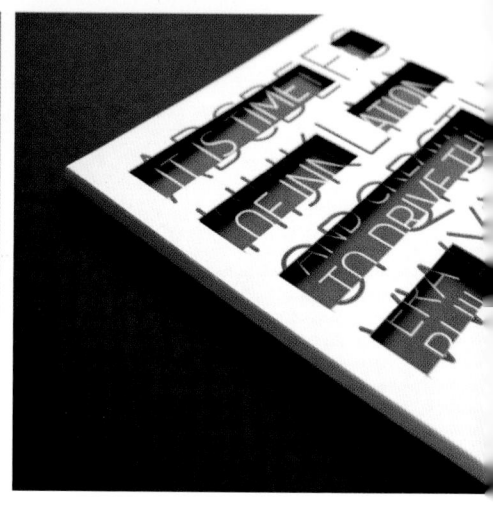

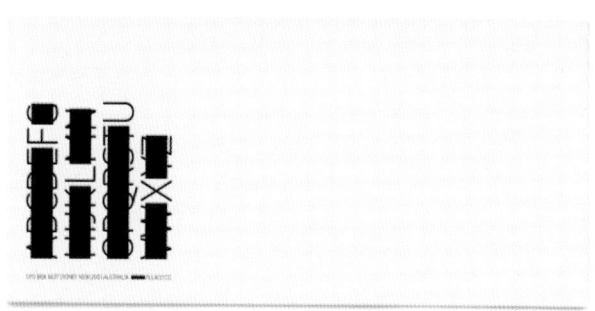

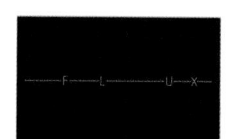

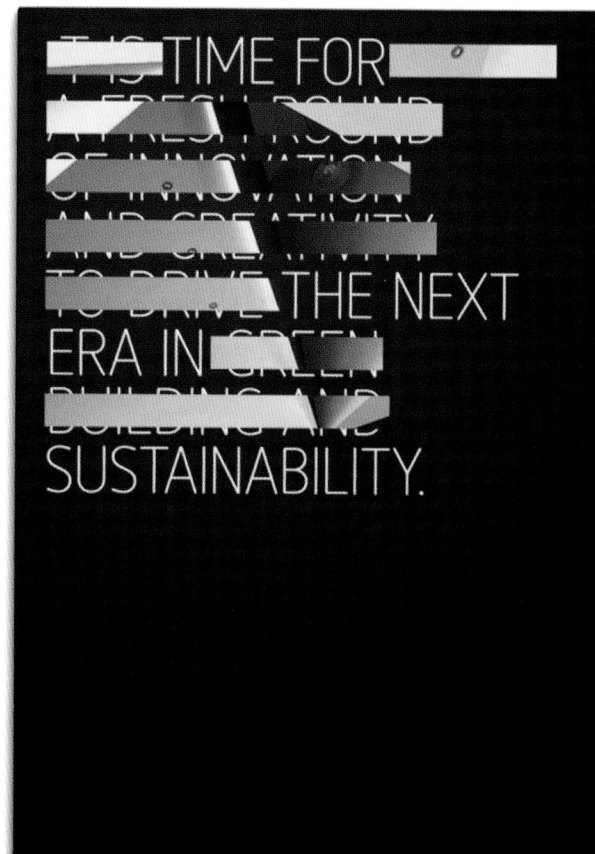

Flux Identity

Australia

Re:
Design Agency

Jason Little
Creative Director

Ellie See
Designer

Flux
Client

Flux is a specialist environmental design and engineering consultancy, dedicated to delivering game-changing sustainable solutions in the built environment.
The flexible identity was developed to portray their innovative approach, and act as a strong signal to their process of simplification and elimination. The graphic strike through device can be used to distill lengthy information to its core message, imply the removal of the unnecessary, and act as a recognizable visual language for the organization.

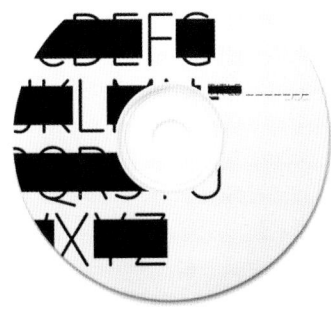

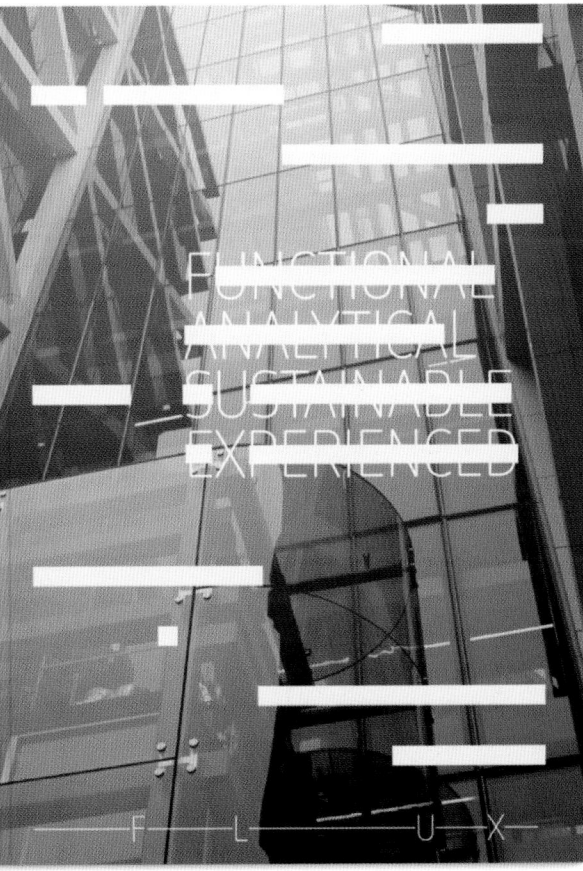

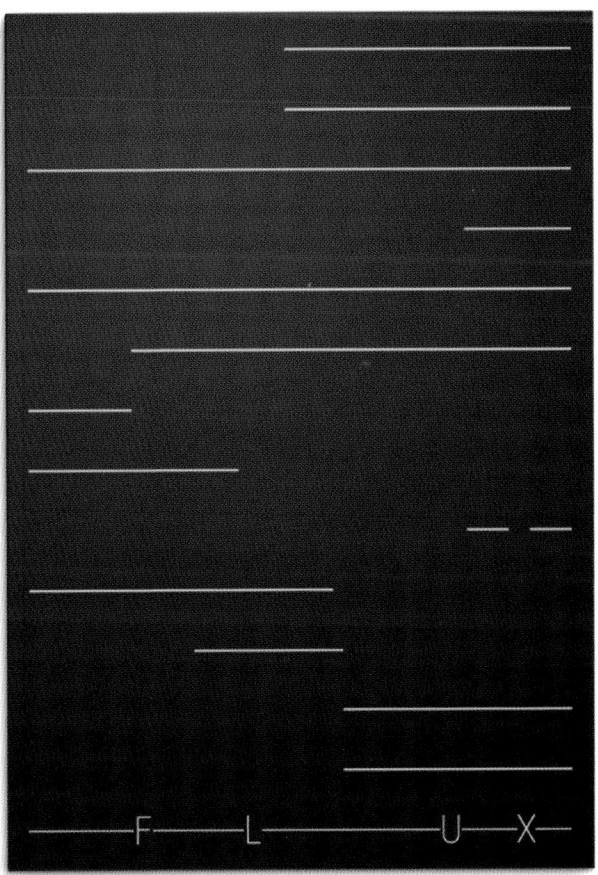

Tsutsumi Comute A/W Flyer

Japan

OUWN
Design Agency

Atsushi Ishiguro
Designer

TSUTSUMI COMUTE
Client

164

Tsutsumi Comute is a men's fashion brand. A natural scene presented in the flyer embodies the brand character and shows a strong connection with monochrome.

EXHIBITION

TSUTSUMI COMUTE
2013-14
Autumn-Winter
EXHIBITION

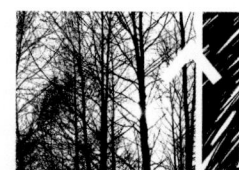

TD

TSUTSUMI COMUTE
2013-14
Autumn-Winter
EXHIBITION

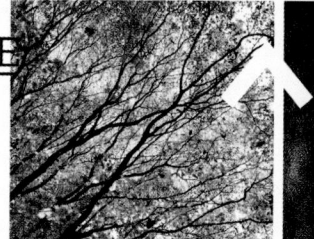

EXHIBITION

TSUTSUMI COMUTE
2013-14
Autumn-Winter
EXHIBITION

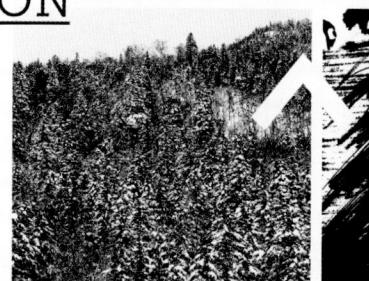

XHIBITION

TSUTSUMI COMUTE
2013-14
Autumn-Winter
EXHIBITION

EXHIBITION

TSUTSUMI COMUTE
2013-14
Autumn-Winter
EXHIBITION

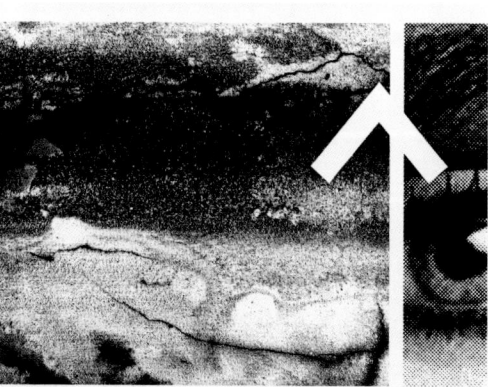

UMI COMUTE

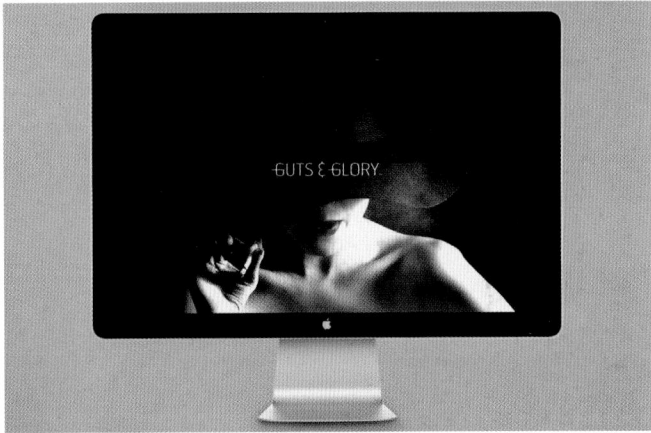

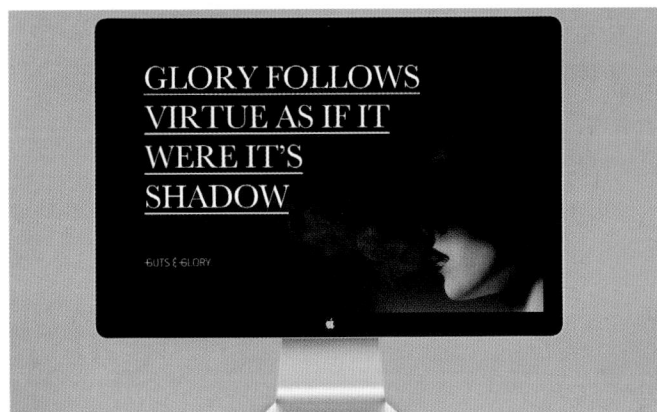

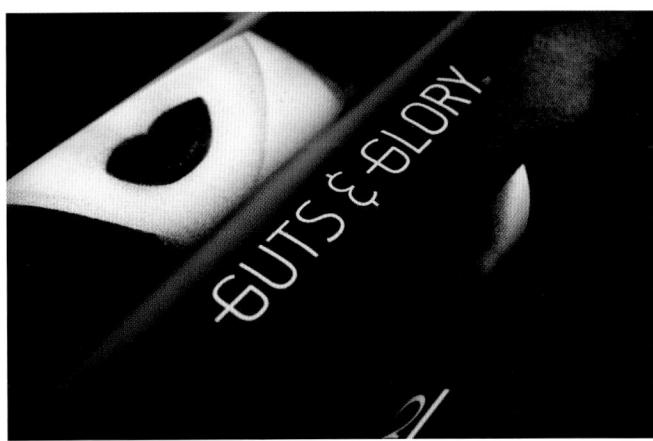

Guts & Glory
Norway

Anti
Design Agency

Kjetil Wold
Creative Director

Martin Stousland
Designer

Guts & Glory
Client

Guts & Glory wants to maintain a luxurious and inaccessible communication image. Instead of screaming for attention they make themselves almost unreachable. Using a black on black, no color solution, the business cards ended up as exclusive as it can get. Surprisingly, their clients love the inaccessibility.

www.anti.as

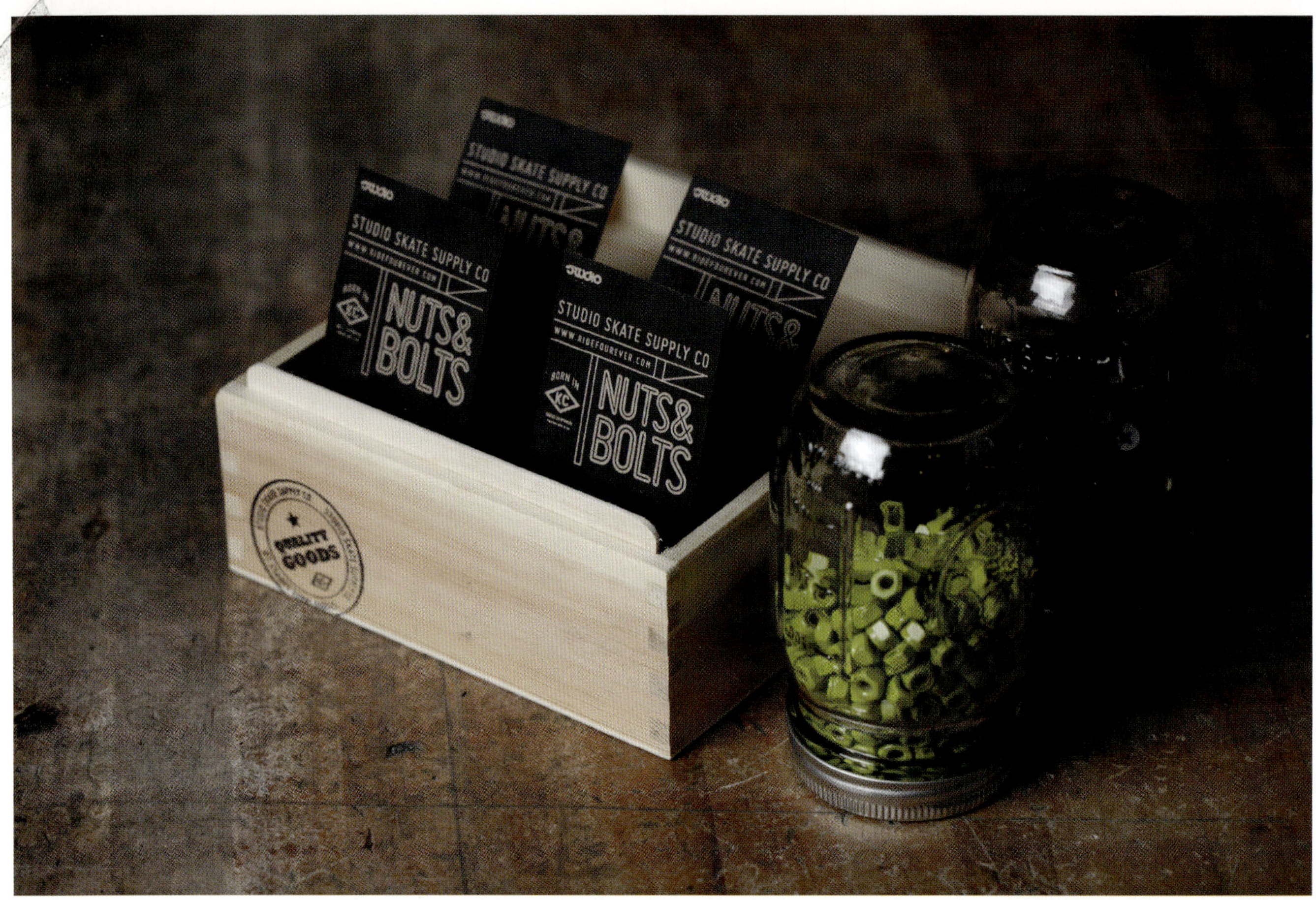

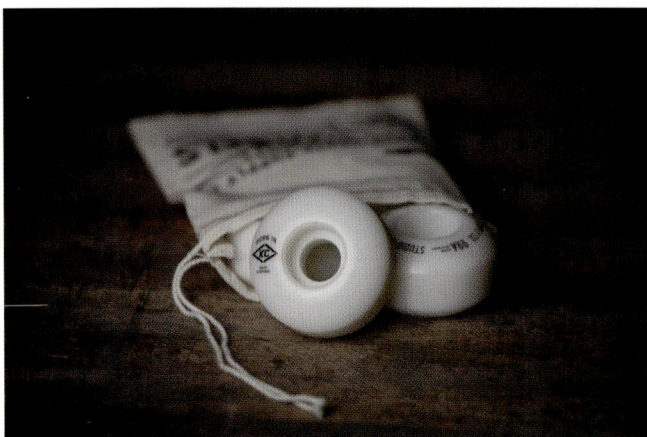

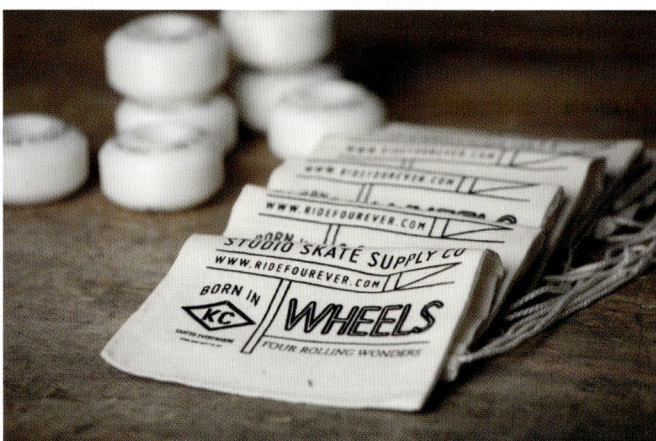

Studio Skate Supply: Hardware Series

United States

Contrabrand.net
Design Agency

Brandon Wilson
Designer

Kenny Swoger
Photographer

The design of this line of essential skateboard gear was inspired by memories of the experiences shared by the designer and his grandfather. They frequented auctions in their hometown to look for old tools, hardware or anything that had a tie to local history. If it was worn, they would spray paint it black and call it new, everything was hand-altered in one way or another.

VIPP Packaging

Denmark

Box House
Design Agency

Lone Wolf Larsen
Designer

VIPP A/S
Client

The new VIPP packaging creates a
unique packaging concept that embodies
VIPP's principles on aesthetics and
function. The packaging is manufactured in
premium matt certified FSC paper and inserts
are in black corrugated cardboard with colored
core all colors are aligned to the VIPP corporate
identity.

167

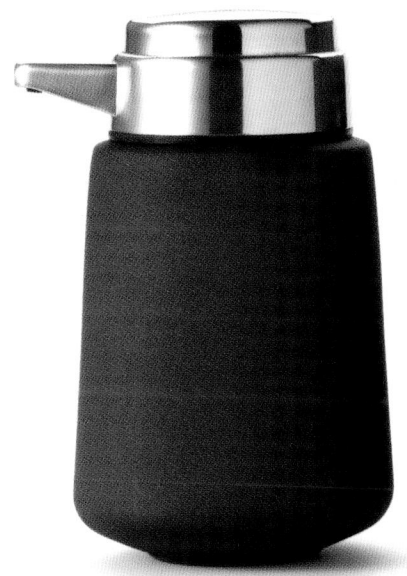

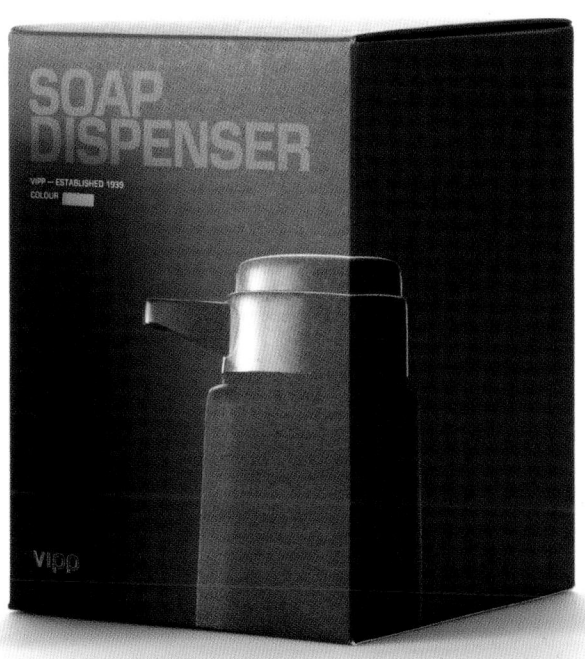

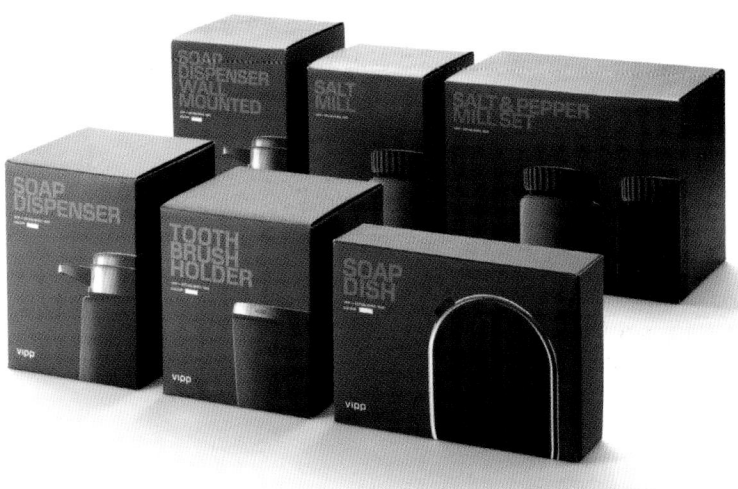

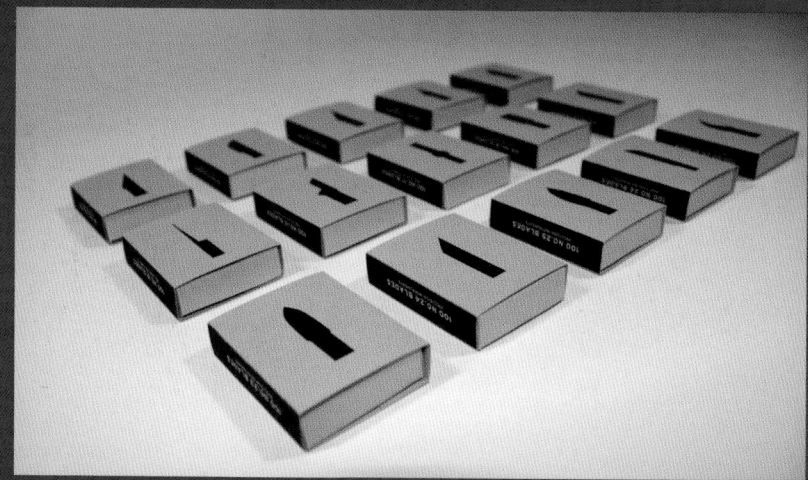

X-acto Blades
South Korea

Heesang Lee
Designer
& Photographer

Carin Goldberg
Creative Director

The 'X' on the X-Acto logo is a stenciled letter that makes a symbolic mark for X-Acto knife. And the blades numbers in the packaging center and the back illustrations show the shape of blades. The minimalistic packaging design for X-acto Blade's boxes simplify exactly what the consumer is getting in each box.

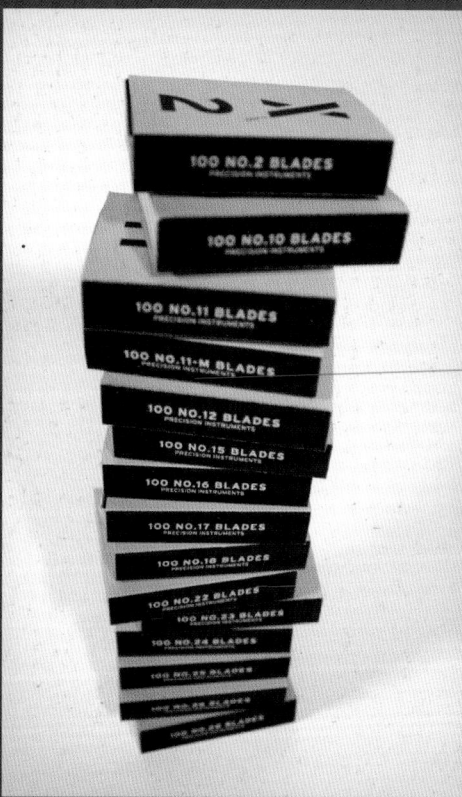

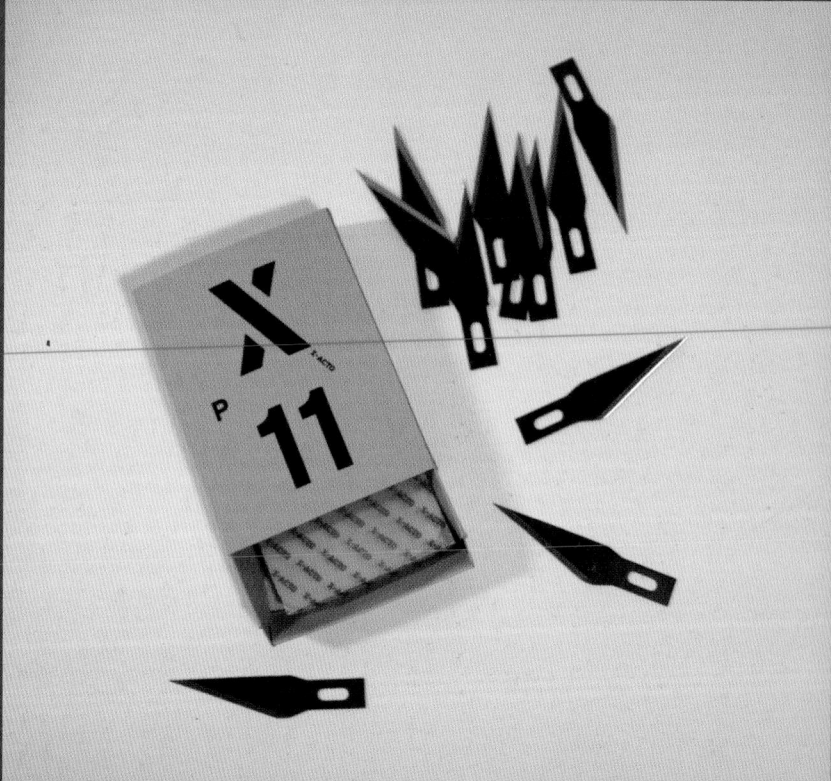

"Black and white is basic but sophisticated."
—Zita Arcq (La Tortillería)

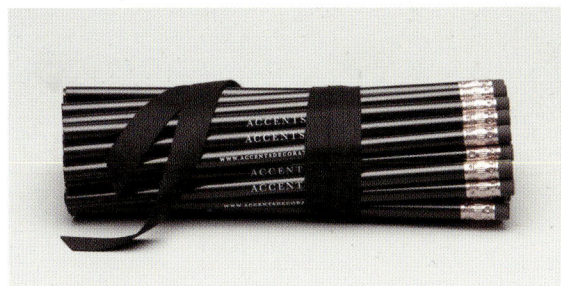

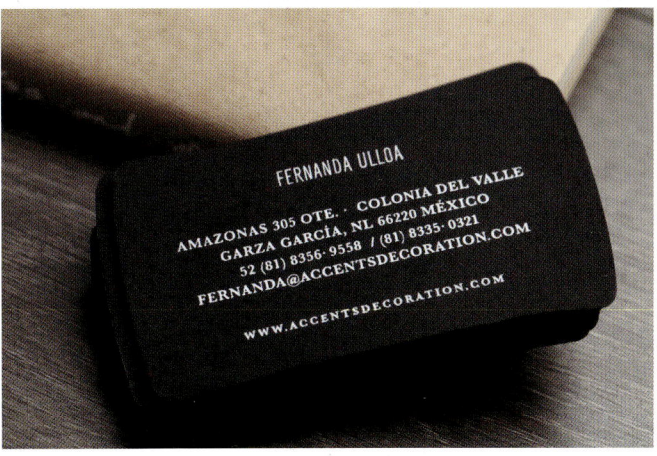

FERNANDA ULLOA

AMAZONAS 305 OTE. · COLONIA DEL VALLE
GARZA GARCÍA, NL 66220 MÉXICO
52 (81) 8356· 9558 / (81) 8335· 0321
FERNANDA@ACCENTSDECORATION.COM
WWW. ACCENTSDECORATION.COM

Accents Decoration
Mexico

La Tortillería
Design Agency

Zita Arcq & Sonia Saldaña
Creative Director

CAROGA
Photographer

Accents Decoration
Client

This is a brand makeover for the store Accents Decoration, aiming to highlight the graceful character of the store while emphasizing how it creates different styles for different settings and tastes.

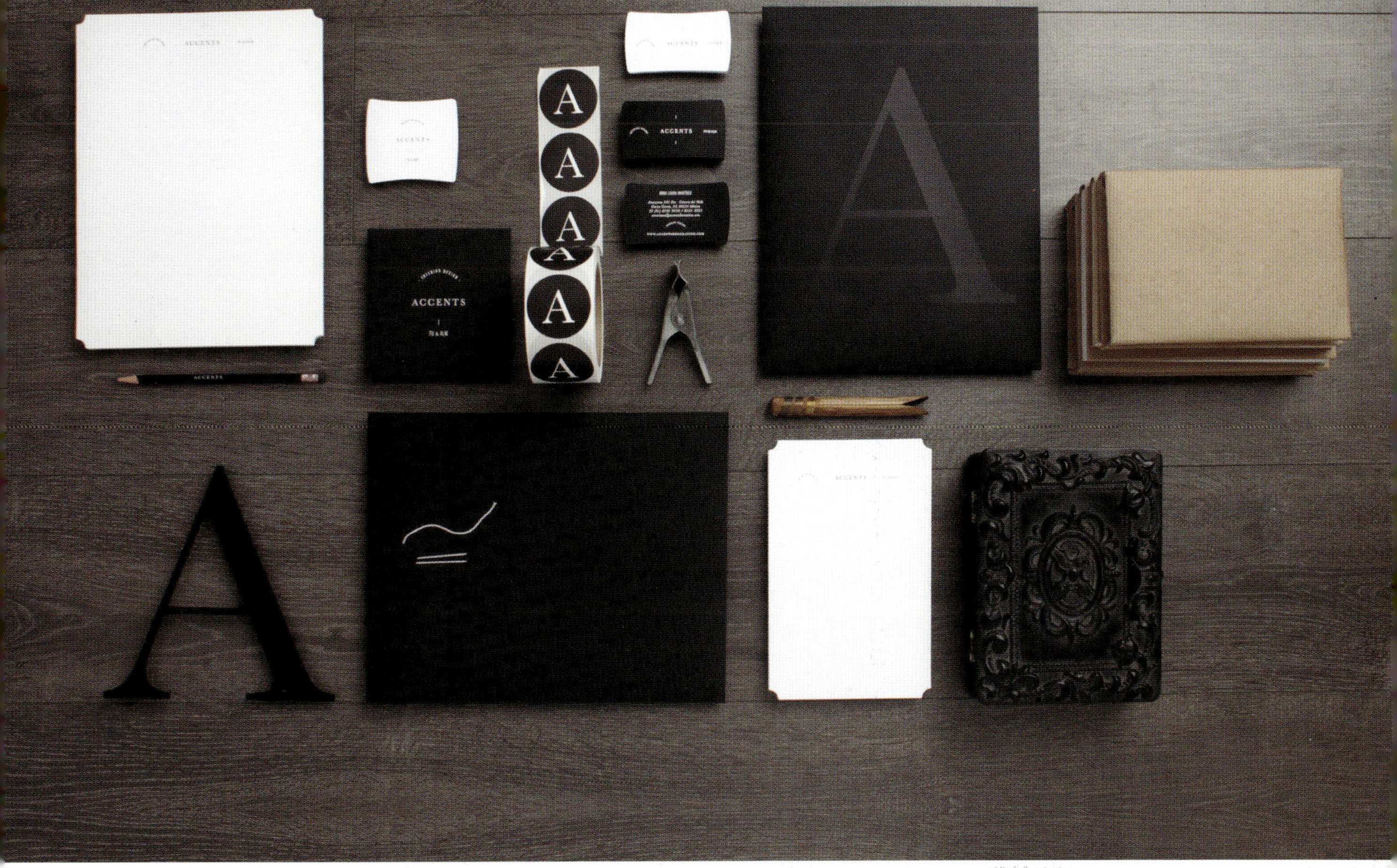

170

Transmediale.11
Germany

+Ruddigkeit
Design Agency

Raban Ruddigkeit
Creative Director

**Dirk Heider,
Kristina Brasseler,
Gianna Pfeifer**
Art Director

Transmediale.11
Client

The campaign for transmediale, an annual festival for media art and digital culture was inspired by the simplicity of one line and one dot, as in the 1 and the 0 - the basic pattern of the binary system – and DNA, thus a code connecting man and machine and allowing for infinite words and images.

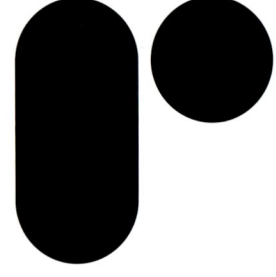

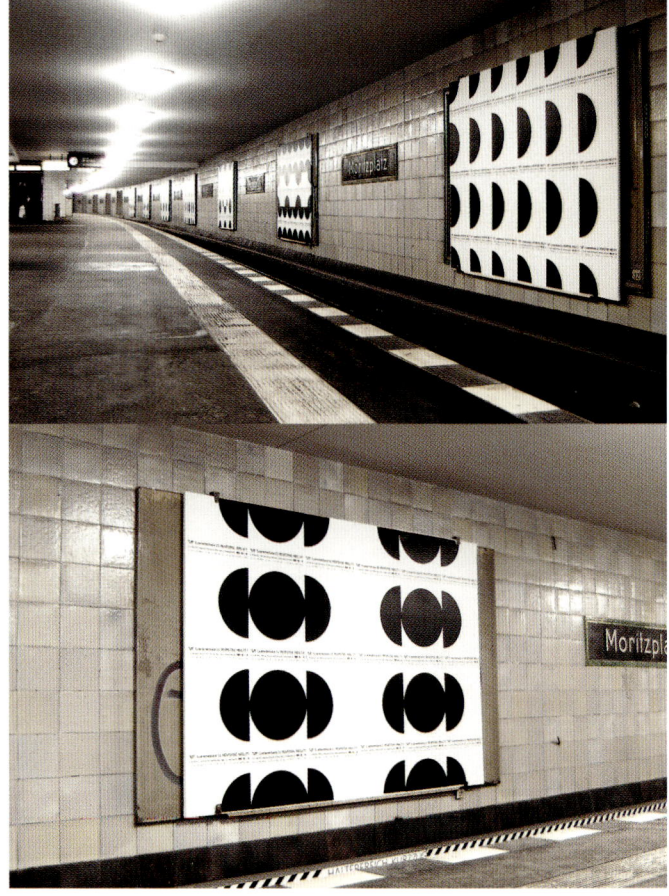

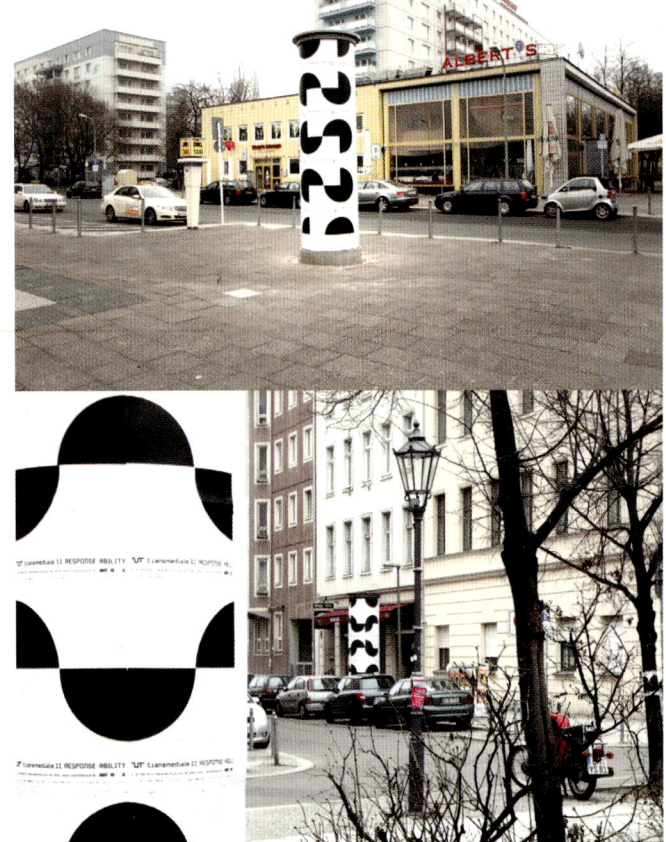

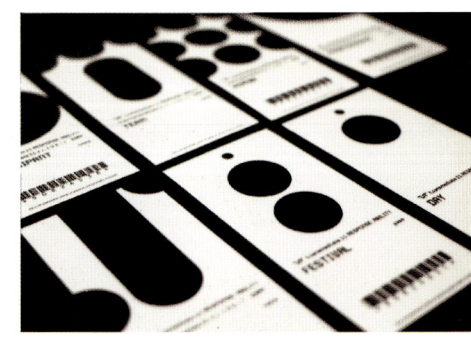

response: ability transmediale.11 — mediale.11 ... Haus der Kulturen der Welt

transmediale.11 RESPONSE:ABILITY, 1 – 6 feb 2011, Haus der Kulturen der Welt, www.transmediale.de

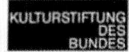 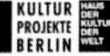   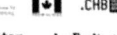

> *"The world is becoming more and more chaotic, making it difficult to tell right from wrong sometimes. The grayscale, however, keeps expanding in our daily life."*
> —Jeffrey Tam (ALONGLONGTIME)

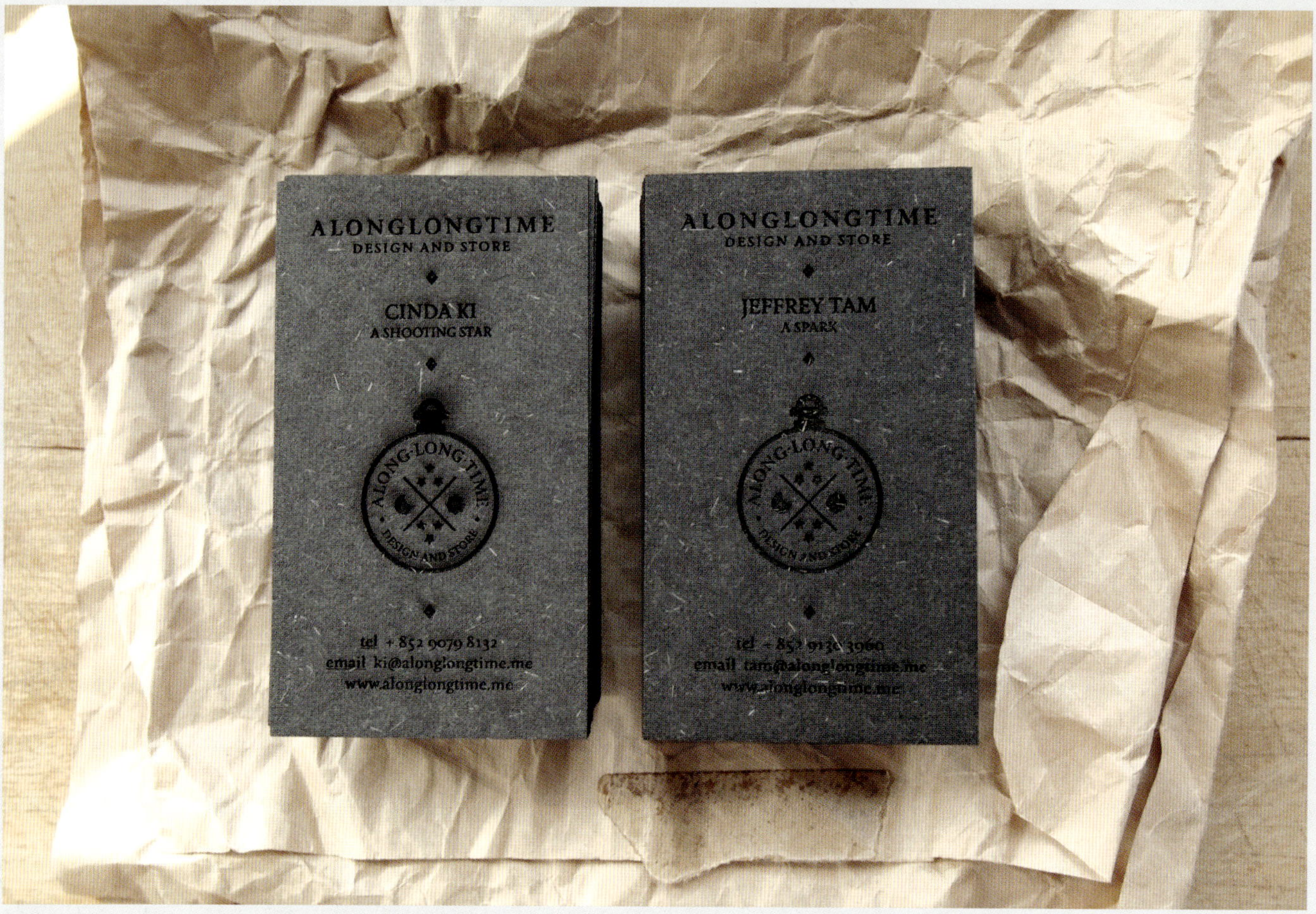

Alonglongtime

Hong Kong, P.R.C.

Alonglongtime
Design Agency

Jeffrey Tam
Designer

The business card design for Alonglongtime, a Hong Kong based multi-disciplinary design house, reflects its belief that not everything lasts forever, but there are something worth fighting for. The fine laser cut engraves the idea on the card, hoping their thoughts and messages will stay in the world long after they are gone.

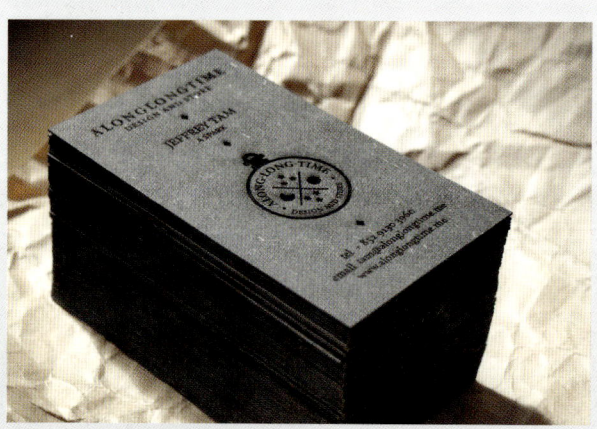

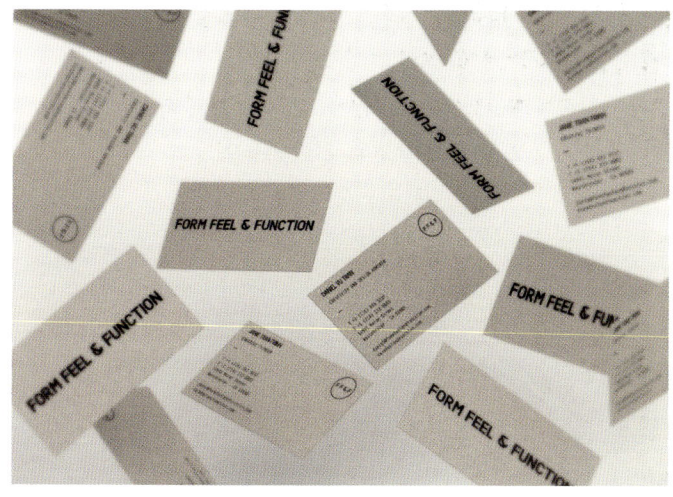

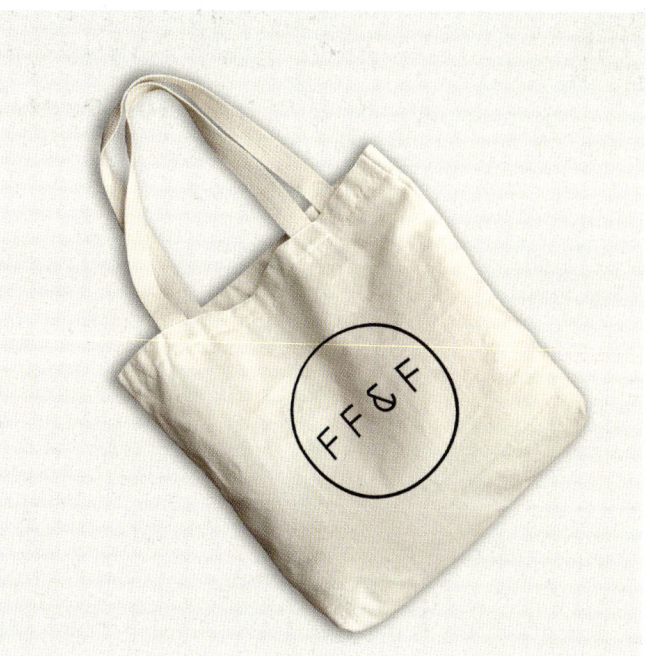

FF&F
Germany

Emanuele Cecini
Designer

Form Feel and Function
Client

This branding is for a startup company named FF&F based in Los Angeles committed to promoting young and talented designers. Combined with a clean logo, single print color and recycled paper stock, the minimalist and modern design allows the identity to be applicable in a wide range of different products.

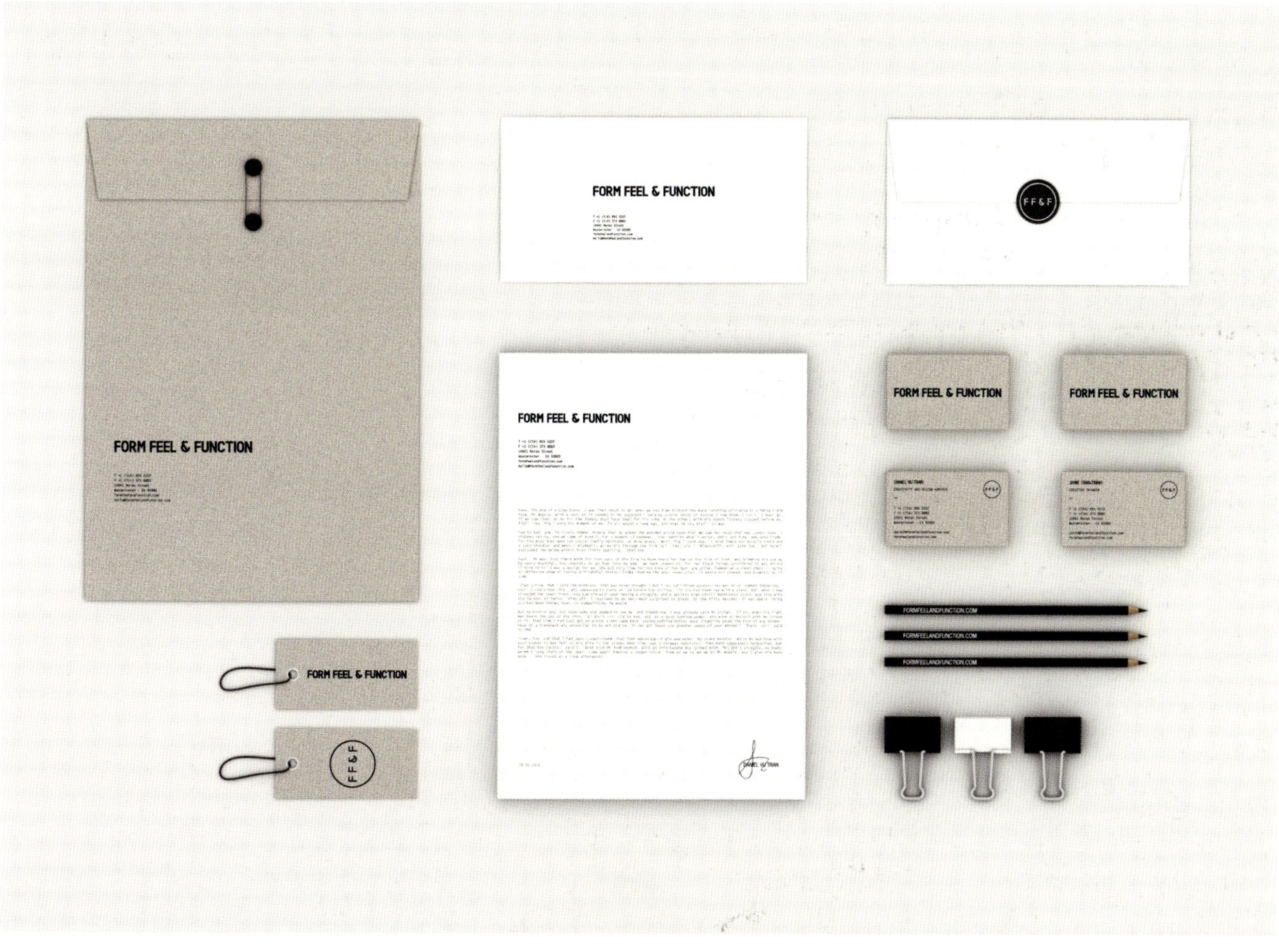

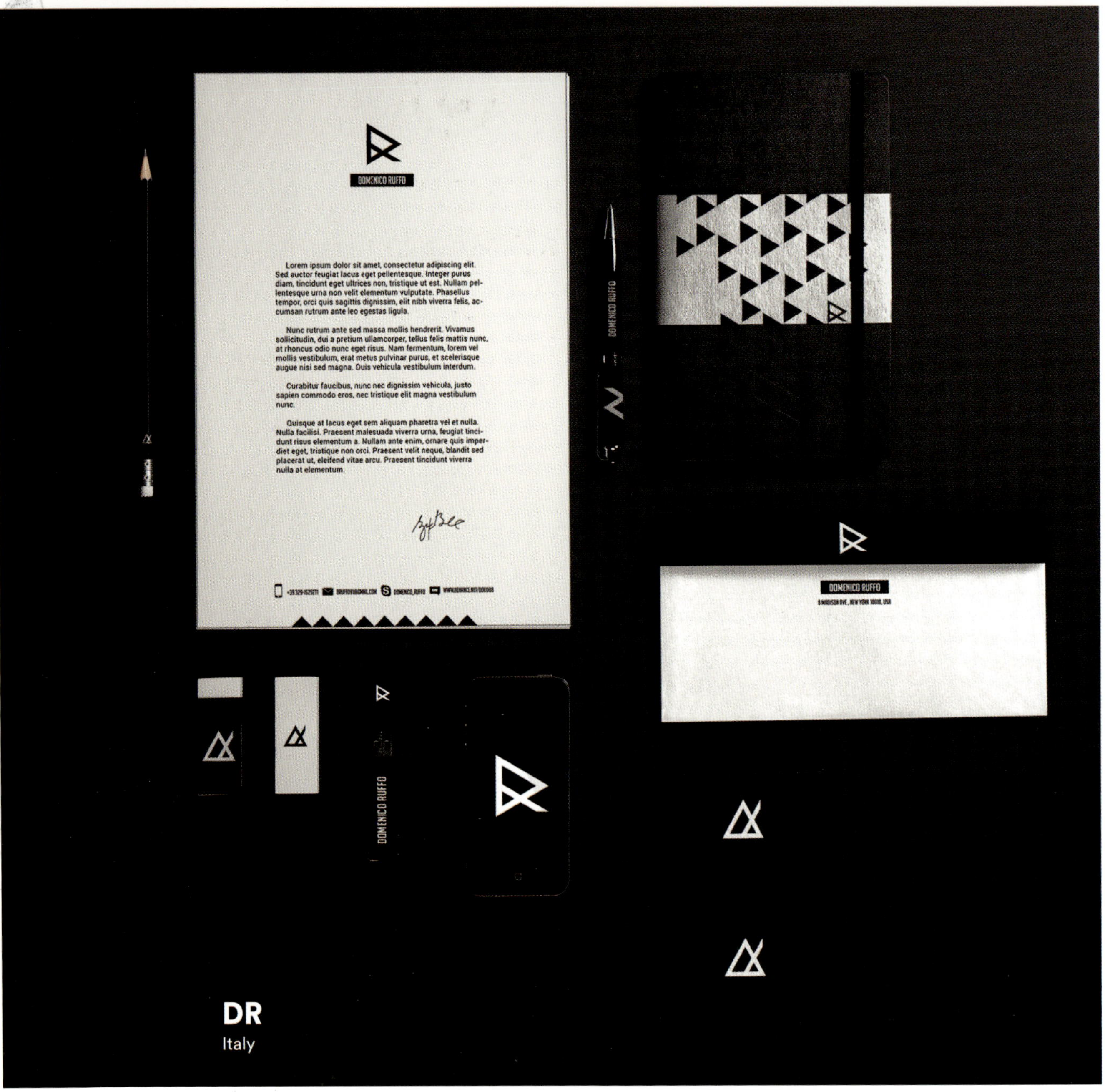

Lorem ipsum dolor sit amet, consectetur adipiscing elit. Sed auctor feugiat lacus eget pellentesque. Integer purus diam, tincidunt eget ultrices non, tristique ut est. Nullam pellentesque urna non velit elementum vulputate. Phasellus tempor, orci quis sagittis dignissim, elit nibh viverra felis, accumsan rutrum ante leo egestas ligula.

Nunc rutrum ante sed massa mollis hendrerit. Vivamus sollicitudin, dui a pretium ullamcorper, tellus felis mattis nunc, at rhoncus odio nunc eget risus. Nam fermentum, lorem vel mollis vestibulum, erat metus pulvinar purus, et scelerisque augue nisi sed magna. Duis vehicula vestibulum interdum.

Curabitur faucibus, nunc nec dignissim vehicula, justo sapien commodo eros, nec tristique elit magna vestibulum nunc.

Quisque at lacus eget sem aliquam pharetra vel et nulla. Nulla facilisi. Praesent malesuada viverra urna, feugiat tincidunt risus elementum a. Nullam ante enim, ornare quis imperdiet eget, tristique non orci. Praesent velit neque, blandit sed placerat ut, eleifend vitae arcu. Praesent tincidunt viverra nulla at elementum.

DR
Italy

Domenico Ruffo
Designer

DR is the initials of the designer Domenico Ruffoc. With his own font Quarz 974 that was inspired by simple and geometric lines as triangles and the use of black and white colors, the designer created a comprehensive brand identity that truly says more with less.

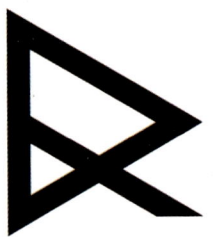

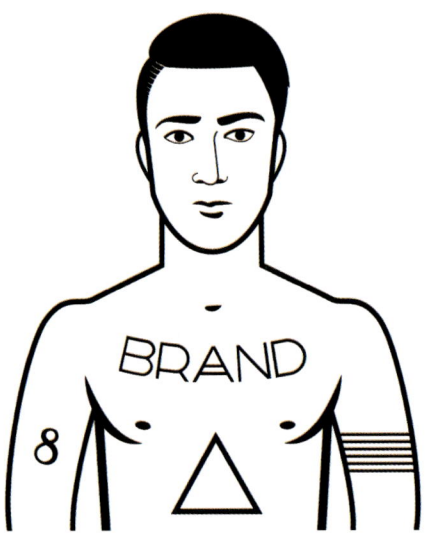

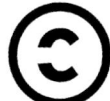 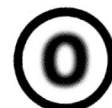 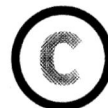

Curiosin   Vitalia Oculo Plus   Cariprazine

=====   =====   =====

CURIOSIN OLDAT   **VITALIA OCULO PLUS**   **CARIPRAZINE**

begek, égési sérülések   szemészeti problémákra   gyógyszer elegrendezési problémákra
hámsérulesek gyógyítására   alkalmazható szer

Medicine Packaging

Hungary

Botond Vörös
Designer

**Hungarian University
of Fine Arts**
Client

In this project, the task was to design a set of
packaging for medicine. It is a clean and strong
identity that reflects the uses of the medicine.
The designer employed basic elements, icons,
signs, lines, colors and the typography to
represent sicknesses and the convalescences.
Black, most commonly associated with power
and serenity, was used to showcase a simple and
elegant look.

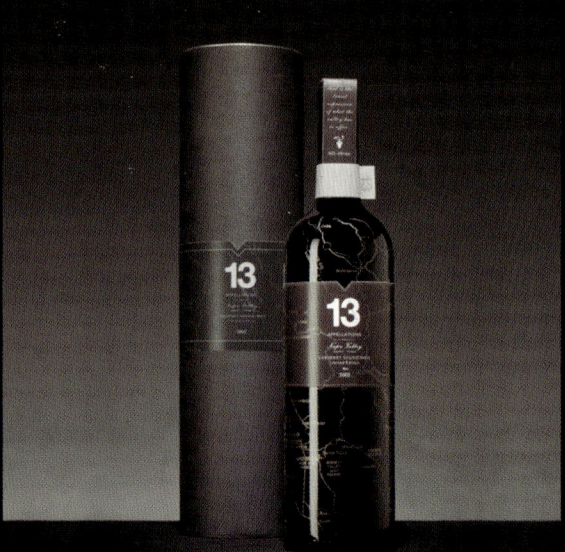

13 Appellations Wines
China

Wei Sun
Designer
& Photographer

Against the trend of vineyard-designated wines, the collective made the wine not from a single vineyard but from a baker's dozen. The idea was to blend one ton of grapes together to create the wine that is connected to Napa Valley, the true expression of what the valley has to offer. The concept of mapping each appellation reflects the idea's complexity, executed to express the boldness of the idea and its true meaning. The bold type reflects the brand's belief, and the intricacies of the map express the width and depth of its idea.

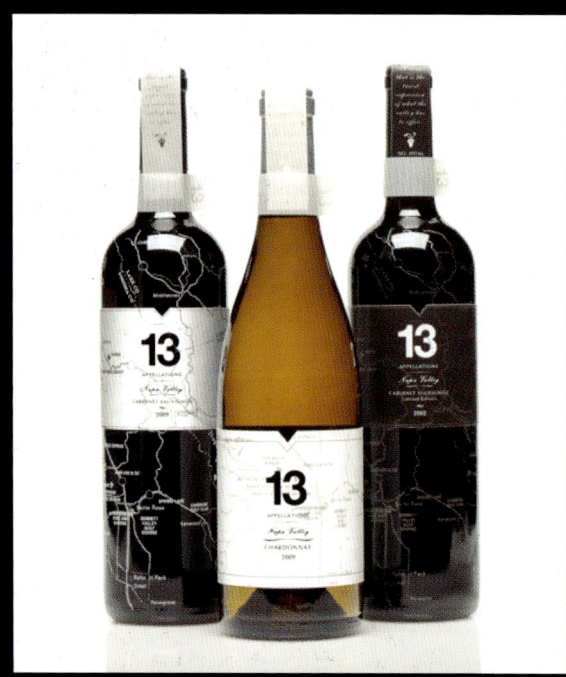

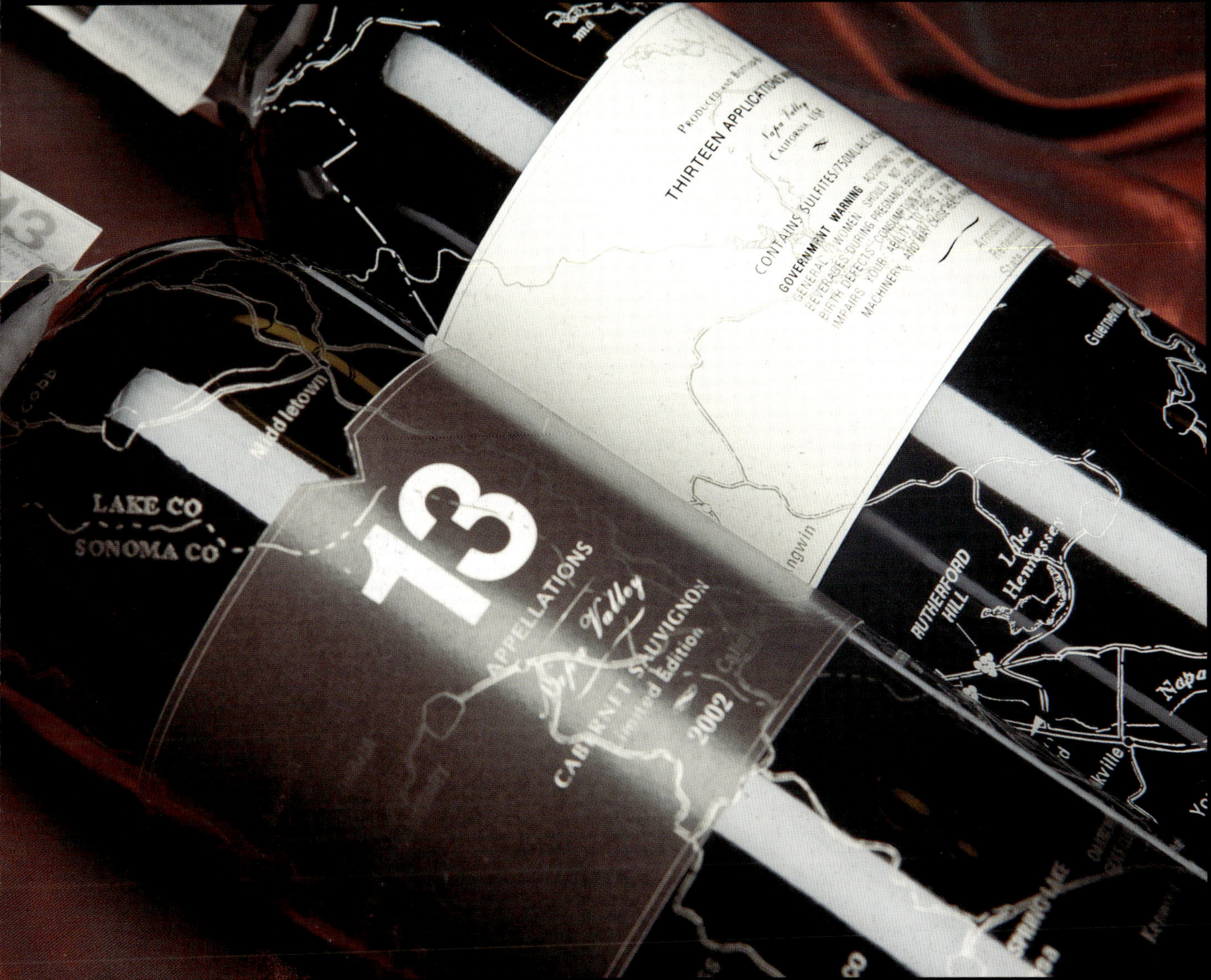
THIRTEEN APPLICATIONS
Produced and Bottled
Napa Valley
California, USA
CONTAINS SULFITES
GOVERNMENT WARNING
13
APPELLATIONS
CABERNET SAUVIGNON
Limited Edition
2002
LAKE CO
SONOMA CO
Middletown
RUTHERFORD HILL
Lake Hennessey
Guerneville
Napa

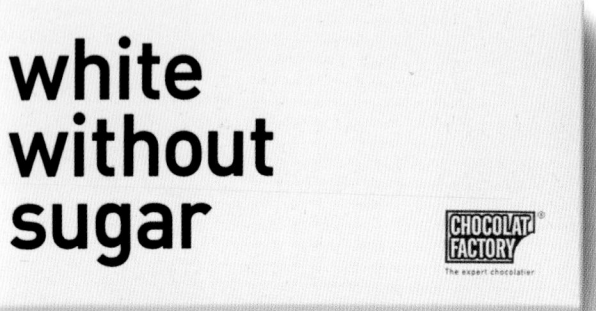

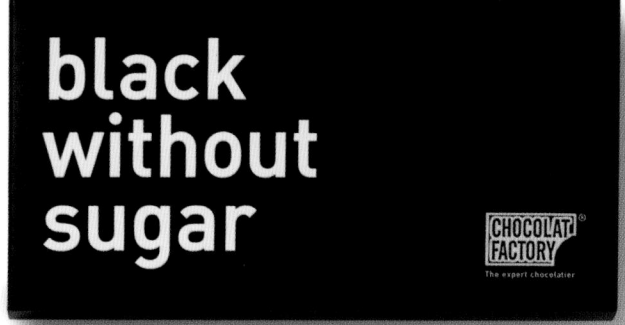

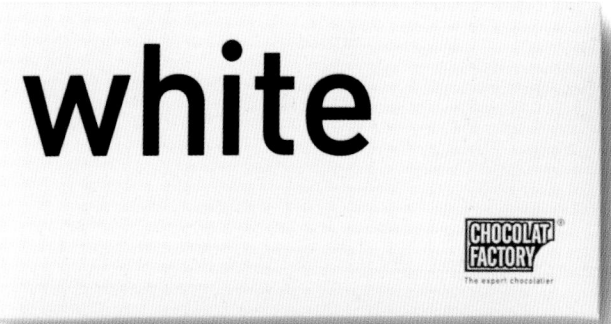

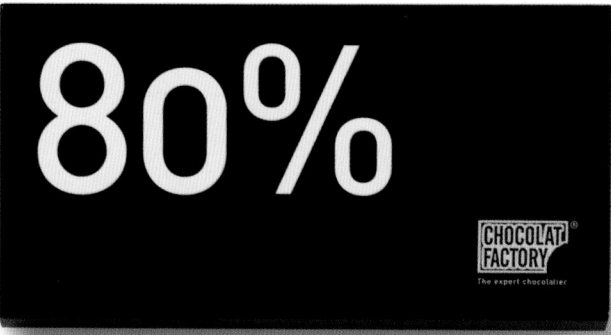

Chocolate Bars

Spain

ruiz+company
Design Agency

David Ruiz
Creative Director

Ainhoa Nagore
Art Director

Chocolat Factory
Client

Following the brand identity's graphic criterion, austere luxury, the new line of bars provides only the information that is absolutely relevant, such as the type of cocoa they use. It is forceful, which differentiates and expresses the brand personality.

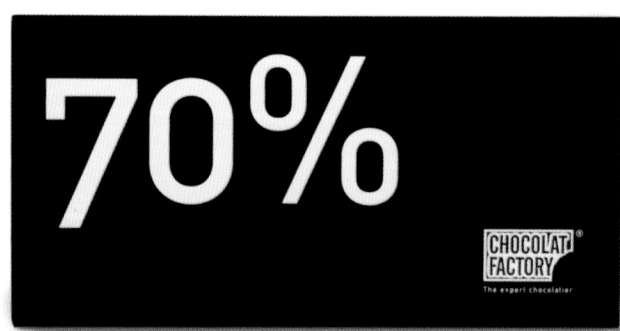

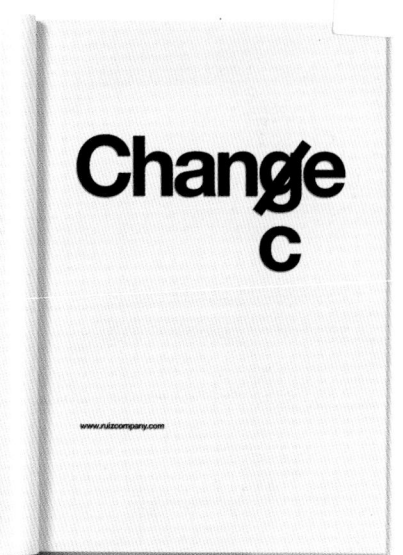

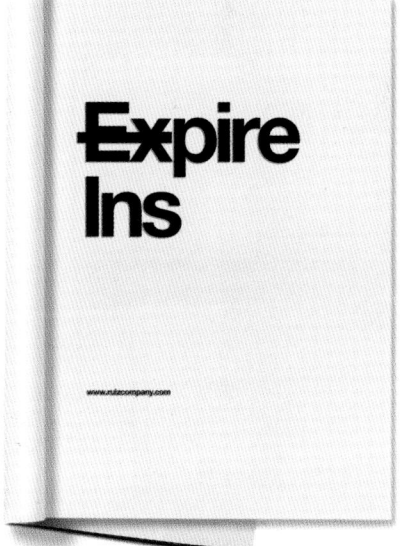

Self-Promotion Campaign
Spain

ruiz+company
Design Agency

David Ruiz
Creative Director

Ainhoa Nagore
Art Director

This self-promotion campaign is for the magazine Yorokobu. In the context of an economic crisis the designers voiced their attitude to the present times, a declaration of intentions in favor of action, change and the adapting of their needs to the market.

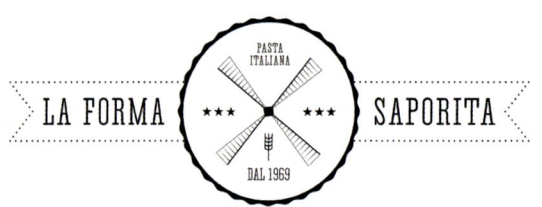

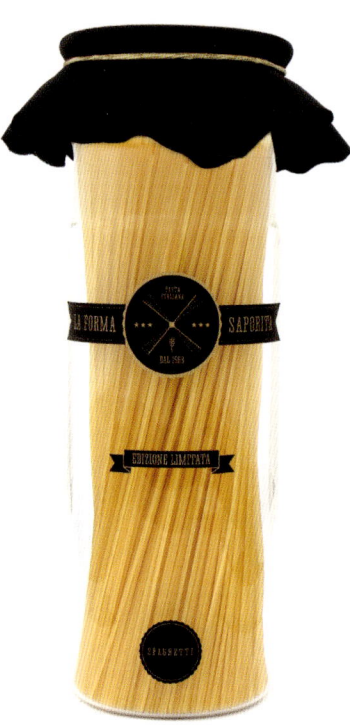

180

La Forma Saporita
Bulgaria

Yanko Djarov
Designer

La Forma is an Italian brand based in Parma that manufactures pastas. The brand name means "the tasty shape" because pasta comes in various shapes and it is always delicious. The designer wanted to create a really simple but elegant and stylish design that represents the high quality of the brand's organic products and its traditions. That effect was even stronger in the classical color scheme – black and white.

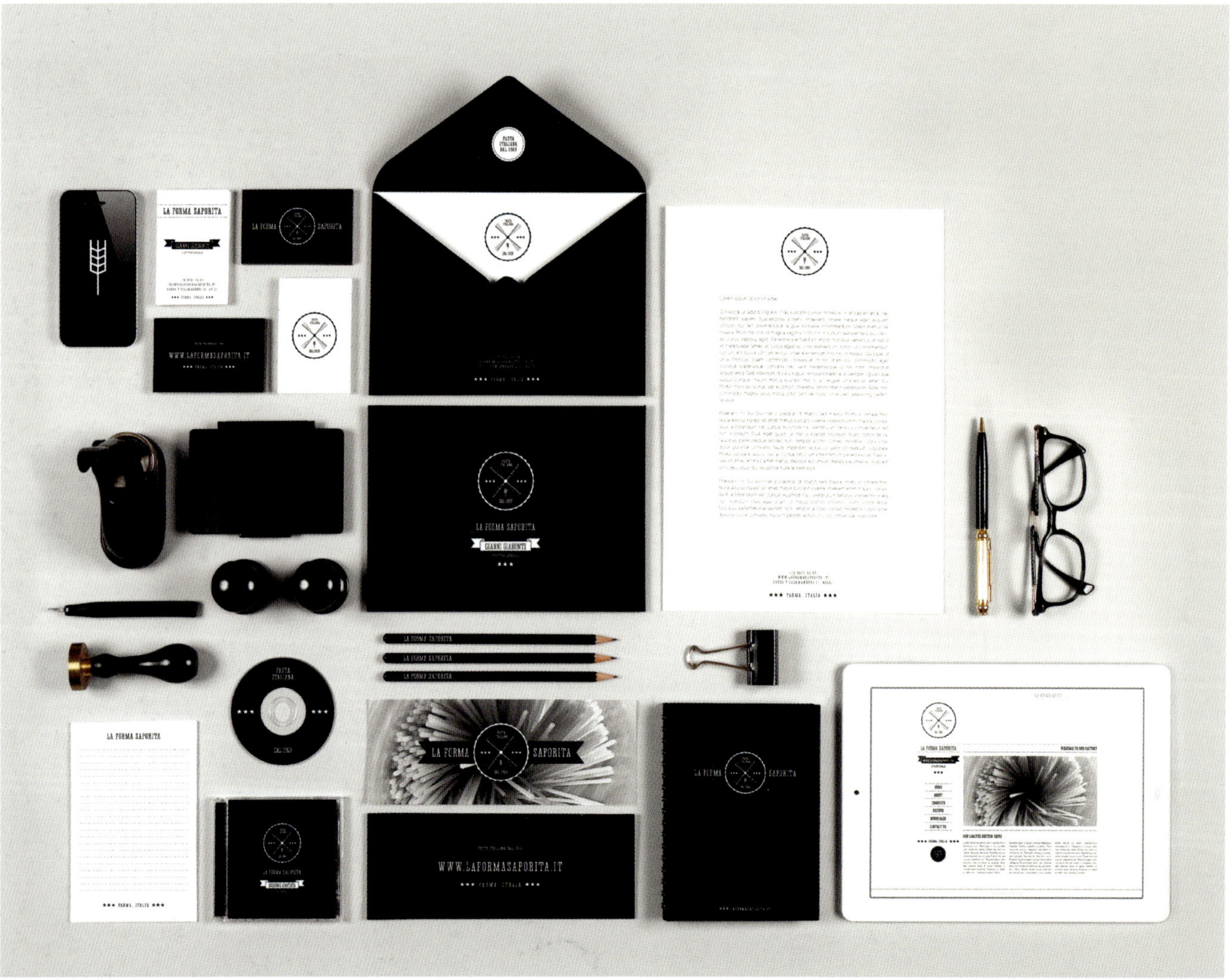

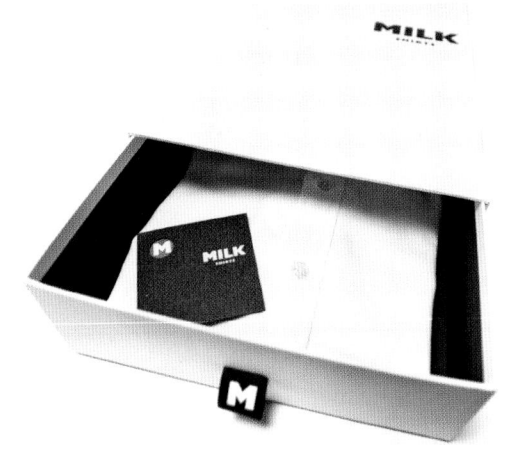

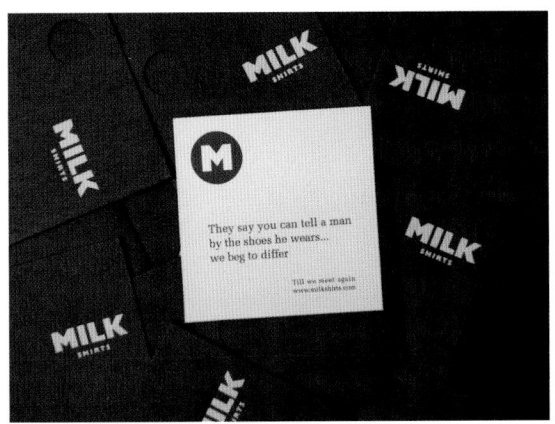

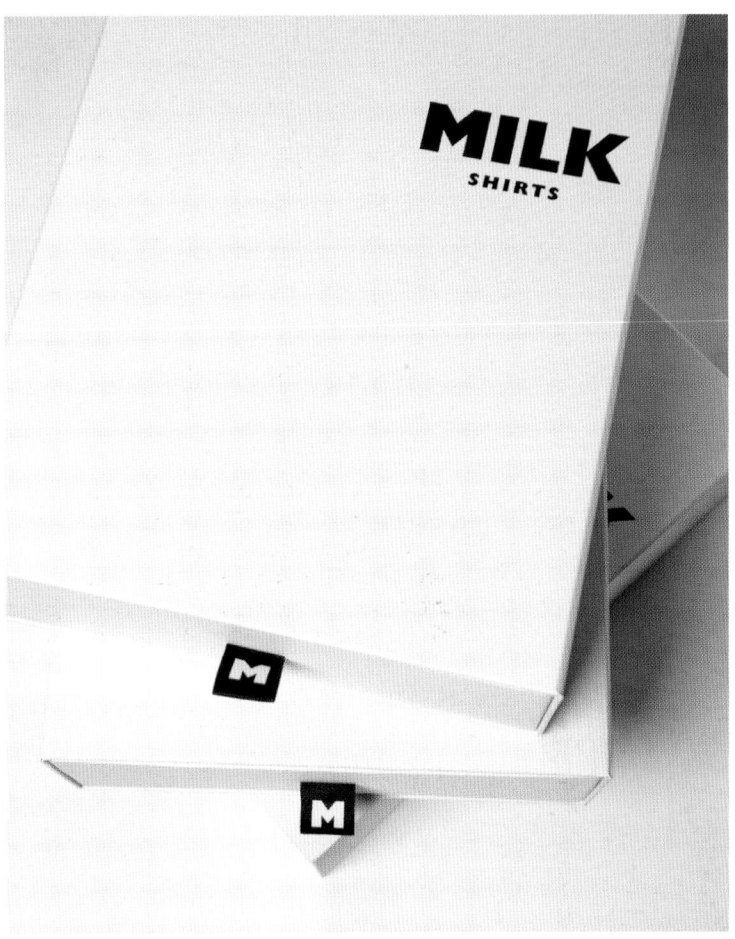

MILK Shirts Packaging

Denmark

Box House
Design Agency

Lone Wolf Larsen
Designer

MILK Shirts
Client

This packaging design aims to reflect the comfort and impeccable quality of the product held within. Therefore, a clean, functional, bold yet understated white packaging was created. It visually supports MILK's brand identity and grabs customers' attention.

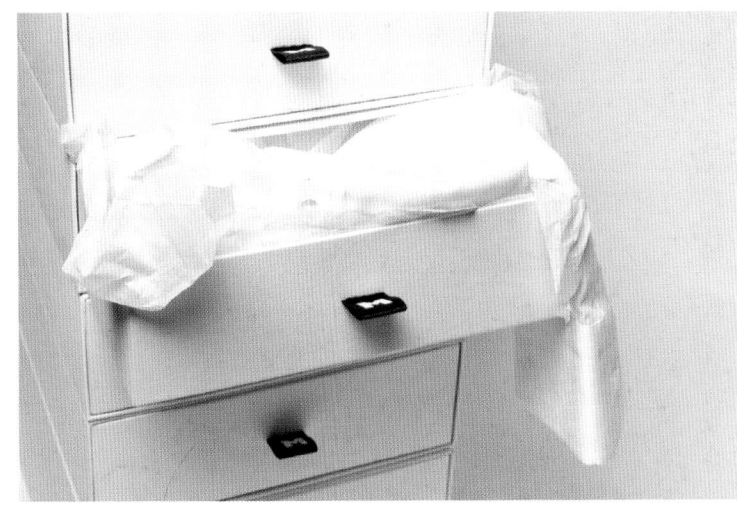

www.about.me/boxhouse

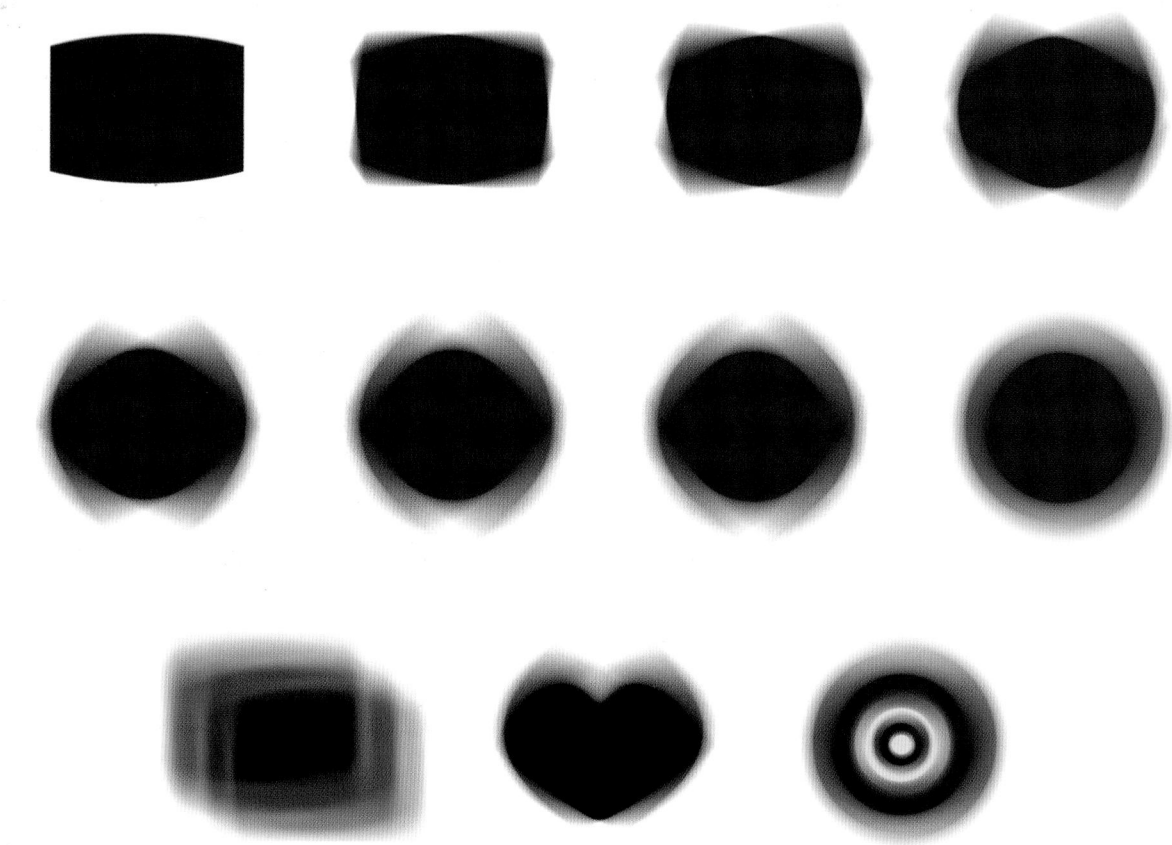

Museum of Moving Image
United States

Jimin Nam
Designer

Museum of Moving Image
Client

Located in Astoria, New York, Museum of Moving Image is a mecca of all the films and motion records in the history. To make a logo for this museum, the designer focused on the beauty of the theater screens' shape and blurry edges.

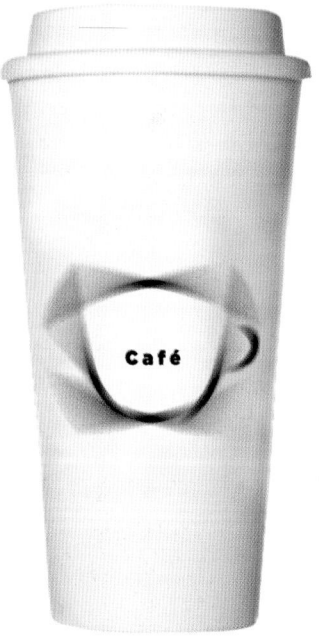

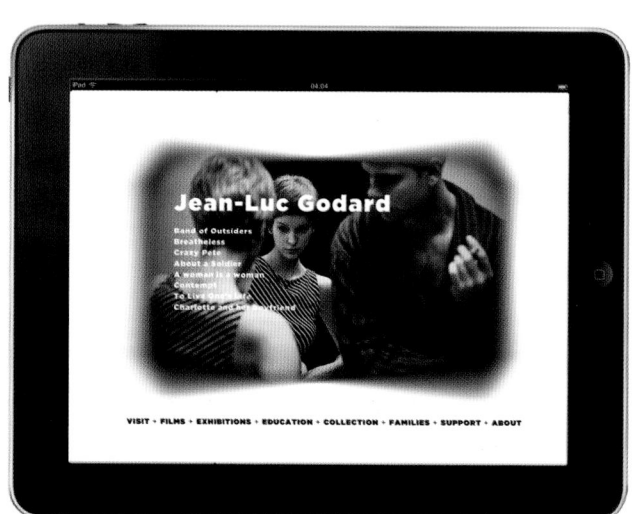

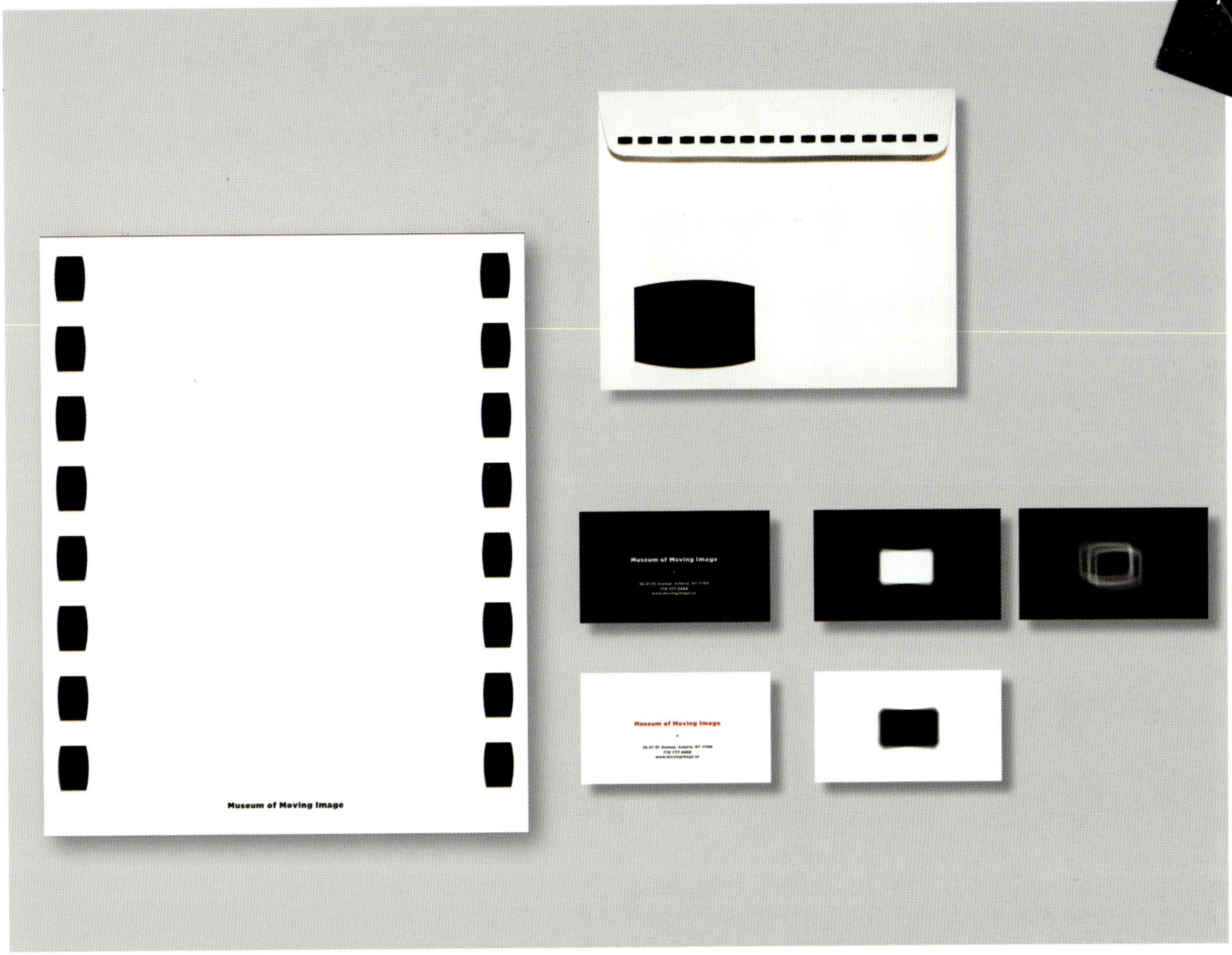

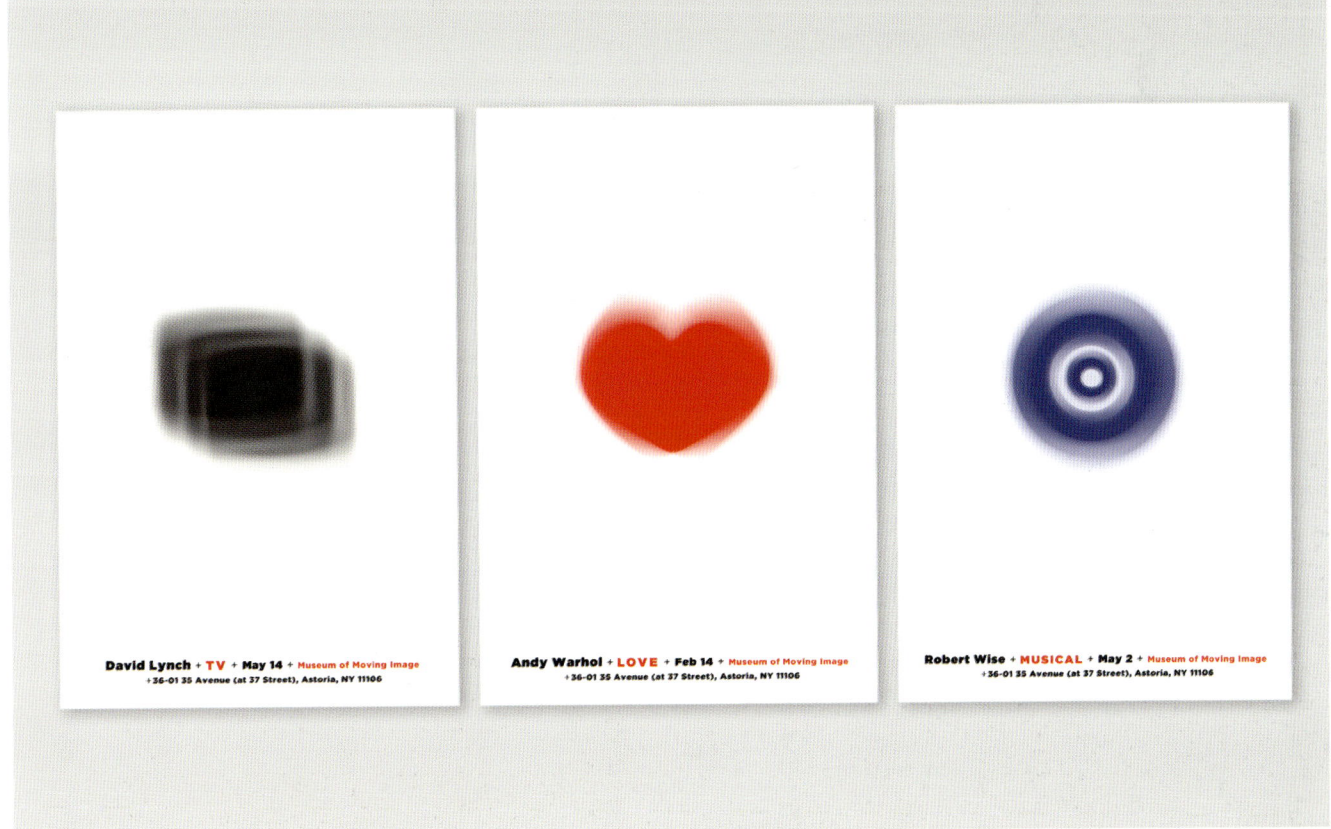

Acknowledgments

We would like to thank all the designers and companies who have in-
volved in the production of this book. This project would not have been
accomplished without their significant contribution to the compila-
tion of this book. We would also like to express our gratitude to all the
producers for their invaluable opinions and assistance throughout this
entire project. The successful completion also owes a great deal to
many professionals in the creative industry who have given us precious
insights and comments. And to the many others whose names are not
credited but have made specific input in this book, we thank you for
your continuous support.

Index

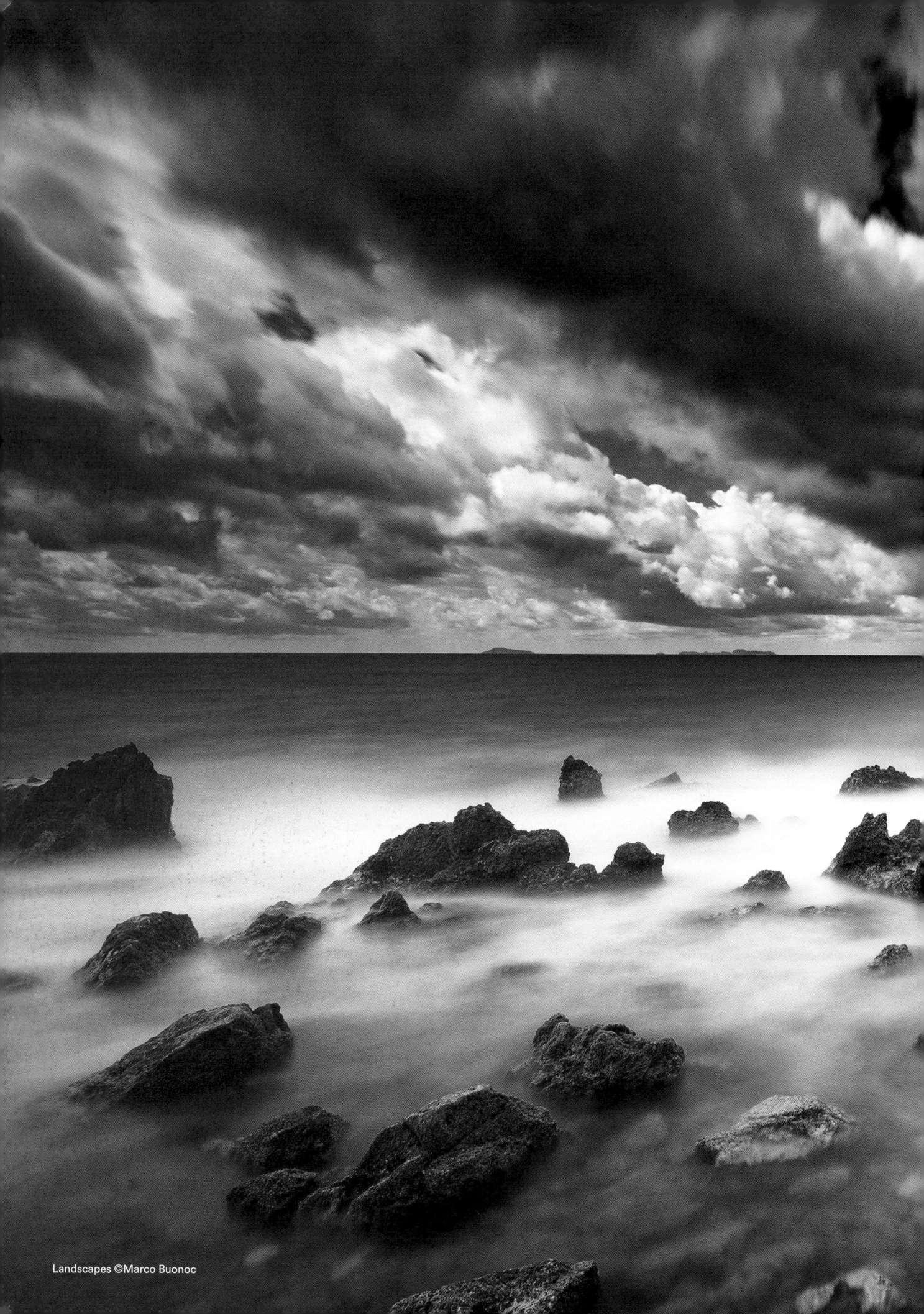

Landscapes ©Marco Buonoc

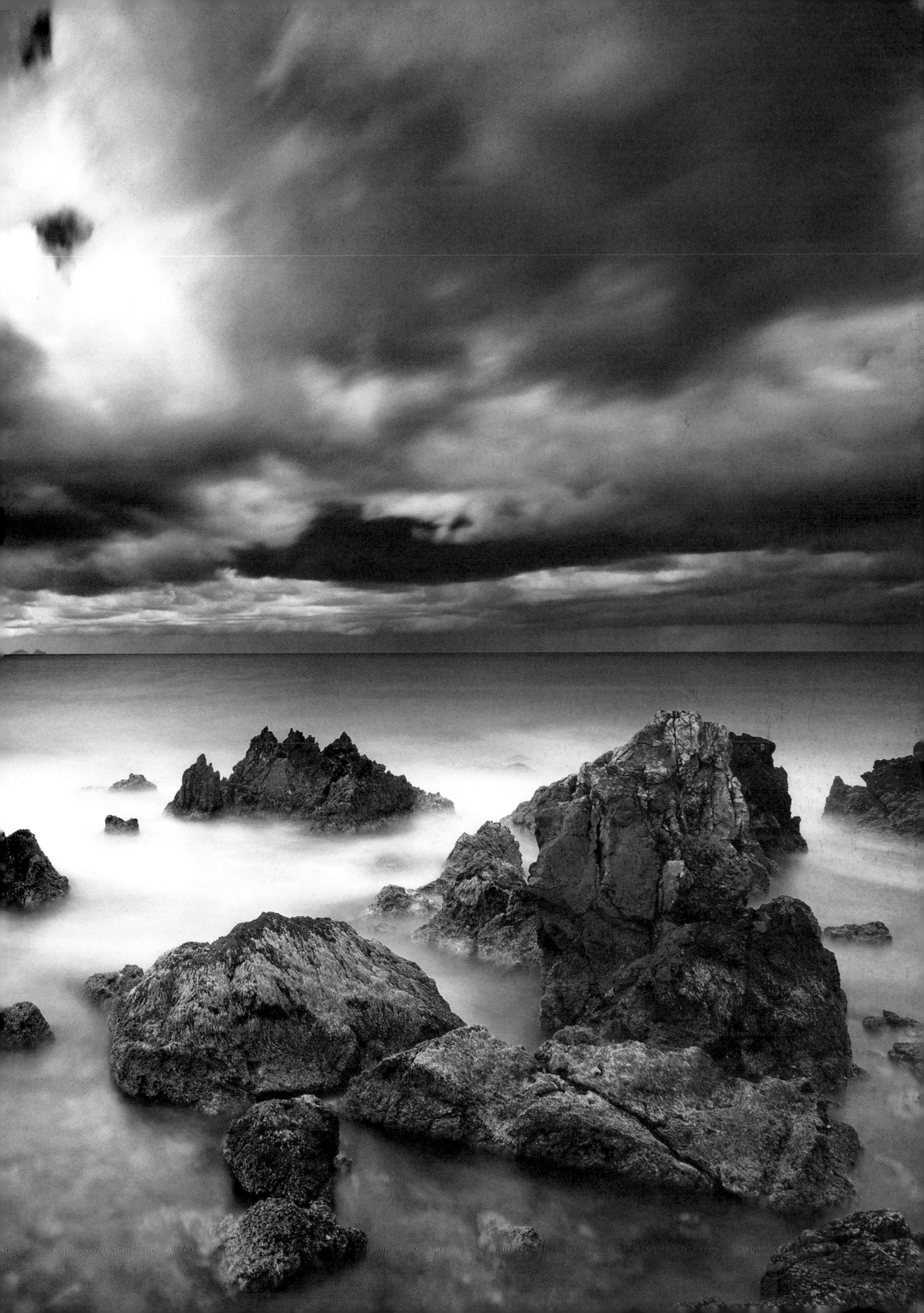

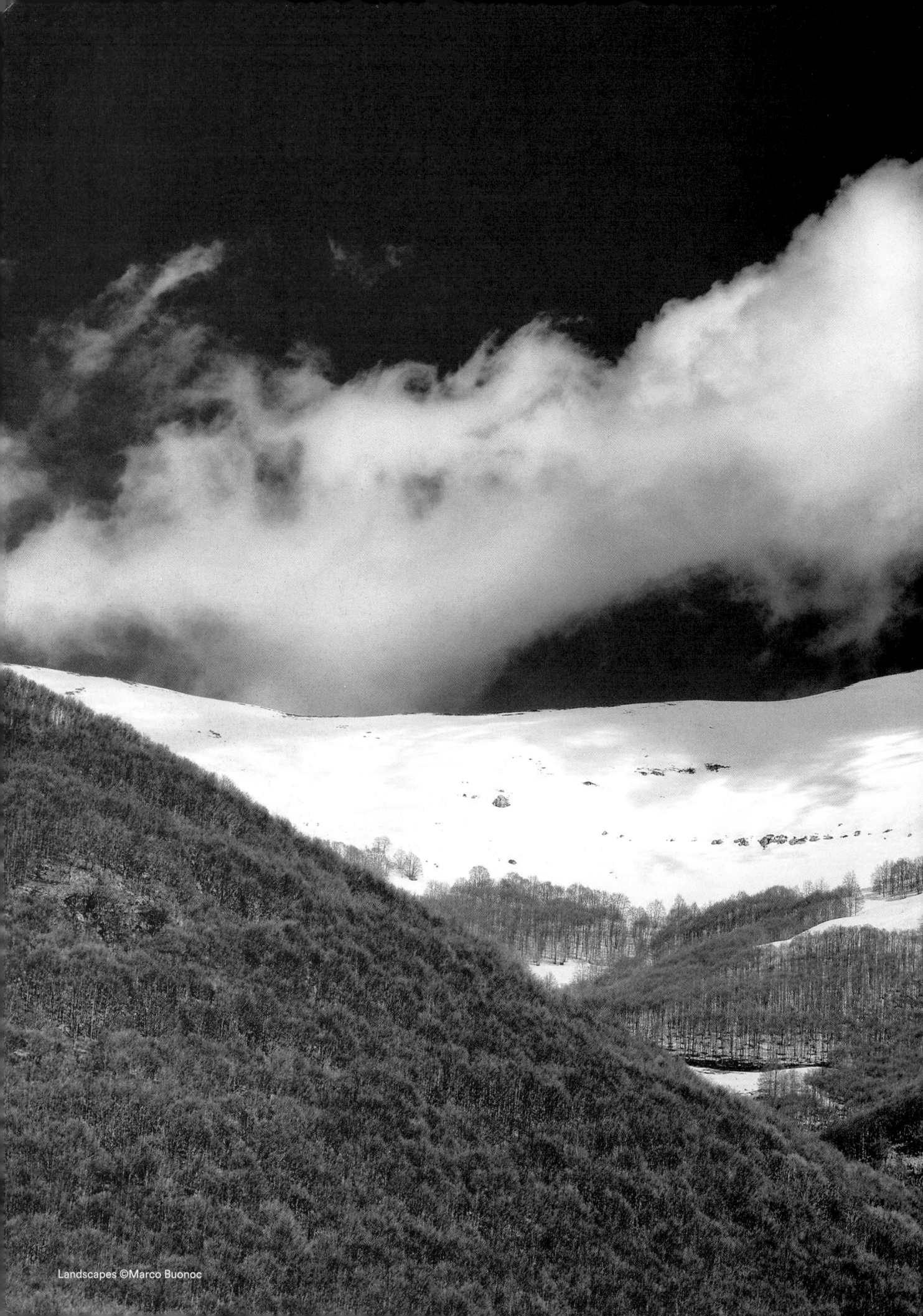

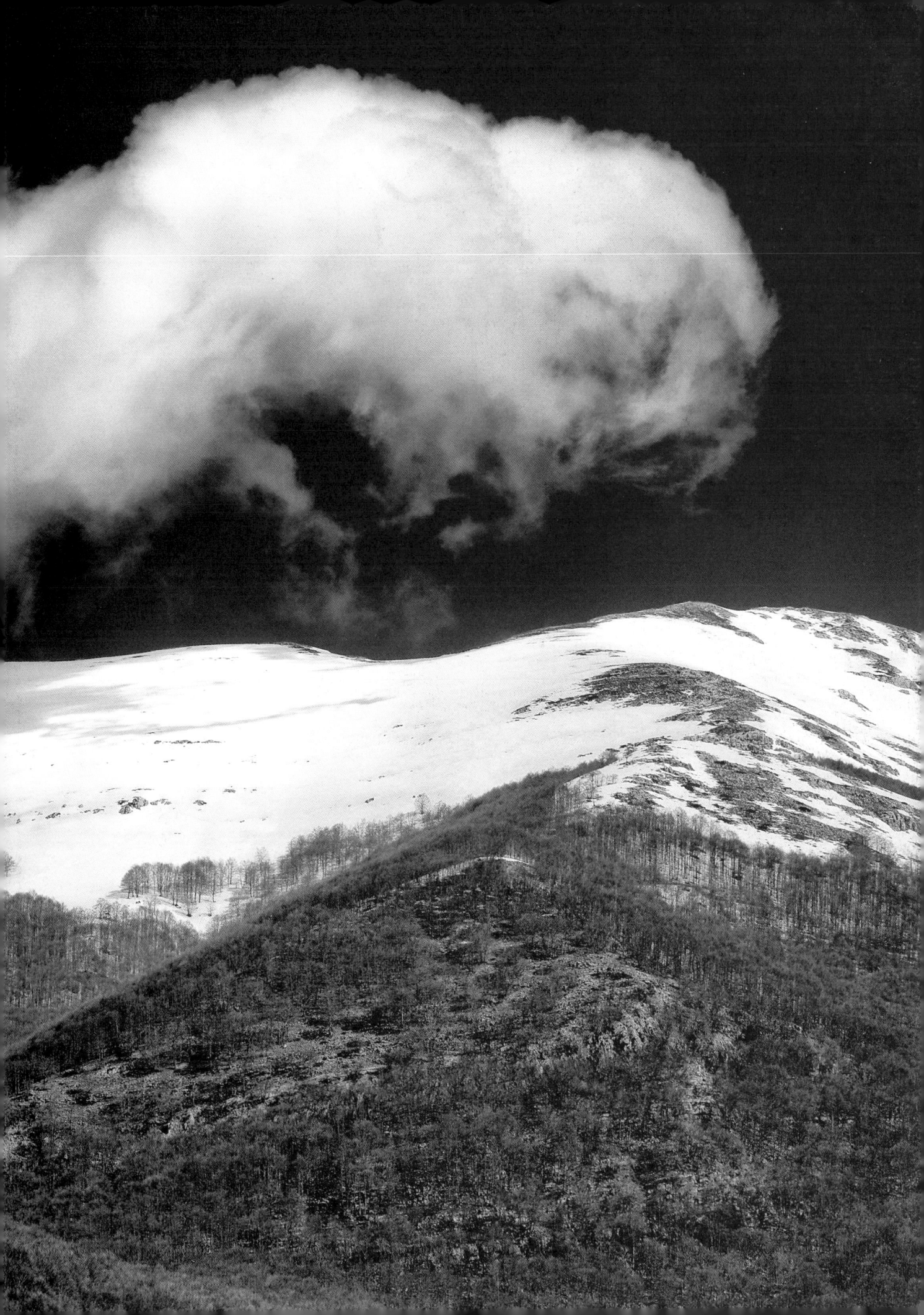

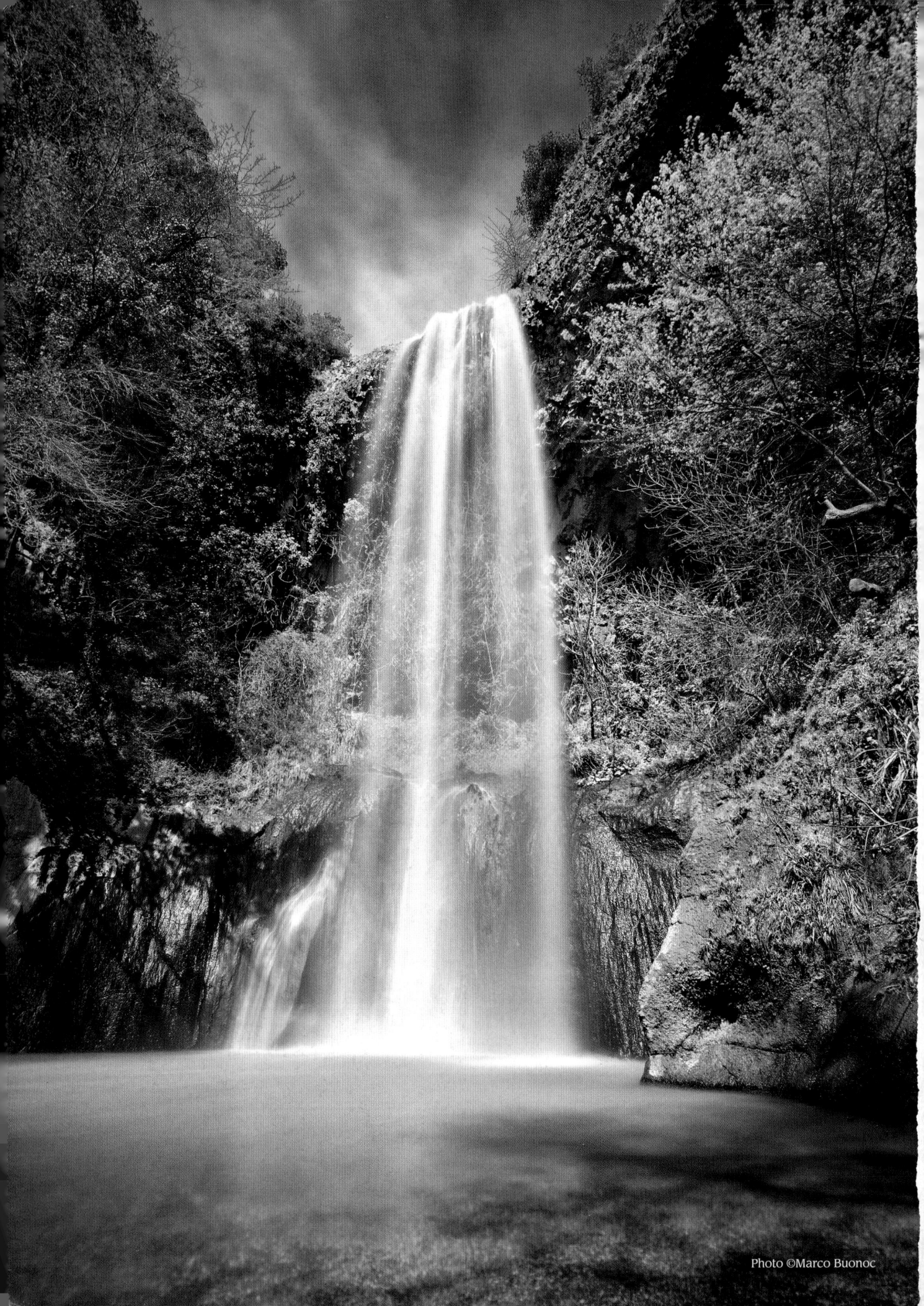